D0930504

ECONOMICS OF WORLDWIDE STAGFLATION

Economics
of Worldwide
Stagflation

MICHAEL BRUNO AND JEFFREY D. SACHS

Harvard University Press

Cambridge, Massachusetts   1985

HB
172.5
.B78
1985

Copyright © 1985 by Michael Bruno and Jeffrey D. Sachs
All rights reserved
Printed in the United States of America
10 9 8 7 6 5 4 3 2 1

This book is printed on acid-free paper, and its binding
materials have been chosen for strength and durability.

LIBRARY OF CONGRESS CATALOGING IN PUBLICATION DATA

Bruno, Michael.
  Economics of worldwide stagflation.

  Bibliography: p.
  Includes index.
  1. Macroeconomics.   2. Unemployment—Effect of
inflation on.   3. Economic development.
I. Sachs, Jeffrey.   II. Title.
HB172.5.B78 1985   339   84-8964
ISBN 0-674-23475-8 (alk. paper)

Acknowledgments

THIS BOOK is the outcome of research work that we have conducted both individually and together over a period of several years. A collaborative effort of this kind between coauthors who live thousands of miles apart requires generous host institutions, adequate funding, modern computer linkups, and, last but not least, the cooperation of numerous helpful and patient individuals. Luckily we were blessed with all of these.

A brief acquaintance between us at Harvard in 1977 led to a prolonged meeting in Jerusalem in the following year and to two joint papers on supply shocks and stagflation. We have since been collaborating intermittently on a joint project carried out at the National Bureau of Economic Research in Cambridge, Massachusetts, and at the Falk Institute and Hebrew University in Jerusalem. We are greatly indebted to these institutions for helping to sustain this research effort. In particular, we would like to thank Martin Feldstein and David Hartman for their continued support of our project at the National Bureau of Economic Research.

Other institutions whose hospitality we enjoyed during brief joint summer visits were the Institute for International Economic Studies in Stockholm (in 1979), headed by Assar Lindbeck, and the Centre for Labour Economics at the London School of Economics (in 1981), headed by Richard Layard. Many of our ideas were first tried out in their seminars. Likewise, thanks go to the Organization for Economic Cooperation and Development (OECD) and the Centre des Hautes Etudes in Paris for hosting Jeffrey Sachs during 1982. The Economics Department of the Massachusetts Institute of Technology as well as its excellent graduate students provided much stimulus and good testing ground for some draft chapters of this book during Michael Bruno's visit in the fall term of 1981. (Our use of the factor price frontier owes a great deal to discussions with Paul Samuelson and Robert Solow during an MIT visit of much earlier vintage.)

Generous funding throughout this period has been provided by the National Science Foundation. Thanks likewise go to the Ford Foundation for partial support during an early phase of this study and to the Binational U.S./Israel Fund during the last phase of the project.

Joint theoretical work requires pencil, paper, and lots of postage stamps. Comparative macroeconomics also requires having large bodies of data and efficient computer systems at one's disposal. This cannot be done at a distance without the most modern computer technology. In this respect as well as others it is hard to surpass DRI (Data Resources, Inc.), whose highly efficient computer system and extensive data banks we were able to work on jointly and simultaneously in Cambridge and Jerusalem. For all of this, we owe great thanks to the late Otto Eckstein, DRI's founder and first president, for his help and care. Otto's untimely death when this book went to press has taken away a friend and colleague who throughout showed keen interest in the progress and substance of this study. May this book be a tribute to the man and his many-sided contributions to macroeconomics.

Machines can only be operated efficiently by knowledgeable individuals, and over the years we have been greatly helped by extremely able research assistants—David Lipton and Louis Dicks-Mireaux at NBER; Oren Sussman and, in particular, Carlos Bachrach, in Jerusalem. Not only have they operated those machines and analyzed masses of data with great expertise, they have also provided valuable comments of their own on the work they were doing.

Work in an area like ours cannot proceed in isolation. Our intellectual debt to other people's work is specifically mentioned at the end of the Introduction. In addition, numerous seminars given at universities or government institutions in the United States, Europe, Japan, and Israel have helped us to improve and modify our approach as we went along; we would like to thank the many colleagues and students who attended these seminars or who commented on papers that preceded this book. We owe a particular debt to Edmond Malinvaud and James Tobin for their comments at the 1979 Kiel Conference.

While benefiting from our earlier papers, most of the material in this book has not appeared in print before. We are particularly indebted to Olivier Blanchard, Stanley Fischer, Ruth Klinov, Robert Solow, Lars Svensson, Philip Weil, Charles Wyplosz, and Yoseph Zeira for carefully reading large parts of the book in draft form and offering many valuable comments.

It may, of course, be easier to read a book than to write it, but given the circumstances, it may be even harder to bring it to press. We thank Manuel Trajtenberg for his friendly advice at critical stages. Michael Aronson, General Editor of Harvard University Press, has our special thanks for patiently prodding us along through ups and downs to the first draft; we also thank Mary Ellen Geer for her highly professional help in editing the book.

Last but not least comes our excellent secretarial and managerial help. To Merriam Ansara at NBER goes very special praise for being a most efficient general manager of the whole operation, typing and shipping floppy discs and papers back and forth between two absent-minded authors across the Atlantic, without misplacing any or losing courage. Thanks go also to Anne Monahan, who with calm and wisdom makes the NBER tick. Margret Eisenstadt, administrative secretary of the Falk Institute in Jerusalem, served intermittently as typist, editor, draftswoman for many of the drawings, and first-class humorist.

Finally, our gratitude goes to our wives and children, who have, in so many understanding ways, helped us to write this book.

We would also like to thank various publishers for permission to use previously published material. Figures 2A.1, 2A.2, 2A.3, and 2.4 first appeared in Michael Bruno, "Raw Materials, Profits, and the Productivity Slowdown," *Quarterly Journal of Economics,* vol. 119, no. 1, 1984, copyright John Wiley and Sons; Figure 11.2 and Table 11.5 first appeared in Jeffrey Sachs, "Wages, Profits, and Macroeconomic Adjustment: A Comparative Study," *Brookings Papers on Economic Activity,* vol. 2, 1979; Tables 11.2 and 11.3 are adapted from C. Crouch, "The Conditions for Trade Union Wage Restraint," in *The Politics and Sociology of Global Inflation,* ed. L. Lindberg and C. Maier (Washington, D.C.: The Brookings Institution, forthcoming); Table 12.5 is adapted from J. W. Kendrick, "International Comparisons of Recent Productivity Trends," in *Contemporary Economic Problems,* ed. William Fellner (Washington, D.C.: American Enterprise Institute, 1981). Excerpts from Chapter 4 also appear in Michael Bruno, "Petrodollars and the Differential Growth Performance of Industrial and Middle-Income Countries in the 1970s," in *Economic Structure and Performance,* ed. M. Syrquin, L. Taylor, and L. Westphal (New York: Academic Press, forthcoming).

Contents

National Bureau of Economic Research

OFFICERS

Franklin A. Lindsay, *chairman*
Richard Rosett, *vice chairman*
Eli Shapiro, *president*
David G. Hartman, *executive director and corporate secretary*

Charles A. Walworth, *treasurer*
Sam Parker, *director of finance and administration*

DIRECTORS AT LARGE

Moses Abramovitz
George T. Conklin, Jr.
Jean A. Crockett
Morton Ehrlich
Edward L. Ginzton
David L. Grove
Walter W. Heller
Saul B. Klaman

Franklin A. Lindsay
Roy E. Moor
Geoffrey H. Moore
Michael H. Moskow
James J. O'Leary
Peter G. Peterson
Robert V. Roosa
Richard N. Rosett

Bert Seidman
Eli Shapiro
Stephen Stamas
Lazare Teper
Donald S. Wasserman
Marina v.N. Whitman

DIRECTORS BY UNIVERSITY APPOINTMENT

Albert Ando, *University of Pennsylvania*
Charles H. Berry, *Princeton*
James Duesenberry, *Harvard*
Marcus Alexis, *Northwestern*
J. C. LaForce, *California, Los Angeles*
Paul McCracken, *Michigan*
Ann F. Friedlaender, *Massachusetts Institute of Technology*

James L. Pierce, *California, Berkeley*
Nathan Rosenberg, *Stanford*
James Simler, *Minnesota*
James Tobin, *Yale*
William S. Vickrey, *Columbia*
John Vernon, *Duke*
Burton A. Weisbrod, *Wisconsin*
Arnold Zellner, *Chicago*

DIRECTORS BY APPOINTMENT OF OTHER ORGANIZATIONS

Carl F. Christ, *American Economic Association*
Robert S. Hamada, *American Finance Association*
Gilbert Heebner, *National Association of Business Economists*
Robert C. Holland, *Committee for Economic Development*
Stephan F. Kaliski, *Canadian Economics Association*
Douglass C. North, *Economic History Association*

Rudolph A. Oswald, *American Federation of Labor and Congress of Industrial Organizations*
G. Edward Schuh, *American Agricultural Economics Association*
Albert Sommers, *The Conference Board*
Dudley Wallace, *American Statistical Association*
Charles A. Walworth, *American Institute of Certified Public Accountants*

DIRECTORS EMERITI

Arthur Burns
Emilio G. Collado
Solomon Fabricant
Frank Fetter

Thomas D. Flynn
Gottfried Haberler
George B. Roberts
Murray Shields

Boris Shishkin
Willard L. Thorp
Theodore O. Yntema

RELATION OF THE DIRECTORS TO THE WORK AND PUBLICATIONS OF THE NATIONAL BUREAU OF ECONOMIC RESEARCH

1. The object of the National Bureau of Economic Research is to ascertain and to present to the public important economic facts and their interpretation in a scientific and impartial manner. The Board of Directors is charged with the responsibility of ensuring that the work of the National Bureau is carried on in strict conformity with this object.

2. The President of the National Bureau shall submit to the Board of Directors, or to its Executive Committee, for their formal adoption all specific proposals for research to be instituted.

3. No research report shall be published by the National Bureau until the President has sent each member of the Board a notice that a manuscript is recommended for publication and that in the President's opinion it is suitable for publication in accordance with the principles of the National Bureau. Such notification will include an abstract or summary of the manuscript's content and a response form for use by those Directors who desire a copy of the manuscript for review. Each manuscript shall contain a summary drawing attention to the nature and treatment of the problem studied, the character of the data and their utilization in the report, and the main conclusions reached.

4. For each manuscript so submitted, a special committee of the Directors (including Directors Emeriti) shall be appointed by majority agreement of the President and Vice Presidents (or by the Executive Committee in case of inability to decide on the part of the President and Vice Presidents), consisting of three Directors selected as nearly as may be one from each general division of the Board. The names of the special manuscript committee shall be stated to each Director when notice of the proposed publication is submitted to him. It shall be the duty of each member of the special manuscript committee to read the manuscript. If each member of the manuscript committee signifies his approval within thirty days of the transmittal of the manuscript, the report may be published. If at the end of that period any member of the manuscript committee withholds his approval, the President shall then notify each member of the Board, requesting approval or disapproval of publication, and thirty days additional shall be granted for this purpose. The manuscript shall then not be published unless at least a majority of the entire Board who shall have voted on the proposal within the time fixed for the receipt of votes shall have approved.

5. No manuscript may be published, though approved by each member of the special manuscript committee, until forty-five days have elapsed from the transmittal of the report in manuscript form. The interval is allowed for the receipt of any memorandum of dissent or reservation, together with a brief statement of his reasons, that any member may wish to express; and such memorandum of dissent or reservation shall be published with the manuscript if he so desires. Publication does not, however, imply that each member of the Board has read the manuscript, or that either members of the Board in general or the special committee have passed on its validity in every detail.

6. Publications of the National Bureau issued for informational purposes concerning the work of the Bureau and its staff, or issued to inform the public of activities of Bureau staff, and volumes issued as a result of various conferences involving the National Bureau shall contain a specific disclaimer noting that such publication has not passed through the normal review procedures required in this resolution. The Executive Committee of the Board is charged with review of all such publications from time to time to ensure that they do not take on the character of formal research reports of the National Bureau, requiring formal Board approval.

7. Unless otherwise determined by the Board or exempted by the terms of paragraph 6, a copy of this resolution shall be printed in each National Bureau publication.

(Resolution adopted October 25, 1926, as revised through September 30, 1974)

ECONOMICS OF WORLDWIDE STAGFLATION

Introduction

THE EARLY 1970s marked a watershed in the macroeconomic performance of the advanced industrial economies. In the 1950s and 1960s almost all the economies of the OECD enjoyed a period of low unemployment, rapid growth of GNP and living standards, and low if gently rising inflation.[1] By the end of the 1960s a leading macroeconomist could plausibly speak of the "obsolescence of the business cycle pattern."[2] Yet shortly into the 1970s, severe and seemingly intractable macroeconomic problems emerged. The Bretton Woods international monetary system collapsed in 1971. An inflationary boom in 1972–73 gave way to deep worldwide recession in 1974–75. In the subsequent period, the OECD economies have sustained rising unemployment, slow economic growth, and continued high inflation, with another deep recession in the early 1980s.

Some measures of the worsening macroeconomic performance are shown in Table I.1. We take 1973 as the breakpoint between the high-growth and low-growth periods, since that was the last boom year in the OECD, though we stress later that many of the problems of the 1970s and 1980s were built up gradually after the mid-1960s. The table shows the pervasiveness of poor performance. It is not that some aspects of macroeconomic life gained at the expense of others; every major dimension worsened significantly after the early 1970s. This pervasiveness also applies across countries. As we show in the second half of this book, *every* economy in the OECD shared in the dismal record, though there are interesting differences in the individual countries' experiences.

The poor macroeconomic performance of the past decade was almost nowhere foreseen and has remained mostly unexplained. Indeed, the recent experience has challenged some of the central tenets of postwar macroeconomics, including the belief in a stable inflation-unemployment trade-off

Table I.1. Measures of Macroeconomic Performance in the
OECD (in percentages)

Economic indicator	1960–73	1973–81
Unemployment rate	3.2	5.5
Inflation	3.9	10.4
GNP growth	4.9	2.4
Productivity growth	3.9	1.4

Sources: Unemployment rate is unemployment as a percentage of the total labor force. Inflation is a weighted average of annual changes in the CPI in the OECD economies. Productivity growth is measured as the annual change in GDP per person employed. All data are for the OECD as a whole and are constructed from the *Historical Statistics of the Main Economic Indicators, 1960–1981* (Paris: OECD, 1983).

and in the efficacy of expansionary macroeconomic policies to reduce unemployment.

In the decade of the 1960s, macroeconomists taught policymakers that a stable Phillips curve describes the menu of choices between inflation and unemployment in an economy. As Figure I.1 shows, the years 1960–69 seemed to provide a striking confirmation of the theory. During that period output rose sharply relative to trend, and very high levels of capacity utilization and low unemployment rates were reached in the major industrial countries. As output expanded, inflation increased as well; the resulting inflation-unemployment locus strongly suggested a stable trade-off, as shown by the dark regression line fit on the observations running from 1960 to 1969.[3]

Milton Friedman and Edmund Phelps cautioned the economics profession against a blithe acceptance of a stable trade-off, arguing that the curve would drift upward if unemployment were held too low for several years, and drift downward in the opposite case.[4] A constant inflation rate could be achieved only at a unique unemployment rate, dubbed the "natural" rate by Friedman. In the long run, in this view, the Phillips curve is vertical at the natural rate. And indeed, the years 1970–73 seemed to give credence to this modified view. But not even their note of pessimism prepared policymakers, macroeconomists, or the public for the sharp simultaneous increases in both inflation and unemployment that then occurred.

The period of "stagflation" (stagnation combined with inflation) broke out with a vengeance during 1973–75. OECD inflation in these years averaged 11.5 percent, up from 6.7 percent in 1971–73, while unemployment rose from 2.5 percent to 5.0 percent in the same two periods. In the next six

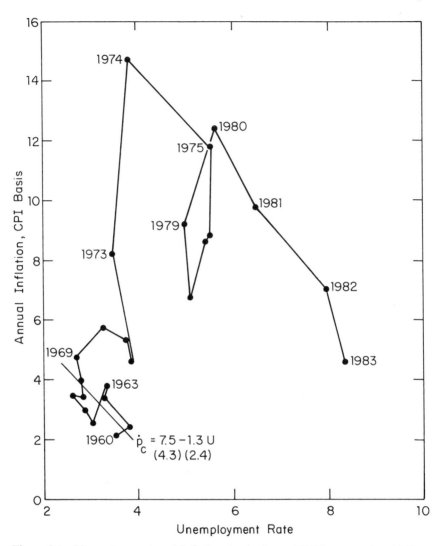

Figure I.1. Unemployment and inflation in the large OECD economies, 1960–1983

years, 1975–81, both unemployment and inflation averaged about double their rates of the 1960s. And as in 1973–75, the end of the 1970s brought in another period of steep simultaneous increases in unemployment and inflation. In 1981–83, unemployment rose while inflation fell.

The Friedman-Phelps "accelerationist" model no doubt improved upon the simple Phillips curve story, but we stress that the modified view does not take us far in explaining the recent experience. The theory predicts that the inflation-unemployment trade-off worsens with "too little" unemployment, but should *improve* with high unemployment. (Precisely, inflation is reduced when unemployment exceeds its "natural" rate.) And yet with a full decade of unemployment at twice the rates of the 1960s, the OECD economies on average still face far less favorable choices than they did fifteen years earlier.

The fact that policymakers still face an unappetizing inflation-unemployment menu helps to account for the second challenge to macroeconomic thinking, the efficacy of countercyclical policies. Some theoretical macroeconomists of the rational expectations, monetarist school have recently argued that expansionary policies could not work to reduce unemployment, even in the short run. A rationally expected monetary policy, so the argument goes, will always and immediately be rendered ineffective by the behavior of forward-looking individuals. Our own reading of the historical evidence firmly rejects this view. We believe that the reluctance of most governments to use Keynesian policies is grounded elsewhere, namely in the inflationary costs that are perceived to accompany such policies. More simply, with a Phillips curve still so far above that of the 1960s, politicians prefer to aim for the lower right end of the curve.

The Critique of Demand Management Policies

In some influential interpretations, particularly those of Friedman (1977) and Feldstein (1982), mistakes in demand management alone account for stagflation in the 1970s. In this view, policymakers pursued expansionary policies from a mistaken belief in a downward-sloping long-run Phillips curve. Higher inflation rather than reduced unemployment resulted. Because of institutional rigidities such as unindexed tax systems, and because of uncertainties surrounding relative prices in a highly inflationary environment, the argument goes, higher inflation actually reduced potential output growth and led to secular stagnation. In effect, the Phillips curve is *upward*-sloping in the time frame in which the rigidities and uncertainties persist. In this view, reduced inflation would lead to higher growth, so that a stable, low rate of money growth is seen as a major long-run stimulative measure.

Both Friedman and Feldstein recognize explicitly that the simultaneous increase in inflation and unemployment might result from independent third factors, rather than as a causal link from inflation to unemployment, but both play down that possibility. In Feldstein's words:

> In trying to identify more basic causes of inflation, it has been common for nonmonetarists to emphasize the series of particular events that were associated with spurts of inflation during the past two decades. There is no doubt that if these events had not occurred or had occurred differently, the path of inflation would also have evolved in a different way. Nevertheless, it would be wrong to put too much emphasis on these specific events. It was not events but *ideas* that propelled the increasing rate of inflation. The upward drift of the inflation rate was the result of a fundamental set of beliefs about the economy and about macroeconomic policy that were shared by economists and policy officials during the past two decades.[5]

This one-factor interpretation of stagflation is problematic on several counts. There is little doubt that policy management from the mid-1960s to early 1970s contributed to rising inflation. It is very difficult, however, to characterize policymakers as having pursued an unrelenting expansionary Keynesian program that kept the economy at the boundaries of full employment after 1973. For *every* year after 1973, for *each* of the six major OECD economies, the unemployment rate was higher than the average unemployment rate during 1960–73.

There is little evidence other than the worldwide stagflation itself to support a causal link from inflation to stagnation. According to the Feldstein-Friedman view, we should expect that countries with the greatest rise in inflation in the 1970s should also be those with the largest slowdown in GNP growth. To check this hypothesis, let us measure the rise in inflation as the average inflation rate for 1973–81 minus the average rate for 1960–73. Similarly, let us measure the slowdown in GNP growth as the average growth rate for 1960–73 minus the average rate for 1973–81.[6] Contrary to the hypothesis, these two variables are not closely related. In Table I.2, we divide twenty-four countries according to their status as above-median or below-median on the inflation rise and GNP slowdown. High-inflation countries did as well as low-inflation countries in terms of real GNP growth. There is also no simple negative relationship between the inflation rate itself during 1973–81 and the growth rate during 1973–81.

When we turn later to the cases of specific countries, these findings will be more clear. Switzerland had among the largest declines in GNP growth in the 1970s, without any increase in inflation on average. Similarly, Japan had

Table I.2.   Changes in Inflation and Unemployment in the
OECD Economies[a]

	Slowdown in GNP growth	
	Larger than median	Less than median
Rise in inflation		
Larger than median	5	7
Less than median	6	6

a. The twenty-four economies of the OECD are listed in note 1 of this chapter.

only a slight inflation increase (which was eliminated by 1978) but has had
the largest persistent slowdown in growth.

Some writers (cited by Stanley Fischer, 1981) have purported to confirm
Friedman's link from high inflation to variable inflation to slow growth.
Fischer neatly disposes of this hypothesis by showing the correlations to be
spurious. He shows that the raw material price shocks of 1974 and 1979
account for almost all of the increased price variability and much of the rise
in inflation in the 1970s. Once the price shocks are included in regressions of
macroeconomic variables on price variability, the latter term loses its explanatory power.

Based on the evidence presented throughout this book, we hold that, as in
the past, expansionary policies reduced unemployment and raised inflation
in the late 1960s and early 1970s, while contractionary policies raised unemployment and reduced inflation since 1973. The failure of inflation to moderate more rapidly in line with the high unemployment should be attributed
to other factors, which we shall introduce, rather than to continued expansionary policies.

Adding Aggregate Supply to the Macroeconomic Model

The inadequacy of purely demand-side models of stagflation has led many
macroeconomists and policymakers to put a new stress on aggregate supply,
and supply disturbances, as key factors in the stagflation. However, no new
consensus has emerged from this different focus, since the nature of supply
behavior, in the output market and particularly the labor market, is subject
to contentious dispute. "Supply-side" arguments have taken many guises. In
the model introduced by Lucas and Rapping (1970), high unemployment is
the result of a voluntary withdrawal of workers from the labor force because

of expectations of a higher wage "next period." The Lucas supply curve seems to us incapable of explaining a decade-long secular increase in unemployment rates throughout the OECD; it has also been refuted in several econometric studies.[7] For others, high taxes and high unemployment insurance benefits account for the rise in unemployment, though such views remain unsubstantiated and seem to be contradicted by the timing and magnitude of the major variables at issue. Indeed, in the United States a group of so-called supply-side economists made so many erroneous claims about the supply effects of tax cuts that the term "supply-side" has been greatly devalued.

We, too, propose that contractionary movements in aggregate supply are needed to explain the slide into stagflation, though our focus is on other aspects of the supply process. We believe that external shocks on a global scale and structural changes in the OECD economies were more important than taxes, or unemployment insurance benefits, or waiting for the illusory higher wage next period, in explaining the abrupt and universal onset of stagflation in the OECD. A clear and central villain of the piece is the historically unprecedented rise in commodity prices (mainly food and oil) in 1973–74 and again in 1979–80 that not coincidentally accompanied the two great bursts of stagflation in Figure I.1. The reactions of the private sector and of macroeconomic authorities to these shocks will be a major focus of our theoretical and empirical work.

The second supply-side focus will be on the institutional environment of wage setting in the OECD economies, both as a locus of independent structural change and as a crucial variable that determines how other shocks (for example, oil) affect the macroeconomy. For instance, one of the variables that set the stage for the 1970s stagflation was a rise in union power and militancy at the end of the 1960s. High employment, changing demographics, and shifting political winds allowed many union movements in Europe to increase their membership, their legal powers, and their plant-level representation. A real wage boom resulted, which started a squeeze on profits even before 1973. When the oil prices did rise, wages reacted in differing ways that depended (as we show in Chapter 11) on the structure of unions and wage-setting procedures. It strikes us as misguided to consider the labor market as a perfectly competitive bourse when in almost every OECD economy much of the labor force is unionized, and governments play an enormous role in affecting labor compensation (through indexation, labor taxes, incomes policies, working hours and vacation legislation, and so on).

In introducing supply considerations into the macroeconomic model, we do not reject the importance of aggregate demand fluctuations or demand policies; indeed, in some ways we vindicate their importance. Some observers have argued that the 1970s "proved Keynes wrong" and that demand policies did not work. But such statements almost always reflect the fallacy of ignoring factors other than demand that were affecting macroeconomic performance in recent years. To ask how demand policies work, we must examine their effects given that oil prices at the same time rose fivefold in real terms. When the question is looked at this way, we find that demand policies have operated largely as traditional models predict, and that such policies bear a major responsibility for the movements in output and inflation in the past decade.

In sum, therefore, we take a middle path between traditional Keynesians and monetarists on the one side, whose stress is almost entirely demand-oriented, and those on the other side who see unemployment and recession as the product of supply behavior alone. If our approach may seem dissatisfying for its doctrinal compromises, we believe that an eclectic view may compensate by trying to apply the most relevant aspects of the rival theories.

A Look at Supply and Demand Factors in the Stagflationary Era

The rest of the book describes how in our view the interaction of various supply and demand factors should enter macroeconomic theory and how these factors can help to explain some of the key developments of the last decade. Here we offer a brief look at some elements of the story that will unfold.

Though the most virulent manifestations of stagflation did not appear until 1973, many OECD economies started down that path several years earlier. In the United States a sustained period of high aggregate demand, fueled by the Vietnam War buildup, pushed the country up the short-run Phillips curve. In 1969 inflation stood at 5.4 percent compared with 1.6 percent in 1960, while unemployment declined from 5.5 percent to 3.5 percent in the course of the decade. Under the fixed-exchange-rate dollar standard, at least part of the U.S. inflation spilled abroad.

In Europe as in the United States, the sustained period of high demand in the 1960s contributed to home-grown inflation and other economic strains. Incomes policies in several economies fell apart in the face of growing labor militancy, which was notable for arising at the grass-roots level, often contrary to the policies of the national unions. The "Events of May" in France (1968), the "Hot Autumn" in Italy (1969), and the wildcat strikes in Germany (1969) all reflected this rising tension. The result in several important economies was a wage explosion, which contributed to a marked shift in income distribution away from profits and toward labor.

As inflation increased, at an uneven pace, among the major economies, the adjustable-peg exchange rate system of the Bretton Woods agreement became more and more shaky. In 1967 the pound was devalued. In 1968 the link of the dollar to gold was weakened when the private and official prices for gold were allowed to diverge. In 1969 France devalued while Germany revalued its currency. With rising inflation in the United States and an overvalued dollar, confidence in the dollar waned in 1970–71, and the dollar was finally devalued in August 1971. From this point until March 1973, when the major currencies began to float, the dollar was under periodic and intense speculative attack, spurred by expansionary U.S. monetary policies in 1972.

The implications for world macroeconomic stability were enormous. Between 1971 and 1973, in attempts to stabilize the dollar, central banks around the world intervened massively, with inflationary consequences for their own money supplies. Annual money (M1) growth in Germany jumped from 7.0 percent from end-'68 to end-'70, up to 13.4 percent from end-'70 to end-'72. Japanese M1 growth went from 18.7 percent (end-'68 to end-'70) to 27.1 percent in the latter period. A weighted-average index of money growth for all industrial countries jumped from 6.5 percent in 1968–70 to 11.6 percent in 1970–72.[8] A world boom fueled by the explosion in world liquidity thus developed in 1972–73.

Before the first oil shock, therefore, the OECD economies already carried the heavy burden of inherited inflation and a growing profit squeeze. A "soft landing" from that situation would have been difficult to manage under any circumstances, but the unprecedented commodity price explosion during 1972–74 immeasurably complicated the picture. The combination of overheated demand and adverse supply conditions caused the nominal and real prices of primary commodities to soar, with one result that the OECD economies imported several percentage points of inflation in 1973–74. Although many raw material prices collapsed in 1975, the higher food and fuel prices proved to be durable and therefore created problems for the rest of the decade.

In subsequent chapters we discuss the various effects of such a commodity price boom, including the direct imported inflation; the inevitable national income loss that accompanies the terms-of-trade deterioration; the shifts in production techniques as firms substitute away from expensive imports; and the downward pressure on profits, real wages, employment, and capital accumulation, with the final allocation of effects among these variables depending on the behavior of real wages. Then there are induced effects as policymakers shift monetary and fiscal policies in response to the shocks. Finally, there are worldwide repercussions through shifts in interest rates and exchange rates which raise problems of policy coordination on a global scale.

In the event, the response to the first oil shock was not impressive. In most countries wage setters attempted to keep pace with higher import prices, with a resulting combination of profit squeeze and inflation spiral. By 1975 in Japan and most countries in Europe, inflation was at a postwar high and real wages were far above market clearing levels. Macroeconomic policies generally turned contractionary, and the combination of tight policies and profit squeeze led to a sharp run-up in unemployment.

The period between the first and second oil shocks, during 1975–79, proved to be difficult for most of the OECD economies. Not only was inherited inflation very high, but sustained real wage growth up to 1975 had resulted in a huge shift in income distribution away from profits. As a consequence, investment growth was far below the rates of a few years earlier. Expansionary policies, in the circumstances, looked unattractive in most economies. Because of high wage indexation or frequent bargaining, an expansionary policy could moderate the profit squeeze only at the expense of significantly higher inflation. In the face of these difficulties, European unemployment rates continued to rise every year between 1975 and 1979.

It is here that one of our major empirical themes, the structural differences between the United States and Europe, first becomes important. In the United States real wages did not keep pace with the foreign shocks, with the result that real wages actually fell in 1974. Moreover, given the pattern of three-year contracts with generally a low degree of effective indexation, U.S. wages were unlikely to accelerate sharply in response to expansionary policies, which were in fact pursued. The United States experienced the only significant recovery in terms of unemployment among the major OECD economies in the intershock period.

The second rise in oil prices, during 1979–80, cut short an incipient recovery in Europe and Japan and stopped the full U.S. recovery in its tracks. Once again the external disturbance caused a run-up in inflation, another turn of the profit squeeze, and a shift to more contractionary policies. The major economies went into an even deeper slump than in 1974–75, with a much larger increase in unemployment rates, very often to double-digit rates. As of 1983 the United States began to recover once again, while Europe seemed locked in a low-growth, high-unemployment equilibrium.

The main stages of this chronology for the OECD countries may be read from the Phillips curve of Figure I.1. Periods of demand shock (for example, the expansionary policies of the mid- to late sixties, the contractionary policies of 1974–75 and 1980–83) are generally movements along a short-run Phillips curve, from southeast to northwest during expansions and northwest to southeast during contractions. Periods of supply shock (particularly 1973–74 and 1979–80) are generally southwest-northeast movements *between* short-run Phillips curves. And, as we explain in Chapter 10 in particular, the profit squeeze (the sustained period of excessive real wages) also helps to account for northeasterly shifts of the curve.

One of the puzzling features of macroeconomic performance among industrial countries has been the marked slowdown not only in output but also in factor productivity in whatever form it is measured. As we shall see, this phenomenon can hardly be explained in terms of the slowdown in capital accumulation or in research and development effort but is, in our view, strongly connected with the timing of the supply price shocks, the increased variability of output fluctuations, and the generally depressed level of output and factor utilization among the industrial countries. When one extends one's view of world developments to a broader group of countries and considers the simultaneous developments of the semi-industrialized, middle-income countries (the MICs), one finds a remarkably better growth performance among those countries during the 1970s. This puts the OECD slowdown in even sharper perspective. The explanation of the MIC performance can be found in another concomitant of the oil price increase and another important macroeconomic trade-off. The recycling of the large post-1974 OPEC surplus largely took the form of massive foreign borrowing, at very low interest rates, by the MICs. Unlike the OECD group, these countries did not enter the 1970s with tight labor markets and the overhang of a profit squeeze. They could thus utilize the current account trade-off to their advantage and continue to invest and pursue generally expansionary domestic policies. For a while, therefore, the MICs managed to avoid the general world slowdown in output and productivity. Only after the second oil shock did the highly contractionary monetary policies in the major OECD economies sharply raise world interest rates, and the inflationary consequences of the earlier expansion also finally caught up with domestic labor markets in some of the MICs (notably Korea and Brazil). The drop in oil prices after 1982 also took its toll (Mexico, Nigeria). At that time the MICs too started joining the world stagflation club amidst growing financial convulsions, accelerating inflation, output cuts, and sharp rises in unemployment.

To sum up, then, what are the main puzzles and theoretical questions that these empirical developments bring up? First and foremost, theory has to account for the simultaneous acceleration of inflation and rising unemployment and the persistence of unemployment, both of which were the major new stagflationary phenomena of the 1970s (which continue into the 1980s). These are pervasive and closely synchronized among countries. Theory also has to account for the medium- and long-term changes in investment and capital accumulation patterns. The differences among countries in macroeconomic performance in the face of common disturbances also have to be explained in terms of comparative macroeconomic theory. To this one might add the marked slowdown in productivity which was common to all industrial countries but not shared by many of the semi-industrialized countries. Finally, global capital movements and sharp fluctuations in real interest rates and exchange rates have to be incorporated into the framework of analysis. Most pervasive of all is the basic underlying question of why, for at least a decade, the industrial world has been performing so poorly in virtually every aspect of macroeconomic life.

Related Studies

Several researchers have made important contributions to the topics of our study, which we are happy to acknowledge here. We also mention some of our own antecedents to this book. We should like to cite three areas of research in particular: the role of raw material price shocks in stagflation; the role of wage-setting institutions in the overall macroeconomic adjustment process; and the formulation of macroeconomic policies under flexible exchange rates, including the issue of policy coordination among a number of economies.

Robert Gordon (1975) was one of the first researchers to indicate both analytically and empirically the role of raw material price shocks in the stagflation process, in a closed-economy model with a focus on the United States. Also working with a U.S. focus, Mork and Hall (1978) built one of the first detailed simulation studies of the oil price shock. Subsequently, Blinder (1979) offered a major econometric study of the role of food and energy prices in the U.S. inflation in the 1970s. Findlay and Rodriguez (1977) provided the first open-economy model of an oil supply shock. The model was rudimentary in structure, focusing on a static one-country environment, with fixed nominal wages and oil inputs used in fixed proportion to output. Bruno (1980) gave the first analytical and econometric discussion of the role of import price shocks for the stagflation in the OECD as a whole. Malinvaud's important study in disequilibrium macroeconomics (1977) put the focus on the conceptual difference between supply and demand shocks in a closed-economy context.

Several papers, including Bruno and Sachs (1979, 1981) Buiter (1979), Rodriguez (1977), and Solow (1980) offered theoretical improvements on the early vintage of models, including the introduction of a second country, dynamics, substitutability in factor demands, and short-run nonmarket clearing. Sachs (1983a) constructed a dynamic perfect-foresight growth model for two economies, which was adapted in modified form by Giavazzi, Odenken, and Wyplosz (1982). Recently, Marion and Svensson (1982, 1983) added further refinements, including a welfare analysis of an oil shock, using duality relations. Van Wijnbergen (1981) and Steigum (1980) likewise provided additional insights on the disequilibrium formulation.

A number of authors have stressed the role of wage-setting behavior for macroeconomic policy and adjustment, in particular comparing nominal and real wage rigidities. Hicks (1974) provided one of the earliest and most lucid discussions of the causes and macroeconomic implications of "real wage resistance" (his term). Gray (1976) showed in a closed-economy context that wage indexation amplifies the price and output consequences of supply shocks, while reducing the output effects of monetary shocks. Papers by Casas (1975), Argy and Salop (1979), Branson and Rotemberg (1980), Modigliani and Padoa-Schioppa (1978), and Sachs (1980b) studied the effects of wage indexation in an open economy and showed that "traditional" policy prescriptions based on rigid (unindexed) nominal wages could be reversed for indexed wages. Recently, the work of Grubb, Jackman, and Layard (1982, 1983) has added valuable theoretical and empirical insight into the links between wage setting and stagflation.

In the mid-1970s several authors began to note the excessive levels of real wages throughout the OECD. John S. Flemming (1976) was probably the first to calculate a "real wage gap" (for the United Kingdom) of the sort used extensively in this book. Corden (1978, 1979), Drèze and Modigliani (1981), Giersch (1981), and Korteweg (1979) argued with respect to individual-country experience that real wage levels were too high (for Australia, Belgium, Germany, and the Netherlands, respectively). Bruno and Sachs (1981), Sachs (1979), and Branson and Rotemberg (1980) made a similar argument on a cross-country, comparative basis. The OECD and the European Economic Community (EEC) also began in the late 1970s to produce "wage gap" measures based on changes in labor's share of income.

The pathbreaking studies of J. M. Fleming (1962) and Mundell (1963) are the bases for policy analysis under flexible exchange rates. Dornbusch (1976) substantially advanced the theoretical frontier by extending this analysis to a dynamic context. Turnovsky and Kaspura (1974), Bruno (1978b), Sachs (1980b), Argy and Salop (1979), and Branson and Rotemberg (1980) examined a range of wage and price dynamics. Several authors, including Hamada and Sakurai (1978) and Mussa (1979), pointed out the strong interdependence of economies under flexible exchange rates, contrary to the view held by some that flexible rates could insulate an economy from foreign disturbances. Hamada (1974, 1979), Johansen (1982), and Canzoneri and Gray (1983) drew a strong lesson from that interdependence by pointing out the importance of international policy coordination in a game-theoretic framework.

Plan of the Book

This book has several aims and therefore, we hope, several types of potential readers. It has been organized to accommodate the varying interests that readers may have in the text. At its most general level it is an extended essay, both theoretical and empirical, on the integration of supply considerations into demand-oriented macroeconomic models and modes of analysis. Its more specific contribution in this regard is its analysis of import price shocks and wage-setting behavior in open and interdependent economies.

The first half of the book is a mostly theoretical, and the second half a mostly empirical, investigation of these topics in terms of comparative macroeconomics. Chapter 1 provides a nontechnical summary of the theoretical work, while Chapter 8 introduces the major empirical findings. Chapter 13 provides a summary, with a discussion of the major policy implications of our findings. For readers mostly interested in the theory, we recommend reading Chapters 1–7, 8, and 13. For those interested in the empirical discussion, we recommend Chapter 1 as a theoretical overview and then Chapters 8–13.

The theoretical chapters build up an understanding of supply shocks through a series of parsimonious models in Chapters 2 through 6. Wherever possible, an attempt is made to keep the discussion at a low level of complexity and leave the technical articulation to appendixes. After the overview in Chapter 1, Chapter 2 introduces the production function and the factor price frontier (FPF) into the analysis. Some econometric estimates of the FPF are presented in an appendix to Chapter 2. In Chapter 3 we study the short-run and long-run supply behavior of the firm, with special focus on the role of intermediate inputs in the production process. Chapter 4 first introduces the demand side into the model, by studying household consumption and savings behavior in an intertemporal context. By linking several countries together in world commodity and capital markets, we study the effects of a raw material price increase on world interest rates and capital flows. In Chapter 5 we abandon the assumption of full short-run market clearing, allowing for various rigidities in output prices and nominal and real wages. The role of Keynesian demand policies in response to various supply shocks is then examined. This short-run emphasis is extended to a two-country setting in Chapter 6, where we show that a global supply shock is likely to induce overly contractionary policies in each economy unless the policy responses are coordinated across the two countries. Finally, in Chapter 7, all of the analytical pieces are pulled together in a series of large-scale simulation models.

The empirical part of the book, Chapters 8 – 12, builds upon the earlier analysis in order to assess the roles of various supply and demand factors in the stagflation. Chapter 8 provides an empirical overview of a large number of OECD economies and describes briefly the genesis of the commodity price shocks in the 1970s. In Chapter 9 our measure of supply-side imbalance, the real wage gap, is presented and its role as an indicator of supply conditions is discussed in several ways. In Chapter 10 the wage gap reappears; together with import prices, it is seen as a major determinant of the shifts in the Phillips curve in the 1970s and 1980s. In addition, the wage gap and monetary policy are shown to be key explanatory variables in the unemployment dynamics of the past decade. In Chapter 11 a cross-country study is made to find the keys to successful macroeconomic performance in recent years. We show that the structural characteristics of the labor market have been an important determinant of overall macroeconomic performance. In Chapter 12 we take up the productivity puzzle to assess the relative importance of oil prices, demand management, and other factors in the weak productivity performance of the past decade. We also consider the differential growth performance of the MICs. Chapter 13 pulls together both halves of the book to reach some conclusions regarding the role of policy in a stagflationary period.

1 Elements of a Theory

IN THIS FIRST chapter we present the major elements of our theoretical framework by means of a simplified diagrammatic exposition. This is done for the benefit of readers who prefer, at first, to skip the detailed and more technical theoretical chapters that immediately follow (Chapters 2–7) and move directly to the empirical part of the study (Chapters 8–13). Our preliminary discussion follows the general order of topics in the detailed theoretical chapters. Detailed derivations for the propositions in this chapter will be found in the theoretical chapters that follow.

Factor Prices and Production Response

The story of macroeconomic upheavals in the last ten to fifteen years will be closely linked in our analysis to the sharp changes that have taken place in the real costs of factor inputs into production—real wages, real interest rates, and, last but not least, the real cost of raw materials, particularly of energy.[1] It is thus natural to start from the most elementary cost accounting of an individual firm, an industry, or the economy as a whole. In each case we may talk, in simplified fashion, of the quantity of and returns to three major factors of production, as shown in Table 1.1.

Our hypothetical production unit hires labor (L) at the cost of W per man-hour; it "imports" materials (N) at the cost of P_N per unit; and it remunerates its owned real stock of productive assets (plant and equipment, denoted by K) at a nominal rate of profit (Z). The profit rate may or may not equal the going rate of interest or rate of return in the economy. By definition, total costs ($WL + P_N N + ZK$) must equal total revenue (PQ) from the sale of Q units of the final good at unit market price P.

Table 1.1. Accounting Framework for Factor Costs

Factor	Quantity	Nominal rate of return (price)	Total cost
Labor (man-hours)	L	W	WL
Capital (real stock of productive assets)	K	Z	ZK
Imported materials	N	P_N	$P_N N$
Total final output	Q	P	PQ

The same accounting identity can, in principle, be applied to a group of firms or a whole industry, provided we net out all purchases of raw materials and intermediate goods which the constituent firms buy from each other, and regard as purchased inputs (N) only those material inputs which are imported from outside the group or industry in question. Finally, one can apply the same identity to the accounting framework of the whole economy, where the final output is the total aggregate use of final goods (for consumption, investment, and exports) and N is total imports of goods and services from abroad. Obviously we now ignore problems of heterogeneity of labor inputs or of types of capital or the many types of raw materials.

Once we have established this basic accounting identity ($PQ = WL + ZK + P_N N$), we may subtract the purchased materials from sales ($PQ - P_N N$) and obtain what is called nominal value added or the nominal product which, by definition, must equal the sum of the wage bill and profits ($WL + ZK$). In general, however, one is not interested in nominal costs and returns, but rather in some *real* measure, that is, after deflating by the price level of some good. Let us use the physical quantities of the final good as our accounting unit and redefine real factor rewards (or costs) in those terms, that is, divide the nominal magnitudes by the price P. The real wage (W/P) will be denoted by W_Q, the real rate of return to capital (Z/P) will be denoted by R, and the real cost of materials (P_N/P) will be denoted by Π_N. This also allows us to define real income in final output units and denote it by $Y[Y = (PQ - P_N N)/P = Q - \Pi_N N]$. This, in turn, will be equal to the real wage bill plus real profits ($W_Q L + RK$).

Much of macroeconomic theory and measurement deals with situations in which the relative price of raw materials (or of imports) does not change, or in which there are fixed proportions between the material input and final output (N/Q). Let us for the moment assume that the "share" of materials in final output stays fixed and equals a number, $\bar{s}_n [s_n = P_N N/(PQ) = \Pi_N N/Q =$

$\bar{s}_n$]. In that case Y is also a fixed proportion of gross output, Q, and it equals $Y = (1 - \bar{s}_n)Q$. Since Y now changes at the same rate as Q, we can suppress the distinction between the two and, for the time being, ignore raw materials altogether. It is as if labor and capital combine to give a net output Y, or $(1 - \bar{s}_n)Q$.

Now let us consider all the possible alternatives of real factor rewards (W_Q, R) that can be sustained by a firm or an industry employing given quantities of labor L_0, and capital, K_0, and obtaining net output, Y_0. These alternative pairs of rewards must obviously lie along a downward-sloping straight line connecting the two axes on which the real wage and real rate of profit are measured (see line YY in Figure 1.1).[2] The line cuts the axes at the intercepts that measure the real income per man-hour (Y_0/L_0) and real income per unit of capital (Y_0/K_0), respectively, and its slope equals the capital/labor ratio (K_0/L_0). At the point C where the real wage is given as W_{Q_1}, the real rate of profit will equal R_1. If a higher real wage (in output units) must be paid, the real rate of profit must of necessity be squeezed to a lower

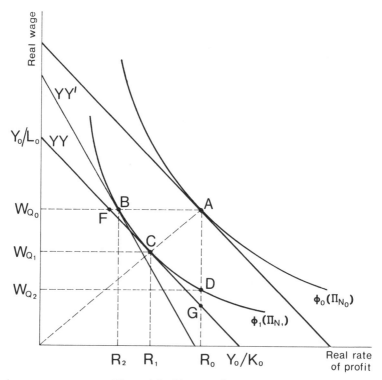

Figure 1.1. Factor price curves

level, such as at point F in the figure. Note that the same set of unit factor reward options would also be applicable to any firm (or industry) which is an exact blow-up of the previous unit, since it is only the *ratios* $(K/L, Y/L)$ that matter in this diagram.

We have just shown almost inadvertently how this particular production unit would respond to a real wage push. If it is forced to keep to the same production technology (represented by the capital/labor ratio), there is only one possible response: the real rate of profit must go down in the short run as indicated by the move from the point C to F. But if the real wage push is a permanent one and no increase in productivity is envisaged, it may want to move to a less labor-intensive and more capital-intensive activity. Suppose that this option is now available to the firm and that this more capital-intensive activity option is represented by the steeper line YY'. Given the permanently higher real wage at W_{Q_0}, the unit will choose to readjust its factor proportions and operate at the point B where the fall in profits is less than at F.

Now suppose that there are infinitely many options available to substitute labor for capital, at least in the long run. Suppose we ask what is the maximal rate of profit that is obtainable by this production unit for any given and fixed real wage cost. We would have to search through all the possible capital/labor ratios like those represented by YY, YY', and similar lines. The envelope of all these lines, the curve ϕ_1 in Figure 1.1, represents this geometric locus. It is called the *factor price frontier* (FPF). As long as technological options obey a basic homogeneity property, namely, that we have constant returns to scale in all factors of production (L, K, and the momentarily suppressed N), there is only one such downward-sloping (and convex to the origin) curve which summarizes all there is to know about the technology and the alternative factor rewards sustainable by it. Given any real wage, it indicates the maximal obtainable rate of return to capital and the appropriate optimal capital/labor ratio. This ratio is always given by the tangent to ϕ_1 at the appropriate point (such as C or B).

Note that the roles of labor and capital are entirely symmetric in this framework. Suppose we now take as our production unit the whole economy. Instead of assuming that the real wage cost is given, we could postulate a situation in which the economy in question borrows the finance for its capital investments from abroad and the real rate of interest on such loans is given on world markets. In that case it makes sense to assume that in the long run the economy will choose a capital/labor ratio which is appropriate to the given rate of interest. Competition among firms in the economy will ensure that the rate of profit will eventually equalize itself to this external rate of interest. The factor price frontier will then tell us what maximal real wage rate workers can expect to get in such an economy. If the external interest rate rises for some reason, the economy will at the given level of technological know-how have to opt for a less capital-intensive technology, reduce its capital/labor ratio, and be forced to pay a lower real wage (for example, consider the reverse movement from B to C in Figure 1.1).

So far we have abstracted from the possibility of technical progress, that is, a situation in which a given quantity of productive factors produces more output as time or technological know-how advances. In the event of such technological progress the whole factor price frontier will shift outward, say from ϕ_1 to ϕ_0 in Figure 1.1. The case depicted in the figure is one in which such progress is neutral as between the factors,[3] namely, at the same capital/labor ratio (note that the tangent through A is parallel to YY) both factor rewards rise by the same proportion ($R_0/R_1 = W_{Q_0}/W_{Q_1}$). If we repeat the earlier scenario under technical progress, then a permanent rise in the real wage will not only be consistent with maintaining the same initial factor intensity but will also enable an equiproportionate increase in the real rate of profit.

At this point we must go back and qualify one basic simplifying assumption that was made when we suppressed the role of raw materials, namely, that the relative price and share of materials stay constant. There is no way in which the developments of the 1970s can be understood without explicit account being taken of the sharp rises in real raw material prices (Π_N) and of the change in the cost share of this important factor.

Let us therefore consider a rise in the relative price of raw materials Π_N and look at the outcome of such a change. The quantity demanded of the raw material (N) relative to the output level (Q) will be reduced. If the rise in raw material prices lowers the quantity ratio N/Q by less than the change in the real cost, Π_N, the share s_n of raw materials in gross output rises and that of domestic real income falls. In fact it can be shown more generally that if the price of raw materials rises, the given input of labor and capital will always yield less real income.[4] Let us now use the analogy of shifts in the factor price frontier due to changes in technological know-how. The case of a rise in Π_N thus is analogous to technical regress or negative technical progress. Suppose ϕ_0 is the relevant factor price frontier when the real price of raw materials is fixed at Π_{N_0}. A rise in the cost of the third factor, N, is tantamount to an *inward* shift (contraction) of the FPF from ϕ_0 to ϕ_1, with real income per unit of labor (Y/L) and real income per unit of capital (Y/K) falling. This is a useful analogy because it also suggests that a rise in the cost of the third factor causes a productivity fall in terms of gross output per unit of labor and capital, a property that we shall return to later on.

Let us now suppose that regular technological progress has already been netted out of Figure 1.1, namely, factor rewards are measured relative to their long-term trends.[5] Thus, shifts in the FPF are due solely to changes in the cost of raw materials, and suppose that the inward shift from ϕ_0 to ϕ_1 is a proportional contraction for both factors of production. Such "homothetic" contraction can be shown to take place whenever the production function can be written in a two-level form: $Q = Q[V(L,K),N]$. Namely, gross output can be written as a function of raw materials and a domestic value-added index (V) which, in turn, can be written as a second tier function of labor and capital. This particular separable form will accompany us throughout much of this study.

Suppose an economy (or industry) starts from an initial point A with a capital/labor ratio K_0/L_0, paying a real wage (relative to trend) of W_{Q_0} and obtaining a real rate of profit on capital of R_0. A rise in raw material prices from Π_{N_0} to Π_{N_1} will entail a downward adjustment in one or both factor rewards and a corresponding factor reallocation in production, all depending on how flexible or rigid is the response of the relevant magnitudes.

If real wages are flexible downward so that the economy can utilize all of its capital and labor, and if these factor supplies are inelastic in the short run, the new short-run equilibrium will be at the point C where the capital/labor ratio is equal to its initial level at A, $K = K_0$, and labor remains fully employed $(L = L_0)$. Both the real wage and the rate of profit fall by the same proportion, which is related to the increase in the raw material price. Likewise, real income (Y) must fall at the same rate.

This particular experiment, in which the quantities of labor and capital remain constant and real income falls, also helps to highlight another important conceptual problem. The real income concept (Y), which is obtained from the single deflation of value added by the final goods price, may serve as a purchasing power yardstick but not as a reliable measure of real GDP output, $V(K,L)$, since that should not change when Π_N changes. Even more important, had we used a conventionally measured double-deflated constant base-year $(P = P_N = 1)$ priced GDP $(Q - N)$, that too could be shown to give a biased measure of real net output when changes in material prices and their share in gross output are large.[6]

Suppose now that real wages are temporarily rigid rather than downward-flexible because workers' wages are linked to the cost of living, and that they are momentarily fixed at W_{Q_0}. In that case the short-run equilibrium is obtained at the point B and not at C. The rate of profit falls even further ($R_2 < R_1$), and labor can no longer remain fully employed. The optimum capital/labor ratio at B (the slope of the tangent) must be higher than at C (and at A). Given the same initial capital stock (K_0), this can only take place if less labor is employed. A rigid real wage, under the assumption made, perforce leads to unemployment.[7] The same framework can be used to show that an autonomous real wage push (moving the economy up along a given factor price frontier, such as from C to B) or a fall in productivity or in the capital stock can likewise lead to unemployment in the short run. We shall subsequently discuss the difference between this "classical" type of unemployment and the more conventional Keynesian variety.

In reality, of course, there will be no pure case of full wage flexibility or complete rigidity; as we shall see, countries cover a fairly wide spectrum of wage responses to an external price shock and also differ in their extent of downward adjustment once unemployment sets in. Likewise, it is important to realize the scope for expansionary monetary policy in a country like the United States or Canada, where *nominal* wages tend to be institutionally sticky but where there is very little formal price indexation. In that case a monetary expansion may temporarily inflate away the real wage and cause an output and employment expansion along the path from B to C. A typical European country, with more real wage resistance, might react to the monetary expansion by price inflation with little trade-off in terms of employment. We shall return to this discussion in the next section.

What happens in the medium and long run? Suppose the long-run borrowing rate is set at the initial rate of return (R_0). The long-run equilibrium is then represented by the point D at which both the capital/labor ratio and the real wage are lower than at C. To maintain full employment in the long run, real wages must fall and capital must be decumulated relative to trend.[8]

Finally, consider the implied assumption that the raw material price increase is a permanent one. If it is perceived as temporary rather than permanent, the FPF is expected to shift back to ϕ_0 after a while and long-run production will be back at A and not at D, while in the short run production will take place at C or B, as before. Total output in the short run will not be affected by this difference in perception but its allocation between consumption and investment will be, because of the differential effect on capital accumulation. In the permanent shock case we have an investment squeeze, whereas in the case of a temporary shock investment need not be affected.

We have so far seen that a raw material price shock (and likewise a real wage push) affects employment in the short run, with the extent and duration of unemployment depending on wage flexibility. The associated profit squeeze will affect the capital accumulation process. Can a country interfere in the transmission process of an external input price shock of this kind? If the domestically produced good (Q) is not a perfect substitute in world trade and it competes in trade with another final good whose international price is P^* and domestic price is EP^* (E = exchange rate between the domestic and foreign currency), then there may be a wedge between the international price ratio of the material input $(P_N^*/P^* = \Pi_N^*$, say) and the domestic relative price Π_N. That wedge, which is the terms of trade between the domestic and international final goods $[\Pi = P/(EP^*) = \Pi_N^*/\Pi_N]$, may be changed by domestic policy. This ratio, after all, is also a measure of the real exchange rate. By a real appreciation of its currency a country may shield itself from the domestic repercussions of an external price shock. It may attenuate the unemployment and inflation effects of such a shock, but, as we shall see, this may come about at the cost of a greater current-account deficit.

Savings, Investment, and International Capital Flows

Suppose we return now to a simple tradable goods world in which the domestically produced final good (Q) is identically the same as everybody else's (that is, purchasing power parity, $P = EP^*$, holds), and the same holds for our one, stylized, raw material (N).[9] But now allow for many countries $(i = 1, 2, \ldots m)$ in a trading world, the ith country producing Q^i and using N^i. We also allow for domestic production (H^i) of the raw material. Countries, of course, differ from one another in the quantities used or produced. Most of them will be net importers $(N^i - H^i > 0)$ but a few ("OPEC") will be net exporters $(H^i - N^i > 0)$ of the material in question. It is the latter that can be assumed to fix either the quantity or the real international price (Π_N) of the input in question.

How is the real income of a country affected by a unit change in the real cost of the raw material? The answer is straightforward. Real income of a representative country (suppress the i superscript for simplicity) will now be $Y = Q - \Pi_N N + \Pi_N H$ or $Y = Q + \Pi_N(H - N)$. When the real price changes by one unit, real income changes by exactly $(H - N)$. A net importer loses and a net exporter gains by such a price change by exactly the amount of his net balance in that good. Moreover, if the real price change is a permanent one, then the country's expected future income will also change by its expected net balance in each period. In other words, a country's total wealth, which is the discounted sum of future net real incomes, will change by the net discounted balance of all present and future net material flows $(H - N)$.

This brings us to the next important question. Countries must obviously trade in final goods (Q) against net imports or exports of the material input. Abstracting from transportation costs and heterogeneity of final goods, a country will be a net exporter ($X^i > 0$) or a net importer ($X^i < 0$) of the final good in question. Now, to be realistic we do not require that each country's net flows in materials $\Pi_N(H - N)$ and in final goods (X) sum up to zero in each period separately. It need only do so in discounted value over the expected planning horizon. In fact, a key feature of the 1970s game is that current accounts did not balance. Some countries were net borrowers [$F = X + \Pi_N(H - N) < 0$] and some were net creditors ($F > 0$). Summed over all countries, the world trade balance must, of course, be zero ($\Sigma F^i = 0$). This is where the important role of foreign borrowing comes in.

Suppose there is a world capital market in which financial imbalances are traded at an intertemporal real interest rate R. It is easiest to conceive of this balancing act as taking place in terms of the obverse side of the balance-of-payments coin, that is, the current account balance as defined in terms of the difference between a country's national savings (S) and national investment (I). The real interest rate (R) will be determined at the intersection of a world savings schedule (S^w) and a world aggregate investment schedule (I^w). But how are savings and investment related to the two key variables Π_N and R?

For each country we may assume, on the basis of our earlier discussion, that investments in production for final goods will react negatively both to a rise in the real interest rate on borrowing and to a permanent rise in Π_N (remember the FPF). Thus, for all countries together (after standardizing for a common efficiency-based labor unit), a downward-sloping world investment schedule can be drawn in an I-R diagram (see Figure 1.2). An increase in Π_N will shift it down and to the left.

The savings story is a more complicated one. As is known from Fisherian theory, for any individual country savings will be positively related to the rate of interest if it is a net debtor. Savings can also be shown to be negatively related to Π_N when a country is a net importer of raw materials (and positively related if it is an OPEC country). As we have seen, a country's wealth contracts or expands according to this basic structural difference. The aggregate outcome for world savings can ultimately be expressed in terms of the following two statements:

1. World savings will be positively related to the rate of interest if the deficit-weighted marginal propensity to consume of the net debtors is greater than (or equal to) the surplus-weighted marginal propensity to consume of the net creditors.

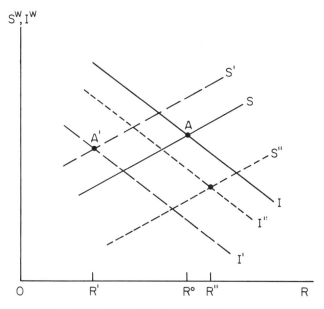

Figure 1.2. Determination of real interest rates

2. Aggregate world consumption falls with an increase in the real price
of the material if the marginal propensity to consume of the net
material exporters (OPEC) is less than the weighted marginal propensity to consume of the net importers.

The first condition is likely to hold empirically if there is a high negative
correlation between deficits and country average income levels (which, in
turn, are probably negatively correlated with marginal propensities to consume). Thus the world savings schedule in *S-R* space is likely to be upward-
sloping (see Figure 1.2). Far more ambiguous is the direction of shifts in
world savings after an oil price shock. After the first oil shock there was a
large investment squeeze (say, *I* shifted to *I'*), but the savings curve probably
rose as the OPEC countries were at first unable to use up their surplus funds
for consumption (see statement 2 above). This can account for the sharp
drop in real interest rates and the emergence of a new extensive world capital
market (see the drop from R^0 to R' in Figure 1.2). The big gainers from this
flow of funds were the middle-income industrializing countries (MICs), who
pursued an expansionary domestic policy, borrowing and investing quite
heavily. A typical net oil-importing country, which also happens to be a net
borrower, obviously suffers from an oil price hike but at the same time gains

from a more readily accessible and lower-priced foreign loan market. Such an economy, especially if it also happened to be more wage-flexible, was likely to suffer much less than a typical industrial creditor country, with a rigid domestic wage structure. It may even have gained for a while from the combination of a rise in Π_N and a fall in R that took place in the mid-1970s.

Things looked different after the second oil price shock as real interest rates started climbing quite rapidly. A set of circumstances that might explain this in terms of Figure 1.2 would be a much smaller investment squeeze[10] and a downward (rather than upward) shift in world savings due to less frugal OPEC savings behavior and a sharper squeeze in industrial country savings (large budget deficits, tighter monetary policy and greater output contraction, and so on). This time, the middle-income countries no longer enjoyed a "free lunch," and their domestic labor markets may also have tightened.

This discussion shows how important the spillover from raw material markets into world financial capital markets may have been. This in turn may be brought back to bear on the factor price frontier (Figure 1.1) and to the differential output and factor allocation responses of countries to such a sequence of external shocks.

Supply Shocks and Demand Management

So far we have dealt only with the supply side of the economy.[11] In a world of complete wage and price flexibility, the analysis of short-run and long-run output, investment, and employment response could proceed without regard to aggregate demand—traditionally a crucial element in macroeconomic theory and policy. But ours is definitely not such a view of the world; indeed, we believe that the role of aggregate demand response is crucial to the understanding of the events of the 1970s and early 1980s. What one can do, therefore, is to superimpose the supply structure discussed earlier on a conventional Keynesian aggregate demand framework.

A macroeconomic framework in which the effects of input price shocks can be analyzed requires the explicit incorporation of raw materials (N) as a separate factor of production along with the conventional labor (L) and capital (K) inputs in the production of final goods (Q). As before, suppose that we can write $Q = [V(L,K),N]$, but this time abandon purchasing power parity and allow for change in the relative prices of home goods (P) and exports or imports of final goods (EP^*). The determination of output and prices in a system like this can be described in terms of aggregate supply (S) and aggregate demand (D) schedules, as drawn in Figure 1.3.

Along the horizontal axis we can measure real GDP (V) in the production of final goods,[12] where $V = V(L,K)$. In the short run the capital stock is fixed so that the horizontal axis can also be used as an ordinal measure of employment. V_f is the GDP level at full employment [$V_f = V(L_0,K_0)$]. Any output level below V_f will signify unemployment. Along the vertical axis we measure the unit price of final goods (P) or the marginal costs of production.

The aggregate supply of goods in the short run can be described as an upward-sloping schedule, S, where the productive capacity (represented here by capital stock, K), the level of technology (T), the international real cost of materials (Π_N^*), the nominal exchange rate (E), and the nominal wage (W) are held constant.[13] Below the full-employment level, the curve S is a marginal short-run cost schedule which assumes rising marginal costs of production with an increase in output. (It can be derived from the same production framework that underlies the FPF of Figure 1.1.) Below a certain output level, as capacity becomes underutilized, the supply curve may be horizontal, while above a certain output level (V_f), S becomes vertical as full em-

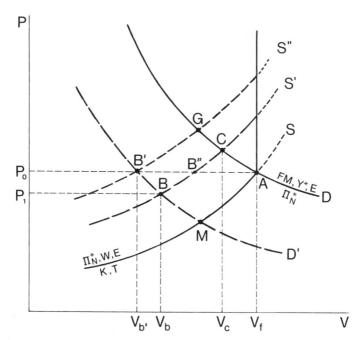

Figure 1.3. Supply and demand determination of output and prices

ployment of all factors in the economy is reached. Under fairly reasonable assumptions it can be shown that an increase in the real cost of materials, in nominal wages, or in the exchange rate (which affects the domestic costs of imports) will shift the supply curve (S) up and to the left, while an increase in the capital stock (K) or in total factor productivity (T) will in the long run shift S down and to the right.[14]

The curve D marks the aggregate demand schedule for this economy. Other things being equal, the demand for final goods (such as consumer goods or exports) rises with a fall in the final goods price (P). What are those "other things" that are held constant when the downward-sloped aggregate demand curve is drawn? One is the relative price of materials (Π_N^*), which affects demand through real income and wealth, and not only on the supply side. When the real price of materials such as oil rises, a net importer of such goods suffers a real income and wealth loss while a net exporter (such as OPEC) benefits. Against this we must weigh the possible substitution of V for N as Π_N^* rises. For a typical industrial country, a rise in the real cost of material inputs on balance shifts the aggregate demand schedule to the left (this is why Π_N^* is placed on the left-hand side of D in Figure 1.3). A rise in world real income (Y^*) or in the exchange rate (E), which affects export demand and expansionary domestic fiscal and monetary policy (briefly denoted FM in Figure 1.3), which affect domestic demand for consumption and investment goods, will each shift the D curve up and to the right. The world export price (P^*) would have a similar effect, but it is assumed constant here and therefore ignored.

We can now use this framework to analyze the output (employment) and price effects of rising material prices as well as the derived effects of the policy response to such input price shocks. As was shown on the factor price frontier, the first impact of rising input prices is a leftward shift of the aggregate supply curve (from S to S'): rising costs of material input or a rise in wages at a given price level reduce profits and the output that producers will be willing to supply at each given price level. Suppose for a moment that there is sufficient compensatory expansionary policy on the demand side to neutralize the contractionary effect of rising material prices on real income, so that the demand curve (D) stays put. In this hypothetical case, with everything else (including wages) held constant, rising material prices or real wages (or a fall in K or T) cause a move of the economy from the initial full-employment equilibrium point A to a new equilibrium point C. There is a fall in output and employment and a rise in prices, which is the essence of a stagflationary impact effect. Such a supply shock is in marked contrast to a shift in aggregate demand, with S held constant, where prices and output (employment) tend to move together (compare, for example, the points M

and A).[15] Note that a similar supply shock effect would be observed if there were an autonomous wage push, exceeding productivity growth, or if there were an autonomous drop in the capital stock or in productivity.

The size of the supply shock depends on what happens to wages (and to the exchange rate). If real wages are downward-flexible, thus mitigating the squeeze on profits, this in itself may prevent the S curve from rising further (the same is true for a currency appreciation, that is, a fall in E). But if real wages are partly rigid relative to productivity (T), so that the nominal wage responds to higher prices with a further rise, the leftward shift in S for a given upward push on prices will be more pronounced (such as from S to S'').[16] The associated profit squeeze which hampers investment depresses capital growth (that is, reduces K), which may further strengthen the supply shock in the medium and long run. The extent of the upward push on wages will depend not only on the degree of wage indexation (real wage rigidity) but also on the size of unemployment, that is, the size of the gap between actual V and V_f, which is a standard Phillips curve argument.

Consider the demand side now. Other things being equal, a rise in Π_N^*, we have argued, depresses real income and demand for a net importer, thus shifting the D schedule leftward and exerting further downward pressure on output (and employment). Contractionary demand management policy (a fall in FM) and the mutual interaction of falling incomes in export markets of other industrial countries (reducing Y^*) cause a further contraction of aggregate demand.

Suppose that D shifts to D'. A new equilibrium in the commodity market, given the configuration of Figure 1.3, will be at the point B, output having fallen further to V_b and the final goods price also adjusting downward in this case to P_1.[17] If P is slow to adjust, production may actually take place at B' (a further fall in demand, output, and employment), where a disequilibrium between supply and demand (potential excess supply of $B'B''$) may for a time persist. As the economy adjusts to the new equilibrium at B, the domestic price level will be adjusting downward (relative to the price of tradables EP^*) while unemployment remains high. This brings us to an important issue, the characterization of the nature of unemployment.

Real Wage Gaps and the Characterization of Unemployment Trade-offs

Once we allow for the possibility that output market prices may not instantly equate supply and demand, we are led to distinguish two types of output shortfalls. If, at a given market price, supply exceeds demand, we speak of pure "Keynesian" unemployment. At given factor and output prices, firms would like to sell more output, but insufficient demand prevents them from doing so. In Figure 1.3, with supply S' and demand D', at given price P_0, firms can only sell B', though they would like to produce B''. The gap $B'B''$ will be termed "Keynesian underproduction." Its counterpart in the labor market, measured by the difference of derived labor demand at B' and B'', can be termed "Keynesian unemployment."

If, on the other hand, output demand exceeds output supply at the market price (and the output supply is less than V_f), then we have pure "classical" unemployment. Thus, with demand D and supply S', we have an excess demand at price P_0 in the magnitude $B''A$. Assuming that at given factor costs suppliers are willing to supply only as much as B'' when the price is P_0, unemployment due to output supply (rather than output demand) insufficiency will result.

In most of the book we assume that output markets clear, so that production occurs at the intersection of supply and demand schedules. Such an equilibrium, illustrated by point B for supply S' and demand D', is evidently at the borderline of Keynesian and classical unemployment. It is in fact the type of equilibrium that Keynes himself described. One characteristic of such an equilibrium is crucial. Since firms are on their supply schedules at B (and thus are not demand-rationed), an expansion from V_b to V_f requires a rise in the quantity of desired *supply,* as well as demand. Not only must demand be raised, but firms must also be induced to raise their output levels. This must be brought about either through a shift along the supply schedule, that is, by raising prices, or by a shift in the supply schedule itself. Either way, the shift in supply will require a fall in one or many real factor prices, or a rise in the capital stock or level of productivity. But demand expansion alone, for *given* real factor prices, capital stock, and technology, cannot restore full employment.

The distinction between pure Keynesian unemployment and the borderline Keynesian-classical variety is therefore that in the latter case, the quantities of both aggregate supply and demand must be increased to restore full employment, while in the former case a demand shift alone can do the job. It must be stressed, however, that "demand" policies (such as monetary or fiscal expansion) may in fact be efficacious in raising the levels of both aggregate supply and demand. A money expansion, for example, may raise output prices for given nominal factor prices. Since real factor prices then fall, desired output supply would rise along with increased demand. In Figure 1.3, such a demand shift might move the economy from B (with demand D') to C (with demand D), along a constant supply schedule S'. The demand expansion raises both demand and supply, and output (as well as employment) rises from V_b to V_c. The fact remains, however, that real factor prices were required to decline (relative to trend, at least) in order to bring about the output expansion. Note, though, that if the nominal wage is highly indexed to the price level, the demand policy would not raise desired supply, or would do so only at the cost of sharply rising prices. The effective supply schedule in this case would be nearly vertical.

In Chapter 9 we attempt to quantify by how much the wage should decline relative to the domestic output price for a given capital stock, technology, and real prices of other inputs, in order to restore full employment. The excess of actual wages over levels consistent with full-employment supply (for given input prices, and so on) is termed the "wage gap." We find the wage gap to be large in several countries, which is consistent with our view that after a supply shock, both aggregate supply and demand must be raised to reach full employment.

Note finally that a negative demand shift generates Keynesian unemployment if output market prices are sticky, while a negative supply shock tends to generate pure classical unemployment. Assuming that prices fall in response to excess supply and rise in response to excess demand, Keynesian unemployment will be associated with falling prices (or decelerating inflation), while classical unemployment will be associated with rising prices (or accelerating inflation). The analysis therefore suggests an explanation as to why, during the periods of supply price shocks, 1973–74 and 1979–80, one observed a simultaneous acceleration in inflation and rise in unemployment (primarily classical), whereas in the post-shock periods, 1974–76 and 1981–83, the demand squeeze was dominant so that inflation decelerated while unemployment continued to rise (this time the increase was mainly of a Keynesian nature). A detailed account of these developments depends on specification of the dynamics of price, wage, and exchange rate adjustment, of which more will be said in later chapters of this book.

Policy Coordination among Countries

When confronted with the external shocks of the 1970s, macroeconomic authorities in most countries responded with significant policy measures, most typically including contractionary monetary policies to fight the imported inflation.[18] The policy responses in the major economies had important macroeconomic effects in other countries as well, sometimes in magnitudes that rivaled the initial supply shocks themselves. Indeed, the tight monetary policy of the United States following 1979 has been termed the "dollar shock" or "third oil shock" in Europe, given its effect of appreciating the dollar and raising European import prices in terms of domestic currencies. Our analysis of the international transmission of macroeconomic policies in Chapter 6 focuses on two issues. First, how do macroeconomic policies get transmitted under flexible exchange rates, and how do alternative assumptions about wage and price dynamics affect those conclusions? Second, what role, if any, exists for the coordination of macroeconomic policies across countries in response to a common external shock?

The basic framework for studying the international effects of macroeconomic policies comes from Mundell (1964). Assuming two countries, with a floating exchange rate between them and nominal wage rigidity in each, Mundell showed that a domestic monetary expansion is likely to lower output and prices abroad, while a fiscal expansion is likely to raise output and prices abroad. In this framework, for example, the post-1979 combination of tight monetary policy and expansionary fiscal policy in the United States is seen to be both expansionary and inflationary in Europe.

In fact, a slight change in the model can have important effects on the conclusions. The Mundell conclusions depend on rigid nominal wages. For example, the domestic monetary expansion at home lowers output abroad essentially by raising foreign real wages and reducing foreign competitiveness in international markets. The monetary expansion causes the home currency to depreciate and thereby reduces foreign import prices. The consumer price index abroad falls, though nominal wages by assumption remain unchanged. Even though world interest rates fall, and therefore world demand rises, the change in relative output prices via the currency depreciation shifts demand toward the home good, and foreign output falls.

Now suppose that foreign wages are partially or fully indexed to a consumer price index (CPI). As the domestic currency depreciates and foreign import prices fall, the foreign CPI will decline, and with it the nominal wage. The movement in the wage will moderate or eliminate the foreign country's loss of international competitiveness, since lower wages feed into greater aggregate supply and lower foreign prices. If indexation is high enough, the shift in world demand toward home goods is sufficiently mitigated that the foreign country joins in the world demand expansion. Formally, we derive a threshold degree of foreign wage indexing such that for indexing below that level a home monetary expansion lowers (and a monetary contraction raises) foreign output, while for a greater degree of foreign indexing, the effect is the reverse. In the latter case, a home monetary contraction would have a *depressing* effect abroad.

The nature of wage-price dynamics has a similar effect on the international transmission of fiscal policies. In the standard model, a fiscal expansion at home appreciates the home currency while raising world interest rates. With complete nominal wage rigidity the foreign country gains in international competitiveness sufficiently to overcome any contractionary effects of higher interest rates, so that its output expands along with the home country's. If wage indexation is important, however, the home expansion can actually *reduce* foreign output. As the home currency appreciates, foreign import prices rise. If foreign nominal wages rise in response, the foreign country's competitive gain is diminished or eliminated. The country then experiences higher world interest rates with little recompense in the form of improved competitiveness, and output may then decline.

Consider in this light the events of the early 1980s, when the United States, with relatively low wage indexation, simultaneously conducted contractionary monetary policy and expansionary fiscal policy. This policy mix caused the dollar to appreciate and helped to reduce U.S. inflation, while Europe, with relatively high wage indexation, was forced to import stagflation from the United States. To fight the inflationary consequences Europe had to conduct a contractionary monetary policy of its own to try to re-export the inflation, thus exacerbating its own unemployment. Such a series of competitive monetary contractions clearly does one thing: it drives up interest rates and thus raises unemployment; but the attempts to export inflation to others may largely cancel out. Obviously, there is a case for welfare improving macro-policy coordination among countries.

Finally, this analysis can be connected back to the section on international capital flows and the role of world interest rate movements in the differential response of the MICs. The post-1979 high interest rate period can be contrasted with the post-1973 low interest rate regime. In fact, the same two-country framework used here can be used to show that an oil price shock which mainly reduces aggregate demand in the "foreign" economy (now representing the OECD group) and only mildly affects the "home" economy (now representing the MIC group) may bring about a fall in world interest rates and result in an actual *rise* in output in the home economy.

In concluding this overview of the relevant theory, let us make one general point. This study will stress the role of the transmission of supply price shocks in the macroeconomic system and the demand response to them, both at the individual economy level and from the point of view of international adjustment. It is important to clarify at the outset that what appears as a supply shock from the point of view of a sector or an economy will, in many cases, have arisen from excess demand pressure in some other (often worldwide) market for a specific factor or group of goods. With the exception of the oil shock, which may have been truly autonomous, most other important shocks, such as the real wage push at the end of the 1960s, the raw material price increases of 1972–74, and the real interest rate hike of the early 1980s, may all reflect such underlying market phenomena. Yet once these real price changes have taken place, their size and duration justify treating them as predetermined, or setting up new initial conditions, from the point of view of the afflicted sector or economy. Moreover, the asymmetry of response to an upward and downward shift and the associated "ratchet" effects give such separate analytical treatment considerable practical relevance, even if in the very long run (remember, Keynes had something to say on that) they may yet appear as nothing but ripples on a smooth trend.

2 Production, Technology, and the Factor Price Frontier

ONE OF THE main objects of our study is to follow through the short-run and long-run effects of changes that take place on the supply side of the economy, in particular the role of real labor costs and the prices of raw materials. For this purpose, we shall first take a look at production and at the way technology and the costs of factor inputs determine profitability, employment, and capital investment. In this chapter we look at the supply framework by detailed exposition of the concept of the factor price frontier (FPF) in a two- and three-factor economy. To show its empirical relevance, we also give an empirical illustration of the FPF in Appendix 2A at the end of the chapter. When prices of raw materials change, conventional measures of real income and real net output have to be carefully reconsidered. This forms another major topic of this chapter and of a subsequent appendix (2B).

The Production Function

Any description of the economic performance of a sector or of an economy must start with production or a production function, relating output or the product to the input of factors of production. Suppose the factors are the conventional pair labor (L) and capital (K), and the output in the form of value added is denoted by V. We can write

(2.1) $V = G(L, K; T)$.

We have added an index T within the parentheses to represent the level of technology, or "time," which for the moment will be assumed to be frozen (later we shall talk about shifts in T).

Conceptually a production function should relate inputs of factors to the *maximal* output levels that can be obtained from the given level of technology (T) and institutions within which production takes place. This is a hard enough concept to define on a micro-, single-activity, or individual-firm level, but it becomes much more complex, if not insoluble, when an aggregate like an industry, let alone the whole economy, is involved. Defining and measuring an aggregate labor input or a capital stock level, and even more so an aggregate output index, is an extremely complex problem. Moreover, it can be shown that to write down an aggregate production function which is, by definition, the outcome of output maximization over many micro-units, one needs highly restrictive assumptions about the distribution of individual cells or the relationship of the various "bits" of the same factor in different activities (for example, we need "composite good" assumptions like fixed proportionality of either quantities or prices of the constituent parts of each aggregate input or output). These obviously do not hold in most realistic situations. Yet there is an established tradition in economics, which has proved quite powerful, to proceed as if such aggregation has already taken place before a production function like (2.1) has been written down. It is only important to remember that such an artifact may at times break down because underlying circumstances have changed, or else it has to be reinterpreted in a way that suits the new circumstances. Two examples with which we shall deal in greater detail as we go along, may briefly illustrate the point.

Suppose we use a production function like (2.1) to describe the relation between an economy's total GDP and its input of labor and capital. With given aggregate labor, L, and capital, K, output may for a time fail to reach the level given by $G(L,K; T)$ not because individual firms in the economy are not using their given inputs of labor and capital efficiently, but because the allocation of labor or of capital among firms has ceased to be efficient. An external shock to the system, such as a change in relative commodity prices or an oil price shock, may have changed the relative profitability of labor or capital use in different activities, and the adjustment process by which labor or capital is reallocated among firms to regain aggregate efficiency fails to take place because of institutional or marketplace price rigidities (for example, labor cannot easily be moved out of place, and real wages are not flexible downward). V will then not be on the aggregate production frontier $G(L, K; T)$. We shall argue later (Chapter 12) that such inefficiencies may in fact have occurred in practice.

Another example has to do with the concept of real GDP itself. Commodities embody the input of materials as well as labor and capital, yet we have been accustomed long ago to sum up value added by labor and capital and call it GDP. For the economy as a whole, real GDP is obtained by subtracting aggregate imports from aggregate uses (for consumption, investment, and exports), all at constant prices of some base year. When is one allowed to write down real GDP as a function of labor and capital inputs irrespective of the material inputs or, in case of the aggregate economy, leaving out imports from the production function? Strictly speaking and in general the concept of real GDP is not independent of relative import prices, yet much of macroeconomics has proceeded as if it were.

Only when imports and output come in fixed proportions or else the relative price of imported inputs does not change can a two-factor production function like (2.1) be written down unambiguously for the conventional measure of GDP. Alternatively, the measure must be changed to suit the circumstances. We discuss this question further in Appendix 2B to this chapter.

For the time being let us stick to the two-factor production function (2.1) and simplify it even further. We shall assume that at each level of relevant labor and capital inputs, the marginal products of labor and capital are well defined ($MPL = V_L = \partial G/\partial L$, $MPK = V_K = \partial G/\partial K$). This "smoothness" assumption is not essential but helps in the exposition. Also we shall for most of the time stick to the assumption that production takes place at constant returns to scale, that is, when the inputs of factors are increased by a certain factor of proportionality (α) output increases by the same factor, that is (leaving out T), $\alpha V = G(\alpha L, \alpha K)$. Therefore, only relative proportions of labor, capital, and output will matter for the marginal products, and the dimensionality of production is reduced from 3 to 2. In terms of the production function this shows itself in two alternative ways. One is that instead of (2.1) we can divide output and capital by labor (let $\alpha = 1/L$) and write $V/L = G(1, K/L)$ or $V/L = g(K/L)$. Alternatively, we can divide by V inside the brackets of Eq. (2.1) and write $1 = G(L/V, K/V)$, which gives the unit isoquant G in Figure 2.1.

The curve G in Figure 2.1 describes all the efficient combinations of labor and capital that yield one unit of output or, alternatively, all the efficient combinations of inputs per unit of output $(L/V, K/V)$. Points above or to the right of this curve are inefficient input combinations. The slope of this curve at any given choice of input use $[(L/V)_0, (K/V)_0]$, at the production point P_0, measures the ratio of marginal products, or the marginal rate of substitution between labor and capital at the given level of factor use. The intercepts of the tangent on the two axes measure the respective reciprocals of the marginal products, which in turn, under cost minimization, are the marginal costs of production expressed, respectively, in the units of each factor.

If we denote the nominal wage rate by W and the nominal rental of capital

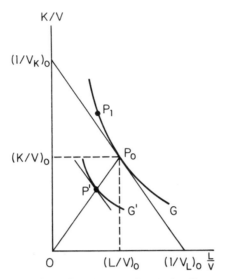

Figure 2.1. Production (primal)

by Z, then producers minimizing production costs will choose that input combination which satisfies

(2.2) $W/V_L = Z/V_K = MC,$

and therefore $1/V_L = MC/W$, $1/V_K = MC/Z$. The slope of the tangent at P_0 is the ratio of the two marginal products or the relative factor prices: $-V_L/V_K = -W/Z$.

Another convenient feature of the diagram is the fact that the relative distances of the pairs of points along the axes measure the product elasticities (or "shares") of the two factors, labor and capital: $s = (L/V) \div (1/V_L) = V_L L/V$ and $1 - s = (K/V) \div (1/V_K) = V_K K/V$. One can also see from the geometry that the point P_0 divides the tangent (and likewise the points $(L/V)_0$ and $(K/V)_0$ divide the respective intercepts) by the ratio of the factor shares $s/(1-s)$, which in turn must sum up to one, a well-known property of linearly homogeneous production functions (Euler's theorem).

In the case in which producers not only minimize production costs for a given output level but also choose their output competitively so as to maximize profits, marginal costs will equal the product price level, P_V. We can then everywhere substitute real factor returns, which we shall denote by $W_V (= W/P_V)$ and $Z_V (= Z/P_V)$, respectively,[1] for marginal products, and actual factor shares for output elasticities, $s = WL/(P_V V)$, $(1-s) = ZK/(P_V V)$. In what follows, however, we shall at times want to distinguish between cost minimization and the more restrictive profit maximization assumption, especially when output will be constrained from the demand side.

The Factor Price Frontier

Under constant returns to scale, the curve G in Figure 2.1 summarizes all there is to know about production technology. Among other attributes, it establishes a one-to-one correspondence between the pair of marginal products and the pair of unit inputs and thus also with the capital/labor ratio. The latter is represented by the slope of the ray OP_0 to the production point, P_0. Under diminishing returns (the curve G is convex to the origin), a higher capital/labor ratio at point P_1 goes together with higher K/V, lower L/V and likewise with lower MPK and higher MPL.

This simple correspondence between intensity of input use and marginal factor products, which in technical language is called "duality," allows us to describe the productive process interchangeably in the space of marginal factor products. The resulting curve, F, in Figure 2.2 is the factor price frontier (FPF). It is the dual of the isoquant G (in Figure 2.1) and represents the pair of maximal combinations of marginal factor products (see Samuelson, 1962). If profits are maximized and factors are paid their real marginal products ($W_V = V_L$ and $Z_V = V_K$), then the FPF represents the maximum rate

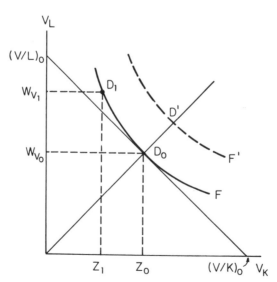

Figure 2.2. Factor price frontier (dual)

of return that can be paid to capital for a given real wage level, independently of the level of activity.

The curve F which is convex to the origin is an alternative, and often a more convenient, way of summarizing all the information we need about the technology in question. It is independent of the level of activity. The slope of the tangent at the "dual" point D_0 measures the corresponding capital/labor ratio and the intercepts of the tangent on the two axes measure the intensity of input use (V/K and V/L), in complete symmetry to Figure 2.1.[2] At a lower V_K the reciprocal ($1/V_K$) rises, and therefore one moves on the isoquant G (on Figure 2.1) to the left from P_0 to P_1. Therefore V_L goes up and K/L goes up. Likewise at a higher point D_1 on F (Figure 2.2), the capital/labor ratio (slope) is higher, the marginal product of labor is higher, and the marginal product of capital is lower, than at D_0. Thus, with a given lower real rate of interest ($Z_{V_1} < Z_{V_0}$) production under profit maximization will take place with a higher capital/labor ratio (the slope at D_1 is steeper than at D_0), and a higher real wage ($W_{V_1} > W_{V_0}$) can be paid. Alternatively, in a system in which the real wage is the dominant exogenous driving force, a rise in W_V will make for capital deepening and a fall in the rate of profit. We shall see in Appendix 2A and in Chapter 8 that a process of this kind took place in the major industrial countries already in the 1960s.

Consider now technical progress, that is, suppose T rises. This will show as an inward shift of the unit isoquant from G to G' (Figure 2.1). Less labor or less capital per unit (or both) is now required. The nature of the shift depends on the nature of technical progress. For example, a proportional ("homothetic") inward shift will take place, that is, the tangent at P' is parallel to that at P_0, when at a given capital/labor ratio technical progress increases the marginal products of both factors proportionately. This is termed Hicks-neutral technical progress.[3]

In complete analogy to the primal system, the dual FPF will shift outward when there is technical progress. In the special, Hicks-neutral case mentioned above, this shift too will be proportionate (homothetic) so that along a given ray OD_0D' (constant relative marginal products) the tangent at D' is parallel to that at D_0, namely, the capital/labor ratio stays the same.

Here and elsewhere in this book we shall adopt the convention of using lowercase letters to represent logarithms of capital letters unless otherwise specified ($v = \log V$, and so on), and we use dots (for example, $\dot{x}$) for the time-rates-of-change of variables.[4] Suppose now that technology shifts with time, so we can write $T =$ time. We can rewrite (2.1) in the form

(2.3) $\dot{v} = s\dot{l} + (1 - s)\dot{k} + \gamma,$

where $\gamma = V^{-1} \partial V / \partial T$ is the rate of technical progress and s, $(1 - s)$ are the output elasticities (factor shares) of labor and capital, as before.

Alternatively this can be written in the form

$(2.3')$ $s(\dot{v} - \dot{l}) + (1 - s)(\dot{v} - \dot{k}) = \gamma.$

Its dual, the shift in the FPF, can be written in the form[5]

(2.4) $s\dot{v}_l + (1 - s)\dot{v}_k = \gamma.$

In the case of steady Hicks-neutral technical progress (t.p.), γ is a pure number and does not depend on k or l.

Harrod-neutral technical progress, alternatively termed as labor-augmenting t.p., is illustrated in Figure 2.3. F shifts to F'' so that at a given rate of return to capital (Z_{V_0}) the output/capital ratio stays the same, while the product-wage expands by the ratio of the height of D'' over D_0. A special case, but empirically relevant, is one in which labor-augmenting t.p. takes place at a fixed time rate (λ) so that the production function can be written in the form of $V = V(Le^{\lambda t}, K)$. The implication is that if we redefine the labor input in intensity units $(Le^{\lambda t})$ and the product-wage axis to be $(e^{-\lambda t}) V_L$ (the product wage per "intensity" unit), the resulting detrended FPF would stay fixed. This procedure will be followed in the empirical work in Appendix 2A.

There is one well-known production function for which Hicks-neutrality and Harrod-neutrality amount to the same thing—the Cobb-Douglas pro-

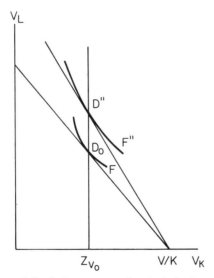

Figure 2.3. Labor-augmenting technical progress

duction function. In Hicks-neutral form we write $\dot{v}=\gamma+\phi\dot{l}+(1-\phi)\dot{k}$. Alternatively, in Harrod-neutral or labor-augmenting form we have: $\dot{v}=\phi(\dot{l}+\lambda)+(1-\phi)\dot{k}$ provided $\lambda=\gamma/\phi$.

Material Inputs and the Analogy of Productivity Change

In a real economy there are more than two primary factors of production, labor and capital, and their value added (V) is not directly observed. There is need to look again at the concept of net output and factor productivity within a broader three-factor framework, which we now take up.

Let us now extend our model to include a third factor of production, purchased materials or intermediate goods, N, in the case of the manufacturing sector, say (or foreign imports in the case of the aggregate economy). The two-factor theory developed in the previous sections could be extended formally to incorporate any number of factors of production. The only problem is that any increase in dimensions beyond two makes the use of simple diagrammatic exposition more difficult. Luckily, however, there is a simple analytical technique, employing the logic of duality in a particular way, which enables us to keep two-dimensional simplicity and at the same time suggests an isomorphism that gives some important insight into the role of a rise in the cost of material inputs, one of the main subjects of our subsequent discussion.

Let $Q=Q(L,K,N)$ now be a well-behaved linearly homogeneous production function for gross output (Q) of a final good using labor, L, capital, K, and a third factor—a raw material, or an intermediate input, N. Let the price of the output be P and that of the material P_N. For the time being we leave out the technological shift factor (T), which will be added later on. In rate-of-change form we can now write

(2.5) $\dot{q} = s_l\dot{l} + s_k\dot{k} + s_n\dot{n},$

where $s_i(i=l, k, n)$ are the output elasticities (or "shares") of the three factors, and under constant returns to scale they sum up to one ($\Sigma s_i=1$).

Assume that the *relative* price of materials $\Pi_N=P_N/P$ is given (as is the case if both N and Q are tradable goods in a small open economy). Let Y be the real income derived by the two remaining factors, $Y=(PQ-P_NN)/P=Q-\Pi_NN$, and assume optimal use of N such that its marginal product equals its relative price (that is, $MPN=Q_N=\partial Q/\partial N=\Pi_N$). Substituting in $Q(L,K,N)$, one obtains what can be termed a *real income function,*[6]

(2.6) $Y = Y(L,K; \Pi_N),$

with the following "semi-dual" properties: (1) The marginal products of labor and capital in Y are the same as in $Q (\partial Y/\partial L = \partial Q/\partial L, \partial Y/\partial K = \partial Q/\partial K)$, and the derivative of the input price is negative and equals the input quantity $(\partial Y/\partial \Pi_N = -N)$. (2) If the Q production function is linearly homogeneous in the three factors L, K, and N, the Y function will be linearly homogeneous in the primary factors L, K, so that the Euler equation holds for $Y(K,L)$:

$$(2.7) \qquad Y_L L + Y_K K = Y.$$

For the factor shares in Y we have $Y_L L/Y = (Q/Y)s_l = (1 - s_n)^{-1} s_l = (s_l + s_k)^{-1} s_l$, and similarly $Y_K K/Y = (s_l + s_k)^{-1} s_k$.

Now consider changes in Π_N. Using lowercase letters to denote logarithms of uppercase variables as before, the proportionate rate of change of Π_N is $\dot{\pi}_n$. It immediately follows that the partial elasticity of real income (as measured by Y) with respect to a real change in the price Π_N is the ratio of the relative shares of the material and value added in gross output. The proof is straightforward. We have

$$\frac{\Pi_N}{Y} \frac{\partial Y}{\partial \Pi_N} = -\frac{\Pi_N N}{Y} = -\frac{P_N N}{PQ - P_N N} = -\frac{s_n}{1 - s_n},$$

where s_n is the input share.[7]

A simple corollary of this proposition is that a policy that aims at keeping relative domestic factor shares constant in the face of a real change in material prices $(\dot{\pi}_n)$ requires both factor rentals to decrease at the rate $\dot{\pi}_n s_n/(1 - s_n)$ for given factor inputs. This may be used to measure real terms-of-trade effects on factor rewards. It does not require that workers receive their marginal product, only that the raw material be used optimally. Note too that the fixed-proportions case $(N = \mu Q)$ can be looked upon as a limiting case for which the proposition holds directly: one obtains $Y = Q(1 - \mu \Pi_n)$ and therefore $\partial Y/\partial \Pi_N = -\mu Q = -N$.

Consider the real income function (2.6) in rate-of-change form. Using its properties from the foregoing discussion, we get[8]

$$(2.8) \qquad \dot{y} = (s_l + s_k)^{-1}(s_l \dot{l} + s_k \dot{k}) - b,$$

where $b = (1 - s_n)^{-1} s_n \dot{\pi}_n$.

What (2.8) says is that the rate of change of real income is composed of the weighted rate of change of the labor and capital inputs (with weights being their respective shares in value added) *minus* a shift factor b which is the weighted rate of change of material input prices.

Compare the real income function (2.6) with our first two-factor production function (2.1), and compare the rate-of-change expression (2.8) with the productivity growth expression (2.3). The analogy is clear. An increase (decrease) in raw material prices acts on real income in a way that is analogous to negative (positive) technical progress on output in a two-factor world.

By way of a short digression from our main discussion, one might note another point that Eq. (2.8) brings up. Although the concept $Y(=Q-\Pi_N N)$ may be relevant for the purpose of measurement of real income, it can certainly not serve as a measure of real net output of labor and capital (V), since it is not independent of the change in input prices (a subject briefly discussed earlier). Y is what is sometimes called single-deflated value added, since the nominal value added ($PQ-P_N N$) is deflated only by output prices. An alternative definition of real value added that uses double deflation (namely, the difference of the real magnitudes of real output and real input, $Q-N$) is the one that is usually used for purposes of real GDP measurement in national income accounting. In Appendix 2B we show that it too is the wrong measure of net output changes, since it is likely to be biased when material prices change. Strictly speaking, changes in real net output (V) must in this case be measured so that they equal exactly the weighted sum of labor and capital inputs (plus pure technical progress, which has been left out here), that is,

$$(2.9) \qquad \dot{v} = (s_l + s_k)^{-1}(s_l \dot{l} + s_k \dot{k}) = (1 - s_n)^{-1}(\dot{q} - s_n \dot{n}).$$

Equation (2.9) suggests measurement of changes in real value added from changes in gross output and material inputs using continuously moving share-weights (since there is no presumption in general that s_n will stay constant over time). This is termed a "Divisia Index" measure of value added and is free of material price bias. For a more detailed discussion of net output measurement, see Appendix 2B.

The FPF in the Three-Factor Case

We now turn to the factor price frontier for this case. As before, this will summarize the information about the technology in terms of the maximal combinations of the three marginal factor products, $F(Q_L, Q_K, Q_N) = 0$. By extension of the two-factor case (Eq. 2.4), we could write it down right away in rate-of-change form (q_l is the log of MPL, and so on):

$$(2.10) \qquad s_l \dot{q}_l + s_k \dot{q}_k + s_n \dot{q}_n = 0.$$

We now denote the real wage (in gross output units) by W_Q and the real rate of return to capital by R. Under profit maximization and perfect competition, marginal products equal real factor returns; substituting $(q_l=w_q, q_k=r, q_n=\pi_n)$ and rewriting, we get

(2.10') $\qquad s_k \dot{r} + s_l \dot{w}_q = - s_n \dot{\pi}_n$, or

$$\dot{r} = - s_k^{-1}(s_l \dot{w}_q + s_n \dot{\pi}_n).$$

Under imperfect competition in the output market, marginal products are proportional to, but not equal to, real factor returns, where the factor of proportionality P/MC measures the degree of monopoly. As long as the degree of monopoly remains constant, the rate of change of marginal products will equal the rate of change of real factor returns, and therefore Eq. (2.10') will remain valid.

The first equation in (2.10') again suggests the analogy of the negative productivity shift in the two-factor case. The second equation is the basis for some empirical estimates of FPF that will be shown in Appendix 2A.

Rather than resorting to the three-factor extension of the previous model, we could make direct use of the analogy established between the value-added function (2.8) and the two-factor production function (2.1). Instead of holding the technology (T) fixed, we now hold the relative input price (Π_N) fixed as we draw an isoquant in L/Y, K/Y space or the FPF in R, W_Q space.

The curve F_0 is drawn in Figure 2.4 for a given relative raw material price Π_{N_0}. It is downward-sloping and convex to the origin, as before. The slope of the tangent at any point measures the capital/labor ratio that corresponds to the pair of factor prices, and its intercept on the W_Q axis (OT) measures Y/L. Likewise, the intercept on the R axis (OS) measures Y/K.

Consider a rise in raw material prices. The FPF shifts inward, like the shift from F_0 to F_1 in Figure 2.4. When will this contraction be homothetic? Economically what is implied is that at a given capital/labor ratio, the ratio of factor prices must also stay invariant to an increase in raw material prices. In strict analogy to the case of Hicks-neutrality of technical progress, this will take place here when the production function is "weakly separable" in the material input, that is, when the production function has the two-level form: $Q=Q[G(L,K),N]$. By a celebrated theorem due to Leontief (1947), this implies that the marginal rate of substitution between labor and capital depends only on L/K and is independent of N. In turn this means that $\partial(W_Q/R)/\partial N=0$, and therefore we must have $\partial(W_Q/R)/\partial\Pi_N=0$ on the FPF. In other words, weak separability of the production function implies weak separability of the dual FPF. F_0 takes the form $F[f(W_Q,R),\Pi_N]=0$. A material input price increase, like Hicks-neutral technical regress, is then represented by a homothetic inward shift of F_0 to F_1. At the point C on the FPF, on

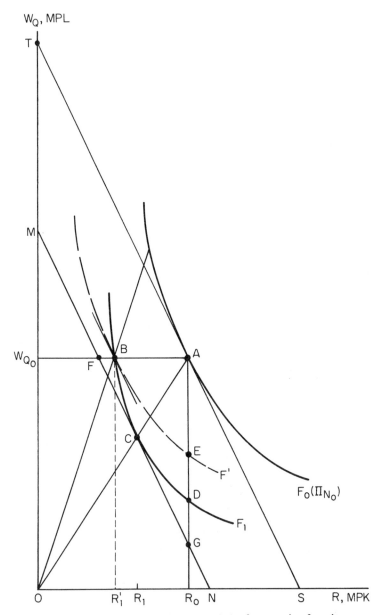

Figure 2.4. Input price increase and the factor price frontier

the ray OA, the capital/labor ratio is the same as at A. Marginal factor products at C are reduced by the same ratio from their original level at A. Total real income per unit of labor (Y/L) falls by the same proportion from OT to OM (and Y/K from OS to ON).

The case of weak separability of intermediate inputs will be discussed further in Chapter 3. Although it may be relevant for most industrial raw materials or for total imports into the aggregate economy, it is probably not applicable to a pure energy input, E, for which some separability may hold, but it could take the alternative form $Q[L,G(K,E)]$ (see Berndt and Wood, 1979). In this case energy combines with capital to form a composite from which labor (and other materials, here left out) are separable. By analogy, the resulting factor price frontier in the R, W_Q space would now contract along the R axis at the rate $\dot{\pi}_e s_e/s_k$ (where s_e is the share of energy and π_e its log price). This rate will be independent of the real wage. For simplicity, consider an even more special case in which the energy input comes in fixed proportions with capital. In this case $Q=Q[(L, \min K,E/\eta)]$, and $R=Q/K- W_Q L/K-\Pi_E\eta$. Suppose F_0 is the initial FPF, for a given Π_E. An increase of $\Delta\Pi_E$ in the real energy price then implies that F will shift to the left by $\eta(\Delta\Pi_E)$, that is, at all levels of the real wage the rate of return falls by the same amount. The resulting FPF denoted by F' will cut F_1 at the point B and will lie to the right of F_1 for all $W_Q < W_{Q_0}$.[9] The implications of the difference in the assumption about the nature of production will be taken up in the next chapter.

Change in Terms of Trade and Demand Rationing

The single-sector analysis of this chapter will subsequently be modified and extended in several directions — we have not yet even considered all aspects of the one-sector model (for example, the composition of demand, the balance of payments, and the role of money and prices). Most of these extensions lie outside the scope of the first empirical illustration, to be given in Appendix 2A. There is one extension, however, which has to be mentioned briefly at this stage: what happens if one removes the assumption that the final goods price P is given from outside the sector, or economy, in question.

If the final good Q is an imperfect substitute for a world good (priced P^*), the relative raw materials price now depends on the terms of trade of the final goods $[\Pi=P/(EP^*)]$, where E is the nominal exchange rate between the currency units in which P and P^* are measured. We then have $\Pi_N=\Pi_N^*/\Pi$, where $\Pi_N^*=P_N^*/P^*$ is the world relative price of raw materials (assumed to be exogenous). Even if one only wants to apply this factor-price analysis to a single large sector, one should keep in mind that the relative input price Π_N may now depend not only on relative world prices but also on the real exchange rate $(1/\Pi)$ and on demand management in the economy as a whole. For example, an external raw-materials price shock (increase in Π_N^*) may be accompanied by a real appreciation (a rise in Π or a decline in P^*E/P), and the FPF may then partly shift back (this, as we shall see, seems to have been important in the case of Germany, for example).

There is another important consideration in this more general case: output may be constrained on the demand rather than on the supply side. Firms may be unable to sell all that they would like at prevailing prices. This case will be taken up in greater detail in Chapter 5. For the moment, however, we note that under such a disequilibrium situation, prices may not move together with marginal production costs. Let us go back to consider the FPF in this more general case.

As long as cost minimization holds, the marginal product of each factor can be written as the product of the real factor return and the ratio of price over marginal cost, to be denoted by D $(D = P/MC)$. This will be unity under commodity market competitive equilibrium. This means that the FPF can always be written in the form $F(W_Q D, RD, \Pi_N D) = 0$, or in rate-of-change version we have (substituting in Eq. 2.10 $\dot{q}_l = \dot{w}_q + \dot{d}$, and so forth),

(2.11) $s_l \dot{w}_q + s_k \dot{r} + s_n \dot{\pi}_n + \dot{d} = 0$,

$\dot{r} = - s_k^{-1}(s_l \dot{w}_q + s_n \dot{\pi}_n - \dot{d})$.

When $\dot{d} = 0$, namely prices and marginal costs move together, we are back at Eq. (2.10′). However, when the economy moves into a demand-constrained phase, there is a presumption that the ratio D $(= P/MC)$ may rise, namely $\dot{d} > 0$. The effect is thus the same as that of negative t.p. or a rise in input price. We must now distinguish between the FPF for *actual* factor prices, which shifts inward, homothetically, and the original FPF in terms of *marginal products,* which stays put. Thus, for a given real wage, profits may be squeezed further when there is a demand shortfall.[10] This property of the FPF will be used in the following empirical study to take account of cyclical effects on profits.

Appendix 2A: Empirical Factor-Price Profiles in Manufacturing

In this appendix we turn to an empirical illustration of factor-price profiles for the manufacturing sector of four major industrial countries: the United

States, the United Kingdom, Germany, and Japan.[11] This is meant to illustrate that the conceptual framework discussed can be given straightforward empirical content. More detailed empirical work is discussed in subsequent chapters of this book.

The data on the real cost of intermediate goods appear in Figure 2A.1. For all four countries, an attempt was made to use an index that is as close as possible to the wholesale price index for the aggregate material input into the manufacturing sector, and to deflate it by the manufacturers' wholesale price. Conceptually the input price should include fuels, unprocessed foods from agriculture, and all other material or intermediate inputs imported from the rest of the economy or from abroad. It is important to stress that in most cases fuels constitute only a relatively small share of this index.

Much of the action in the exceptional input price behavior over this period is not fully accounted for by oil prices although their role may in part have been indirect (for example, raising extraction and production costs for other materials). To show this, we have also included an international index of nonfuel primary export prices relative to manufacturing export prices. This index was constructed by Kravis and Lipsey (1981),[12] and shows a pattern broadly similar to that of the overall index including fuel prices. Obviously the individual country patterns need not be identical, because of the movements in relative exchange rates and the different domestic government pricing policies. A particular case in point is Germany, which had a sharp real appreciation in the 1970s and which also kept internal energy and agricultural prices low.

Two basic facts stand out from Figure 2A.1. One is the sustained and unambiguous real price shock of the early 1970s (on the order of 40 percent for the United Kingdom and Japan, 30 percent for the United States, and only 10 percent for Germany). With some fluctuations and one or two additional mini-shocks, the high level was, by and large, maintained to the end of the decade. The other fact worth pointing out is that for three of the countries (excluding Japan), this unprecedented shock was preceded by fifteen years of steady decline (on the order of 1 percent a year) in the relative cost of the material input, closely associated with the relative decline of these prices (and of oil) in the world market.

Specification of the factor price frontier depends on the choice of an underlying production function; its estimation could be done jointly with estimation of the quantity model (this was done in Bruno, 1981, and Bruno and Sachs, 1982b). We confine ourselves here to the analysis of factor price profiles based on single-equation estimation. The choice of the functional form is consistent with a simple production model, and the empirical esti-

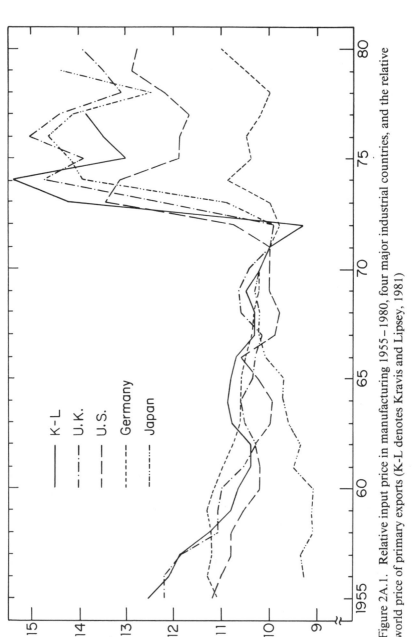

Figure 2A.1. Relative input price in manufacturing 1955–1980, four major industrial countries, and the relative world price of primary exports (K-L denotes Kravis and Lipsey, 1981)

mates are not substantially altered with the use of an alternative estimation technique.

A number of authors have used a general four-factor (K,L,E,M) translog production framework for estimation purposes. Although this may be the best approach for some purposes (for example, specific concern for the energy input), the results of such estimates also suggest that for a broad view of developments, a simplified model may do no worse, and for our present purposes may be better. We shall lump all intermediate goods, including energy, into one input and choose the simplest production function that still seems a sufficiently realistic approximation.[13]

The size of the direct energy share in total manufacturing output is on the order of 2 to 3 percent, compared to an order of magnitude of 30 to 65 percent for all other material inputs, depending on the degree of aggregation or consolidation of the manufacturing sector from its constituent parts.[14] If the nonenergy input can be assumed to be separable while energy may not be, the extent of overall error coming from imposing separability on the aggregate input cannot be large.

Another simplification involves the implicit assumption that the prices of the aggregate input of intermediate goods from the manufacturing sector into itself move at the same rate as the wholesale price of the manufacturing output. This enables one to net out this input and consider manufacturing production as using only labor, capital, and materials (and intermediate goods) purchased from outside the sector. This is certainly not an ideal choice but is one that can be made in lieu of a detailed and fully consistent time-series account of input quantities and prices.[15]

Finally, we come to the choice of functional specification. The simplest approach would be to use a linearized level form of Eq. (2.5) with an independent term for technical progress. If the underlying production function were Cobb-Douglas in all three factors, this would be precisely correct. While this is a reasonable assumption for the pair of labor and capital inputs in net product $V(K,L)$, it makes no a priori empirical sense for the substitution between N and V. We shall choose a two-level production function with an unrestricted constant elasticity of substitution (CES) between the material input N and the net product index V, where the latter in turn is assumed to be a Cobb-Douglas function for K and L.[16] The second-order approximation to the FPF of this function yields a functional form which is like that of the general Cobb-Douglas with only one second-order (π_n^2) term, which, however, can be ignored for empirical reasons.[17] We end up estimating the following profit function (in log level form):

$$(2A.1) \qquad r = a_0 - a_1(w_q - \lambda t) - a_2\pi_n + a_3 j.$$

The first coefficient (a_1), measuring the relative labor/capital shares (s_l/s_k), is expected to be constant by assumption, while the second (a_2) should measure the relative materials-capital share (s_n/s_k) evaluated at a base point (for which $\log \Pi_n = 1$). The additional intensity variable $j = \log J$ is a proxy for cyclical variations, here measured by deviation of the average hours per employee per week from the long-run trend. Its role can be linked to the $D\ (=P/MC)$ measure discussed in this chapter. It is of importance in explaining the fluctuations of profits primarily in the case of the United States.

Table 2A.1 gives a selection of the relevant regressions for Eq. (2A.1). The estimates for the labor-augmenting productivity factor, λ, the share of capital in value added, $1 - \phi = s_k/(1 - s_n)$, and the share of intermediate goods in total costs, s_n (bottom section), all have the right orders of magnitude. Figures 2A.2 and 2A.3 give a graphic representation of the factor price profiles for the various countries. For the United States, the figure corresponds to the first regression shown in Table 2A.1.

Each of the charts is drawn in terms of the actual rate of profit (R) on the horizontal axis and the detrended product wage ($W' = W_Q e^{-\lambda t}$) on the vertical axis, using the λ coefficient estimated from the regression. The solid curves represent estimated factor price frontiers drawn for given levels of Π_N (and normal hours per employee, that is, $J = 1$), one representing an average pre-1973 level, the other an average post-1973 level of raw materials prices (the implicit rate of change, $\Delta \pi_n$, is noted in each graph). For the two countries represented in Figure 2A.2 (the United Kingdom and Germany), the regression estimates (dotted lines) are shown along with the actual observations, and the horizontal distance between corresponding annual points measures the regression errors. For the United States (Figure 2A.3), the underlying "decycled" observations are also plotted; these correct the profit rate by the intensity factor ($19 \times j$) from the regression (column 1 of Table 2A.1), and thus uncover an underlying long-run pattern which is not markedly different from that of the United Kingdom or Japan.

For all countries, a schematic description would suggest that until 1972 there was an upward movement in W_Q' (downward in R) more or less along a given FPF (this real wage push will be discussed further in Chapter 8), a clear shift to a new FPF after 1972, and movement down the new curve after 1973–74. Clearly there are some differences between countries in the timing and extent of the downward adjustment of the real wage after 1974 (and the upward readjustment of the rate of profit).[18] The United Kingdom initially showed greater real wage rigidity than Japan and the United States (with a correspondingly tighter profit squeeze) and then overreacted in 1977 (figures for 1978–80 show that the product wage rose back and the profit rate

Table 2A.1. Factor Price Frontier: Equation (2A.1)[a]

Regression results	United States 1955–1978		United Kingdom 1961–1977		Germany 1960–1976		Japan 1966–1978
	(1)	(2)[b]	(3)	(4)	(5)	(6)	(7)
Regression coefficients of:							
t(time)	0.018	0.036	0.183	0.168	0.173	0.220	0.134
	(0.016)	(0.022)	(0.065)	(0.072)	(0.063)	(0.070)	(0.073)
w_q	−1.413	−2.061	−3.518	−4.994	−2.672	−3.698	−1.426
	(0.636)	(0.838)	(1.695)	(1.757)	(0.969)	(1.019)	(0.626)
π_n	−1.177	−1.648	−2.269	−2.364	−1.910	−2.902	−1.686
	(0.297)	(0.483)	(0.548)	(0.618)	(0.834)	(0.849)	(0.517)
j	19.001	19.347	14.035	—	2.449	—	—
	(1.598)	(1.837)	(6.499)		(1.016)		
Statistics:							
$\overline{R}^2$	0.91	0.89	0.83	0.78	0.91	0.88	0.78
D.W.	1.97	2.04	2.21	2.29	1.37	1.80	1.25
S.E.	0.08	0.09	0.21	0.24	0.05	0.06	0.14
Estimated parameters[c]							
λ	0.016	0.019	0.031	0.034	0.057	0.059	0.094
$s_k/(1-s_n)$	0.414	0.326	0.221	0.167	0.272	0.213	0.407
s_n	0.328	0.350	0.334	0.283	0.342	0.382	0.410

a. Second row numerals (in parentheses) are standard errors.
b. Column (2) is a two-stage least-squares variant.
c. λ is corrected for time trend of j.

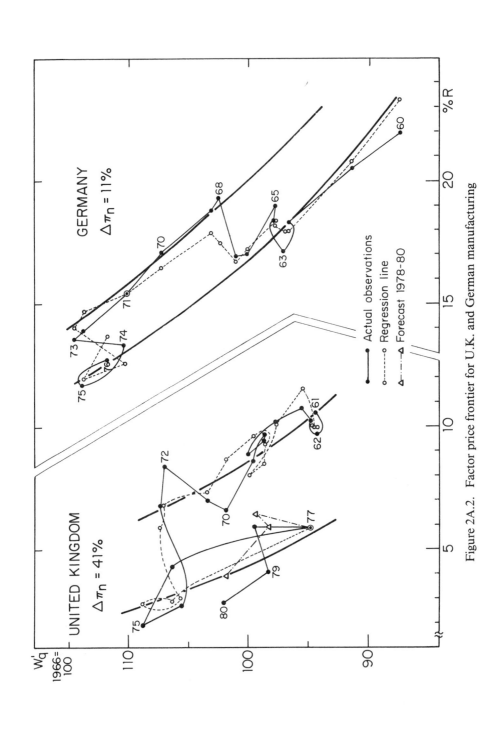

Figure 2A.2. Factor price frontier for U.K. and German manufacturing

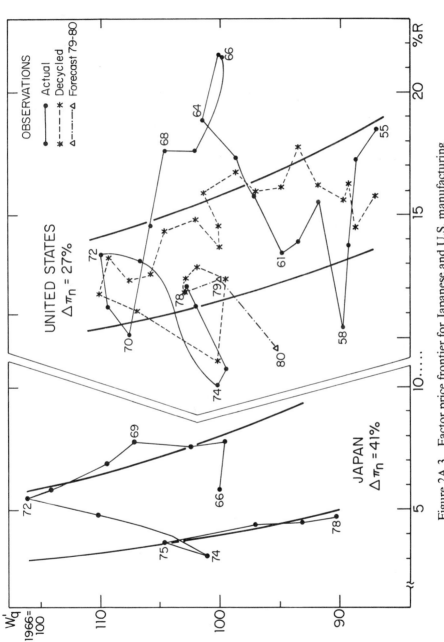

Figure 2A.3. Factor price frontier for Japanese and U.S. manufacturing

continued to fall; the picture also shows an out-of-sample forecast of R to 1980). Japan shows the most marked reduction in real product wage (relative to the 11 percent trend, which may be somewhat excessive). By 1977–78, it had in fact undergone a drop of about 15 percent in both R and W_Q'' [$= W_Q$ exp $(-0.11t)$], more or less *pari passu* with the rise in the cost of raw materials, $\Delta \pi_n s_n/(1 - s_n)$, as suggested by the earlier analysis of this chapter.

In some ways the case of the United States (Figure 2A.3) is the most interesting. It is not surprising that the debate about whether the rate of profit in the United States has been falling over time (see Feldstein and Summers, 1977) has been inconclusive. In the United States more than in any of the other countries, the fluctuations in the rate of profit turn out to be dominated by the cycle. However, once the J variable is introduced, the same long-run structural features emerge. Note that the 1974–75 dip in profits (to about 8 percent) was mostly, though not entirely, cyclical. A comparison of 1978 with 1972 gives an approximate view of the total net effect of the raw materials price hike on the profit-maximizing level, a drop in the rate of profit by about 10 percent (namely 1.4 percentage points). The trend fall in R from 1955 to 1971 is estimated at about 15 percent (2.5 percentage points out of 16 percent; compare the asterisked observations for the two years). This took place *pari passu* with a 20 percent rise in W_Q'' which was partly moderated by a 12 percent drop in Π_N (the asterisked 1971 observation lies much closer to the first FPF than the 1955 point).[19] The figure also includes an out-of-sample forecast of R to 1980 indicating a further fall in the rate of profit, which, according to later data, did in fact take place.

In view of the very strong role of the cyclical variable in the United States, various alternatives were tried out to see how robust the results are. Using the measure of capacity utilization published by the Federal Reserve Board, one gets essentially the same results except that the coefficients for w_q and π_n are less significant.[20]

The case of Germany also merits a brief separate discussion. In spite of a much smaller rate of change in real raw materials cost, the resulting elasticity with respect to Π_N came out highly significant, and the estimated coefficients of the production function are very reasonable. However, the response to the 1973–74 events was much milder than in the other three countries. The Π_N values of the two curves in Figure 2A.2 are only 11 percent apart.[21] The main secular change observed on the factor price profile is the upward trend in W_Q'' and the accompanying downward movement of R, in which the raw materials price had only a minor role to play. The 1973–74 shift seems to have moved the sector back to the FPF on which it had been in the 1960s. The accompanying changes in factor rewards were relatively minor, and as we shall see again later, the same is true for the shift in productivity change in manufacturing. This relatively minor effect is directly related to the small-ness of the shift in real raw materials prices (see Figure 2A.1), which in turn is related to the appreciation of the German exchange rate after the first oil shock.

The German case brings out the point that our discussion of the FPF for the manufacturing sector is of necessity limited here by the fact that we are ignoring the links of the major factor prices with the rest of the economy. Short of embedding the relationship within a more complete general equilib-rium model for the main markets (commodities, labor, and foreign ex-change), one could at least try to assess the possible simultaneity bias in the estimates. For the United States, Table 2A.1 lists an alternative regression that was estimated by two-stage least squares (using lagged values of the variables and l as instruments for w_q and π_n). The model does not seem to be much affected by this modification. A similar attempt for the United King-dom and Germany leaves the coefficient for π_n unaffected but suggests some simultaneity problem in j and w_q. These questions will be taken up in greater detail in subsequent empirical chapters.

Appendix 2B: Product Measurement

In principle, we have seen, the output of a three-factor production system could be measured in several ways. The following measures have been men-tioned in the text:

1. Gross output, Q.
2. Real income, $Y=(PQ-P_N N)/P$.
3. "Double-deflated" value added, $V_d=Q-N$.
4. "True," or Divisia, index of real value added $= V$,
   where $\dot{v}=(1-s_n)^{-1}(\dot{q}-s_n\dot{n})$.

We have already seen that the second measure (Y) cannot be a true measure of net output, although it could be a good measure of real income to the consumer of the final good. We now show that the third measure, which is the one most commonly used for national accounting purposes, may be biased when intermediate goods prices change from the base year (a dia-grammatic representation is also given in Figures 12.1 and 12.2).

Suppose the production function is separable, $Q=Q[V(K,L),N]$, and CES in V and N where the elasticity of substitution between V and N is σ. We thus have $\dot{q}=(1-s_n)\dot{v}+s_n\dot{n}$ and $\dot{n}=\dot{q}-\sigma\dot{\pi}_n$, so we can write:

(2B.1) $\dot{v}=\dot{q}+\sigma\dot{\pi}_n s_n/(1-s_n).$

For double-deflated value added (V_d), we have $V_d=Q-N$ (assuming $\Pi_N=1$ at $t=0$). Therefore,

(2B.2) $\dot{v}_d = \dfrac{Q\dot{q}-N\dot{n}}{Q-N} = \dot{q}+\dfrac{N}{Q-N}\sigma\dot{\pi}_n = \dot{q}+\sigma\dot{\pi}_n s_n/(\Pi_n-s_n).$

Comparing (2B.1) and (2B.2), we get the size of the bias in the measured growth rate of real value added.[22]

(2B.3) $\dot{v}_d-\dot{v}=-\dfrac{\sigma s_n}{1-s_n}\dfrac{\dot{\pi}_n(\Pi_N-1)}{\Pi_N-s_n}.$

Inspection of Eq. (2B.3) leads to several conclusions. First, there will be no bias only if we have fixed proportions ($\sigma=0$), or if there is no change in raw material prices ($\dot{\pi}_n=0$). Next, for all monotonic changes in Π_N (both up and down), the bias is always negative ($\dot{v}_d<\dot{v}$) and grows as we move away from $t=0$ ($\Pi_N=1$). This follows from the fact that $\dot{\pi}_n(\Pi_N-1)>0$ whenever Π_N consistently rises or falls over time, and from the fact that $(\Pi_N-1)/(\Pi_N-s_n)$ is an increasing function of Π_N.

This bias is likely to be small when the share of the material input is small, as would be the case of inputs to GDP in a large economy like that of the United States. For a heavy material-using sector like manufacturing or a heavily import-dependent aggregate economy, double deflation may be more problematic. For example, computation of the GDP slowdown of ten smaller OECD countries[23] between the period 1960–73 to 1974–80 shows a slowdown of 2.83 percent when calculated at constant 1972 prices and only 2.42 percent when calculated at 1975 prices. A Divisia Index calculation shows the estimated slowdown to be close to the 1975 price-based estimate: 2.47 percent (see Bruno 1982c).

3   Factor Adjustment to Supply Price Shocks

IN THIS CHAPTER we present a simplified analysis of the short-run and long-run effects of an exogenous change in factor prices on the productive framework of a single-sector economy.[1] For the moment no regard will be paid to the demand side of the economy nor to the mutual interaction of such shocks among several economies, topics that will be taken up later. We confine the present discussion to the output and factor input response. This is spelled out in a form that will become useful in our subsequent empirical analysis.

We start off with a single-sector, one-final-good, three-factor framework, which is the simplest model appropriate for the problem discussed here. The economy produces one tradable final good (of quantity Q and price P) and uses a material (for example, oil) input, N, whose relative price ($\Pi_N = P_N/P$) is given, together with labor, L, and capital, K. The supply of labor is given ($\bar{L}$), and so is the initial quantity of capital ($\bar{K}$). The production function is assumed to be linearly homogeneous, and all factors are assumed to be cooperant, in the sense that an increase in the quantity of any factor raises the marginal productivities of the other two factors.[2]

Analysis in Terms of the Factor Price Frontier

We are now ready to return to the factor price frontier (see Figure 2.4). Consider a permanent increase in the relative raw material price ($\Delta\pi_n$) which permanently shifts the FPF from F_0 to F_1, and suppose that material inputs in production are weakly separable from labor and capital.

Real wages may be downward-sticky in the short run. Without going into a more exact specification of such stickiness, we shall at first distinguish, for expositional purposes, between the rigid short run (RSR) in which W_Q (along with K) is strictly fixed while labor may not be fully employed $(L < \bar{L})$, and the flex short run (FSR) in which the real wage adjusts to whatever level warrants full employment of labor $(L = \bar{L})$ and capital $(K = \bar{K})$. In the long run both real wages and capital will be assumed to be flexible.

If real wages are downward-flexible, the new short-run equilibrium (FSR) will take place at the point C where the capital/labor ratio is equal to its initial level at A, $K = \bar{K}$, and labor remains fully employed $(L = \bar{L})$. Both the real wage and the rate of profit fall at the same percentage, which we have shown must be equal to $-[s_n/(1 - s_n)]\Delta\pi_n$, where $\Delta\pi_n$ is the one-time shift in π_n. Y/L and Y/K must fall at the same rate. It will subsequently be shown that gross output also generally falls.

Suppose now that real wages are rigid rather than downward-flexible, and that they are momentarily fixed at W_{Q_0}. In that case the short-run equilibrium takes place at the point B and not at C. The rate of profit falls by more $(R'_1 < R_1)$, and labor can no longer remain fully employed. The optimum capital/labor ratio at B (the slope of the tangent) must be higher than at C (and at A). Given the same initial capital stock $(\bar{K})$, this can only take place if less labor is employed. A rigid real wage, under the assumption made, must lead to unemployment. This is classical, and not Keynesian, unemployment since it comes from too high a real wage and not from any deficiency in demand.[3] There is, of course, another possibility. If producers are unable to reduce the labor input for institutional or technological reasons (for example, putty-clay technology), then the production possibilities lie along the tangent MCN, and with rigid wages production will take place at F and not at B. Full employment is then retained, but profits must fall by even more than at B.

What happens in the long run (LR)? Suppose the long-run borrowing rate is set at the initial rate of return (R_0). The LR equilibrium is then represented by the point D at which the capital/labor ratio is lower than at C, and so is the real wage. To maintain full employment in the long run, capital must be decumulated relative to trend. It is, of course, by no means necessary that the real rate of interest in world capital markets remain invariant when a raw material price shock occurs, and part of the adjustment may take place through a downward shift in the real rate of interest. This did in fact happen after the first oil shock (the reverse seems to have happened after the second). In that case the LR point will lie to the left of D on the new FPF. This possibility will be discussed in Chapter 4; for the moment we ignore it. Finally, consider the assumption that the raw material price increase is a permanent one. If it is temporary, rather than permanent, the FPF shifts back to F_0 and long-run production will be back at A and not at D, while in the short run production will take place at C or B, as before.[4]

The implication that there is unemployment in the short run under real wage rigidity depends on the specification of the production function.[5] For an illustration of a case in which this need not happen, consider the example of energy-capital complementarity that was discussed briefly in Chapter 2. When energy is the only material input and it comes in fixed proportions with capital, the FPF, as we have seen, shifts to F', which is parallel to F_0 along the R axis. Under real wage rigidity, therefore, equilibrium will take place at B, and in contrast to the previous model, full employment can in the short run be maintained at the initial real wage W_{Q_0} since the optimum capital/labor ratio stays the same while the net rate of return to capital[6] falls by the amount $\Delta R = -\eta \Delta \Pi_e$. In the long run, if the real interest rate equals R_0, the capital stock and the real wage must adjust downward to equilibrium at the point E. The new steady-state real wage at E is clearly above, and the capital/labor ratio below, the respective long-run equilibrium levels under the previous technology (compare the points E and D and the respective tangents at these points), but otherwise the long-run implications remain the same. The short-run effect on labor demand is, of course, different.

Finally we may note that the same framework can be used to analyze the effect of exogenous shocks to the real wage or to the real interest rate, and likewise for an exogenous productivity slowdown, cases that we shall encounter as we go along.

Changes in Labor Demand and Output Supply

For the analysis of employment response under the general three-factor production function $Q = Q(L,K,N)$, one can appeal to standard price theory and derive labor demand equations for given nominal prices of labor (W) and materials (P_N) and a given quantity of capital (K). In our subsequent discussion we shall want to distinguish between rationed labor demand L_Q^d, when the firm chooses L to minimize costs for a given Q, and so-called notional labor demand L^d, when the firm chooses both L and Q in order to maximize profits.

Under short-run cost ($= WL + P_N N$) minimization we obtain the conditions

(3.1) $$\frac{\partial Q}{\partial L} = \frac{W}{MC}, \quad \frac{\partial Q}{\partial N} = \frac{P_N}{MC},$$

where MC is the marginal cost. Thus the *ratio* of the marginal products equals the *ratio* of factor prices:

$$(3.2) \qquad \frac{\partial Q}{\partial L} \bigg/ \frac{\partial Q}{\partial N} = W/P_N.$$

Equation (3.2) together with the production function for given $\overline{Q}[\overline{Q} = Q(L,K,N)]$ allows us to derive the first type of output-constrained labor demand relation in terms of given output, quantity of capital, and the given variable factor price ratio,

$$(3.3) \qquad L_Q^d = L_Q^d(\underset{+}{\overline{Q}}, \ \underset{-}{W/P_N}; \ \underset{+}{K}).$$

When output is free to adjust to a profit-maximizing level, we can equate marginal costs (MC) to the price level (P) in Eq. (3.1). This allows one to apply the two first-order conditions separately and obtain notional labor demand (L^d) in terms of the two real factor returns (and capital):

$$(3.4) \qquad L^d = L^d(\underset{-}{W/P}, \ \underset{-}{P_N/P}; \ \underset{+}{K}).$$

A similar demand function can be written down for N. Likewise one obtains an output supply function of the general form

$$(3.5) \qquad Q^s = Q^s(\underset{-}{W/P}, \ \underset{-}{P_N/P}; \ \underset{+}{K}).$$

In this chapter we shall from now on stick to the profit-maximizing case. Rather than staying at the level of generality (for which more detail is given in Appendix 3A), we shall narrow down the functional forms to be used here. First consider the case of value-added separability.

Suppose that the production function can be written in the two-level form; that is, gross output is a linearly homogeneous function of a value-added index (V) and materials (N), while value added can be written, as before, as a function of labor and capital (for the time being we leave out technical progress):

$$(3.6) \qquad Q = Q(V,N), \qquad V = V(L,K).$$

The advantage of this two-level formulation is that it allows one to consider in stages the two separate production functions and obtain a simple relationship for labor demand. The problem is how to define a price index P_V for value added, since neither V nor P_V is separately observable in the market (although their product is). Suppose, for the moment, that both of these exist and that the relative price of V in Q units is denoted by $\Pi_V = P_V/P$ and the first-order condition for profit maximization holds, namely $\partial Q/\partial V = \Pi_V$. As before, assume also that $\partial Q/\partial N = \Pi_N$. We can now apply the factor price frontier concept to the first-level production function $Q(V,N)$. In rate-of-change form we can write

$$(3.7) \qquad s_n(\dot{p}_n - \dot{p}) + s_v(\dot{p}_v - \dot{p}) = s_n\dot{\pi}_n + (1 - s_n)\dot{\pi}_v = 0.$$

Equation (3.7) can serve as the definition of an index P_V with its rate of change defined as

$$(3.7') \qquad \dot{p}_v = (1 - s_n)^{-1}(\dot{p} - s_n\dot{p}_n).$$

Having defined P_V, the product wage (W/P_V) is also defined and labor demand can be written in the form

$$(3.8) \qquad L^d = L^d(W/P_V; K).$$

Thus, if capital is given in the short run, labor is a function of a single variable, the real wage in value-added units $(W_V = W/P_V)$. How does this relate to the more general form given by (3.4)? The answer is simple. We know from Eq. (3.7) that the two relative prices Π_V and Π_N must be negatively related. Since $W_V = W/P_V = (W/P)/(P_V/P) = W_Q/\Pi_V$, and Π_V is a negative function of Π_N, it is clear that (3.8) could also be written in the form

$$(3.8') \qquad L^d = L^d(\underset{-}{W_Q}/\underset{+}{\Pi_V}; K) = L^d(\underset{-}{W_Q}, \underset{-}{\Pi_N}; K).$$

Thus (3.8') is a special case of Eq. (3.4).

Using these two formulations interchangeably will be helpful in our subsequent discussions. There are times when the use of a value-added formulation will be more straightforward, and there are problems for which the full-fledged gross output formulation is a more convenient one to handle. We also note in passing that for the value-added separable case we could conduct the FPF analysis of rising raw materials prices (Π_N) alternatively in terms of falling relative GDP prices (Π_V).

For given real output wage (W_Q) a rise in Π_N or a fall in Π_V implies a rise in $W_V = W_Q/\Pi_V$ and thus a rise in real product wage.[7] Generally, the employment response after a raw material price increase can conveniently be summarized by looking at the effect on W_V (see Chapter 9). Employment will stay constant in the face of a raw material price shock if and only if W_V stays constant. If, for any reason, there is an independent total productivity fall (negative technical progress) or a drop in capital stock, then W_V, too, will have to fall to maintain full employment.

Analysis in Terms of the Two-Level CES Function

At this point it will help to specialize our formulation even further and consider a more detailed analysis of response in terms of an empirically useful production function, the two-level (or "nested") CES. Suppose the Q function in Eq. (3.6) exhibits constant elasticity of substitution (σ) between V and N and the V function likewise is also CES with elasticity σ_1, that is, the production function takes the form

$$(3.9) \qquad Q^{-\rho} = aV^{-\rho} + (1-a)N^{-\rho}; \qquad V^{-\rho_1} = bL^{-\rho_1} + (1-b)K^{-\rho_1},$$

where $\sigma = (1+\rho)^{-1}$ and $\sigma_1 = (1+\rho_1)^{-1}$ are the respective elasticities of substitution. The important property of CES is the simple relationship between relative quantity and relative price change. Thus for the V function we can write

$$(3.10) \qquad \dot{l} - \dot{k} = \sigma_1(\dot{z} - \dot{w}) = \sigma_1(\dot{r} - \dot{w}_q),$$

where z and w are, as before, the log nominal rental prices of labor and capital and r, w_q are the respective p-deflated rentals ($r = z - p$, $w_q = w - p$).

Similarly, we can write down the FPF as in Eq. (2.10'):

$$(3.11) \qquad \dot{r} = -s_k^{-1}(s_l \dot{w}_q + s_n \dot{\pi}_n),$$

where s_l, s_k, s_n can be worked out explicitly.[8]

Substituting for $\dot{r}$ in (3.10) we obtain the labor demand equation directly in rate-of-change form:

$$(3.12) \qquad \dot{l}^d = \dot{k} - s_k^{-1}\sigma_1[(1 - s_n)\dot{w}_q + s_n \dot{\pi}_n].$$

Similarly, using (3.12) together with Eq. (2.9) we obtain the gross output supply equation:[9]

$$(3.13) \qquad \dot{q}^s = \dot{k} - s_k^{-1}\sigma_1(s_l \dot{w}_q + \eta s_n \dot{\pi}_n),$$

where $\eta = (1 - s_n)^{-1}(s_l + \sigma_1^{-1}\sigma s_k)$ and $\eta \leqslant 1$ for $\sigma_1 \geqslant \sigma$.

We can now apply these quantitative formulas to the analysis of the response to a raw material price shock. For small changes in $\dot{\pi}_n$ we thus find that in the wage-rigid short run (RSR), at given real output wage ($\dot{w}_q = 0$), and given capital stock ($\dot{k} = 0$), employment must fall at the rate $s_k^{-1}\sigma_1 s_n \dot{\pi}_n$ while gross output falls by η times the same rate (where $\eta \leqslant 1$ if $\sigma_1 \geqslant \sigma$). This is represented by the shift from A to B on Figure 2.4.

When the real wage becomes downward-flexible in the short run (that is,

$$\dot{w}_q = -\frac{s_n}{1 - s_n}\dot{\pi}_n \text{ when } \dot{k} = 0), \text{ Eq. (3.12) obviously tells us that } \dot{l}_d = 0 \text{ so that}$$

full employment can be maintained at the point C. Output reduction is mitigated and now falls only by the amount $(1 - s_n)^{-1} s_n \sigma \dot{\pi}_n$.

What can we say about the drop in output in the "long-run" case $\dot{r} = 0$ (point D in Figure 2.4)? This can be readily obtained from an equation that is the long-run analog to (3.12); just interchange the role of labor and capital, since now labor is kept constant while capital is made to adjust to the long-run rate of interest. The result is that $\dot{q} = - s_l^{-1} s_n \sigma_1 \eta' \dot{\pi}_n$, where $\eta' = (1 - s_n)^{-1}(s_k + \sigma_1^{-1} \sigma s_l)$. A comparison of the two expressions for the short-run drop in gross output (for fixed real wage, fixed capital) with the long-run drop (fixed r, fixed employment) shows that the long-run fall is less than the short-run if and only if $s_k < s_l$, a condition on the relative labor share which usually holds empirically.[10]

Empirical estimates for labor demand and output supply based on the two-level CES production function were given in Bruno and Sachs (1983).

Some Simple Dynamics

To see the implications of a permanent raw material price shock within a simple continuous-time framework, one may consider the dynamics in terms of the two key variables, the real wage and the capital stock (w, k, in log terms).

The log of labor demand can be written in the form $l^d = k + h(w_q, \pi_n)$,[11] and the dynamic equation for the real wage can be written as a positive function of excess demand for labor (some version of an augmented Phillips curve):

(3.14) $\dot{w}_q = \phi[h(w_q, \pi_n) + k - \bar{l}]$,

where $\phi' > 0$ and $\bar{l} = \log \bar{L}$.

Next we may postulate an investment function (again using small letters for logarithms) taking the form

(3.15) $\dot{k} = \psi[r(w_q, \pi_n) - r_0] - \delta$,

where $\psi' \geq 0$, $\psi(0) = \delta$, δ = rate of depreciation. $r(w_q, \pi_n)$ is the log value of the rate of return in terms of the FPF. Since $\dot{k} = \dot{K}/K$, this equation implies that gross investment ($\dot{K} + \delta K$) is proportional to the capital stock, and the factor of proportionality (ψ) is a function of the distance of the actual rate of return from the long-run rate (r_0).[12] For $r < r_0$ one could, as a special case, assume $\psi \equiv 0$, that is, that there is zero gross investment when the (log) rate of return falls below r_0 (and capital is nonshiftable).

The phase diagram for the set of two dynamic equations (3.14), (3.15) is given in Figure 3.1. The labor-market equilibrium curve LL is given for $\dot{w}_q = 0$. The equilibrium real wage is a positive function of the capital stock and a negative function of the relative raw material price. Above LL there is unemployment; below LL there is excess demand for labor. The line KK ($\dot{k} = 0$) marks the equilibrium real wage for given r_0 and initial π_n (based on FPF). Above KK, $\dot{k} < 0$, and below it, $\dot{k} > 0$. The equilibrium intersection point A may be a stable node or the focus of a spiral.[13]

Figure 3.2 shows the case of a raw material price shock under the weak separability case. The equilibrium curves are shifted to $L'L'$ and $K'K'$, respectively, with the new long-run equilibrium represented by the point D. The points C and D correspond to the respective points C (short-term, flexible wage) and D (long-term, flexible capital) on the new FPF (F_1) in Figure 2.4. Under complete real wage flexibility ("very high" $\phi'h'$), the economy shifts first from A to full employment at C (preserving the initial capital and labor levels). Subsequently the capital stock and the real wage fall gradually along $L'L'$ until long-run equilibrium is reached at D.

The case of a focus in which the economy spirals toward equilibrium is represented by initial real wage rigidity ("very low" $\phi'h'$) causing low r and persistent capital decumulation (see the movement from A to B along KK in Figure 3.2). Once unemployment has reached a critical level the real wage starts falling, but by now there is undershooting of the capital stock. The economy may go through a sequence of unemployment with decumulation (region I) or accumulation (II), overfull employment (III), decumulation (IV), and so on until the long-run equilibrium is eventually reached at D. Note that in terms of the FPF (F_1 in Figure 2.4) the economy will be fluctuating back and forth along F_1 on both sides of the point D.

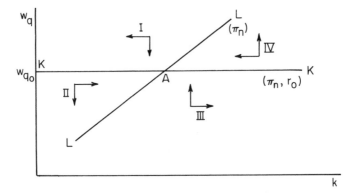

Figure 3.1.   Real wage and capital stock dynamics

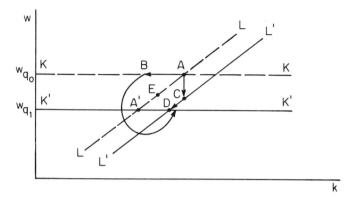

Figure 3.2. Dynamic response to an input price increase

How might the process differ under alternative technological assumptions? Consider the dynamics for full capital-energy complementarity. This would be represented in Figure 3.2 by a case in which the curve LL does not move with a change in π_n, but only the line KK, with equilibrium represented by an intersection point like A'. Here the "flex short run" and the "rigid short run" coincide and the economy stays at A, which is a full-employment point, and then drifts toward the new equilibrium in one of the possible ways depending on the extent of real wage rigidity. Strictly speaking, the point A' does not exactly represent the case just discussed since we have seen that the real wage must fall by less under capital-energy complementarity than under value-added separability. Therefore the KK line also shifts down by less. A point like E marked on the line LL between A' and A may represent the correct equilibrium in this case (imagine a line drawn parallel to KK through E), in full correspondence to the point E on the curve F' in Figure 2.4 (the real wage at E is higher than at D).

We have thus illustrated in greater detail the argument made earlier. A price increase in raw materials in the single-sector economy must, in the long run, entail a fall in the real wage and in the equilibrium capital stock. This is qualitatively the case under both alternative technological assumptions made. Whether there may be unemployment in the short run or not does depend on the technology, and whether there is unemployment along the dynamic path to equilibrium in either model depends on the extent of real wage rigidity.

One can use the same framework to analyze the effect of other exogenous changes in supply. Thus, a permanent drop in productivity could be modeled as a downward shift in the $h(w_q,\pi_n)$ and $r(w_q,\pi_n)$ functions in Eqs. (3.14)–(3.15), just like the increase in π_n. An exogenous rise in real wage could be represented as a shift of the initial point upward into the unemployment region (I) from the point A. This could start a process of gradual adjustment (unless the real wage stays put at the higher initial level). Finally, an exogenous change in the real rate of interest r_0 involves a shift in the KK line—a shift up (down) when r_0 falls (rises), with a corresponding adjustment process in the two state variables w_q and k. For example, a rise in r_0 could be represented as a move of the KK line down to $K'K'$ with the new long-run equilibrium switching from A to A' in Figure 3.2. At the initial stage the economy moves from A toward B; there is a fall in k, and unemployment initially emerges (depending on real wage persistence). The process of k, w_q adjustment will eventually lead the economy to A', in which both the product wage and the capital/labor ratio are below their initial values at A.

Appendix 3A: General Derivation of Input Demand and Output Supply Functions

Consider any m-factor constant-returns production function whose output (in logs) is q; let the log quantity and log product price of factor i be denoted by a_i, $w_i (i = 1, 2, \ldots , m)$, respectively. Next denote the cost share of the ith factor by s_i and let the Hicks-Allen elasticity of substitution[14] be σ_{ij}, where $\sigma_{ij} s_j = \partial a_i / \partial w_j$. Using dots for rates of change, the unit factor demand functions are

$$(3A.1) \qquad \dot{a}_i - \dot{q} = \sum_{j=1}^{m} \sigma_{ij} s_j \dot{w}_j$$

and $\sum_{j=1}^{m} \sigma_{ij} s_j = 0$ for all $i = 1, 2, \ldots , m$.

Next we write down the factor price frontier in rate-of-change form:

$$(3A.2) \qquad \sum_{j=1}^{m} s_j \dot{w}_j = 0.$$

Equation (3A.2) can be substituted into (3A.1) to solve out for the case in which one of the factors (say, the mth) is fixed (in our case, capital is fixed in the short run). Thus (3A.1) can be rewritten as

$$(3A.1') \qquad \dot{a}_i - \dot{q} = \sum_{j=1}^{m-1} (\sigma_{ij} - \sigma_{im}) s_j \dot{w}_j \qquad (i = 1, 2, \ldots , m).$$

Applying (3A.1') to the three-factor case (L,N,K) we get

$$(3A.3) \qquad \dot{l} - \dot{q} = s_l (\sigma_{ll} - \sigma_{lk}) \dot{w}_q + s_n (\sigma_{ln} - \sigma_{lk}) \dot{\pi}_n,$$

(3A.4) $\dot{n} - \dot{q} = s_l(\sigma_{nl} - \sigma_{nk})\dot{w}_q + s_n(\sigma_{nn} - \sigma_{nk})\dot{\pi}_n,$

(3A.5) $\dot{k} - \dot{q} = s_l(\sigma_{kl} - \sigma_{kk})\dot{w}_q + s_n(\sigma_{kn} - \sigma_{kk})\dot{\pi}_n.$

Equation (3A.5), when reversed in sign $(\dot{q} - \dot{k})$, is the short-run supply function. Since $\sigma_{kk} < 0$, this readily shows that output (per unit of capital) is a negative function of the raw material price (π_n) when capital and raw materials are cooperant factors $(\sigma_{kn} > 0)$. Also, output is a negative function of the real wage if capital and labor are cooperant factors $(\sigma_{kl} > 0)$.

By subtracting Eq. (3A.3) from (3A.5) we get an expression for the labor/capital ratio and likewise find that $(\dot{l} - \dot{k})$ is negatively related to $\dot{w}_q$ (for a given $\dot{\pi}_n$) if $\sigma_{lk} > 0$, and is negatively related to $\dot{\pi}_n$ (at given $\dot{w}_q$) as long as $\sigma_{kn} + \sigma_{lk} \geq \sigma_{ln} + \sigma_{kk}$. The latter condition is automatically satisfied in the case of raw material separability $(\sigma_{ln} = \sigma_{kn})$, to which most of our discussion in this chapter was confined. It is even satisfied for the capital-energy complementarity case $(\sigma_{kl} = \sigma_{nl})$ as long as $(-\sigma_{kn}) \leq (-\sigma_{kk})$.

When material separability $Q[V(L,K),N]$ is assumed, these questions can be further simplified. Since now $\sigma_{nl} = \sigma_{nk}$, Eq. (3A.4) becomes

(3A.4') $\dot{n} - \dot{q} = -\sigma\dot{\pi}_n,$

where $\sigma = s_n(\sigma_{nk} - \sigma_{nn}) = \sigma_{nl} = \sigma_{nk}$ is the elasticity of substitution between V and N in Q. Similarly, one can show that $s_l(\sigma_{kl} - \sigma_{ll}) = s_k(\sigma_{kl} - \sigma_{kk}) = \sigma_1$ is the elasticity of substitution between L and K in V. We can now write the output supply per unit of capital and labor demand per unit of capital in the simplified form:

(3A.5') $\dot{q} - \dot{k} = \sigma_1\dot{w} - s_k^{-1}s_n\sigma_1\eta\dot{\pi}_n,$

(3A.6) $\dot{l} - \dot{k} = -\sigma_1(1 + s_k^{-1}s_l)\dot{w}_q - s_k^{-1}s_n\sigma_1\dot{\pi}_n,$

where $\eta = (1 - s_n)^{-1}(s_l + \sigma_1^{-1}\sigma s_k) \leq 1$, as in the text equations (3.12)–(3.13). These equations, we have seen, can also be obtained more directly.

4 Savings, Investment, and Capital Flows

IN THIS CHAPTER we take a major leap into general equilibrium analysis. We study the intertemporal allocation of output between present and future consumption and investment, also allowing for international borrowing and lending, and we analyze the effect of changes in raw material prices and in real interest rates on wealth and asset formation. First this is done within a single open economy that also produces a raw material and then within a multicountry trading world. This framework enables the study of simultaneous changes in world prices of raw materials and real interest rates, a problem of much relevance in the 1970s. It also helps to consider the differential response of borrower countries—middle-income countries (MICs)—which may have suffered by being net importers of oil (or other raw materials) but which also for a time benefited from the recycling of the cheap financial OPEC surplus.

While most of the analysis in this chapter is still confined to the real economy, we introduce domestic money (and bonds) in one intermediate section, to take up the role of domestic monetary policy in output expansion when there is nominal wage rigidity. A more general treatment of the role of domestic demand management will be deferred to the next chapter.

Production, Investment, and the Balance of Payments

Let us continue with the open-economy, one-final-good, three-factor framework and consider now the allocation of output and investment over time in a simple extension of this model. As earlier, the country produces one tradable final good (of quantity Q and price P) and uses a material (for example, oil) input, N, whose relative price ($\Pi_N = P_N/P$) is given, in production, $Q =$

$Q(L,K,N)$, together with labor, L, and capital, K. Linear homogeneity and factor cooperancy (positive cross-derivatives) are assumed. The final good can be traded (net exports $= X$) and is used for domestic private (C) and public (G) consumption as well as for investment (I) in future capacity.

A useful procedure, to be followed here, is to confine the discussion to a two-period horizon.[1] Subscripts will denote the period ($t = 1, 2$). Period 1, the short run, is characterized by the fact that the capital stock is fixed ($K = \overline{K}$). By period 2, the expected long run, the capital stock may be augmented or contracted by the amount of investment or disinvestment[2] carried out in period 1 ($K_2 = \overline{K} + I_1$). Zero depreciation and no investment are assumed in period 2, since K_2 stays on for posterity. Labor supply in both periods is assumed to be given, and labor-augmenting technical change is allowed for by measuring labor (L_t) in intensity units.

The commodity balance in the two periods takes the form

(4.1) $C_t + G_t + I_t + X_t = Q_t,$

where $t = 1, 2$ and, by assumption, $I_2 = 0$. All these magnitudes are measured in real output units.

While a single-sector specification for production of final goods is maintained, the model is extended by introducing domestic production of the raw material N. Its output will be assumed to be fixed at the quantity H_t in both periods and will have the exogenous nominal market price P_{N_t} (and *relative* price Π_{N_t}). Since the production of H is held fixed in this country, the input of factors into it can be ignored, and it is only taken into account in the calculation of real income (Y_t) and the trade balance (F_t). Total real income will be $Y_t = Q_t - \Pi_{N_t}N_t + \Pi_{N_t}H_t = Q_t + \Pi_{N_t}(H_t - N_t)$. It can be expressed as a real-income (or revenue) function:

(4.2) $Y_t = Y_t(L_t, K_t; \Pi_{N_t}, H_t),$

where $\partial Y_t/\partial L_t = \partial Q_t/\partial L_t$, $\partial Y_t/\partial K_t = \partial Q_t/\partial K_t$, $\partial Y_t/\partial \Pi_{N_t} = H_t - N_t$, and $\partial Y_t/\partial H_t = \Pi_{N_t}$.

Note that ($H_t - N_t$) is net exports of the material (this is negative for a net importer). The trade balance in traded-goods units (F_t) can be written as

(4.3) $F_t = X_t + \Pi_{N_t}(H_t - N_t) = X_t + Y_t - Q_t = S_t - I_t,$

where $S_t = Y_t - C_t - G_t =$ domestic savings.

Assume now that the country's residents are free to borrow or lend between the two periods at a given interest factor R or (real) rate of interest ($R - 1$). (This particular "small-economy" assumption will be relaxed later in the chapter when more countries are introduced.) This implies the inter-temporal borrowing or lending constraint

$$(4.4) \qquad F_1 + F_2/R = 0.$$

Another way of stating this equation is to say, for the case of borrowing, that the second period's current account surplus, $F_2 + (R - 1)F_1$, which consists of the trade surplus corrected for net interest payments, must exactly match the first period's deficit, $-F_1$.

Using Eq. (4.3), the intertemporal borrowing constraint can alternatively be stated as a household budget constraint,

$$(4.5) \qquad C_1 + C_2/R = Y_1 + Y_2/R - T - I_1 = \Omega,$$

where $T = G_1 + G_2/R$ = total government budget (taxes).

This again states the well-known property that the present value of the consumption flow must equal the present value of the income stream minus the change in physical wealth, which is net household wealth, Ω. Alternatively, if firm investment is financed by selling financial assets to households (which must bear the same rate of interest, $R - 1$), Eq. (4.5) states that the total consumption flow of households plus total incremental investment in the asset must equal total income accruing to households.

Firm Behavior

Before returning to household behavior, let us digress for a moment to consider the firm's investment behavior. It is assumed here, along with much of the optimum investment literature, that firms in the Q industry choose I_1 so as to maximize their discounted cash flow:

$$[Q_1(\overline{K}, L_1, N_1) - W_1 L_1 - \Pi_{N_1} N_1] - I_1$$
$$+ [Q_2(\overline{K} + I_1, L_2, N_2) - W_2 L_2 - \Pi_{N_2} N_2]/R,$$

subject to the labor and production constraints.

Such intertemporal optimization leads to two kinds of conditions. One is the usual set of static first-order conditions for the marginal products of the two variable factors in each period separately,

$$(4.6) \qquad \partial Q_t/\partial L_t = W_{Q_t}, \qquad \partial Q_t/\partial N_t = \Pi_{N_t}.$$

The second, intertemporal, condition comes from maximization with respect to investment in the first period, that is, choice of the capital stock in the second period. This gives

$$(4.7) \qquad \partial Q_2/\partial K_2 = R, \qquad I_1 = L_2\kappa(\Pi_{N_2},R) - \bar{K},$$

where κ is the capital/labor ratio at the relative prices Π_{N_2} and R.

What (4.7) implies is that while the marginal product of capital may shift in the short run (fixed capital), in the long run (second period) the capital stock must be adjusted[3] so that its marginal product equals the long-run external interest factor, R. With constant returns to scale the product wage in period 2 (W_{Q_2}) is thus also determined exogenously. We shall make use of these simplifying properties.

Having stated the equilibrium conditions for firm behavior, one can now deduce some simple properties of the net wealth (Ω) concept introduced in Eq. (4.5). Using (4.2) and (4.5) and the fact that $K_2 = \bar{K} + I_1$, one can write

$$(4.5') \qquad \Omega = Y_1 + Y_2/R - T - I_1 = \Omega(\Pi_{N_1}, \Pi_{N_2}, R, \bar{K}, H_t, L_t; I_1).$$

For optimum investment (4.7), we have $\Omega^* = \Omega^*(\Pi_{N_1}, \Pi_{N_2}, R, \bar{K}, H_t, L_t)$, which is net wealth optimized with respect to investment. Differentiating with respect to I_1, one gets $\partial\Omega/\partial I_1 = [\partial Y_2/\partial K_2]/R - 1 = 0$. $\partial\Omega^*/\partial x = \partial\Omega/\partial x + (\partial\Omega/\partial I)(\partial\Omega/\partial x)$ for any x. Since $\partial\Omega/\partial I = 0$, Ω and Ω^* must have the same response to the exogenous variables.

The response of net wealth to changes in the price of the raw materials is

$$(4.8) \qquad \partial\Omega^*/\partial\Pi_{N_1} = \partial\Omega/\partial\Pi_{N_1} = \partial Y_1/\partial\Pi_{N_1} = H_1 - N_1,$$
$$\partial\Omega^*/\partial\Pi_{N_2} = \partial\Omega/\partial\Pi_{N_2} = (\partial Y_2/\partial\Pi_{N_2})/R = (H_2 - N_2)/R.$$

This is a simple and intuitively plausible result. It says that an increase in the price of raw materials in either period increases or decreases net wealth by the net export of the material input $(H - N)$, properly discounted. A net exporter gains in net wealth, and a net importer loses. The welfare implications of such changes and responses to changes in R will be discussed later. Let us first turn to consumption and savings behavior.

Household Consumption and Savings Behavior

Suppose now that household behavior can be represented as maximization, by a representative household, of a concave intertemporal utility function $U(C_1,C_2)$ subject to given net wealth, Ω. The consumption goods of the two periods are assumed to be gross substitutes $(U_{12} \geqslant 0)$, implying that both consumption goods are normal with respect to increases in wealth. The consumption function is

(4.9) $C_t = C_t(\underset{+}{\Omega}, R)$.

As is well known from Fisherian theory, an increase in the rate of interest will in general lead to ambiguous effects on present consumption since the substitution and wealth effects of an interest-rate change may work in opposite directions. Only for a net borrower (or initial balance) can we make unambiguous statements. This also applies in the present model.

Differentiating the budget constraint (4.5) and the first-order condition for utility maximization $u_1 = Ru_2$ (where $u_i = \partial U/\partial C_i$) with respect to R, one can get the following version of the Slutsky equation:

(4.10) $\partial C_1/\partial R = -u_2/A + (\partial C_1/\partial \Omega)F_1/R$,

where A is the (positive) bordered Hessian determinant of U and the related first term in (4.10) is the pure compensated substitution effect. C_1 is a normal good $(\partial C_1/\partial \Omega > 0)$. Thus $\partial S_1/\partial R = -\partial C_1/\partial R > 0$ if $F_1 \leqslant 0$.

Since investment is negatively related to the rate of interest, it follows that $\partial F_1/\partial R = \partial S_1/\partial R - \partial I_1/\partial R > 0$ for $F_1 \leqslant 0$. Thus *a net borrower will borrow more (less) when the interest rate falls (rises)*.

Temporary and Permanent Input Price Shocks

We can now analyze the effect of changes in relative raw material prices. Suppose we start from an initial equilibrium situation as at the point A of the FPF in Figure 2.4. Thus the assumption is that initially $\partial Q_1/\partial K_1 = \partial Q_2/\partial K_2 = R = R_0$.

Consider first a change in Π_{N_1}, Π_{N_2}, each taken separately. The first event in which $\Delta\Pi_{N_1} > 0$ (Π_{N_2} constant) marks the case of a *temporary* price shock. The relative price rises in the short run but is expected to return to the starting point in the future. In this case the factor price frontier (F_0 in Figure 2.4) contracts temporarily to F_1, and under the separability assumption and real wage flexibility the economy moves from A to C. In period 2 the economy is expected to move back to A, however. There is thus no change in investment plans. By (4.8) there is a temporary fall (rise) in total first-period real income (Y_1) and wealth (Ω) if the country is a net importer (exporter) of the raw material in the first period: $\partial\Omega/\partial\Pi_{N_1} = \partial Y_1/\partial\Pi_{N_1} = H_1 - N_1 \lessgtr 0$. For the trade surplus we get

$$(4.11) \quad \partial F_1/\partial \Pi_{N_1} = \partial Y_1/\partial \Pi_{N_1} - \partial C_1/\partial \Pi_{N_1} = (H_1 - N_1)(1 - \partial C_1/\partial \Omega)$$
$$= (\partial C_2/\partial \Omega)(H_1 - N_1)/R_0.$$

$\partial F_1/\partial \Pi_{N_1} \lessgtr 0$ according to whether $H_1 \lessgtr N_1$. Thus, for a net importer of raw materials the current account worsens in the first period (and improves in the second period).

Consider now the case in which only $\Delta \Pi_{N_2} > 0$ (Π_{N_1} constant), that is, a price increase is *expected* in the future. By strict analogy to the previous case, second-period expected real income, and therefore present net wealth, will rise or fall according to whether the country is expected to be a future net exporter or net importer of N (see Eq. 4.8): $\partial \Omega/\partial \Pi_{N_2} = (\partial Y_2/\partial \Pi_{N_2})/R_0 = (H_2 - N_2)/R_0$.

In this case present real income is not affected, but on the other hand investment falls in anticipation of a fall in $K_2/\overline{L}$. The FPF stays put now but is expected to shift next period, with the economy ending up at the point D. The current account in period 1 this time unambiguously *improves* for a net importer as a result of the fall in investment and a rise in savings, in expectation of falling future income:[4]

$$(4.12) \quad \partial F_1/\partial \Pi_{N_2} = -(\partial C_1/\partial \Omega)(H_2 - N_2)/R_0 - \partial I_1/\partial \Pi_{N_2}.$$

The case of a *permanent* price shock can be represented as a combined change in both Π_{N_1} and Π_{N_2} at the same rate ($\partial \Pi_N$). The resulting change in the current account can be written as the *sum* of the two previous expressions (4.11) and (4.12):

$$(4.13) \quad \partial F_1/\partial \Pi_N = (H_1 - N_1) - (\partial C_1/\partial \Omega)[(H_1 - N_1)$$
$$+ (H_2 - N_2)/R_0] - \partial I_1/\partial \Pi_N.$$

The three components of (4.13) are, respectively, the real income (output) effect, the wealth effect on consumption (due to valuation of net total resource gains or losses), and the investment effect. The total effect will in general be ambiguous, since the different components pull in conflicting directions. However, there are some special cases (pointed out by Svensson, 1981) in which the sum of the first two terms is nonnegative. If the country is initially in a stationary net import or net export position, the first two terms of (4.13) can be written in the form

$$(\partial C_2/\partial \Omega - \partial C_1/\partial \Omega)(H - N)/R_0.$$

This is nonnegative if $\partial C_1/\partial\Omega \geq \partial C_2/\partial\Omega$ and $N \geq H$, or if both inequalities are reversed. In these cases the current account unambiguously improves. The case $\partial C_1/\partial\Omega > \partial C_2/\partial\Omega$ may indicate some kind of "consumer impatience," the marginal propensity to consume today being larger than that expected in the future.

Welfare Analysis

One can summarize the effects of changes in relative prices by looking at the components of welfare change in terms of the utility function. Again making use of Eq. (4.5) and the first-order condition, and remembering that changes in I_1 do not affect the value of Ω, we get

$$dU = u_1 dC_1 + u_2 dC_2 = Ru_2(dC_1 + dC_2/R)$$

$$= Ru_2(dY_1 + dY_2/R + \frac{C_2 - Y_2}{R^2} dR)$$

$$= u_2(R dY_1 + dY_2 + F_1 dR).$$

Thus one can write

(4.14) $$dU/u_1 = (H_1 - N_1)d\Pi_{N_1} + \frac{H_2 - N_2}{R} d\Pi_{N_2}$$

$$+ \frac{F_1}{R} dR + \Pi_{N_1}dH_1 + \frac{\Pi_{N_2}}{R} dH_2.$$

As one would expect, the welfare indicator depends on the respective raw material price changes weighted by the self-sufficiency measure for each period. The third term in (4.14) stands for the welfare effect of a change in the interest rate (that is, the rate of intertemporal substitution). *A net debtor gains while a net creditor loses from a fall in R (and conversely for an increase in R).*[5]

This finding suggests an interesting application to the effect of the oil price shock on a net importer who also happens to be a net debtor in the world capital market, the situation of a large number of MICs. It may very well be that after the first oil shock, the welfare gain from the fall in the real interest rate could in some of these countries have compensated for or even outweighed the direct loss due to the rise in real oil prices. We return to this topic in the last section of this chapter.

Wages, Prices, and Monetary Policy

As long as real wages are instantaneously downward-flexible in response to excess supply of labor, an input price shock, whether temporary or permanent, will bring about a downward adjustment of the real wage so as to maintain full employment at the short-run, fixed capital point (point C in Figure 2.4). In the second period, as capital adjusts, there will also be a further downward adjustment in the real wage, as long as the long-run real rate of return to capital remains above the level consistent with the use of the initial capital level $\overline{K}$.

Consider now the case of short-run wage rigidity. We shall assume that in the long run the real wage is fully flexible, but that in the short run, due to institutional factors (wage contracts, union behavior, and so on) this does not hold. Two kinds of wage rigidity may be discussed. One is the extreme case of *real* wage rigidity (the very short run) which occurs if there is 100 percent price indexation. Unemployment emerges, and real income (Y_1), net wealth (Ω), and total welfare (U) will be lower than under wage flexibility. No welfare-improving demand stimulus is possible here (tax measures, such as a wage subsidy, could improve welfare). A more interesting case occurs when the *nominal* wage (W) is rigid. Here a demand expansion may drive the real wage down, increasing output supply and employment. There is obviously room for intermediate cases of partial wage indexation.

We shall leave fiscal policy considerations to the next chapter, where we introduce a semitradable good, since in the present tradable goods model all that temporary fiscal policy can do is to change the pattern of consumption (and the trade deficit) over time; it cannot change the employment level. It does pay, however, to consider monetary policy since it will affect the price level and through the latter the level of the short-run real wage. Again we keep the analysis to essentials.

We introduce money and a nominal domestic bond. Let us assume that (log) money demand is linear in (log) gross output of final goods and in a nominal interest rate j, and that the money market clears so that we can write (in log form):[6]

$$(4.15) \qquad m_t - p_t = aq_t - bj_t,$$

where $t = 1, 2$.

To overcome the indeterminancy of money demand and interest rates in the second period, we shall assume that the second period's interest factor is equal to the exogenous nominal world interest rate, which under subsequent price stability will be the same as the real rate (r_2): $j_2 = j_2^* = r_2$. In the short run, however, the world nominal rate, j_1^*, and the real rate, r_1, may differ.

To complete the system, we write down the intertemporal asset arbitrage condition,

$$(4.16) \qquad j_1 = j_1^* + e_2 - e_1 = j_1^* + p_2 - p_1 - (p_2^* - p_1^*)$$
$$= p_2 - p_1 + r_1,$$

where $e_t = \log E_t$, the log of the exchange rate, and we have made use of the purchasing power parity condition $p_t = p_t^* + e_t$.

We can now rewrite the money market equilibrium conditions for the two periods:

$$m_1 - p_1 = aq_1 - br_1 - bp_2 + bp_1; \qquad m_2 - p_2 = aq_2 - br_2.$$

Substituting for p_2 in the first equation from the second, we get the following conditions for the respective price levels in the two periods:

$$(4.17) \qquad p_1 = (1 + b)^{-1}[(m_1 + bm_2) - a(q_1 + bq_2) + b(r_1 + br_2)],$$

$$(4.18) \qquad p_2 = m_2 - aq_2 + br_2.$$

Equation (4.17) makes it clear that in a two-period model with perfect foresight, present prices depend on both present and future money stocks, output levels, and exogenous world interest rates. This clearly is a special example of multiperiod rational expectations theory, to which we return in Chapter 7.

Ignoring possible changes in the real interest rate (see the following section), we can now reconsider the effect of a supply shock. The main route through which this will affect the price level equation (4.17) is the depressing effect on output in one or both periods. With given money supply the transactions motive for holding money is weakened, and since real rates are given exogenously, the domestic price level must rise to balance real money holdings. It is interesting to note that for a *temporary* rise in material prices the increase in the domestic price level is less than it would be under a permanent shock, since with p_2 held constant a rise in p_1 also signals a temporary fall in the domestic interest rate (see Eq. 4.16), thus taking up part of the slack.

We are now ready to return to the discussion of *nominal* wage rigidity. Since it is unlikely that the output drop will by itself bring about a price level increase of sufficient magnitude to reduce the real wage to full employment equilibrium, the impact effect of a material price shock will tend to be stagflationary, that is, it will bring about a price increase as well as some unemployment (in terms of the FPF, Figure 2.4, the economy will upon impact be somewhere between the points B and C).

Real income (Y_1) and employment can now be increased by a monetary *expansion* which will inflate away the sticky nominal wage, bringing about a real wage reduction to the extent desired (that is, bringing the economy to the point C). Obviously there is room for alternative strategies, depending on whether this expansion is perceived to be temporary (only m_1 is made to change, keeping m_2 unchanged), permanent (both m_1 and m_2 to be changed at the same rate), or somewhere in between. Similarly, one can extend this analysis to intermediate cases in which real wages are partially sticky, thus making for more inflation.

Determination of the Real Interest Rate in a Multicountry World

The model will now be extended to a world with many countries; each of them has the same basic technology as the single economy described in the preceding section, but different initial factor endowments are allowed. We preserve the simplicity of a single final tradable good and an exogenous relative price, Π_N, confronting all countries. However, one country ("OPEC," superscript 0), which is a net exporter of the material input, is singled out, while all other countries (superscript $i = 1, 2, \ldots , m$) are net importers. The output of the raw material by all other countries is assumed to be exogenously fixed ($H_t^i = \overline{H}_t^i$), while that of country 0 will be endogenously determined by world demand given the fixed relative price, Π_{N_t}, which is assumed to be set by country 0. We thus have

$$(4.19) \qquad H_t^0 - N_t^0 > 0, \qquad \overline{H}_t^i - N_t^i < 0, \qquad \sum_{i=0}^{m} (H_t^i - N_t^i) = 0,$$

where $t = 1, 2; i = 1, 2, \ldots , m$. For simplicity, assume that $\overline{H}_t^i$ ($i = 1, 2, \ldots , m$) are sufficiently small, relative to N_t^i, that the status of a net importer will not be reversed.

An alternative procedure, not followed here, would be to have OPEC set H_t^0 and let Π_{N_t} be endogenous.

In aggregating real income over all countries, using the world balance equation (4.19) for the material, we find that world income (Y_t^w) equals world production of final goods (Q_t^w), and the world market balance of final goods can be written as

$$(4.20) \qquad Y_t^w = Q_t^w = \sum_{i=0}^{m} Q_t^i = C_t^w + G_t^w + I_t^w,$$

where $C_t^w = \Sigma_{i=0}^{m} C_t^i$, and so on.

While the exogeneity of the real price of oil is kept for simplicity, the real rate of interest now becomes endogenous. It will be assumed that R is determined by the world equilibrium of savings supply and investment demand in the first period. The main object of this section is thus to consider the factors determining the world savings and investment schedules. Consider first aggregate investment demand, which is obtained by aggregating the investment function of the individual countries (we continue to ignore investment in the production of H). Assuming constant returns to scale and summing I_1 from (4.7) over countries, world investment can be written as

(4.21) $\quad I_1^w = \sum_{i=0}^{m} I_1^i = \kappa(\Pi_{N_2}, R)L_2^w - K_1^w,$

where L_2^w is the second period's world labor input (in intensity units) in final goods production.

Figure 4.1 shows the world investment schedule as a downward-sloping curve in $[I^w, R]$ space. An increase in the expected cost of oil or in the capital stock will shift the I curve down and to the left.

The world savings schedule raises more ambiguities. Consider aggregate savings as the difference between world income and consumption. Assume

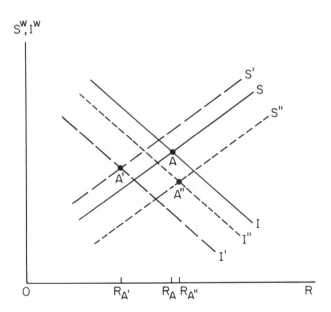

Figure 4.1. World capital market equilibrium

first that labor markets clear. Then

$$(4.22) \qquad S_1^w = Q_1^w(\Pi_{N_1}) - C_1^w[\Pi_{N_1}, \Pi_{N_2}, H_1^0(\Pi_{N_1}), H_2^0(\Pi_{N_2}), R] - G_1^w$$
$$= S_1^w(\Pi_{N_1}, \Pi_{N_2}, R).$$

From the earlier analysis we know that gross output in each country in the first period depends only on the first-period relative price Π_{N_1} and on the given quantities of labor and capital (here omitted). Private consumption in each country depends on R and on wealth, which in turn varies with the various relative prices. We have also inserted H_t^0 to express the indirect dependence of OPEC consumption on its own price through the real income effect on total oil revenues. The C^w function is where the aggregation ambiguities come in, so it will be discussed in greater detail.

Consider first the aggregate response of C_1^w (and of S_1^w) to changes in the rate of interest. Aggregating (4.10) over countries, we can write

$$(4.23) \qquad \partial S_1^w/\partial R = -\partial C_1^w/\partial R = \sum_{i=0}^{m} [u_2^i/A_i] + 1/R \sum_{i=0}^{m} (\partial C_1^i/\partial \Omega^i)(-F_1^i).$$

The first term on the right-hand side of (4.23) is positive, as in the single-country case. For the second term we know that the aggregate current-account balance for the whole world must be zero ($\sum_{i=0}^{m} F_1^i = 0$). The second summation is the world aggregate propensity to consume out of wealth. Let us divide the countries into net debtors ($F_1^i < 0$) and net creditors ($F_1^i > 0$). A simple proposition follows: *World savings will be positively related to the rate of interest if the deficit-weighted marginal propensity to consume of the net debtors is greater than (or equal to) the surplus-weighted marginal propensity to consume of the net creditors.* This is a sufficient though by no means necessary condition to guarantee $\partial S_1^w/\partial R > 0$.

Empirically, one is more likely to find net debtors among the lower-income countries, for which one would assume that marginal propensities to consume tend to be higher than in countries with higher levels of income. It thus makes sense to assume that the world savings schedule is upward-sloping (or flat).

The dependence on input price changes is more problematic. Consider first the first-period price. We have

$$(4.24) \qquad -\partial C_1^w/\partial \Pi_{N_1} = \sum_{i=0}^{m} (\partial C_1^i/\partial \Omega^i)(N_1^i - H_1^i)$$
$$+ (\partial C_1^0/\partial \Omega^0)(-\Pi_{N_1} \partial H_1^0/\partial \Pi_{N_1}).$$

The second term on the right-hand side of (4.24) is the negative real income effect of OPEC consumption coming from the fall in demand for H_1^0 as Π_{N_1} is raised. For the first term we apply an argument very similar to the one underlying (4.23), that is, the first term is

$$\sum_{i=1}^{m} (\partial C_1^i/\partial \Omega^i)(N_1^i - H_1^i) - (\partial C_1^0/\partial \Omega^0)(H_1^0 - N_1^0),$$

where $\Sigma_{i=1}^{m} (N_1^i - H_1^i) = H_1^0 - N_1^0$. Therefore, $-\partial C_1^w/\partial \Pi_{N_1} > 0$ if

$$\partial C_1^0/\partial \Omega^0 < 1/(H_1^0 - N_1^0) \sum_{i=1}^{m} (\partial C_1^i/\partial \Omega^i)(N_1^i - H_1^i).$$

Thus we have the proposition: *Aggregate world consumption falls with an increase in the real price of oil if the marginal propensity to consume of the net oil exporter(s) is less than the weighted marginal propensity to consume of the net importers.*

Although the condition may have held immediately after the oil price shock of 1973–74, it can at best be assumed to have been temporary, as OPEC countries may have taken time to adjust consumption (for instance, the absence of infrastructure may have held up imports). Even if it holds, however, there is another force working in the opposite direction, that is, current oil prices reduce real income and output (Q_1^w). A temporary price increase may thus move world savings either way. This argument does not hold for an anticipated price increase (Π_{N_2}), which will affect C_1^w but not Q_1^w.

Now consider a permanent increase in price ($d\Pi_N = d\Pi_{N_1} = d\Pi_{N_2}$). Suppose $H_t^i - N_t^i = H^i - N^i(t = 1, 2)$. Repeating the derivation of (4.24) for Π_{N_2}, and using the fact that $\partial C_1^w/\partial \Pi_{N_2} = \Sigma_{i=0}^{m} (H^i - N^i) + \Pi_{N_1}\partial H_1^0/\partial \Pi_{N_1}$ and $\partial C_1^i/\partial \Omega^i + (1/R)\partial C_2^i/\partial \Omega^i = 1$ (for all i), we eventually get

(4.25)
$$R(\partial S_1^w/\partial \Pi_N) = \sum_{i=0}^{m} (\partial C_2^i/\partial \Omega^i - \partial C_1^i/\partial \Omega^i)(H^i - N^i)$$
$$+ [\Pi_{N_1}(\partial H_1^0/\Pi_N)(\partial C_2^0/\partial \Omega^0)$$
$$- \Pi_{N_2}(\partial H_2^0/\partial \Pi_N)(\partial C_1^0/\partial \Omega^0)].$$

The first term in (4.25) will be positive (or zero) if $\partial C_2^0/\partial \Omega^0 \geqslant \partial C_1^0/\partial \Omega^0$ (no "impatience" for OPEC) and $\partial C_2^i/\partial \Omega^i \leqslant \partial C_1^i/\partial \Omega^i$ for all oil importers ($i = 1, 2, \ldots, m$). The second term in (4.25) represents net savings of OPEC from the real income effect of a change in Π_N in both periods; it will be positive if the fall in the demand for H_2^0 is sufficiently more negative than the fall in the demand for H_1^0 (note that the demand for the material will contract in period 2 because the reduced capital input bears part of the adjustment to higher material prices in that period).

So far we have assumed full wage flexibility in the face of an oil shock. To the extent that real wages are sticky in at least some oil-importing countries, Q_1^w, now dependent on real wages in different countries, will fall by more, with a further depressing effect on aggregate savings.

The analysis has been conducted all along under the assumption that producers always operate on their supply schedule and equate prices to marginal costs. There is good reason to suggest that the contractionary policies pursued by the major industrial countries after the first oil shock and again after the second oil shock temporarily placed some of them in a short-term Keynesian disequilibrium (excess supply) situation. The analysis of output determination in a demand-constrained situation will be given in the following two chapters. For the present purpose it suffices to state that contractionary demand policies in response to an input price shock may further reduce aggregate savings along with aggregate output.

The two cases just described may be relevant for an explanation of the differences in real-interest behavior after the two oil shocks. As is well known, one of the concomitants of the first supply shock (1973–74) was a sharp reduction in real interest rates in the financial markets of most industrial countries. Very small or negative rates were recorded throughout the period 1974–77. As noted in Sachs (1981) and elsewhere, this drop can mainly be attributed to the sharp fall in investments in the industrial countries that followed the profit squeeze. Although savings also contracted substantially during 1974–75 in the industrial countries, it seems that the temporary increase in OPEC savings more than compensated for the fall in OECD savings, so the representation of the movement from point A to A' in Figure 4.1 seems pertinent. The combined surplus of OPEC countries and of OECD was matched by a rising deficit in the oil-importing countries, financed to an increasing degree by private commercial loans which, in turn, were funded by the recycling of petrodollars. Between 1972 and 1978 the flow of nonconcessional finance to LDCs more than quadrupled, from $13 billion to $56 billion at current prices. By 1978 this formed over 50 percent of total external finance in the oil-importing and over 60 percent in the oil-exporting MICs (see World Bank, 1981, p. 53, fig. 5.3). All of this increase was obtained at zero or negative real interest rates.

After the second oil shock both the I and S curves seem to have shifted differently. There was apparently a much smaller downward shift in the aggregate investment schedule than after 1973, while the aggregate savings schedule may have shifted downward on account of a smaller OPEC savings response and a bigger savings squeeze in the OECD group (also exacerbated by large budget deficits in several countries). A point like A'', on the intersection of the new curves I'' and S'', may illustrate this situation.

We should point out, however, that the large rise in nominal (and also real) short- and medium-run rates of interest in 1980–82 was connected with the monetary squeeze (coupled with fiscal expansion) in the United States, to which the other industrial countries responded in kind. This aspect of country interdependence will be discussed in detail in Chapter 6.

We end this section by noting that our procedure here was to assume that OPEC set the price, Π_{N_t}, and let the quantity produced, H_t^0, adjust to world demand. Though simple, this procedure has the drawback that it leaves open the question of oil depletion, or what happens to oil that is left over at the end of the second period (here it is valueless). Obviously, there is room for a more sophisticated treatment of OPEC behavior as well as game-theoretic considerations that lie outside the scope of the present discussion (see, for example, Dixit, 1981).

The Differential Response of ICs and MICs

Let us go back to consider some additional aspects of the differential response of individual countries to the combination of a raw material price shock and a concomitant fall in real interest rates, a situation pertinent to the aftermath of the first oil and raw material price shock.

The question to which we address ourselves now is how one might account for a different response by two types of countries, an industrial country (IC) and a middle-income industrializing country (MIC), to a similar exogenous shock. To keep the analysis as simple as possible and also stay within the framework discussed earlier, let us assume that production in both types of countries uses the same technology in terms of the basic production function $Q = Q(L,K,N)$, but that they might differ in the (intensity units) × (employment) decomposition of the labor input (L) and in its rate of growth. An IC (superscript a) would initially have more intensity units represented by each employed person than an MIC (superscript m), while the time rate of change of total $\bar{L}^m$ supplied exogenously would be higher than that of $\bar{L}^a$ on account of faster population growth and faster labor-augmenting technical progress (being further away from the technology frontier).

As long as we confine ourselves to the measurement of labor in intensity units, the factor price frontier for both types of countries will be the same. The curve ϕ in $[R,W]$ space (see Figure 4.2) is drawn for a given initial relative price of the raw material (Π_N). Suppose the IC is initially producing at the point A^a on the FPF, being in equilibrium at the real rate of interest (= rate of return on capital), R^a, and applying a real wage W^a per (intensity) unit of labor. The slope of the tangent TS to the FPF at the point A^a measures

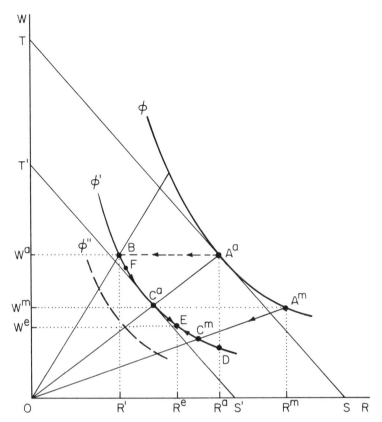

Figure 4.2.   The factor price frontier and macroeconomic adjustment in the ICs and MICs

the capital/labor ratio ($K^a/L^a = \kappa^a$), and the intercept OT measures real income per unit of labor (Y^a/L^a). For simplicity assume that the initial rate of return to capital in the IC is also the world rate of interest on borrowing. It is also realistically assumed that an MIC initially operates at a lower relative wage/profit ratio than the representative IC (or a higher relative profit rate, due to risk and capital market segmentation). The MIC thus produces at the point A^m with rate of return $R^m > R^a$, real wage $W^m < W^a$, capital/labor ratio $K^m/L^m < K^a/L^a$, and real income per unit of labor $Y^m/L^m < Y^a/L^m < Y^a/L^a$.[7]

Consider now a permanent shock to the relative price, Π_N. This will show as an inward contraction of the FPF from ϕ to ϕ', as shown in Chapter 3. The way in which the FPF contracts depends on the general specification of the production function. As long as one considers a general increase in raw material prices, the assumption of weak separability is probably empirically valid, and it is made here, that is, it is assumed that $Q = Q[N; V(K,L)]$. In this case the FPF shifts inward homothetically, and the tangent at C^a on the new FPF would be parallel to TS. In other words, C^a represents the new short-run, full-employment, full-capacity equilibrium point for the IC, and C^m fulfills the same role for the MIC.

The immediate response of the two economies to the same exogenous price shock is probably different. Consider the extreme case in which real wages are rigid in the IC and fully flexible in the MIC. In that case the IC moves from A^a to B, there is a sharp profit squeeze (with quasi-rents falling from R^a to R'), and unemployment emerges (at B the capital/labor ratio is higher than at A^a). In the MIC, on the other hand, the movement is from A^m to C^m as real wages adjust downward, and employment need not fall.[8]

One can also tell a short-run story about differential demand management in the two types of countries. A contractionary fiscal or monetary policy may push the IC away from ϕ' and cause an even tighter profit squeeze (see the discussion in Chapter 2). This undoubtedly characterized most ICs after 1973 but did not happen in a typical MIC. As will be shown in Chapter 12, the MICs pursued expansionary policies and were willing and able to incur higher current-account deficits and higher rates of inflation, an option not pursued by the major industrial countries. In any case, even if real wages were temporarily rigid in many ICs, unemployment helped to reduce real wages with varying lags. In terms of Figure 4.2, the implication of IC short-run adjustment is a gradual movement along ϕ' from B toward C^a.

The long-run behavior depends, as we have seen, on what happens to the real rate of interest. Suppose it falls from R^a to R^e. In that case a new long-run equilibrium for the IC would be at the point E, at which the capital/labor ratio is lower than at C^a (or A^a). In our simplified two-period model this move will take place in one period; in a more realistic model it will be a gradual development. One would thus observe a slowdown in capital accumulation (K^a/L^a falls but since L^a goes on rising, K^a need not fall but investment will). Note that the new long-run equilibrium need not lie to the right of C^a but could be at a point such as F, if the real rate of interest falls enough. In the latter case real wages (relative to productivity trend) might first fall in response to unemployment and then rise again as the capital/labor ratio adjusts upward. This is less likely to have actually happened, especially since the sharp fall in real interest rates did not last very long.

The long- or medium-run story may again be different for the MICs. The rate of return at C^m is higher than the newly established rate of interest, R^e, and the extended private capital market has now become fully accessible to

MICs. There is an incentive to borrow, invest, and increase the capital/labor ratio toward its long-run level at E. The movement along the FPF is from C^m to E. In the process the real wage may or may not rise above its original level W^m (it will obviously rise per *employed person*).

The analysis is thus consistent with a marked difference in the effect of the same exogenous shocks on the two types of countries.[9] Clearly, there was also a third type of country. A net importing country that does not have access to the private capital market would obviously not enjoy the full benefits of recycling and would suffer the terms-of-trade loss due to rising oil and raw material prices. This probably happened in most of the lower-income LDCs in the 1970s. However, quite a few of the MICs may have benefited, at least temporarily, from the combination of events after the first oil shock. This does not seem to have happened after the second shock. An increasing number of MICs ran into trouble at the end of the 1970s (for example, Korea, Brazil, Mexico), which, at least partly, came as a result of the sharply rising cost of foreign borrowing after the second oil shock and the rising real cost of labor in the domestic market of some of these countries (notably Korea).

5 Stagflation and Short-Run Adjustment

THE SIMPLE tradable goods model analyzed so far suffers from one major deficiency. Being a single-final-good world, it cannot allow for proper treatment of demand management under Keynesian, as distinct from classical, unemployment. Though supply shifts played a major role in the 1970s, the story of short-run adjustment under stagflation remains very incomplete if shifts in aggregate demand and in terms of trade of final goods are not explicitly accounted for.[1]

There is one obvious way in which the model of the previous chapter could be extended — by adding another, nontradable-goods sector to the economy. Such a two-period, two-commodity framework can then be applied to both the short-term issues as well as the intertemporal questions taken up in the previous chapter. This model, however, is not transparent.[2] To preserve single-sector simplicity for our present discussion, we therefore opt for another modification of the basic framework.

The single final good (Q) with domestic price, P, which is used for domestic consumption or investment, will be assumed to be an imperfect substitute in the export market of final goods, where the economy will be facing a downward-sloping demand curve. At the same time we shall also allow for imperfect substitution in consumption between the domestic good and the import of the final good. To keep the short-term discussion as simple as possible, we also give up the intertemporal aspects of the theory in this chapter. We shall subsequently return to a more complete framework in the context of a simulation model (Chapter 7). Finally, we concentrate here mainly on a simplified diagrammatic exposition, leaving the algebra and a quantitative amplification to Appendix 5A.

While discussing the individual economy it is easiest to consider external market conditions as given exogenously; this assumption is relaxed in

Chapter 6. We distinguish between two exogenous nominal commodity prices: the foreign price of intermediate goods and the foreign price of final goods. These prices will be denoted by p_n^* and p^*, respectively. Their relative price will be denoted by $\pi_n^* (= p_n^* - p^*)$. (These prices, as well as subsequent quantity variables, are in logarithms.) Intermediate goods are used as a major input (n) in the domestic production of final goods (q), together with labor (l) and capital (k). Intermediate goods may also be produced domestically at the given world price, and such import substitution (or even net export) may provide one source of international differences in industrial structure. The single domestic final good, q, whose price is p, will be an imperfect substitute for the foreign final good in both consumption and exports. The domestic price of the foreign good is $(p^* + e)$, where e is the exchange rate in domestic currency per unit of foreign exchange. The relative price of the final good $(\pi = p - p^* - e)$, or the final goods terms of trade, will be one important endogenous variable to be determined in the commodity market.

The Commodity Market

Determination of $\pi (= p - e - p^*)$ is tantamount to the determination of the real exchange rate $(e - p)$. In order to conclude something about the behavior of the absolute price level (p) we still need a theory to determine the *nominal* exchange rate, e. Under a fixed-exchange-rate regime it can be considered exogenous, while under a float it will be determined by money and asset markets in conjunction with the commodity market. Exchange rate determination will be discussed separately. For the moment we have only to remember that $p = \pi + p^* + e$, and that for given final goods price (p^*) and given exchange rate (e) any change in the terms of trade (π) implies an equal change in the price level (p).

For the quantity axis of the final goods market one may use the gross output measure q, since this obviously corresponds most closely to the measure of final goods actually transacted in the market. Most of the detailed analysis in Appendix 5A is in fact done in those terms. For ease of exposition, however, it is convenient to make explicit use of the value-added separability assumption and translate quantities supplied and demanded into value-added terms. Since in the short run the labor input is related one-to-one to value added $[v = v(l,\bar{k})]$, such transformation makes it easy to read the labor market conditions simultaneously from a commodity market diagram. It is expositional convenience that suggests using π and v here, rather than another pair like p and q, on the two axes in Figure 5.1.[3]

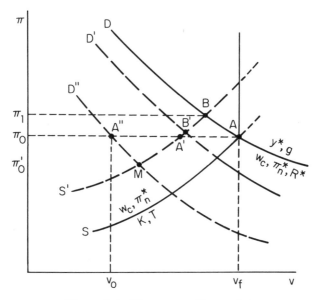

Figure 5.1. The commodity market

We shall linearize the production and demand relationships that are discussed in detail both in Appendix 5A and in earlier chapters, and simply suppress the dots (rates of change) whenever it is convenient.[4]

For the supply schedule of final goods we may write

(5.1) $q = -a(w - p) - b(p_n - p) + k,$

and remember that (5.1) can be built up from a set of underlying relations in which Q is a CES function of V and N (elasticity σ) and V is a CES function of K and L (elasticity σ_1). Specifically, one can always move from a q-formulation to a v-formulation and vice versa by making use of the fact that $v - n = \sigma(p_n - p_v)$ and $q = (1 - s_n)v + s_n n$ to get

(5.2) $v = q + s_n\sigma(p_n - p_v).$

Note that (5.2) only requires cost minimization. When profit maximization holds, we may make use of the fact that

(5.3) $p = (1 - s_n)p_v + s_n p_n,$

and thus rewrite (5.2) in the form[5]

(5.2′) $v = q + \sigma(p - p_v) = q + (1 - s_n)^{-1}s_n\sigma(p_n - p),$

an equivalence relation that we have already encountered in Chapter 3.

Now consider the supply schedule in terms of value added. We may write, from the earlier analysis,

(5.4) $v^s = k - a_1(w - p_v)$,

where $a_1 = s_k^{-1}s_l\sigma_1$.

Now

$$w - p_v = (w - p) + (p - p_v) = (w - p) + (1 - s_n)^{-1}s_n(p_n - p).$$

This suggests another way of showing that v, just like q, can be represented as a negative function of the two real variable factor prices $(w - p)$ and $(p_n - p)$. At this point, however, there are two additional transformations to be made. One is to decompose $\pi_n(=p_n - p)$ into its exogenous and endogenous elements: $\pi_n = \pi_n^* - \pi$. The other has to do with the replacement of the output wage $w_q = w - p$ by the consumption wage $w_c = w - p_c$, where the consumer price (p_c) is assumed to be a log-linear index of domestic and importable goods:

(5.5) $p_c = \psi p + (1 - \psi)(e + p^*) = p - (1 - \psi)\pi$.

Thus $w_c = w_q + (1 - \psi)\pi$, and we can finally rewrite (5.4) in the form

(5.6) $v^s = k - a_1 w_c - b_1\pi_n^* + c_1\pi$,

where $b_1 = (1 - s_n)^{-1}s_n a_1$, $c_1 = b_1 + (1 - \psi)a_1$, and $a_1 = s_k^{-1}s_l\sigma_1$, as before. The real wage may be considered the equilibrating variable when the labor market is in disequilibrium, but it is often characterized by temporary downward rigidity. Its relatively slow speed of adjustment justifies using it as a given parameter in drawing an aggregate short-run supply curve for the commodity market, rather than assuming labor market clearance.[6]

The curve marked S in Figure 5.1 indicates the aggregate supply for final goods in terms of v^s and π on the axes. In the short run, with capital, k, held fixed, supply should in principle be upward-sloping. However, one would expect the curve to be reasonably flat at low levels of output. As indicated by (5.6), the curve is drawn here with the international relative price of the intermediate good $(\pi_n^* = p_n^* - p^*)$ and the domestic real wage (w_c) as given parameters. Any increase in one of these factor prices raises variable production costs and therefore shifts the S curve up and to the left, unless the price of the other factor falls. Any increase in the capital stock or in total productivity will shift the curve down and to the right. The curve ends in a vertical portion at $v = v_f$, indicating the full-employment production level $v_f = v(\bar{l},\bar{k})$ when both capital and labor become fully employed.[7]

Let us next briefly summarize the demand side of the model. (This is analyzed in greater detail in Appendix 5A.) Consider the main components of final demand: private and public consumption, investment, and exports. Private consumption of the domestic good is considered a positive function of disposable real income and a negative function of the terms of trade ($\pi = p - e - p^*$). Exports are similarly a positive function of world income (y^*) and a negative function of π. Investments are considered a negative function of the externally given real interest rate (R^*) and a positive function of the rate of profit.[8]

Once this subsystem is solved out, it can be summarized in the form of a demand schedule:

(5.7) $v^d = -c_2\pi - a_2 w_c - b_2\pi_n^* + d_2\zeta,$

where ζ represents various demand-shift factors.

This is drawn in Figure 5.1 as a downward-sloping curve D for a given set of parameters (ζ). It will be shifted up and to the right by an increase in external demand (y^*), or by domestic fiscal policy (g).[9] A shift of curve D down and to the left will be caused by an increase in the real interest rate (R^*) or by an increase in the real wage (w_c). The assumed sign of w_c comes from its role in the domestic production and use of intermediate goods and through its effect on profits and investment demand.[10]

The role of the relative foreign price of intermediate goods is ambiguous because of conflicting forces at work. A rise in π_n^* at a given production level of intermediate goods will depress real income and consumption for a net importer of these goods, while the substitution effect and a possible increase in the domestic production of intermediate goods will work in the other direction. For a net importer of intermediate goods and a low degree of substitutability, the demand curve is thus likely to shift to the left with an increase in π_n^*. For a net exporter of intermediate goods or for an economy in which there is considerable domestic substitutability, the shift may go in the other direction.[11] For most OECD countries the first is the more likely.

Consider now the effects of two kinds of possible changes in the system. A factor price shock, such as an increase in the relative price π_n^* (or in w_c) shifts the supply curve unambiguously to the left (see the shift from S to S' in Figure 5.1), leading to excess demand of the amount AA' at the initial price π_0. If D stays put, the new equilibrium at B will involve a rise in π to π_1 and a fall in v and l. If, as was suggested, demand also contracts (from D to D') as a direct effect of the rise in π_n, excess demand will be reduced, but the new equilibrium at point B' will in any case involve a reduction in output, and unemployment will therefore emerge (in the figure we took the initial point

A to be at full employment, v_f). What will happen to the relative price π is not clear: if, as is likely, the supply curve is relatively flat and the effect of supply dominates over the demand shift, π will rise;[12] in the opposite (and for an OECD economy less likely) case, where import prices are demand-expanding, the terms of trade will obviously rise but the net effect on output becomes ambiguous.

Consider the importance of the degree of real wage stickiness in this analysis. Although we have not yet considered the labor market, it is clear that an output contraction will reduce labor demand and press downward on real wages. Assume now that nominal wages are downward-flexible or that the unexpected price shock causes a momentary reduction in *real* wages (w_c). In that case there will be a countervailing force working in the commodity market in exactly the opposite direction to that of the import price shock, and the stagflationary effect will be mitigated. One expects to find different patterns of real wage response to an import price shock in different countries, as we in fact do in our subsequent empirical study (see Chapters 9 and 11).

It is important to point out that this analysis of the effect of a rise in a factor price is confined to the short-run implications. As we have seen, a fall in the rate of profit and a contraction in output, in addition to their immediate effect on investment demand, may eventually cause a fall in the capital stock, k. These changes may also have repercussions on domestic real wealth, thereby affecting the demand curve. These wealth effects were discussed in the previous chapter and for the time being are not further analyzed here.

The commodity market representation of the effect of a supply shock is the key to an understanding of the difference between stagflationary effects of the kind that affected OECD economies during the two oil shocks and the more conventional business-cycle demand fluctuations which are either inflationary *or* deflationary in both commodity and labor markets. A rightward shift in the demand curve by itself raises prices (unless we are in a flat section of the supply curve), as well as final output and employment (unless we are hitting against the full employment ceiling, v_f). In the case of a demand contraction coming from either domestic demand restraint (g) or a contraction in world demand (y^*), both prices and employment would tend to fall. In Figure 5.1 such a contraction is represented as a further shift of the demand curve from D' to D'', causing excess supply at the given initial price ratio π_0. If prices are downward-flexible the relative price would fall to π_0', with equilibrium at M. But suppose prices (p) are rigid so that at given p^* and e the relative price stays temporarily at π_0. In that case output would be constrained by demand and would fall further to v_0, with unemployment of the more conventional Keynesian kind resulting. (This was discussed in

Chapter 1; see further discussion in the next section in the labor market context.) Firms would like to sell more but are unable to do so. At point A'' they are, at least temporarily, not on their supply curves. This is in marked contrast to the previous case, in which output contraction originates purely from a supply shock.

During the 1974–75 recession and then again in 1980–81, there was clearly a combination of a supply shock with a concomitant demand contraction coming from the cumulative income reduction in all OECD countries. This contraction was compounded by a fall in investment and in some countries by domestic monetary or fiscal restraint as well. For this reason it is easy to fall into the trap of attributing *all* of the unemployment to a more conventional demand contraction combined with downward price rigidity. As pointed out by Malinvaud (1977), in the 1950s and 1960s the experience of the industrial countries was confined to alternations between situations of Keynesian unemployment and inflation activated primarily by shifts in aggregate demand. The developments of the 1970s mark a departure from this pattern, with supply shifts playing a much more prominent role.

As we shall see later, one may identify the "perverse" upward-moving portions of the Phillips curve (1973–74, 1979–80) with periods in which the supply shift dominated (so that simultaneously unemployment rose and inflation accelerated), while the post-shock periods, 1974–75 and 1980–83, may have been dominated by the contractionary aggregate demand response (unemployment continued to rise and inflation decelerated). Wage rigidity played an important role throughout the period.

An important price shock, as we have seen, is most likely to cause a rise in the relative domestic price level, $p - e - p^*$. For a given e and p^*, the *nominal* domestic price level will rise. (Of course, since the shock is also occurring abroad, p^* will change as well. Multicountry considerations are taken up in the following chapter.) However, it is important to note that neither the observed price rise nor the intercountry differences in inflation rates since 1973 can be explained without recourse to the monetary mechanism and exchange-rate behavior under a flexible-rate regime. For the determination of e, attention must focus on the asset markets, to which we turn briefly.

Current theory and available evidence stress that the exchange rate is the relative price of national moneys. One important element of exchange-rate determination, then, is the relative growth rates of money stocks. Our model, like most, has the characteristic that a money supply increase in one country leads in the long run to an equiproportional depreciation of its exchange rate and a rise in its domestic prices. Since p and e rise by the same amount,

$p - e - p^*$ and output are unaffected in the long run by the money supply increase.

In the short run, though, the determination of domestic prices and the exchange rate is more complicated. Let us trace through the effect of a one-shot increase in the domestic money supply. Initially, domestic interest rates tend to fall. But given world capital mobility, there is an attempt to transfer funds to foreign assets, which have a temporarily higher rate of return. With floating rates, the exchange rate depreciates (e rises); in fact, e continues to rise until the expected returns of domestic and foreign assets are again equalized.

As e rises, import prices and the consumer price level rise. If nominal wages are sticky, $w - p_c$ falls, and the terms of trade worsen, that is, $p - e - p^*$ falls. Domestic prices do not immediately rise in equal proportion to e. Over time, if real wages are restored, w increases, pushing up the domestic price level in the process. Eventually, p and e rise in the same proportion as the original money supply change. If the real wage is fixed in the *short run,* then the domestic price level almost immediately rises in proportion to the depreciation. This is, of course, the familiar vicious circle of depreciation and domestic inflation.[13]

Once it is recognized that the recessions in 1974–75 and 1980–82 were in significant part classical and supply-determined, that is, directly tied to too high real wages protected by indexation arrangements, the inflationary consequences of expansionary monetary policy are highlighted. It is important to remember, though, that expansionary monetary policy may have some effect on output in the short run, and that for countries like Canada and the United States, with sluggish nominal wage change (see Chapter 11), the inflationary effects of the money expansion might initially be small.

Now let us consider the implications of the analysis in the labor market, which in many ways mirrors the effects already considered in the commodity market.

The Labor Market

The curve L^d in Figure 5.2 represents the usual downward-sloping marginal product curve, here expressed in terms of the consumption real wage (w_c) rather than the output wage ($w - p$). This is derived from the commodity supply schedule (see Appendix 5A). The direction of the shift caused by changes in the relative price π_n^* is again ambiguous since L^d includes em-

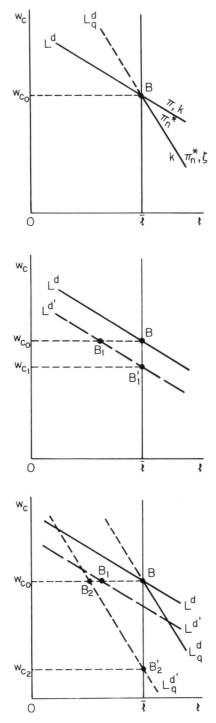

Figure 5.2. (*top*) The labor market; (*middle*) classical unemployment; (*bottom*) Keynesian unemployment

ployment in both final and intermediate goods production. Final goods production will fall with a rise in π_n^* and yet total labor demand may rise if the increase in employment from domestic production of the material input is large enough (see, for example, Hudson and Jorgenson, 1978). However, the most likely case for an OECD country with low elasticity of energy and raw material production is an unambiguous leftward shift in the demand curve for labor. In the middle part of Figure 5.2, which illustrates such a shift, the result is excess supply (unemployment) of the amount $B_1 B$ at the initial level of real wage w_{c_0}.

A new equilibrium full employment at B_1' could be reached after a process of downward real wage adjustment. Alternatively, if capital is a cooperant factor, capital accumulation might eventually help to shift the labor demand curve back and thus reduce unemployment. It is doubtful whether such a corrective mechanism could occur by itself, and in any case either adjustment process would be slow to come about.[14] Another option for a single country, at least in theory, would seem to be the adoption of an expansionary fiscal policy.[15] In the commodity market this is represented by a rightward shift of the demand curve, leading to an increase in both output (v) and prices (π and therefore p). Since the final goods price ratio π also appears as a parameter of the labor demand curve (see the top part of Figure 5.2), this expresses itself as a shift back to the right of the L^d curve and a reduction in unemployment. The implied cost in a greater current-account deficit may make this a difficult policy to follow for any length of time. Besides, as we shall see in Chapter 6, it cannot be adopted by all supply-shocked countries simultaneously; when the relative price, π, rises in one country it must fall in the rest of the world.

If output in the commodity market happens to be temporarily constrained on the demand (and not on the supply) side, which is the Keynesian case discussed earlier, producers will not be on their supply curve; the relevant demand schedule for labor will be represented by the steeper curve marked L_q^d in the top part of Figure 5.2, whose position will be determined mainly by the demand variables (ζ).[16]

The case of a pure demand shock (see the leftward shift from L_q^d to $L_q^{d'}$ in the bottom part of Figure 5.2), with a rigid real wage, brings about *Keynesian* unemployment of the amount $B_2 B$, if L^d stays put. The case represented in the middle part of the figure may more appropriately be termed *classical* unemployment, having been caused by a shift in the whole marginal product schedule. With both types of shocks present in the major recessions of the 1970s, it is, of course, difficult to assess how much of the unemployment at any point in time or in any specific country may have been Keynesian or classical.[17]

General Equilibrium

The commodity and labor markets can, as usual, be combined into one general equilibrium framework in w_c, π space (see Figure 5.3).[18] The line QQ describes commodity market equilibrium when there are no other constraints. It is upward-sloping; to the right of it there is excess supply and to the left excess demand in the commodity market. Both of these properties are best shown by considering the expression for excess demand $(v^d - v^s)$ obtained by subtraction of Eq. (5.6) from Eq. (5.7):

$$(5.8) \qquad v^d - v^s = -k + (a_1 - a_2)w_c + (b_1 - b_2)\pi_n^* - (c_1 + c_2)\pi + d_2\zeta.$$

Since $a_1 > a_2$ by assumption, we have $\dfrac{\partial(v^d - v^s)}{\partial w_c} > 0$. Similarly, $\dfrac{\partial(v^d - v^s)}{\partial \pi} < 0$. Therefore we find that $\left.\dfrac{\partial w_c}{\partial \pi}\right|_{v^d=v^s} > 0$.

The QQ line shifts to the right with $\zeta > 0$ and to the left with $k > 0$. The sign of $\dot\pi_n^*$ is ambiguous (for reasons mentioned earlier) but is likely to be positive $(b_1 > b_2)$.

Likewise we obtain the full employment curve for the labor market. We show in Appendix 5A that the demand for labor under profit maximization

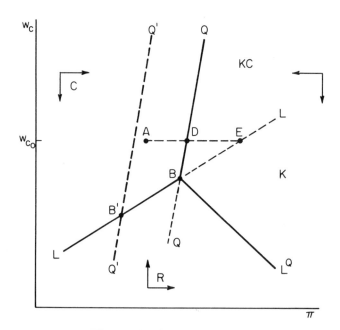

Figure 5.3. General equilibrium

can be written in the form

(5.9) $l^d = k - a_3 w_c - b_3 \pi_n^* + c_3 \pi,$

and under the output-constrained (cost-minimized) case we can write

(5.10) $l_q^d = d_4 v^d - a_4 w_c + b_4 \pi_n^* - c_4 \pi - e_4 k.$

Assuming the supply of labor to be fixed at $\bar{l}$, we thus get LL as the regular or "notional" full employment line for the labor market.[19] Its slope must be less than that of QQ (see Appendix 5A). There is unemployment above and excess demand for labor below LL. Each market equilibrium curve must depart from the notional equilibrium whenever the other market imposes a constraint. Thus the labor market equilibrium curve has a kink and turns downward to the right of the intersection of QQ and LL. (Consider the signs of the coefficients of w_c and π in Eq. (5.10) and the corresponding curve BL^Q in Figure 5.3.) Likewise, when labor is fully employed this imposes a constraint on the commodity market, so that the segment BL^Q in Figure 5.3 is also the continuation of the commodity market equilibrium curve into the full-employment region.

The space is thus divided into three major regions. The arrows in Figure 5.3 point in the direction of dynamic adjustment implied by the state of excess demand (supply) in respective markets. However, one may divide the region of generalized excess supply into two subregions below and above the notional full employment curve LL (denoted by K and KC, respectively). The K region unambiguously represents a Keynesian unemployment regime. At given relative prices a demand expansion without a reduction in real factor prices is enough to restore full employment. The KC region is the borderline between Keynesian (K) and classical (C) unemployment regimes. Employment can be increased by a demand expansion, but a change must take place in w_c, in π, or in both to get back to full employment.[20]

The C region represents the pure form of classical unemployment. Demand expansion alone does nothing to increase employment, and a change in relative prices is required. The R region is that of generalized excess demand ("repressed inflation" in Malinvaud's terminology).

Let us consider the effect of an increase in π_n^* within the general disequilibrium framework. Suppose the economy is initially in equilibrium at the point A, with LL representing the post-shock position of the labor market. For the commodity market there are in principle two alternative outcomes (assuming the country is a net importer), depending on the relative strength of the direct supply effect (shifting QQ to the right) and the wealth and demand contraction effects (shifting it to the left). The two outcomes are represented in Figure 5.3 by QQ and $Q'Q'$, with Walrasian equilibrium taking place at B or B', respectively. Upon impact the economy may thus be in either a C or a KC regime.

Consider the case of a C regime, and assume that there is real wage rigidity in the form of a temporarily rigid w_c. Dynamic adjustment must thus take place along a horizontal line. If the nominal exchange rate stays fixed, nominal wages and prices must rise proportionately to bring about commodity market equilibrium at the point D on QQ.[21] After an initial spurt of inflation the commodity market would return to equilibrium, but unemployment would still remain, a situation not unlike the developments of the 1970s (w_c relative to trend has, of course, fallen, but only slowly).

We note that an economy may find itself in a C regime not merely by the impact of a rise in π_n^*. An autonomous real wage push at given π from an initial equilibrium point (such as at B) will lead to a similar stagflationary impact effect. Likewise, a sudden drop in π (real depreciation), at given w_c, may come about as a result of a sudden drop in a country's foreign borrowing potential (or a rise in borrowing rates). This, too, may lead to a shift into the C regime. The case of a real wage push may be applicable to developments in some OECD countries in the late 1960s, while the case of the cut in foreign lending may be applicable to some semi-industrialized economies in the early 1980s.

The dynamics of adjustment to a raw material price shock in terms of prices, exchange rates, and wages will be spelled out in greater detail with the help of a simulation model to be presented in Chapter 7. For the time being, we only note again that unemployment for a single country could in principle be removed by fiscal expansion. In Figure 5.3 this would show as a shift of the QQ curve to the right and a further movement of the economy from D to E. Such an attempt to "ride the storm" and a hope that the commodity crisis would soon be over characterized the initial post-1973 macro-response of a few smaller countries, such as Sweden or Italy. The cost of such policy is greater inflation or worsening of the current account, or a combination of both.

Finally, the trade balance could be represented within the same framework, but for our present discussion let us only consider its general determinants. If C_N denotes the imports of final goods and H the output of domestic raw materials, the trade surplus (F) can be written as

$$(5.11) \qquad F = (P/E)X - P^*C_N - P_N^*(N - H).$$

After substituting for the various elements of the model, one can show that F

can be expressed as a function of the same variables as before:[22]

$$(5.12) \qquad F = F(\Pi, \ W_c, \Pi_N^*, \ Y^*, \ \zeta).$$
$$\qquad\qquad\quad - \quad - \quad \pm \quad + \quad -$$

The response of the trade balance to a rise in Π (real appreciation) is certainly negative, while the change with respect to Π_N^* may be ambiguous on account of the conflicting income and substitution effects. Whichever way the initial impact goes, it is most likely that an expansionary policy would run the economy into a deficit region.

Would it be possible for all countries to pursue an expansionary policy simultaneously and thus extricate themselves from an unemployment situation? To answer this question we must turn back to a multicountry world, which is the subject of our next chapter. Let us point out right away that when the terms of trade (π) rise for one country, they must by definition turn in the opposite direction for the group of its trading partners. Thus an expansionary policy pursued by one country must, at least to some extent, come at the expense of the others. To what extent this happens will depend on the degree of real wage rigidity prevalent among the trading partners.

Appendix 5A: The Detailed Model

THE BASIC MODEL: OUTPUT SUPPLY

This appendix works out the underlying model of Chapter 5 in greater detail. The aggregative structure of the model is as follows. A small open economy, with a flexible exchange rate, faces given world prices of intermediate (P_N^*) and imported final (P^*) goods. Their relative price is denoted by $\Pi_N^*(= P_N^* / P^*)$. The economy produces intermediate goods at the world price, and a single final good with price P. The final domestic good is an imperfect substitute in consumption with the foreign final good; consumption and export demand for the domestic final good vary negatively with the relative price of the two final goods $\Pi = P/(EP^*)$, where E is the exchange rate. There are thus three different goods in the system, one fully tradable intermediate good and two imperfectly substitutable final goods, but to maintain simplicity only one final good is domestically produced.

As in the previous discussion, domestic production of the final good (Q) is a function of labor input (L), input of the tradable intermediate good (N), and exogenously fixed capital (K); and we again assume a nested CES function, $Q = Q[V(L,K),N]$, with parameters σ, σ_1, and η as defined in Chapter 3.

Assuming profit maximization, we obtain the following supply log-linearized equation:

(5A.1) $q^s = -a_1(w-p) - b_1(p_n - p) + k,$

where $a_1 = s_k^{-1}s_l\sigma_1 > 0$, $b_1 = s_k^{-1}s_n\sigma_1\eta > 0$.

One may note that Eq. (5A.1) could also be turned around to represent a supply price equation:[23]

(5A.2) $p = (a_1 + b_1)^{-1}(a_1 w + b_1 p_n + q - k).$

Equation (5A.1) expresses changes in output supplied as a negative function of changes in the product wage and the relative price of the intermediate input. The real wage variable in terms of which we analyze the labor market is the consumption wage ($w_c = w - p_c$), where the consumption basket determining p_c may consist of both domestic as well as imported final goods (with prices p and $p^* + e$, respectively). Define the consumer price index as a log-linear fixed-weight function of the domestic and foreign final goods prices, where the weights ψ and $(1 - \psi)$ represent the shares of domestic and foreign final goods in domestic final consumption:

(5A.3) $p_c = \psi p + (1 - \psi)(p^* + e).$

We may rewrite (5A.1) in the form $p_c - p = -(1 - \psi)(p - p^* - e) = -(1 - \psi)\pi$ and note that $w - p = w_c - (1 - \psi)\pi$. Also, $p_n - p = \pi_n^* - \pi$. We can thus express the supply equation in terms of the change in the price of the final goods terms of trade ($\pi = p - p^* - e$), with the change in the international price ratio ($\pi_n^* = p_n^* - p^*$) and the real consumption wage ($w_c = w - p_c$) as parameters:

(5A.4) $q^s = \gamma_1\pi - \gamma_2\pi_n^* - \gamma_0 w_c + k,$

where $\gamma_1 = a_1(1 - \psi) + b_1 > 0$, $\gamma_2 = b_1$, $\gamma_0 = a_1$, and a_1, b_1 are defined as in Eq. (5A.1). Note that $\gamma_1 > \gamma_2$, a property of which use will be made later.

According to (5A.4), domestic final goods production is an *increasing* function of the final goods terms of trade, a decreasing function of the international price ratio of intermediate inputs, and a decreasing function of the real consumption wage. The international price ratio π_n^* is exogenous for the small economy, so that fluctuations in its level can be termed external shocks in intermediate good costs. The real wage will in general not be exogenous but must be determined from conditions in the labor market.

COMMODITY DEMAND

We first derive the aggregate demand schedule on the assumption of a fixed level of domestic production of the intermediate good. This simplification considerably clarifies the workings of the model. We subsequently allow for endogenous determination of domestic intermediate goods supply.

The total demand for domestic final good is given by

(5A.5) $Q^d = C + I + G + X,$

where $C + I + G$ represents that part of total domestic final expenditure falling on the *domestic* final good (that is, imports have already been netted out from C, I, G). Nominal gross national product is less than PQ by the value of net imports of the intermediate good. To see this, note that value added in the domestic final goods industry is $PQ - P_N N$. Value added in the intermediate goods industry is $P_N H$.[24] Ignoring inventory changes, $N - H$ equals net imports of the intermediate good. GNP in value terms is then given as the sum of value added in the final and intermediate goods industries:

(5A.6) $PY = P_V V = PQ - P_N(N - H).$

The components of Q^d in (5A.5) are assumed to follow standard macroeconomic specifications. To avoid intertemporal complications here, consumption of home goods will be expressed as a function of current real income, in domestic good units $(Y = \Pi_V V,$ where $\Pi_V = P_V/P)$ net of (real) taxes (T) and the final goods terms of trade $[\Pi = P/(EP^*)]$:

(5A.7) $C = C(Y - T, 1/\Pi).$

We will assume $1 > C_1 > 0$, $C_2 \geq 0$, though the second inequality need not hold.[25]

Interest rate effects on consumption are ignored here, and investment will, for the time being, be treated as exogenous (this is modified later). Export demand for the domestic final good is a function of world income (Y^*) and the final goods terms of trade (Π):

(5A.8) $X = X(Y^*, 1/\Pi),$ $X_1 > 0, X_2 > 0.$

For the time being, domestic production of the intermediate good is taken as fixed:

(5A.9) $H = \overline{H}.$

Equations (5A.5)–(5A.9) determine an aggregate demand schedule. Substituting (5A.6)–(5A.9) into (5A.5), logarithmically differentiating and substituting for $n[n = q - \sigma(p_n - p)]$,[26] we eventually obtain an aggregate demand schedule which can be written as

(5A.10) $q^d = \delta_2(p_n - p) - \delta_3(p - p^* - e) + \delta_0\zeta$

or

(5A.11) $q^d = -\delta_1\pi + \delta_2\pi_n^* + \delta_0\zeta,$

where $\zeta = Q^{-1}[I + G - C_1T + X_1Y^*]$ and ζ represents a general demand shift index. $\pi = p - p^* - e$ and $\pi_n^* = p_n^* - p^*$, as before, are the rates of change of the two respective relative prices. The coefficients are as follows:

$\delta_0 = [1 - (1 - s_n)C_1]^{-1} > 0$ (Keynesian multiplier)

$\delta_1 = \delta_2 + \delta_3$

$\delta_2 = \delta_0C_1(s_n\sigma - \theta_n) \gtreqless 0$ where $\theta_N = P_N(N - H)/(PQ) =$ share of intermediate imports in gross output, and

$\delta_3 = \delta_0Q^{-1}\Pi^{-1}(C_2 + X_2) > 0$

(this is the response of final demand to a change in Π^{-1}), and therefore $\delta_1 > \delta_2$.

The aggregate demand multipliers implied for the components of $(I, G, - T, Y^*)$ are familiar. Our attention turns rather to the multipliers on the final goods terms of trade (π) and the relative price of intermediate goods (π_n^*). Consider the effect of a rise in π_n^* (that is, the sign of δ_2). At a *given* level of gross output Q, real income will change according to changes in $(P_N/P)(N - H)$. Two effects are manifest. For given Q, a rise in P_N/P will reduce the input of N if technology permits (that is, $\sigma > 0$), in the amount $\sigma(\dot{p} - \dot{p}_n)$, which will raise GNP by $(1 - s_n)^{-1} s_n\sigma(\dot{p}_n - \dot{p})$ on account of substitution. The reduction of N allows the economy to reduce its net imports of the intermediate good, or perhaps to increase its net exports. In either event, real income *rises* relative to gross output. The other effect is a direct price effect on income, at given N and H. At initial Q, N, H, the relative price movement $\dot{p}_n - \dot{p} > 0$ changes income in the amount $-\theta_n(\dot{p}_n - \dot{p})$, where θ_n is the share of intermediate imports. For net importers of N, real income falls by the share of net imports in gross output. For net exporters, income rises.[27] The sign $\delta_2 < 0$ or $\delta_2 > 0$ thus depends crucially on whether the positive substitution effect is outweighed by the negative income effect $(s_n\sigma < \theta_n)$.[28] For most OECD economies, at least in the short run, with little possibility for technical substitution, we should suppose that $\sigma < \theta_n/s_n$ and $\delta_2 < 0$.

The effects of final-goods term-of-trade shifts on aggregate demand $(\delta_1 = \delta_2 + \delta_3)$ are similarly ambiguous. The consumption and export substitution effects cause an increase in demand for domestic final goods, when $\dot{\pi} < 0$, of $\delta_3 \ [= \delta_0 Q^{-1}\Pi^{-1}(C_2 + X_2)]$. The coefficient δ_2, we have argued, is likely to be negative. δ_1, which is the sum of δ_2 and δ_3, may be positive even when $\delta_2 < 0$. Plausible parameter values suggest that it is in fact positive. (See the next section.) For the theoretical development we will assert this condition unless otherwise stated.

COMMODITY MARKET EQUILIBRIUM

Equations (5A.4) and (5A.11) are readily solved algebraically. Equating q^d and q^s, assuming $k = 0$, and solving, we get:

(5A.12) $q = (\gamma_1 + \delta_1)^{-1}[(\delta_2\gamma_1 - \delta_1\gamma_2)\pi_n^* + \delta_0\gamma_1\zeta - \delta_1\gamma_0 w_c]$,

$\pi = (\gamma_1 + \delta_1)^{-1}[(\gamma_2 + \delta_2)\pi_n^* + \delta_0\zeta + \gamma_0 w_c]$.

The reader can trace out analytically the sign indeterminacies of the multipliers. Although γ_1 can be negative, we definitely require $\gamma_1 + \delta_1 > 0$. Note that for $-\gamma_1 < \delta_1 < 0$, it is theoretically possible that $(\delta_2\gamma_1 - \delta_1\gamma_2)/(\gamma_1 + \delta_1) > 0$, so that $\partial q/\partial\pi_n > 0$ even for $\delta_2 < 0$. Graphically this is the case of an upward-sloping aggregate demand schedule, with absolute slope less than the S slope. Now, the upward shift of the D curve which follows $\dot{\pi}_n > 0$ increases q. Depending on the dynamic specification of the model, this configuration may be unstable (akin to the failure of the Marshall-Lerner condition). Empirically, we trust, this is a mere curiosity. If, as seems most likely, $\delta_1 > 0$ and $\delta_2 < 0$, output definitely falls as π_n^* rises (for given ζ and w_c).

Until now everything has been expressed in terms of effects on gross output (Q) rather than on GNP (V). The analysis of impact effects can readily be extended to the latter by using a suitable measure of GNP. Suppose this is measured as a Divisia Index. We can then write, on the basis of (5A.6), that $(P_V V)\dot{v} = (PQ)\dot{q} - P_N(N-H)(\dot{n} - \dot{h})$. After suitable substitution it follows that in log-linear form

(5A.13) $v = (1 - \theta_n)^{-1}[(1 - s_n)q + s_n\sigma(p_n - p)]$

$= (1 - \theta_n)^{-1}[(1 - s_n)q + s_n\sigma\pi_n - s_n\sigma\pi]$.

This is the extension of Eq. (5.2′) for the case in which $\overline{H} \neq 0$. Since $\theta_n < s_n$, the coefficient of q is less than one, and thus any change in q will be reflected in a smaller rate of change in v on account of the concomitant change in intermediate imports. In addition, there is the direct positive substitution effect of a change in the relative price of intermediate goods ($p_n - p = \pi_n^* - \pi$) on value added.

By appealing to the original supply and demand functions (5A.4) and (5A.11), one can readily calculate the new coefficients (denoted by γ_i' and δ_i', respectively) for the modified supply (v^s) and demand (v^d) curves in terms of GNP rather than gross output. For the supply curve (see Eq. 5.6), we now find:

$$c_1 = \gamma_1' = \alpha_0[1 - \psi(1 - s_n)] > 0,$$
$$b_1 = \gamma_2' = \alpha_0 s_n > 0 \qquad \text{(and } c_1 > b_1 \text{ as before),}$$
$$a_1 = \alpha_0(1 - s_n) > 0,$$

where $\alpha_0 = (1 - \theta_n)^{-1} a_1 = (1 - \theta_n)^{-1} s_k^{-1} \sigma_1 s_l > 0$ so that all the previous signs are maintained. For the demand curve (see Eq. 5.7), we have

$$\delta_0' = (1 - \theta_n)^{-1}(1 - s_n)\delta_0 = d_2,$$
$$\delta_1' = (1 - \theta_n)^{-1}[\delta_1(1 - s_n) + s_n\sigma] = c_2,$$

so that $\delta_1' > 0$ if $\delta_1 > 0$ and the slope of the demand curve remains negative. Finally, $\delta_2' = (1 - \theta_n)^{-1}[\delta_2(1 - s_n) + s_n\sigma] = b_2$. Here we may find $\delta_2' > 0$, even though $\delta_2 < 0$ so that the shift of the corresponding demand curve may be upward rather than downward. For the analog to the equilibrium solution (5A.12), using δ_i' and γ_i' rather than δ_i and γ_i, it can be seen that $dv/d\pi_n^*$ will still be negative provided $\delta_2'(\gamma_2' - \gamma_2') < \delta_3'\gamma_2'$. (Remember that $\delta_1' = \delta_2' + \delta_3'$, where $\delta_3' = (1 - \theta_n)^{-1}(1 - s_n)\delta_3 > 0$.) This will always be true provided θ_n is large enough.

One modification to be briefly mentioned comes from allowing variations in the output of the domestic intermediate-goods industry (H) in response to changes in π_n^*. This case was taken up in Bruno and Sachs (1979), where it was shown that the final output demand curve (q^d) will now (1) be steeper, (2) shift downward by less (or upward by more) for a given $\dot{\pi}_n^* > 0$,[29] and (3) shift down in response to a real wage increase ($\dot{w}_c > 0$) while the previous q^d was unaffected.

Again, it can be shown that the equilibrium gross output (and GNP) will be reduced by an increase in π_n^* provided the import share of intermediate goods (θ_n) is large enough relative to the combined effect of substitution between N and V and the income effect of increased domestic supply of H.

Finally, we may consider the effect of letting investment become an endogenous variable in the analysis. One simple way of extending the model is to allow the real interest rate on foreign borrowing ($R*$) to enter the investment function (negatively) and allow for positive dependence on the domestic profit rate.

Using the factor price frontier, we may thus write:

$$(5A.14) \quad I = I(\underline{R}*, \underline{W}_C, \underline{\Pi}_N).$$

This adds $R*$ as a negative demand shift factor and also gives an additional argument in favor of making W_c and Π_N negative demand shift factors (as was in fact done in the text).

THE LABOR MARKET

Consider first the conventional ("notional") demand for labor, which can be obtained from the commodity output side under profit maximization.[30]

Using Eq. (3.11) for labor demand and switching from w_q to w_c and from π_n to π_n^*, we get (after linearizing):

$$(5A.15) \quad l^d = k - s_k^{-1}\sigma_1\{(1 - s_n)w_c + s_n\pi_n^* - [1 - \psi(1 - s_n)]\pi\}.$$

Thus notional labor demand depends negatively on w_c and π_n^* and positively on π.[31]

What can we say about labor demand in the case in which producers are constrained from the commodity demand side? Limiting ourselves to cost minimization, it can be shown from Chapter 3 that $\eta l - n = \sigma(w - p_n) - (1 - \eta)k$, and thus:

$$(5A.16) \quad l_q^d = \eta_1^{-1}[q^d - s_n\sigma(w - p_n) - (1 - \eta_1)k]$$
$$= \eta_1^{-1}[q^d - s_n\sigma(w_c + \psi\pi - \pi_n^*) - (1 - \eta_1)k],$$

where $\eta_1 = s_l + s_n\eta = (1 - s_n)^{-1}(s_l + \sigma_1^{-1}\sigma s_k s_n)$.

In the output-constrained case, labor demand thus depends positively on π_n^* (and q) and negatively on π and k(and w_c). Once the H-industry output is allowed to vary we have to add its derived demand for labor (l_h), which will rise when $\dot{\pi}_n > 0$. In that case the analysis has to be modified along the following lines (see Bruno and Sachs, 1979). Denoting the labor elasticity in H by α_h and the elasticity of substitution (between labor and capital) by σ_h, we have:

$$(5A.17) \quad l_h = -(1 - \alpha_h)^{-1}\sigma_h(w - p_n) = (1 - \alpha_h)^{-1}\sigma_h(-w_c - \psi\pi + \pi_n^*).$$

If the share of the Q-industry labor (call it L_1 now) in total employment is μ_1, we now have $l^d = \mu_1 l_1^d + (1 - \mu_1)l_h$, where l_1^d is given by Eq. (5A.15) and l_h by (5A.17). This will keep the sign on the coefficients of w_c but could reverse the sign on π_n^* for large enough import substitution effects. Empirically, this is an unlikely case for a typical OECD country.

6 Macroeconomic Adjustment and Policy Coordination in a Global Setting

In Chapter 4 we introduced some global aspects to the analysis of supply shocks. In a full-employment context we examined the effects of a rise in Π_N on world interest rates and capital flows, showing, for example, the presumption that world interest rates might tend to fall after a rise in Π_N. In this chapter we study other aspects of the global adjustment process, focusing particularly on short-run macroeconomic issues. We address three topics here: First, what is the short-run pattern of adjustment to higher Π_N in a world economy with nominal and real wage rigidities? Second, how do macroeconomic policies undertaken by one economy in response to the supply shocks affect macroeconomic performance in others? And third, is there a role for policy coordination after a supply shock? In answer to the first two questions we will once again find that the nature of macroeconomic transmission depends heavily on the form of wage setting. In a world of high capital mobility and flexible exchange rates, domestic fiscal expansion or monetary contraction will cause an exchange rate appreciation in the home market which is an exchange rate depreciation for the rest of the world. If real wages are sufficiently rigid abroad, this will be transmitted just like a stagflationary supply shock to the rest of the world. In answer to the third question, we show that almost surely a cooperative response to supply shocks will dominate a noncooperative response by the separate economies. Moreover, the bias seems to lie in a particular direction: noncooperative macro-policies are undesirably *contractionary* following a supply shock, in the sense that economic welfare in all the economies can be improved by *joint* monetary reflation relative to the noncooperative equilibrium.

The global setting makes analysis particularly difficult, and therefore it is necessary to proceed through a number of stages of argument. In this chapter we employ a stripped-down model to get qualitative answers to the three questions. We first examine the simple economics of a rise in Π_N when there is one N-importing region that is large in the world capital market. This region might be thought of as the OECD as a whole. Next we divide the N-importing regions into two economies, which might be thought of as "the U.S." and "Europe," or the Developed and Non-oil Developing Economies, with OPEC kept in the wings. In this two-country setting we determine the effect of policy responses in one economy on macroeconomic adjustment in the other, and we discuss the analytical justification for policy coordination.

A "World" Model with One N-Importing Region

We will utilize a simplified version of the model of Chapter 5. We assume that there is an N-exporting region ("OPEC") which sets a real price of N: $\Pi_N = P_N/P$. Π_N is taken to be exogenous. Since the industrial world is now one country, Π_N is for the moment the same as Π_N^* (that is, $\Pi = 1$). We also assume that there is no domestic production of N. Although much of the discussion for the one global economy resembles our discussion in Chapter 5, the global model allows an endogenous determination of the world interest rate and sets the stage for the more complex two-country model in the following section.

For the global oil importer, we begin again with the log-linear aggregate supply schedule:

(6.1) $q^s = -a(w - p) - b(p_n - p) + k.$

Remember that (6.1) can be built up from a set of underlying relations in which Q is a CES function of V and N (elasticity σ), and V is a CES function of K and L (elasticity σ_1). Specifically:

(6.2) $q = v - \sigma(p - p_v),$

(6.3) $v = k - \alpha(w - p_v),$

where $\alpha = \sigma_1 s_l/s_k$ and, denoting the share of V in Q by $s_v (= 1 - s_n)$,

(6.4) $p_v - p = -[(1 - s_v)/s_v](p_n - p).$

Thus in (6.1) we may write $a = \alpha$ and $b = (\alpha + \sigma)(1 - s_v)/s_v.$

Aggregate demand is here written in semireduced form as a negative function of the nominal interest rate, i (ignoring price expectations); a negative function of the real price of n, π_n; and a positive function of a fiscal demand variable (g):

(6.5) $q^d = - \psi i - \xi \pi_n + \gamma g.$

As we have seen in Chapter 5, there are a number of channels through which higher π_n reduces aggregate demand. To these we might here add a global argument similar to the one given in Chapter 4: to the extent that OPEC has a lower marginal propensity to consume than domestic residents, a shift of income to OPEC reduces demand for the home final good.

We study once again a range of wage behavior varying from nominal wage rigidity to real wage rigidity but this time do it in a slightly different form. Since there is only one final good in the model, consumer prices p_c equal output prices p. There remains, of course, the distinction between p and p_v, given by (6.4). Thus we consider two cases of indexing, the standard link to consumer prices ($\lambda = 1$) and alternatively a link to value-added prices ($\lambda = 0$):

(6.6) $w = \bar{w} + \theta[\lambda p + (1 - \lambda)p_v].$

θ is the degree of indexation, with $0 \leqslant \theta \leqslant 1$. Note that when $\theta = 1$, $\lambda = 0$, $w - p_v$ is fixed at $\bar{w}$, which in turn fixes GDP and employment.

The model is closed by specifying the money demand relationship, which we write once again as

(6.7) $m - p = \phi q - \beta i.$

The full model is shown in Appendix 6A at the end of this chapter. Note that there are nine equations, to determine w, p, p_v, q, l, n, p_n, v, and i, as functions of π_n, m, g, $\bar{w}$, and k.

The signs of the most important multipliers are shown in Table 6.1. (They are worked out in detail in Appendix 6A.) In general, we can make the following points. Negative demand shocks (for example, a downward shift in

Table 6.1. Signs of Multipliers for the Global Oil-Importing Economy

Endogenous variables	Exogenous variables			
	m	g	π_n	$\bar{w}$
q	$+^a$	$+^a$	$-$	$-$
v	$+^a$	$+^a$	$\pm^b$	$-$
p	$+$	$+$	$\pm$	$+$
i	$-^a$	$+$	$\pm$	$+$

a. When $\theta = 1$ there is a zero effect.
b. When $\theta = 1$ the sign is necessarily zero ($\lambda = 0$) or negative ($\lambda > 0$).

fiscal policy, $dg < 0$) reduce output and lower prices and interest rates. Negative supply shocks (for example, a rise in the base wage, $d\overline{w} > 0$) reduce output and raise prices and interest rates. A rise in π_n is both a negative supply shock and a negative demand shock, so that output necessarily falls while prices and interest rates may rise or fall, depending upon whether supply effects are large or small relative to demand effects. Thus, $dq/d\pi_n < 0$ while $di/d\pi_n \gtrless 0$ and $dp/d\pi_n \gtrless 0$, with $di/d\pi_n$ and $dp/d\pi_n > 0$ when the supply effect predominates.[1]

Figures 6.1 and 6.2 provide a graphic interpretation of these results. By combining Eq. (6.6) with (6.1) and (6.4), and using the definitions of a and b shown after (6.4), we may derive a world aggregate supply schedule. By combining (6.5) and (6.7), we find a world aggregate demand schedule. These are given, respectively, as

(6.8) $q^s = \alpha(1 - \theta)p - \alpha\overline{w} - [(1 - s_v)/s_v] [\alpha(1 - \theta + \theta\lambda) + \sigma]\pi_n + k,$

(6.9) $[1 + \psi\phi/\beta]q^d = -(\psi/\beta)p - \xi\pi_n + (\psi/\beta)m + \gamma g.$

Thus, aggregate supply is an upward-sloping function of p (and is vertical for $\theta = 1$), and aggregate demand is a downward-sloping function of p. These schedules are shown in Figure 6.1.

As in the single-country case (Chapter 5), negative demand shocks ($d\pi_n > 0$, $dg < 0$, $dm < 0$) shift q^d down and to the left; negative supply shocks ($d\overline{w} > 0$, $d\pi_n > 0$, $dk < 0$) shift q^s up and to the left. A rise in π_n is both a negative supply shock and a negative demand shock. When both schedules shift to the left (as in Figure 6.2), q necessarily falls while p may rise or fall. It may seem surprising that higher π_n could reduce p. This will occur only when demand contracts sharply after π_n rises, so that output falls by an enormous amount. If policymakers try to use expansionary policy to main-

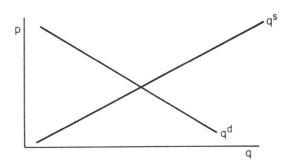

Figure 6.1. Aggregate supply and demand in the world economy

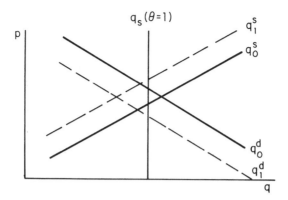

Figure 6.2. A rise in Π_N in the world economy

tain q, then prices must rise (because q^s shifts to the left, prices are higher at any given level of output than before the shock).

To analyze $d\pi_n > 0$ more fully, consider the case of full indexation (given by the vertical supply curve, $\theta = 1$, in Figure 6.2). Then, from (6.8):

$$(6.10) \qquad dq = - [(1 - s_v)/s_v](\sigma + \lambda\alpha)d\pi_n.$$

Likewise,

$$(6.11) \qquad dv = - [(1 - s_v)/s_v](\lambda\alpha)d\pi_n.$$

Output effects are now a function of supply characteristics alone; the aggregate supply curve is vertical. Shifts in demand (for example, $dm > 0$, $dg > 0$) have no effect on output, only on prices. The output effect of $d\pi_n > 0$ is the sum of two components. For *given* v, there is a reduction in q as firms substitute away from n. This effect is measured by $- \sigma[(1 - s_v)/s_v]d\pi_n$. Second, there may be a reduction in v. Since wages are indexed to $\lambda p + (1 - \lambda)p_v$, w_v $(= w - p_v)$ rises when π_n increases, by an amount $dw_v = \lambda[(1 - s_v)/s_v]\, d\pi_n$. The reduction in v as a result of dw_v is αdw_v. Thus, the total reduction in q is $\sigma\,[(1 - s_v)/s_v]d\pi_n + \lambda\alpha[(1 - s_v)/s_v]\, d\pi_n$, as shown in (6.10). When $\theta = 1$ and $\lambda = 1$, output is reduced by the amount of the pure substitution effect.

Note that when $\theta = 1$, dq/dm and dq/dg equal zero, and $dp/dm = 1$ (see Table 6.1 and Appendix 6A). Full indexation renders demand policies ineffective. An increase in demand simply causes prices to move up a vertical aggregate supply schedule. The ineffectiveness of monetary policy when $\theta = 1$ is a robust result. Higher m simply translates into equiproportional increases in wages and prices. We will see shortly that the ineffectiveness of fiscal policy is partly an artifact of our assumption of only one global oil-importing economy. In the two-economy model in the next section, a fiscal expansion in one of the two economies is always effective, for all values of θ. In that model, fiscal policy works in part by bringing about a terms-of-trade improvement for the expanding country (and a terms-of-trade loss in the other country). In the present model, with one final good and an exogenous real price of intermediate inputs, this particular channel is blocked. But even in the two-economy model, a fiscal expansion in *both* countries will be ineffective under conditions of full indexation, since neither country will achieve a terms-of-trade improvement vis-à-vis the other.

When $\theta < 1$, demand factors as well as supply factors affect q and v, and monetary and fiscal policy can be effective in responding to a rise in π_n. Expansionary monetary and fiscal policies shift the demand curve along an upward-sloping aggregate supply schedule.

It is interesting to ask whether higher or lower indexation leads to a more moderate output decline following a rise in π_n. From the supply curve (6.1) we know that $dq/d\pi_n = - a(dw_q/d\pi_n) - b$, so that the real issue is the effect of alternative indexation formulas on $dw_q/d\pi_n$. In general, if $d\pi_n > 0$ raises prices, indexation will protect the real wage, and the fall in output will be *greater* the higher is θ. If $d\pi_n > 0$ reduces prices (which is a theoretical possibility if demand falls sharply relative to supply at the initial price level), indexation decreases nominal wages in step with prices, and the fall in output will be *smaller* the higher is θ. To show this formally, consider the case of p-indexation, (that is, $\lambda = 1$). If we examine $\partial/\partial\theta[dq/d\pi_n]$ we find

(6.12) $\partial/\partial\theta[dq/d\pi_n] = -(a\psi/\Delta)[dp/d\pi_n],$

where Δ is a positive factor given in Appendix 6A. Thus, when the supply shock raises prices ($dp/d\pi_n > 0$) $dq/d\pi_n$ becomes more negative as θ increases.

We can also observe that higher indexation results in a greater rise in prices (or a smaller decline) following a rise in π_n. That is, $\partial/\partial\theta[dp/d\pi_n]$ is necessarily positive, as can be verified in Appendix 6A. Thus, taking the likely case that the rise in π_n raises prices, we can conclude that an increase in indexation worsens the stagflationary consequences of the input price shock: output declines more, while the price level rises further.

Also interesting are the pure supply shock effects of $d\overline{w} > 0$ shown in Table 6.1. A rise in the base wage rate, *ceteris paribus,* lowers output and value added, raises prices, and raises interest rates.

A World Model with Two Oil-Importing Economies

We now subdivide the oil-importing region into two economies (H, for "home"; F, for "foreign"). There are three types of questions to examine in the expanded model. First, how does the effect of higher π_n on H depend on the economic structure of F? Second, how do policy responses in H or F to the supply shock affect macroeconomic performance in the other economy? And third, given that both H and F will vary their policy instruments after a rise in π_n, is there a case for *coordinated* policy action in response to the common shock?

We take the economic structure of F to be like that of H, though we let the specific parameter values differ across the two economies (particularly in the wage equations). We also assume that the final goods produced in H and F are imperfect consumption substitutes, with the share of demand falling on one or the other final good a function of the relative price $\pi = p - e - p^*$. The price of oil p_n is fixed in real terms, relative to a basket of the home and foreign final goods (with weights μ, $1 - \mu$). Letting π_n^w be the real price of oil in terms of this basket, we write:

(6.13) $p_n = \pi_n^w + [\mu p + (1 - \mu)(p^* + e)]$.

This can alternatively be written in the form

(6.13') $\pi_n = \pi_n^w - (1 - \mu)\pi.$

The structure of the oil-importing economies is like that described in the country model of Chapter 5. The full model and its solution are given in Appendix 6A at the end of this chapter. The principal changes from the one-global-economy model of the previous section are the following.

1. *Aggregate Demand:* This is now a negative function of the country's relative price of final goods (π). Thus a term $- \delta\pi$ is added to Eq. (6.5) to give

(6.14) $q^d = -\delta\pi - \psi i + \gamma g - \xi(p_n - p).$

Substituting for ($p_n - p$) from Eq. (6.13') and for i from a money equation like (6.7), this can alternatively be written as

(6.14') $q^d(1 + \psi\phi/\beta) = -h\pi + \psi(m - p)/\beta + \gamma g - \xi\pi_n^w$

$= -(h + \psi/\beta)p + h(e + p^*) + (\psi/\beta)m + \gamma g - \xi\pi_n^w,$

where $h = \delta - (1 - \mu)\xi$ and assume $h > 0$.

2. *Consumer Prices:* These are a weighted (η) average of home and for-

eign final goods prices:

(6.15) $p_c = \eta p + (1 - \eta)(p^* + e) = p - (1 - \eta)\pi.$

3. *Aggregate Supply:* Using a supply curve for the home economy like (6.1) and substituting for π_n from (6.13′) and for $(w - p)$ from a wage indexation equation like (6.6) with p replaced by p_c, we get for the case of p_c indexation $(w = \bar{w} + \theta p_c)$

(6.16) $q^s = a(1 - \theta)p + [b(1 - \mu) + a\theta(1 - \eta)]\pi - a\bar{w} - b\pi_n^w + k$
   $= [a(1 - \theta) + b(1 - \mu) + a\theta(1 - \eta)]p$
   $- [b(1 - \mu) + a\theta(1 - \eta)](e + p^*) - a\bar{w} - b\pi_n^w + k.$

We note that the pair of equations (6.16) and (6.14′) give an upward-sloping supply curve q^s and a downward-sloping demand curve q^d just as in Figure 6.1. The only difference now is that there is an additional exchange rate shift variable, π or e, moving the q^d curve rightward and the q^s curve leftward as π or e rises. For given *real* exchange rate (π) q^s will again be vertical if $\theta = 1$ (full indexation), while for given *nominal* exchange rate (e) q^s will be vertical if $\theta = \mu = \eta = 1$.

4. *The Foreign Country:* In exactly analogous fashion, we can draw q^{*d} and q^{*s} curves for the F economy in q^*-p^* space, the only difference being that $e^* = -e$ and therefore a rise in e shifts the two curves in the opposite direction to that of the H country.[2]

5. *Capital Mobility and Interest Rates:* We assume perfect capital mobility between the two oil-importing economies. Combining the assumption that $i = i^*$ with two analogous money market equations like (6.7) for the two economies,[3] we obtain the following international money market equilibrium condition:

(6.17) $p - (\beta/\beta^*)p^* = (m - \phi q) - (\beta/\beta^*)(m^* - \phi^* q^*).$

In this way we can reduce the full fifteen-equation model shown in Appendix 6A to a more concise five-equation model consisting of the q^d and q^s equations (6.14′) and (6.16) plus their starred counterparts (not shown separately here) plus the capital flow equilibrium condition (6.17). These five equations solve for the five variables p, p^*, q, q^*, and e (or π).

To keep a manageable number of cases under discussion, we will consider only one form of wage indexing, with w linked to p_c rather than to p_v (that is, $\lambda = 1$).

COMPARATIVE STATICS

If the two countries are identical in structure, the effects of a rise in π_n^w will be the same as those we analyzed in the previous section of this chapter. The variables π and e will be unaffected by the supply shock, so that we can aggregate over the final outputs of the two oil-importing economies and treat the two economies as one. The extended model is useful only if the economies differ in some interesting way, or if they pursue distinct policies following a rise in π_n^w.

To explore these issues, we may solve for output, prices, and the interest rate as a function of the exogenous variables m, m^*, g, g^*, and π_n^w. The signs are displayed in Table 6.2, and the detailed solutions are given in Appendix 6A. In each case the result is shown for the home variable, though the multipliers for the foreign economy can be found simply by replacing all starred variables (those with a superscript asterisk) by unstarred counterparts, and vice versa, given the symmetry of the model with respect to H and F. Thus, if $a_1 = \phi + \mu^*$, then $a_1^* = \phi^* + \mu$. (To apply this rule consistently, we also add the convention that $\mu^* = (1 - \mu)$, where μ is the weight of the home good in the pricing of p_n.)

As long as home and foreign parameters are close in magnitude, a supply-price shock ($d\pi_n^w > 0$) has the expected effect of lowering output in both economies. As we observed in the case of one oil-importing region, the effect on world interest rates is ambiguous and depends on whether the contractionary supply effects of $d\pi_n^w > 0$ exceed the contractionary demand effects

Table 6.2. Signs of Multipliers for the Two-Country Model

Endogenous variables	Exogenous variables				
	m	g	m^*	g^*	π_n^w
q	$+^a$	$+$	$\pm^b$	$\pm^c$	$\pm^d$
π	$-^a$	$+$	$+^b$	$-$	$\pm$
i	$-^a$	$+$	$+$	$+$	$\pm$
p_c	$+$	$\pm$	$\pm^e$	$\pm$	$\pm$
p	$+$	$\pm$	$-$	$+$	$\pm$

a. $= 0$ when $\theta = 1$.
b. $= 0$ when $\theta^* = 1$, > 0 when $\theta = 1$ and $\theta^* < 1$.
c. < 0 if $\theta = 1$.
d. < 0 for identical economies.
e. < 0 if $\theta^* = 1$.

(in which case i rises), or vice versa. But in fact, once we drop the assumption that the two economies' parameters are the same, other possibilities arise. An increase in π_n^w can actually raise output in one of the two economies under plausible circumstances.

Suppose the home supply and demand are not directly affected by π_n ($\xi = b = 0$), while abroad demand is more sharply affected than supply, that is, $\xi^* > b^*$. Furthermore, assume full wage indexation in both economies ($\theta = \theta^* = 1$). Then from Appendix 6A we see that $dq/d\pi_n^w (= a_5)$ reduces to ($\xi^* - b^*)d\psi/\Delta$, which would be positive. Thus, home output would rise after the supply shock. (Similarly, the domestic price level falls.) To understand this result, note that because $\xi^* > b^*$, foreign interest rates (i^*) tend to decline after $d\pi_n^w > 0$ and there is domestic exchange appreciation.[4] The home country benefits indirectly from higher π_n^w through a world interest rate decline.

This case is relevant to the differential behavior of the non-oil MICs and the ICs in the 1970s, which was already discussed in Chapter 4. The drop in aggregate demand in the developed economies in the 1970s reduced world real interest rates, which in turn stimulated borrowing and demand in the developing countries. The decline in world interest rates and increased access to borrowing helped in several developing countries to compensate for higher π_n. Thus, between 1973 and 1979, growth rates in the non-oil MICs remained at high levels. After the 1979–80 oil price increases, this group of countries suffered both from $d\pi_n^w > 0$ and $di > 0$. The rise in interest rates at this point was largely the result of the macro-policies pursued in the developed economies in response to $d\pi_n^w > 0$.

There are two other uses of immediate interest for the two-country extension. We will argue at length later that differences in wage behavior across economies help to explain different patterns of adjustment in the major economies. Thus, one aspect to examine is how world adjustment proceeds when indexation is high in one region (empirically, most of western Europe) and low in the other region (North America). Second, we should examine how differential policy responses in the two economies affect world equilibrium. These are the topics of the next section.

THE INTERNATIONAL TRANSMISSION OF MACROECONOMIC POLICIES

When π_n^w rises, it is likely that output falls while prices increase. This stagflationary event may well induce a policy response ranging from an aggressive expansion to counteract rising unemployment, to a contractionary policy to put the lid on rising inflation. For a variety of reasons, some of which we discuss in the next section, the contractionary option was the typical response, both in 1973–74 and 1979–80. Domestic policy changes have important repercussion effects in other countries, leading to two problems of great significance. First, in choosing a response to a supply shock, each country must estimate the impact of foreign policies on the home economy. In both 1973–74 and 1979–80, most governments probably failed to judge the breadth and depth of contractionary policies around the world, with the result that output levels everywhere fell below target. Second, because of the interdependence of economies, the choice of policies itself depends on policies pursued elsewhere. We will find that *coordinated* selection of policies after a supply shock can raise economic welfare in all economies.

The supply shocks occurred in a setting of flexible exchange rates, which conditioned in an important way the attitudes to macroeconomic policies and the policy choices that were actually made. Until the mid-1970s, conventional views about the international transmission of monetary and fiscal policies under flexible exchange rates were based on models of full nominal wage rigidity ($\theta = \theta^* = 0$), in which intermediate inputs played no role. In such models, of which Mundell (1963) provided the original and most important one, certain striking results were derived. A domestic monetary contraction, for example, was shown to *raise* income abroad. In such models, lower m causes a currency appreciation which raises the home terms of trade π under conditions of nominal wage rigidity. Home competitiveness worsens, and demand is shifted to foreign final goods from home goods. Foreign output actually rises. The home appreciation (or foreign depreciation) lowers home prices and raises foreign prices. Such results seem to suggest that European economies, for example, should expect a boom, not a recession, from tight U.S. monetary policies under flexible exchange rates. A fiscal expansion, on the other hand, raises the relative price of home final goods (π rises), thus causing demand to shift from home goods to foreign goods. In this way the domestic fiscal expansion raises output in the foreign economy in Mundell's model. Thus, in this model the European economies should experience a boom in response to expansionary U.S. fiscal policies.

These results turn out to be extraordinarily sensitive to a change in assumptions. As soon as $\theta^* > 0$ or $b^* > 0$, it is quite possible that a domestic monetary contraction *lowers* foreign income, so that monetary policies are positively transmitted (by "positive" transmission we mean that the direction of effect on foreign output is the same as on domestic output). Also, with $\theta^* > 0$ or $b^* > 0$, it is possible that a domestic fiscal expansion causes a contraction in output abroad, so that fiscal policy is negatively transmitted.

In both cases, the difference with respect to standard analysis is that domestic factor prices are induced to change following shifts in m or g.

In the traditional model, the fact that a domestic money contraction raises q^* results from the foreign gain in competitiveness when m falls. The decline in m causes π to rise (and e to fall) and thus shifts demand toward the foreign economy. But the rise in π lowers foreign real wages. Implicitly, the tight monetary policy at home imposes a real wage decline abroad, and this decline allows foreign aggregate supply to increase. Since nominal wages are fixed in the traditional model, there is no response of w^* to the real wage decline. Once wages are even partially indexed, the monetary contraction at home may lower q^*. As π rises (e falls), w^* also rises, and this undercuts some of the basis for foreign expansion. Similarly, p_n^* rises as well, with the same effect. If $\theta^* = 1$, then q^* definitely declines. As θ^* rises, it becomes more likely that a domestic money contraction will reduce income abroad.[5]

The transmission of fiscal policy also depends on the degree of wage indexation, but in the opposite direction to monetary policy. For a given θ, low values of θ^* result in the positive transmission of a domestic fiscal contraction to the foreign country (that is, $dq^*/dg > 0$), while high foreign indexation makes it more likely that $dq^*/dg < 0$. To see how $dg > 0$ can reduce foreign income, consider the case in which w_c^* is fixed (that is, $\theta^* = 1$). Since we can write w_v^* as $w_c^* + [(1 - s_v^*)/s_v^*]\pi_n^w + [(1 - \eta^*) + \mu(1 - s_v^*)/s_v^*]\pi$, an increase in π *raises* w_v^* if w_c^* is fixed, and thereby lowers aggregate supply of value added in the foreign country. Since $dg > 0$ tends to raise π, it tends to reduce foreign aggregate supply when the foreign consumption wage is fixed. Moreover, since $\pi_n^* (= p_n^* - p^*)$ equals $\pi_n^w + \mu\pi$, the rise in π also increases the real price of intermediate inputs to the foreign economy. Since v^* falls, and $q^* = v^* - [\sigma(1 - s_v^*)/s_v^*](\pi_n^w + \mu\pi)$, we conclude that q^* falls as well. In sum, $dq^*/dg < 0$ for $\theta^* = 1$.

In Table 6.3 we summarize the direction of effect of economic policies in H on output and prices in F. Most interesting, perhaps, is the case in which the home economy has $\theta = 0$, and the foreign economy $\theta^* = 1$, for this provides a stylized version of interactions between the United States and Europe (of course, in reality we have $0 < \theta < \theta^* < 1$). Here we see two things: a U.S. monetary *contraction* would be stagflationary in Europe (that is, $dq^*/dm > 0$, $dp_c^*/dm < 0$); and a U.S. fiscal *expansion* would be stagflationary in Europe (that is, $dq^*/dg < 0$, $dp_c^*/dg > 0$). Since this was the U.S. policy mix pursued after 1980, it was not surprising to hear the chorus of complaints from European governments over U.S. macroeconomic management.

A glance at the signs of multipliers in Table 6.2 will show that if we confine

Table 6.3. International Transmission of Macroeconomic Policies

Policy	Low indexation	High indexation
	Effect on foreign output	
Domestic money expansion	Negative	Positive
Domestic fiscal expansion	Positive	Negative
	Effect on foreign prices	
Domestic money expansion	Negative	Negative
Domestic fiscal expansion	Positive	Positive

Note: Indexation refers to θ^*, not θ; prices refer to the consumer price level, p_c^*, not p^*. Results in all cases are for $\theta < 1$. The low indexation case refers to $\theta^* = b^* = 0$. The high indexation case refers to $\theta^* = 1$, $b^* > 0$. All results may be derived from Appendix 6A.

our attention to the foreign output price level p^* rather than to that of the foreign consumption basket (that is, $\eta = 1$), the above result is obtained even under more general conditions. As long as the F country (Europe) is highly indexed ($\theta^* = 1$) and the raw material is indexed to the home (U.S.) price ($\mu = 1$), domestic (U.S.) monetary contraction or fiscal expansion will always be stagflationary abroad.

This simple two-country model can be modified in several ways, and with some of these modifications, it is possible that $dq^*/dg > 0$ even when $\theta^* = 1$. For example, in the aggregate demand equation (6.14), q^* does not appear explicitly as an argument. Multiplier effects from a home expansion to foreign output, and from q^* to q, are forced to work solely through interest rates and the exchange rate. Including foreign output in the aggregate demand equation reduces the possibility that q^* falls when g is raised, because the direct effect of the domestic expansion now tends to raise q^*. However, it remains true that as θ^* rises, the expansionary effect of g is strongly diminished, and perhaps reversed.

The Role for Policy Coordination after a Supply Shock

A SIMPLE ILLUSTRATION

Early advocates of flexible exchange rates emphasized their "insulating" properties for the home economy.[6] Insulation took one of two meanings:

that foreign disturbances would not affect the home economy because of offsetting exchange rate movements; or that flexible exchange rates freed up policy instruments so that macroeconomic policy could actively offset foreign disturbances. Our analysis to this point strongly rejects the first interpretation of insulation. We have seen that external disturbances almost inevitably affect domestic prices and output.[7] In the large-country models of this chapter, changes in monetary and fiscal policy abroad almost surely affect q and p_c, whether wages are indexed or not. A rise in world energy prices, similarly, affects output and raises prices in both countries.

The second interpretation of insulation has more merit, but it can be overstated. Flexible exchange rates increase the potential for insulation, by freeing monetary policy to respond to external disturbances. But this fact is sometimes taken to mean that under flexible rates, each country can safely be left alone to pursue its macroeconomic goals, independent of the actions of others. In this interpretation, since flexible exchange rates allow each economy to select a preferred inflation rate (and presumably other macroeconomic targets), policy coordination is redundant at best, misguided, and perhaps actually harmful. The analysis in this section disputes such a view. Policy coordination is almost always desirable and may be particularly important after a supply shock.

The importance of coordination depends on two facts: (1) that there are not enough independent policy instruments available to allow each country to hit all of its macro-targets; and (2) that policy instruments of one economy affect macroeconomic outcomes in others. In these circumstances we can show that a "Nash policy equilibrium," in which each country chooses its preferred policies taking the other countries' actions as *given,* will be Pareto-suboptimal. Policy coordination, in which all countries agree to adjust their policy instruments away from the Nash equilibrium, can raise welfare everywhere.

Let us consider a simple version of the two-country model to illustrate the problems here. First, instead of the supply curves we write p as *fixed* markup over w and p_n, and the same for p^*:[8]

$$(6.18) \qquad p = \zeta w + (1 - \zeta)p_n,$$
$$p^* = \zeta w^* + (1 - \zeta)p_n^*.$$

(In this and the remaining equations of this illustration, *all* home and foreign coefficients are set equal.) Second, we assume zero indexation ($\theta = \theta^* = 0$). Third, we ignore g and g^*, by setting $\gamma = \gamma^* = 0$. The remaining equations are the same as before (though we do not need the money equations).[9]

The source of inefficiency of noncooperative policymaking in this model lies in the price equations, which are derived from (6.6), (6.15), and (6.18):[10]

(6.19) $p_c = \overline{w} + \beta_0 \pi_n^w - \beta_1 \pi, \quad \beta_0, \beta_1 > 0,$

$p_c^* = \overline{w}^* + \beta_0 \pi_n^w + \beta_1 \pi.$

By the fixed nominal wage and fixed markup assumptions, the price level is determined only by the predetermined wage ($\overline{w}$), the world relative price of inputs π_n^w, and the terms of trade. Higher π reduces p_c but raises p_c^*. An attempt to reduce p_c by altering π can be successful only if p_c^* is increased. *Therefore, successful anti-inflationary policy here means exporting inflation abroad.* This factor is at the heart of the inefficiency of noncooperative policymaking: each side tries to export inflation, but together the two sides merely create a deep recession.

By subtracting the two economies' aggregate demand schedules from each other, we get an equation for π in terms of $q - q^*$:

(6.20) $\pi = - [1/(2\delta - \xi)](q - q^*).$

We assume that $2\delta - \xi > 0$, which is the condition that a real appreciation reduces aggregate demand.[11]

For convenience, we write the coefficient $[1/(2\delta - \xi)]$ as γ_0. Substituting (6.20) into (6.18) and (6.19), we can write p_c and p_c^* as a function of $\overline{w}$, π_n^w, and $(q - q^*)$:

(6.21) $p_c = \overline{w} + \beta_0 \pi_n^w + \beta_1 \gamma_0 (q - q^*),$

$p_c^* = \overline{w} + \beta_0 \pi_n^w - \beta_1 \gamma_0 (q - q^*).$

We assume that policymakers in each country use monetary policy to set q, q^* *taking as given* the level of output in the other economy. Thus q and q^* are the decision variables, and q, q^*, p_c, and p_c^* are the targets.

Now let us write the utility functions of each country as a quadratic loss function in the level of prices and output:[12]

(6.22) $\Omega = -(q)^2 - v(p_c)^2,$

(6.23) $\Omega^* = -(q^*)^2 - v^*(p_c^*)^2.$

The variables p_c and q should be thought of as deviations from an optimal path, so that utility is highest when $p_c = q = 0$.

In this model it is trivial to find the symmetric Pareto-optimal solution for demand management after a supply shock. Suppose that we begin with an equilibrium in which $q = q^* = p = p^* = \pi_n^w = 0$. A supply shock occurs so that $\pi_n^w > 0$. In any symmetric equilibrium, $q = q^*$. From (6.21) this implies that $p_c = \overline{w} + \beta_0 \pi_n^w = p_c^*$, so that price levels in the symmetric solution are independent of q and q^*. There is no way to reduce both p_c and p_c^* below the level $(\overline{w} + \beta_0 \pi_n^w)$ in the short run. Thus, $\Omega = -(q)^2 - v[(\overline{w} + \beta_0 \pi_n^w)]^2 = \Omega^*$. Given that higher price levels are therefore unavoidable after the supply shock $\pi_n^w > 0$, the symmetric optimum is clearly reached by setting $q = q^* = 0$.

In the noncooperative setting the economies will reach the *same* prices, but with q and $q^* < 0$, which makes utility lower than at the symmetric Pareto optimum. The reason here is straightforward: if the foreign country sets $q^* = 0$, the home country will have an incentive to reduce q below 0, thereby improving the home terms of trade and exporting some inflation. Of course, if $q < 0$ then the foreign country will no longer want to peg $q^* = 0$. In the end, both q and q^* are equal and negative in the noncooperative setting.

To find the noncooperative equilibrium, simply substitute the price equation (6.21) into the utility functions (6.22) and (6.23). Thus, for example, $\Omega = -(q)^2 - v[\overline{w} + \beta_0 \pi_n^w + \beta_1 \gamma_0 (q - q^*)]^2$. In the Nash noncooperative game, the home country chooses $\partial \Omega / \partial q = 0$, yielding

(6.24) $q = -v(\beta_1 \gamma_0)(\overline{w} + \beta_0 \pi_n^w)/[1 + v(\beta_1 \gamma_0)^2]$
$\qquad + v(\beta_1 \gamma_0)^2 (q^*)/[1 + v(\beta_1 \gamma_0)^2].$

Clearly, when $(\overline{w} + \beta_0 \pi_n^w) > 0$ (that is, when inherited inflation is high), optimum q is reduced. If $q^* = 0$ and inherited inflation is positive, then q will be set below zero. The foreign country chooses a similar rule:

(6.25) $q^* = -v(\beta_1 \gamma_0)(\overline{w} + \beta_0 \pi_n^w)/[1 + v(\beta_1 \gamma_0)^2]$
$\qquad + v(\beta_1 \gamma_0)^2 q/[1 + v(\beta_1 \gamma_0)^2].$

The noncooperative equilibrium is the pair (q, q^*) that satisfies (6.24) and (6.25), and it is easy to see that the solution is

(6.26) $q = q^* = -v(\beta_1 \gamma_0)(\overline{w} + \beta_0 \pi_n^w).$

The cooperative equilibrium is $q = q^* = 0$. Thus supply shocks (or any situation in which both countries inherit a high exogenous rate of inflation) lead to overcontraction relative to a joint optimum for the two economies. Everybody loses from the lack of coordination.

Equations (6.24) and (6.25) are known as reaction functions for the home and foreign economies, for they describe the optimal choice of output in "reaction" to the choice taken abroad. Figure 6.3, a standard diagram in this sort of analysis, presents a graph of the two reaction functions. The point of intersection is the Nash noncooperative equilibrium. The cooperative equilibrium is given by (0,0). Note that for each country, if the other country sets output at zero, the best choice of output is negative. Thus each country has a

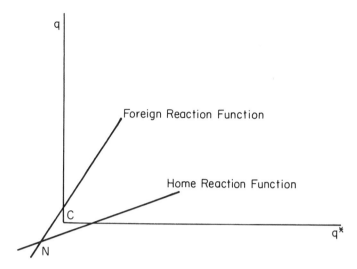

Figure 6.3. Reaction functions and Nash (N) and cooperative (C) equilibria in the policy game

unilateral incentive to break away from the cooperative outcome by reducing output.

The static model is illustrative but in many ways unsatisfactory. It specifies that domestic inflation control comes *only* at the expense of higher inflation elsewhere, an assumption that is clearly extreme. It fails to reflect the fact that inflation control is typically an intertemporal problem of trading off higher unemployment in the short run for a long-term reduction in inflation. A more satisfactory, dynamic extension of our model is introduced in Sachs (1983b), in which inflation is reduced both through domestic slack and through terms-of-trade improvements. It turns out, not surprisingly, that the noncooperative anti-inflationary policy that is selected is still too contractionary, in the sense that both economies can benefit from a coordinated moderation of anti-inflationary policy.

Using that dynamic model, it is demonstrated that noncooperative (Nash) policymaking will lead to too rapid a disinflation, with excessive output losses in the period immediately following a supply shock. Consider specifically a case in which $\pi_n^w > 0$ leads to high levels of inflation at $t = 0$ in the two economies, and suppose that $\dot{\pi}_n^w = 0$ for $t > 0$. In this case we show that:

1. The best cooperative policy is to reduce the inflation at a constant geometric rate (denoted as v_1^c). Thus,

$$\dot{p}_t = v_1^c \dot{p}_{t-1}, \qquad t > 0$$

(where $\dot{p}_t$ is $p_t - p_{t-1}$, and $\dot{p}_{t-1}$ is $p_{t-1} - p_{t-2}$ in this difference equation).

2. The noncooperative equilibrium also results in a geometric reduction in inflation, but now at a *faster* rate (denoted as v_1^{nc}):

$$\dot{p}_t = v_1^{nc} \dot{p}_{t-1}, \qquad t > 0,$$

with $\quad v_1^{nc} < v_1^c.$

3. Therefore, the Nash equilibrium leads to an initial overcontraction (that is, excessive disinflation of both economies relative to the Pareto-optimal path).

SOME EMPIRICAL EVIDENCE

The empirical evidence seems to support the potential role for coordination, at least on the key point that a money-led economic expansion *relative* to one's trading partners imposes an inflation cost. We consider the crucial link between π and $q - q^*$. Since q and q^* are GNP relative to potential, we appeal to Okun's law to write q and q^* as linear functions of the unemployment rates U and U^*. Then, our hypothesis is that

(6.27) $\pi = \alpha_0 + \alpha_1 U - \alpha_2 U^*, \qquad \alpha_1 > 0, \alpha_2 > 0,$

that is, a rise in domestic unemployment is associated with an improvement in the home terms of trade, and a rise in U^* is associated with a worsening of the home-country terms of trade. Remember that (6.27) is derived by subtracting the foreign aggregate demand schedule from the domestic aggregate demand schedule, assuming that $f - f^*$ is unchanging. Thus, the relationship should only hold over periods in which fiscal policies across countries are roughly similar.

Regressions for Germany, Japan, and the United States during the floating rate period, 1973–81, show the following:[13]

	$\hat{\alpha}_1$	$\hat{\alpha}_2$	$\hat{\rho}$	$\overline{R}^2$
Germany	0.06	−0.09	−0.68	0.19
	(2.06)	(2.35)	(1.30)	
(6.28) Japan	0.17	−0.05	−0.45	0.60
	(4.43)	(4.15)		
U.S.	0.07	−0.10	−0.67	0.67
	(5.80)	(4.90)	(1.80)	

For each country, rising unemployment abroad has been associated with a worsening of the terms of trade, on the order that 1 percentage point higher

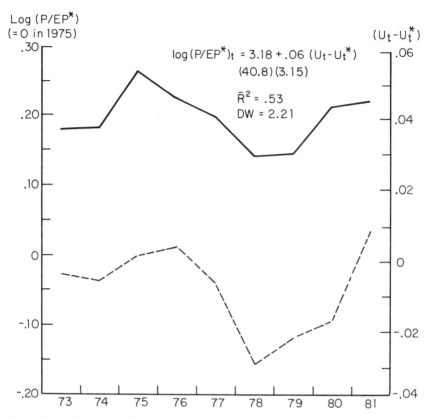

Figure 6.4. U.S. terms of trade and relative unemployment rate, 1973–1981. Solid line is $U_t - U_t^*$; dashed line is log $(P/EP^*)_t$

unemployment abroad is associated with a 5 to 10 percent terms-of-trade deterioration, and presumably a worsening inflation. Figure 6.4 further highlights this pattern in the case of the United States. When the United States reduced unemployment during 1975–79, at a time of rising foreign unemployment, it experienced a sharp terms-of-trade deterioration. This deterioration was reversed when U rose in the United States in 1980–81 while falling in Germany and Japan.

Conclusions

This chapter has explored the global macroeconomic adjustment to a world-wide supply shock. It extends the standard analysis of macroeconomic inter-dependence in several directions: (1) introduction of an intermediate, traded input into production; (2) partial or full wage indexation in the economies;

and (3) policy reaction functions, based on policy optimization subject to national social welfare functions.

Starting with the case of a single N-importing region, we show the following important results. A rise in Π_N reduces output but may raise or lower interest rates and prices. Interest rates and prices tend to rise when the contractionary *supply* effects of the rise in Π_N dominate the contractionary *demand* effects, and tend to fall in the reverse case. Indexation worsens the output consequences of the supply shock to the extent that it helps to preserve high levels of W_Q after a supply shock. Indexation certainly worsens the price level consequences.

In a model with two N-importing economies, we show how macroeconomic policies are transmitted across international borders. Standard macroeconomic models, following Mundell (1963), have often found that under flexible exchange rates, one country's contractionary monetary policies result in output expansion in the other country; and that a fiscal expansion in one country also results in output expansion abroad. We show, however, that these conclusions are *reversed* when wage indexation is high, a relevant empirical assumption for most OECD economies outside of North America. In this light we show that a U.S. policy mix of expansionary fiscal policy and contractionary monetary policy may have reduced output and raised prices in Europe, a complaint heard with much frequency after 1981.

The fact that macroeconomic policies in one economy strongly affect policies in the others leads to a situation in which decentralized policymaking is likely to result in inefficient macroeconomic equilibria for the world as a whole. We demonstrate this point rigorously in the final section of this chapter, by showing that macroeconomic policies are likely to be overly contractionary following an inflationary supply shock. Under flexible exchange rates, policymakers in each country have an incentive to reduce the supply-shock inflation by pursuing contractionary policies to achieve a currency appreciation. On an international scale these attempts by separate countries cancel out, with the result that all countries end up pursuing excessively contractionary policies relative to a Pareto optimum.

Appendix 6A: The Detailed Models

WORLD MODEL WITH ONE OIL-IMPORTING ECONOMY

Aggregate Supply

$$(6A.1.1) \quad q = - a(w - p) - b\pi_n + k$$

$$a = \alpha$$

$$b = (\alpha + \sigma)(1 - s_v)/s_v$$

(6A.1.2) $v = -\alpha(w - p_v) + k$

(6A.1.3) $l = v - \sigma_l(w - p_v)$

(6A.1.4) $n = q - \sigma\pi_n$

Aggregate Demand

(6A.1.5) $q = -\xi\pi_n + \gamma g - \psi i$

Wages and Prices

(6A.1.6) $w = \overline{w} + \theta[\lambda p + (1 - \lambda)p_v]$

(6A.1.7) $p = s_v p_v + (1 - s_v)p_n$

(6A.1.8) $p_n = p + \pi_n$

Money Market Equilibrium

(6A.1.9) $m - p = \phi q - \beta i$

MULTIPLIERS FOR THE MODEL WITH ONE OIL-IMPORTING ECONOMY

Output

(6A.2.1) $dq = a_1 dm + a_2 dg + a_3 d\pi_n + a_4 d\overline{w}$

$\qquad\qquad a_1 = (1 - \theta)\psi/\Delta \geq 0$

$\qquad\qquad a_2 = \gamma b\, \alpha(1 - \theta)/\Delta \geq 0$

$\qquad\qquad a_3 = -[B\psi + \xi\alpha\beta(1 - \theta)]/\Delta < 0$

$\qquad\qquad a_4 = -a\psi/\Delta < 0$

$\qquad\qquad \Delta = \psi + \alpha(1 - \theta)(b + \psi\phi) > 0$

$\qquad\qquad B = [(1 - s_v)/s_v]\{\sigma + \alpha[1 - \theta(1 - \lambda)]\} > 0$
$\qquad\qquad\quad (B = b \quad \text{for} \quad \lambda = 1)$

Value Added

(6A.2.2) $dv = b_1 dm + b_2 dg + b_3\pi_n + b_4 d\overline{w}$

$\qquad\qquad b_1 = a_1 \geq 0$

$\qquad\qquad b_2 = a_2 \geq 0$

$\qquad\qquad b_3 = a_3 + \sigma(1 - s_v)/s_v \gtreqless 0 \qquad$ (when $\theta = 1$,

$\qquad\qquad\quad b_3 = -\alpha(1 - s_v)\lambda/s_v \leq 0)$

$\qquad\qquad b_4 = a_4 < 0$

Prices

(6A.2.3) $dp = c_1 dm + c_2 dg + c_3 d\pi_n + c_4 d\overline{w}$

$c_1 = \psi/\Delta > 0$ (when $\theta = 1$, $c_1 = 1$)

$c_2 = b\gamma/\Delta > 0$

$c_3 = [(B - \xi)\beta + \beta\psi\phi]/\Delta \gtrless 0$

$c_4 = a(\beta + \psi\phi)/\Delta > 0$

Interest Rate

(6A.2.4) $di = d_1 dm + d_2 dg + d_3 d\pi_n + d_4 d\overline{w}$

$d_1 = -\alpha(1 - \theta)/\Delta \leqslant 0$

$d_2 = b\gamma/\Delta > 0$

$d_3 = \{B - \xi[1 + a(1 - \theta)\phi]\}/\Delta \gtrless 0$

$d_4 = \{a + \psi[1 + a(1 - \theta)]\}/\Delta > 0$

WORLD MODEL WITH TWO OIL-IMPORTING ECONOMIES

Aggregate Supply

(6A.3.1) $q = -a(w - p) - b(p_n - p) + k$

(6A.3.2) $q^* = -a^*(w^* - p^*) - b^*(p_n^* - p^*) + k^*$

Aggregate Demand

(6A.3.3) $q = -\delta(p - e - p^*) - \psi i + \gamma g - \xi(p_n - p)$

(6A.3.4) $q^* = -\delta^*(p^* + e - p) - \psi^* i^* + \gamma^* g^* - \xi^*(p_n^* - p^*)$

Wages and Prices

(6A.3.5) $w = \overline{w} + \theta[\lambda p_c + (1 - \lambda)p_v]$

(6A.3.6) $w^* = \overline{w}^* + \theta^*[\lambda^* p_c^* + (1 - \lambda^*)p_v^*]$

(6A.3.7) $p = s_v p_v + (1 - s_v)p_n$

(6A.3.8) $p^* = s_v^* p_v^* + (1 - s_v^*)p_n^*$

(6A.3.9) $p_c = p - (1 - \eta)\pi$

(6A.3.10) $p_c^* = p^* - (1 - \eta^*)\pi^*$

(6A.3.11) $p_n = \pi_n^w + [\mu p + (1 - \mu)(p^* + e)]$,
$\quad\quad$ i.e., $p_n - p = \pi_n^w - (1 - \mu)\pi$

(6A.3.12) $p_n^* = p_n - e$

Money-Market Equilibrium

(6A.3.13) $m - p = \phi q - \beta i$

(6A.3.14) $m^* - p^* = \phi^* q^* - \beta^* i^*$

(6A.3.15) $i = i^*$

MULTIPLIERS FOR THE WORLD MODEL WITH TWO
OIL-IMPORTING ECONOMIES

Output

$$dq = a_1 dm + a_2 dg + a_3 dm^* + a_4 dg^* + a_5 d\pi_n^w$$

$$a_1 = a(1 - \theta)\{[1 + a^*\phi^*(1 - \theta^*)](\psi^* h + \psi h^*)$$
$$\quad + ha^*(1 - \theta^*)\beta^* + d^*\psi\}/\Delta \gtrless 0$$

$$a_2 = \gamma\{d^*a(1 - \theta)\beta + da^*\beta^*(1 - \theta^*)$$
$$\quad + [1 + a^*\phi^*(1 - \theta^*)][h^*a(1 - \theta)\mu + d\psi^*]\}/\Delta > 0$$

$$a_3 = a^*(1 - \theta^*)[- ha(1 - \theta)\beta + d\psi]/\Delta \gtrless 0$$

$$a_4 = \gamma^*[1 + a^*\phi^*(1 - \theta^*)][ha(1 - \theta)\beta - d\psi]/\Delta \gtrless 0$$
$$\quad (a_4 < 0 \text{ if } \theta = 1)$$

$$a_5 = - \{[b/a(1 - \theta)]a_1 + [b^*/a^*(1 - \theta^*)]a_3\} + (\xi/\gamma)a_2$$
$$\quad + (\xi^*/\gamma^*)a_2^* \gtrless 0$$

$$\Delta = [1 + a\phi(1 - \theta)]\{[1 + a^*\phi^*(1 - \theta^*)](\psi^* h + \psi h^*)$$
$$\quad + ha^*(1 - \theta^*)\beta^* + d^*\psi\}$$
$$\quad + \{d^*a(1 - \theta)\beta + da^*\beta^*(1 - \theta^*)$$
$$\quad + [1 + a^*\phi^*(1 - \theta^*)]$$
$$\quad + [h^*a(1 - \theta)\beta + d\psi^*]\} > 0$$

$$h = \delta - \xi(1 - \mu), \quad\quad h^* = \delta^* - \xi^*\mu$$
$$\quad (h \text{ and } h^* \text{ assumed to be positive})$$

$$d = \mu b + a\theta(1 - \eta) > 0$$

Terms of Trade

$$d\pi = b_1 dm + b_2 dg + b_3 dm^* + b_4 dg^* + b_5 d\pi_n^w$$

$$b_1 = -a(1 - \theta)\{[1 + a^*\phi^*(1 - \theta)]\psi + a^*(1 - \theta^*)\beta^*\}/\Delta \leqslant 0$$

$$b_2 = \gamma[1 + a\phi(1 - \theta)]\{[1 + a^*\phi^*(1 - \theta)]\psi^*$$
$$+ a(1 - \theta^*)\beta^*\}/\Delta > 0$$

$$b_3 = -b_1^* \geqslant 0$$

$$b_4 = -b_2^* < 0$$

$$b_5 = -\{[b/a(1 - \theta)]b_1 + [b^*/a^*(1 - \theta^*)]b_3 + (\xi/\gamma)b_2$$
$$+ (\xi^*/\gamma^*)b_2^*\} \gtrless 0$$

Interest Rate

$$di = c_1 dm + c_2 dg + c_3 dm^* + c_4 dg^* + c_5 d\pi_n^w$$

$$c_1 = -a(1 - \theta)\{[1 + a^*\phi^*(1 - \theta^*)]h^* + d^*\}/\Delta < 0$$

$$c_2 = \gamma[1 + a\phi(1 - \theta)]\{[1 + a^*\phi^*(1 - \theta^*)]h^* + d^*\}/\Delta > 0$$

$$c_3 = c_1^* < 0$$

$$c_4 = c_2^* > 0$$

$$c_5 = -\{[b/a(1 - \theta)]c_1 + [b^*/a^*(1 - \theta^*)]c_3 + (\xi/\gamma)c_2$$
$$+ (\xi^*/\gamma^*)c_4\} \gtrless 0$$

Prices

$$dp_c = d_1 dm + d_2 dg + d_3 dm^* + d_4 dg^* + d_5 d\pi_n^w$$

$$d_1 = 1 - \phi a_1 - (1 - \eta)b_1 + \beta c_1 > 0$$

$$d_2 = -\phi a_2 - (1 - \eta)b_2 + \beta c_2 \gtrless 0$$

$$d_3 = -\phi a_3 - (1 - \eta)b_3 + \beta c_3 \gtrless 0$$
$$(d_3 < 0 \text{ if } \theta = 1)$$

$$d_4 = -\phi a_4 - (1 - \eta)b_4 + \beta c_4 \gtrless 0$$
$$(d_4 > 0 \text{ if } \theta = 1)$$

$$d_5 = -\phi a_5 - (1 - \eta)b_5 + \beta c_5 \gtrless 0$$

7 Simulation Models

THE PREVIOUS chapters have set forth a general equilibrium model of a supply shock in a two-period model. In this chapter we show how to extend the model to a multiperiod or infinite-horizon case. The purpose of this extension is more than theoretical; an empirical calibration of our model requires an accurate treatment of the timing of economic decisions. Though we can completely characterize the behavioral relations in a multiperiod context, we will no longer be able to solve the model analytically as in the earlier chapters, so the extended model is solved by means of numerical simulation.

As in the two-period setting, the multiperiod model allows for many possible assumptions with respect to output markets, dynamics, and so on. In this chapter we consider two versions of the model, first with and then without instantaneous output market clearing. In the first section we develop a one-sector, semitradable model in an infinite horizon, assuming continuous output market clearing. The problems of the firm and household are reexamined in the infinite-horizon context, and the parallels with the two-period horizon are spelled out. The rest of the model is then set forth, and some simulations are presented. In the second section we extend this model to allow for disequilibrium in the output market. In this version of the model, agents optimize based on rational anticipations of future prices and quantity constraints.

Since this chapter has methodological aims as well as substantive economic aims, it is more mathematically oriented than the other chapters. Readers not interested in the detailed derivations of the general equilibrium models may turn directly to the subsections entitled "Simulation Exercises." Appendix 7A provides a list of definitions of the variables used in the simulation models.

Various extensions to the simulation models of this chapter may be found in our previously published work: in Sachs (1983a) and Lipton and Sachs (1983) we describe two-country versions of the model; in Bruno and Sachs (1982a) we present a multisector version of the one-country, market-clearing model; in Blanchard and Sachs (1982) the disequilibrium model is treated in greater detail, but in a closed-economy context.

The Semitradable Model in an Infinite Horizon

THE INFINITE-HORIZON MODEL

In this section we extend the semitradable model of Chapter 5 to an infinite-horizon case. It is convenient to analogize to the two-period model of Chapter 4, though that model treated the case of a pure tradable good. In the two-period model, firms and consumers made various decisions in the first period based on expectations of key variables in the second period. For firms, first-period investment decisions were based on expected factor prices in the second period (as well as on the current interest rate). For households, consumption and savings decisions were based on expected future income as well as current income. In the infinite-horizon model these decisions are now based on the entire expected future paths of key variables. In the simulations we study models without uncertainty and assume that the expectations of future variables are made with perfect foresight.

Let us turn first to the firm's infinite-horizon problem. As explained earlier, the goal of a competitive firm under certainty is value maximization. In the two-period model, value V_1 can be written as

(7.1) $V_1 = [Q - W_Q L - \Pi_N N - I]_1 + \Delta^{-1}[Q - W_Q L - \Pi_N N]_2,$

where Δ^{-1} is the one-period discount factor $[\Delta = P_1(1 + i)/P_2]$, where i is the one-period nominal interest rate. (All variables used in this chapter are defined in Appendix 7A.) V_1 is then maximized subject to the constraints that $Q_t = Q[K_t, L_t, N_t]$ and $K_2 = K_1(1 - d) + I_1$.

An analogous expression for the infinite-horizon case is now presented. (The infinite-horizon analysis is conducted in continuous rather than discrete time. Corresponding discrete-time expressions are easy to derive.) The firm's value can be written as a discounted integral of future cash flow:

(7.2) $V(t_0) = \int_{t_0}^{\infty} \Delta(t_0,t)[Q(t) - W_Q(t)L(t) - \Pi_N(t)N(t) - I(t)]dt,$

where $\Delta(t_0,t) = \exp[-\int_{t_0}^{t} r(z)d(z)]$ is the discount factor. The firm maximizes

$V(t_0)$ subject to various constraints, including an accumulation equation for capital (describing $\dot{K}$ as a function of new investment expenditure and depreciation) and the production technology. In maximizing $V(t)$, we assume until the next section that the firm is never demand-constrained in the output market, or supply-constrained in the factor markets.

Before describing the firm's optimal policy, we must add one more assumption: costs of adjustment of the capital stock. We have already seen the usefulness of distinguishing a short run with capital stock fixity and a long run with capital stock flexibility. In a two-period framework it is natural to associate these phases with the first and second periods. In a continuous-time setting the same effects are achieved by positing that there are costs to a rapid change in the level of a firm's capital, so that firms have an incentive to smooth the path of capital accumulation (or decumulation) over time. One important implication of this smoothing is that anticipated *future* events will affect current investment decisions, as in the two-period case. To be specific, we denote the rate of gross capital formation as J and the rate of depreciation as d, so that $\dot{K} = J - dK$. Total investment expenditure, I, includes payments on J as well as adjustment costs. Let P_J be the nominal cost of a unit of physical capital (not including adjustment costs), and $\Pi_J (= P_J/P)$ be its real price. Following Hayashi (1983), adjustment costs per unit of J are assumed to rise as a function of J/K, so that $I = \Pi_J J + \phi(J/K)J$, where $\phi(\,\cdot\,)$ is the per-unit adjustment cost. In our model we will treat the capital good and domestic final output as identical, so that $\Pi_J = 1$. Also, we take the per-unit adjustment cost to be proportional to J/K, in particular: $\phi(J/K) = (\phi_0/2) (J/K)$, where ϕ_0 is a positive constant.

With these assumptions, the results of maximization are straightforward: for a given K, the firm should engage in short-run profit maximization, hiring L and N to the point where marginal productivities equal current factor costs. Investment should be undertaken as a function of the entire future profit stream, which depends on the entire future path of factor costs. The dependence of L and N on *current* costs, and of I on expected *future* costs, results from the assumption about costs of adjustment.

The specific conditions for optimization are easily derived. The optimal policy of the firm is the solution to:

(7.3)   max $V(t_0)$ in (7.2)

subject to:

$I = J[1 + (\phi_0/2)(J/K)]$,

$\dot{K} = J - dK$.

The first-order conditions are as follows:

(7.4)   (a) $Q_L = W_Q$,

        (b) $Q_N = \Pi_N$,

        (c) $J = [(\tau - 1)/\phi_0] \cdot K$,

        (d) $\tau = \displaystyle\int_{t_0}^{\infty} \Delta(t_0,t)[Q_K + (J/K)^2(\phi_0/2)]dt$,

        (e) $V = \tau K$,

        (f) $\dot{K} = J - dK$.

(a) and (b) define short-run factor demands. (c) is the investment equation, with J/K a rising function of Tobin's q, denoted as τ, the real equity value of a unit of the firm's capital. The value of τ may be written as in (d), as the discounted value of the marginal productivity of capital. Note that this marginal product is the sum of Q_K and $(J/K)^2(\phi_0/2)$, where the latter term is the contribution of an increment of K to a reduction in adjustment costs. (e) shows that the value of the firm is simply τK.

Let us now turn to the household's problem. As in the two-period model, we assume that farsighted households maximize an intertemporal utility function subject to a lifetime budget constraint. In the two-period model, the value of lifetime consumption is equal to household wealth A_1, according to Eq. (7.5):

(7.5) $C_1 + \Delta^{-1}C_2 = A_1$.

In turn, household wealth can be written as the sum of human wealth (H_1) and financial wealth (F_1), where human wealth is the discounted value of net-of-tax labor income, and F_1 is the sum of equity claims to capital and foreign bond holdings $(E_1 B_1^*/P_1)$:

(7.6) $H_1 = W_{Q_1}L_1 + \Delta^{-1}W_{Q_2}L_2 - T_1 - \Delta^{-1}T_2$,

(7.7) $F_1 = \tau_1 K_1 + E_1 B_1^*/P_1$.

τ_1 is the real price of an equity claim to a unit of capital. Since $\tau_1 K_1 = (Q_1 - W_{Q_1} L_1 - I_1) + \Delta^{-1}(Q_2 - W_{Q_2} L_2)$, we have $A_1 = F_1 + H_1 = (Q_1 - T_1) + \Delta^{-1}(Q_2 - T_2) + E_1 B_1^*/P_1$.

These expressions find direct analogs here. Following the Sidrauski (1967) framework, we add real balances to the household utility function in order to derive a money demand equation. "Expenditures" on real balances are then measured by the foregone interest earnings $i(M/P)$. The discounted value of total expenditure, including C and iM/P, must equal $H(t_0) + F(t_0)$, where $F(t_0)$ now includes real money balances $M(t_0)/P(t_0)$:

(7.8) $$\int_{t_0}^{\infty} \Delta(t_0,t)[C(t) + \dot{i}(t)M/P(t)]dt = H(t_0) + F(t_0).$$

Human wealth is defined as

(7.9) $$H(t_0) = \int_{t_0}^{\infty} \Delta(t_0,t)[W_Q(t)L(t) - T(t)]dt,$$

and financial wealth is

(7.10) $$F(t_0) = M/P + \tau(t_0)K(t_0) + E(t_0)B^*(t_0)/P(t_0).$$

Households maximize an additively separable intertemporal utility function subject to the wealth constraint in (7.8). Consumption expenditure is divided between purchases of home goods (C^H) and imports (C^M), with $C = C^H + C^M/\Pi$. In the continuous-time model, we write U as the discounted integral of future instantaneous utility levels $u(i)$:

(7.11) $$U(t_0) = \int_{t_0}^{\infty} \exp[-\delta(t - t_0)]u(t)dt,$$

where $u(i)$ is $u(i) = \alpha \log C^H + \beta \log C^M + (1 - \alpha - \beta) \log (M/P)$, with α, $\beta \geqslant 0$ and $\alpha + \beta \leqslant 1$.

The optimal policy of the household is the solution to

(7.12) $\quad$ max $U(t_0)$ in (7.11)

$\qquad$ subject to:

$\qquad u(i) = \alpha \log C^H + \beta \log C^M + (1 - \alpha - \beta) \log (M/P),$

$\qquad \int_{t_0}^{\infty} \Delta(t_0,t)[C(t) + i(t)M(t)/P(t)]dt = H + F.$

The first-order conditions are

(7.13) $\quad$ (a) $\quad U_{C^H} = \alpha/C^H = \lambda,$

$\qquad$ (b) $\quad U_{C^M} = \beta/C^M = (P^*E/P)\lambda,$

$\qquad$ (c) $\quad U_{M/P} = (1 - \alpha - \beta)/(M/P) = i\lambda,$

$\qquad$ (d) $\quad \dot{\lambda} = (\delta - r)\lambda.$

When we substitute these first-order conditions into the household's budget constraint, we get the final form for consumption:

(7.14)   (a) $C^H = \alpha \cdot \delta \cdot (H + F)$,

(b) $C^M = (P/EP^*) \cdot \beta \cdot \delta \cdot (H + F)$,

(c) $M/P = (1/i) \cdot (1 - \alpha - \beta) \cdot \delta \cdot (H + F)$.

The main result of the optimization is that current consumption, and hence current savings, depend (through H and F) on the entire future stream of income. With the specific utility function that we have assumed here, we find that current expenditure is linear in wealth:

(7.15) $C^H + (P^*E/P)C^M + i(M/P) = \delta \cdot A$,

where $A = H + F$ is household wealth. Also, the separate components of expenditure, C^H, C^F, and iM/P, are fixed proportions (α, β, and $[1 - \alpha - \beta]$, respectively) of total expenditure.

In specifying the labor-market behavior, we consider the three alternatives treated in earlier chapters: full labor-market clearing (with $L = L^f$), nominal wage rigidity, and real wage rigidity. The respective equations are

(7.16)   (a) $L = L^f$,

(b) $W_t = W_{t-1} + W_{t-1} \cdot \psi \cdot (L - L^f)_{t-1}$,

(c) $W_{C_t} = W_{C_{t-1}} + W_{C_{t-1}} \cdot \psi \cdot (L - L^f)_{t-1}$,

where $W_C = W/P_C$. (Note that these equations are written in discrete time, in the form in which they appear in the simulation exercises.) The consumer price index depends on home and foreign goods in the semitradable model:

(7.17) $P_C = P^{\alpha/(\alpha+\beta)} (EP^*)^{\beta/(\alpha+\beta)}$,

where α and β are the parameters in the utility function (7.16). (Note that a true price index would include i, as a measure of the price of "consuming" real money balances. We ignore this effect. As it is, M/P is separable from C^M and C^H, so (7.17) is still meaningful as a subindex of goods prices.)

To complete the infinite-horizon small-country model, we must add a few equations dealing with market clearing and the balance of payments. In all the models of this chapter we assume perfect international capital mobility, so that home and foreign assets must have the same expected rate of return. Thus, with a foreign nominal interest rate of i^*, we assume

(7.18) $i = i^* + \dot{E}/E$,

a condition that is known as "uncovered interest arbitrage." This equation is analogous to the two-period model assumption that $(1 + i) = (E_2/E_1)$ $(1 + i^*)$. The real rate of interest in terms of home goods is r, equal to $i - \dot{P}/P$.

Analogously we write $r^* = i^* - \dot{P}^*/P^*$. Since $\Pi = P/EP^*$, $\dot{\Pi}/\Pi = \dot{P}/P - \dot{E}/E - \dot{P}^*/P^*$. From (7.18) and the definitions of r and r^*, we find $r - r^* = -\dot{\Pi}/\Pi$; that is, the home and foreign real interest rates differ by the proportional change in the final goods terms of trade.

The current account equation is given as

(7.19) $CA = [Q - C^H - C^M/\Pi - I - G] + i^*EB^*/P^*.$

The term in brackets is the trade surplus, and the second right-hand side term is the service account surplus. Since the foreign bond is, by assumption, the only tradable asset, we have that the change in B^*, measured in the domestic currency, equals the current account balance:

(7.20) $E\dot{B}^*/P = CA.$

THE COMPLETE MODEL

The complete infinite-horizon semitradable model is shown in Table 7.1. Though there are twenty-eight equations (including transversality conditions) in the model, in fact the full-employment version can be considered to be a nonlinear difference equation system of only six variables: B^*, K, H, E, τ, λ. (In the rigid-wage cases, W or W_C must be added to the list, so that the system becomes seven-dimensional.) In practice, the dynamic equations are now rewritten in discrete time, by writing $\dot{x}_t$ as $x_{t+1} - x_t$ for all variables x_t. The discussion here will proceed, however, with the continuous-time version, to remain consistent with the earlier derivations.

It can be shown that once $B^*(t_0)$, $K(t_0)$, $H(t_0)$, $E(t_0)$, $\tau(t_0)$, and $\lambda(t_0)$ are known, the model delivers the values of $\dot{B}^*(t_0)$, $\dot{K}(t_0)$, $\dot{H}(t_0)$, $\dot{E}(t_0)$, $\dot{\tau}(t_0)$, and $\dot{\lambda}(t_0)$, so that the model may be integrated forward to find the values of B^*, K, H, E, τ, and λ in the future periods. Unfortunately, only the starting values of B^* and K may be taken as given (they are considered an "inheritance" of the past). Starting values of the other four variables are more difficult to find, since they are in fact equal to the discounted integrals of other variables in the model. Consider human wealth, for example. Equations (7.1.14) and (7.1.15) are *equivalent* to defining H as $\int_{t_0}^{\infty} \Delta(t_0,t)[(W/P)L - T]dt$, that is, as the discounted value of net-of-tax labor earnings (the integral form was shown in Eq. 7.9). $H(t_0)$ is known only by knowing the values of W/P, L, T for $t > t_0$. But these values are themselves functions of $H(t_0)$, so that solving the model in any period apparently requires solving the entire general equilibrium model for the infinite horizon.

Table 7.1. The Semitradable Model in the Infinite Horizon

Firm Behavior

(7.1.1) $Q = F(L, K, N)$

(7.1.2) $F_L = W/P$

(7.1.3) $F_N = P_N/P$

(7.1.4) $\dot{K} = J - dK$

(7.1.5) $J = [(\tau - 1)/\phi_0]K$

(7.1.6) $I = J[1 + (\phi_0/2)(J/K)]$

Household Behavior

(7.1.7) $U_{C^H} = \lambda$

(7.1.8) $U_{C^M} = \lambda/\Pi$

(7.1.9) $U_{M/P} = \lambda i$

(7.1.10) $\dot{\lambda} = \lambda(\delta - r)$

(7.1.11) $\lim_{t \to \infty} \Delta(t_0, t)\lambda(t) = 0$

(7.1.12) $A = EB^*/P + M/P + H + \tau K$

(7.1.13) $\lim_{t \to \infty} \Delta(t_0, t)B^*(t) = 0$

(7.1.14) $\dot{H} = rH - [(W/P)L - T]$

(7.1.15) $\lim_{t \to \infty} \Delta(t_0, t)H(t) = 0$

Asset Market Equilibrium

(7.1.16) $i = i^* + \dot{E}/E$

(7.1.17) $r = i - \dot{P}/P$

(7.1.18) $\dot{\tau} = r\tau - [Q_K + (J/K)^2(\phi_0/2)]$

(7.1.19) $\lim_{t \to \infty} \Delta(t_0, t)\tau(t) = 0$

(7.1.20) $\lim_{t \to \infty} \exp[-i^*t] \log[E(t)] = 0$

Output Market Equilibrium

(7.1.21) $\Pi = P/EP^*$

(7.1.22) $P_N = EP_N^*$

(7.1.23) $Q = C^H + I + G + C^{M*}$

Labor Market Equilibrium

(7.1.24)

  (a) $L = L^F$

  (b) $(W/P_C)_t = (W/P_C)_{t-1} + (W/P_C)_{t-1} \cdot \psi \cdot (L - L^f)_{t-1}$

  (c) $W_t = W_{t-1} + W_{t-1} \cdot \psi \cdot (L - L^f)_{t-1}$

(7.1.25) $P_C = Pq(P^*E)^{(1-\alpha)}$

Balance of Payments

(7.1.26) $CA = [Q - C^H - C^M/\Pi - I - G] + i^*EB^*/P$

(7.1.27) $E(\dot{B}^*)/P = CA$

Government Sector Budget Balance

(7.1.28) $T = G$

Certain numerical methods allow us to cut through this problem rather effectively. The method of "multiple shooting" is used here (a full description of this method can be found in Lipton et al., 1982). We take the equations in Table 7.1 *except* for the transversality conditions. Let Z be the vector of exogenous variables, Ω the vector containing E, τ, λ, and H, and Γ the vector containing K and B^* (Γ contains W or W_C, as well, in the rigid-wage cases). The system of equations implicitly can be reduced to equations of the form:

$$(7.21) \qquad \dot{\Omega} = F[\Omega, \Gamma, Z], \qquad \dot{\Gamma} = \Psi[\Omega, \Gamma, Z].$$

At any moment t_0, the values of Γ, that is, $K(t_0)$, $B^*(t_0)$, are inherited from the past. The values of Ω are not known, since they are defined by future values of Z, Γ. But if we *do* know $E(t_0)$, $\tau(t_0)$, $\lambda(t_0)$, and $H(t_0)$ at any instant, it is evident from (7.21) that the system can easily be integrated forward to find the values of E, τ, λ, and H for all later times.

The values of $E(t_0)$, $\tau(t_0)$, $\lambda(t_0)$, and $H(t_0)$ are determined as the unique values that will satisfy the transversality conditions when the system is integrated forward. These values are found by sophisticated guesswork. Trial values of E, τ, λ, and H are proposed, and (7.21) is used to integrate the system forward. Then we check whether $E(T)$, $\tau(T)$, $\lambda(T)$, and $H(T)$ satisfy the transversality conditions for very large T. For example, we determine whether $\tau(T)$ is close to $1 + \phi d$, which we know to equal $\bar{\tau}$. If not, then new guesses are tried for the starting values of the variables and the process is repeated. The iterations continue until the transversality conditions are met.

SIMULATION EXERCISES

The first set of simulations uses the semitradable model to explore the unemployment consequences of a rise in Π_N^*. We focus on the case in which the wage responds slowly to the level of unemployment, to compare the cases of nominal versus real wage rigidity. Specifically, we study the effect of a permanent doubling of Π_N^*, from 0.05 to 0.10, that begins in year 1, quarter $1(1:1)$. The four simulations are as follows: in simulation 1, we assume real wage rigidity and no policy response to the supply shock; in simulation 2, nominal wage rigidity and no policy response; in simulation 3, real wage rigidity with monetary accommodation; and in simulation 4, nominal wage rigidity with monetary accommodation. For the simulations with monetary accommodation, we assume that the monetary authorities respond to the one-shot rise in Π_N^* by a one-shot increase in the money supply of 4.8

percent. Initial values for several variables in the model are shown in Table 7.2.

The simulations are shown in Table 7.3. Simulation 1, which studies the oil shock under real wage rigidity, is the classic case of a stagflationary shock. The doubling of oil prices leads to a 12.7 percent unemployment rate upon impact and a jump of 13.0 percent in consumer prices. The high unemployment slowly reduces real wages, while the profit squeeze reduces the capital stock. In principle, unemployment the year after the shock can either rise or fall, depending on whether the employment-increasing effect of falling W_C is greater or less than the employment-reducing effect of falling K. With the specific parameters of the model, unemployment is reduced, while K falls 1.1 percent the first year after the shock. Over time, prices fall slowly, and K continues to drop to its long-run value (not shown in the table) of 3.4 percent below the initial level. Unemployment falls steadily over time as well.

In simulation 2, the same shock occurs under a structure of nominal wage rigidity. The output response is sharply reduced, because real wages are squeezed by the rise in Π_N^*. Prices jump again, but now only by 8.0 percent. In this case the falling capital stock leads to declining production in the short run, and to very slightly rising prices. While the long-run decline in K is 3.4 percent, as in simulation 1, the long-run price level and terms-of-trade effects are now different because the economy ends up with a different steady-state level of indebtedness from that of the previous simulation.

In simulation 3, the home monetary authorities expand the money supply in a one-shot increase, in the hope of reducing the unemployment conse-

Table 7.2. Parameter Values and Initial Conditions in the Simulation Model

Factor Shares in Gross Output	*Production Technology*
$s_K = 0.239$	$Q = F[V(K,L),N]$
$s_L = 0.713$	$\sigma = 0 (V \text{ and } N \text{ in } Q)$
$s_N = 0.048$	$\sigma_1 = 1.0 (K \text{ and } L \text{ in } V)$
Expenditure Shares in GNP	*Parameters*
$(\text{GNP} = P_V V + i^* E B^*)$	$\delta = 0.112$ (annual rate)
$PC/\text{GNP} = 0.885$	$i^* = 0.112$ (annual rate)
$PI/\text{GNP}_Y = 0.115$	$\phi_0 = 2$ (annual rate)
$i^* E B^*/\text{GNP} = 0.002$	
$P_N N/\text{GNP} = 0.024$	
$iM/\text{GNP} = 0.029 (M/\text{GNP} = 1.074)$	

Table 7.3. Oil Price Increase in the Semitradable Model (percentage deviations from base case)

Simulation	Year and quarter							
	1:1	1:2	1:3	1:4	2:1	3:1	4:1	5:1
1. Real wage rigidity								
Q	−9.8	−8.6	−7.6	−6.7	−5.9	−3.8	−2.5	−1.7
L	−12.7	−10.9	−9.3	−8.0	−6.8	−3.5	−1.7	−0.7
P_C	13.0	12.7	12.4	12.1	11.9	11.2	10.8	10.5
K	0.0	−1.1	−1.9	−2.6	−3.2	−4.5	−4.9	−4.9
2. Nominal wage rigidity								
Q	−0.1	−0.2	−0.2	−0.3	−0.4	−0.5	−0.6	−0.7
L	−0.1	−0.1	−0.1	−0.1	−0.1	−0.1	−0.1	0.0
P_C	8.0	8.1	8.2	8.3	8.4	8.6	8.8	9.0
K	0.0	−0.3	−0.6	−0.8	−1.0	−1.8	−2.3	−2.6
3. Real wage rigidity with money supply increase								
Q	−9.8	−8.6	−7.6	−6.7	−5.9	−3.8	−2.5	−1.7
L	−12.7	−10.9	−9.3	−8.0	−6.8	−3.5	−1.7	−0.7
P_C	18.4	18.1	17.8	17.5	17.3	16.5	16.1	15.8
K	0.0	−1.1	−1.9	−2.6	−3.2	−4.5	−4.9	−4.9
4. Nominal wage rigidity with money supply increase								
Q	3.6	3.1	2.7	2.3	2.0	1.0	0.3	−0.1
L	4.9	4.2	3.6	3.1	2.7	1.5	0.8	0.4
P_C	11.3	11.5	11.7	11.9	12.0	12.6	13.0	13.4
K	0.0	0.0	0.0	−0.1	−0.2	−0.6	−1.1	−1.6

quences of higher Π_N^*. With the output market clearing and wages fully indexed, the result is simply to raise the price level relative to simulation 1 by the exact proportion of the money stock increase. The real economy is unaffected by the money stock increase.

In simulation 4, the same money stock increase raises output under the conditions of nominal wage rigidity. Prices rise initially (relative to simulation 4) by less than the increase in M. Unemployment is more than eliminated, with L now 4.9 percent above L^f. Of course, the money supply increase forestalls but does not prevent the long-run decline in K and W/P_C caused by higher Π_N. K once again falls 3.4 percent in the steady state, though capital decumulation now is not perceptible until four quarters after the shock.

The One-Country Disequilibrium Model

In this section we take a key step toward realism: we abandon the assumption of continuous output market clearing. The semitradable model of the previous section is altered by assuming that domestic prices move too slowly to guarantee $Q^D = Q^S$. In place of the market-clearing assumption we specify that price change is a function of the gap between Q^D and Q^S. In Chapter 5 we observed some of the effects of this change in a static model; the shift to the multiperiod case is a tricky and somewhat subtle extension.

We start with the following important assumptions. We assume that firms can always hire the desired level of labor at the market wage, even when that demand, L^D, exceeds the full-employment level of labor input L^f (implicitly workers are willing, in the short run, to supply the desired overtime). This assumption is made to simplify the discussion of the model and could be removed in a straightforward way. The domestic market for gross output is the only market for which demand may exceed supply (in the labor market supply may exceed demand, but not vice versa). The foreign final good and the imported intermediate input can be purchased in desired quantities, at the going world prices P^* and P_N^*. The asset markets are assumed to clear continuously, so that interest arbitrage holds, and money demand equals money supply at all times.

Without specifying, as yet, how demands are formed, we set $Q^D = C^{HD} + G^D + I^D + X^D$. Desired supply Q^S will be the same as before: a decreasing function of W_Q and Π_N (or W/P_V) and a linear function of K. Actual output is assumed to be determined as

$$Q = \min(Q^D, Q^S),$$

which is the standard "short-side" rule in disequilibrium models. In fact this is not an innocent assumption; the empirical evidence of Chapter 10 suggests that configurations such as $Q^D > Q > Q^S$ are evident in the data. Following standard terminology, as used in Chapter 5, we term $Q^D < Q^S$ the Keynesian regime, and $Q^D > Q^S$ the classical regime. Actual levels of C^H, G, I, and X are then determined according to a *rationing* rule, which maps C^{HD}, G^D, I^D, and X^D into a vector C^H, G, I, X such that $Q = C^H + G + I + X$. We adopt a simple linear rationing rule, so that

(7.22)   (a) $C^H = C^{HD} - \alpha_C(Q^D - Q) = C^{HR}$,

           (b) $G = G^D - \alpha_G(Q^D - Q) = G^R$,

           (c) $I = I^D - \alpha_I(Q^D - Q) = I^R$,

           (d) $X = X^D - \alpha_X(Q^D - Q) = X^R$,

where $\alpha_C + \alpha_G + \alpha_I + \alpha_X = 1$, and α_C, α_G, α_I, $\alpha_X > 0$.

The quantities C^{HR}, G^R, I^R, X^R are the ration levels as perceived by the economic agents (we must assume that the ration rules operate at the level of the household). Households optimize, for example, with the knowledge that $C^H(t)$ must be less than $C^{HR}(t)$ in each period. Although C^{HD} actually helps to determine C^{HR}, we assume that individual households treat the constraint $C^H \leq C^{HR}$ as a *datum that cannot be changed* by announcing a high level of C^{HD}. In the technical jargon of disequilibrium models, we assume that agents do not "manipulate" the ration constraints that they face.

We will, by analogy, define rationing for firms according to $Q^R = \min(Q^D, Q^S)$, with firms optimizing subject to the perceived constraint that sales must be less than or equal to Q^R; that is, firms maximize value subject to $Q^S \leq Q^R$. Note that in (7.22), when $Q^S > Q^D$ (so that $Q = Q^D$), we have $C^H = C^{HD} = C^{HR}$, $G = G^D = G^R$, $I = I^D = I^R$, and $X = X^D = X^R$; that is, when supply exceeds demand, all demands are satisfied. Similarly, when $Q^S < Q^D$, then $Q^S = Q = Q^R$, and the firms sell all that they desire.

The concept of demand in this model is somewhat subtle. Agents can only expend up to their ration limits. What, then, is the meaning of "demands" in excess of the ration limits, demands that agents know cannot be satisfied? We define current demand as the optimal level of current expenditure for an agent (household or firm), taking into account all *future* (expected) prices and rationing constraints facing the agent but ignoring *current* rationing in the output market. It is the level of current expenditure that the agent would choose, given all future prices and quantity constraints, if there were no limit on current expenditure. To put it differently, C^{HD} and I^D are the lowest levels of today's ration constraint, C^{HR} and I^R, such that the constraints are not binding.

THE DYNAMIC EQUATIONS

Let us now describe the firm and household problems in greater detail.

Firm Behavior. In the first section of this chapter we modeled the firm as maximizing firm value subject to technology, factor prices, and the accumulation relation $\dot{K} = J - dK$. We now add two more constraints to the firm's problem: the firm can sell no more than Q_t^R in any period t, and it can invest no more than I_t^R in any period. Firms anticipate all sales constraints in the future. Formally, the decision problem is to choose the paths $\{J(t)\}$, $\{L(t)\}$, $\{N(t)\}$ to maximize

$$(7.23) \qquad V = \int_{t_0}^{\infty} \Delta(t_0,t)[Q(t) - W_Q(t)L(t) - \Pi_N(t)N(t) - I(t)]dt$$

such that

    (a) $Q(t) = F[K(t), L(t), N(t), t]$,

    (b) $\dot{K}(t) = J(t) - dK(t)$,

    (c) $I(t) = J(t) \cdot [1 + (\phi_0/2)(J/K)]$,

    (d) $Q(t) \leq Q^R(t)$,

    (e) $I(t) \leq I^R(t)$.

To find the optimal policy, it is useful to introduce the variable-cost function $VC(K, Q, W_Q, \Pi_N) = \min \{W_Q L + \Pi_N N \text{ such that } Q = F(K,L,N)\}$. We can also write the variable-cost-minimizing factor demands $L(K, Q, W_Q, \Pi_N)$ and $N(K, Q, W_Q, \Pi_N)$ which are the solution to the cost-minimization problem. Then we can write the optimal policy as

(7.24) (a) $Q = \min (Q^S, Q^R)$,

    (b) $I = \min (I^D, I^R)$,

    (c) $I^D = J^D[1 + (\phi_0/2)(J^D/K)]$,

    (d) $J^D = [(\tau - 1)/\phi_0] \cdot K$,

    (e) J such that $I = J[1 + \phi(J/K)]$,

    (f) $L = L(K, Q, W_Q, \Pi_N)$; $N = N(K, Q, W_Q, \Pi_N)$,

    (g) $\dot{\tau} = (r + d)\tau - \partial[VC(W_Q, \Pi_N, Q, K)]/\partial K - (J/K)^2(\phi_0/2)$.

The solution to this problem can now be related to the one derived earlier. According to the solution, the firm's preferred short-run supply Q^S is the same as before, a function of factor prices and K. The firm then produces the minimum of Q^S and Q^R. Similarly, the firm selects the preferred level of investment I^D, and then invests the minimum of I^D and I^R. Once actual output is determined as min (Q^S, Q^R), the firm optimizes by selecting L and N to produce Q at minimum cost. Finally, the *shadow* price of capital τ evolves according to (7.24)(g). One can then show that the shadow price of capital no longer necessarily equals the market price of an equity claim to capital. (Formally, Tobin's "marginal q"—the shadow price of capital— need not equal "average q"—the market price of capital.)

Household Behavior. Once again the household maximizes intertemporal utility, but subject to the constraint that the household may be rationed in the domestic commodity market. The maximizing household may be thought of as following a two-step procedure. First it finds C^{HD}, the desired level of C^H assuming no current rationing in that market. Then consumers choose $C^H = \min (C^{HD}, C^{HR})$. Remember that the household is never constrained in the market for Q^* (that is, C^M is never rationed). Formally, the household's problem is

$$(7.25) \qquad \max U = \int_{t_0}^{\infty} \exp[-\delta(t - t_0)][\alpha \log (C^H) + \beta \log C^M$$

$$+ (1 - \alpha - \beta) \log (M/P)]dt$$

$$\text{such that} \quad \int_{t_0}^{\infty} \Delta(t_0, t)[C^H + C^M/\Pi + iM/P]dt = A$$

and

$$C^H(t) \leqslant C^{HR}(t), \qquad t \geqslant t_0.$$

With λ equal to the marginal utility of wealth (that is, $dU(t)/dA(t) = \lambda(t)$), we find the following two-step solution to this problem. In the first stage, households equate the marginal utility of *desired* consumption of C^H, C^M, and M/P to the marginal utility of wealth multiplied by the respective output price:

$(7.26) \qquad$ (a) $\quad U_1[C^{HD}, C^{MD}, (M/P)^D] = \lambda,$

$\qquad\qquad$ (b) $\quad U_2[C^{HD}, C^{MD}, (M/P)^D] = \lambda/\Pi,$

$\qquad\qquad$ (c) $\quad U_3[C^{HD}, C^{MD}, (M/P)^D] = i\lambda.$

This set of equations yields C^{HD}, which is used in the next step, as well as C^{MD} and $(M/P)^D$, which are not. In the next step, households set actual levels of C^H, C^M, and M/P:

$(7.27) \qquad$ (a) $\quad U_2[C^H, C^M, (M/P)] = \lambda/\Pi,$

$\qquad\qquad$ (b) $\quad U_3[C^H, C^M, (M/P)] = i\lambda,$

$\qquad\qquad$ (c) $\quad C^H = \min (C^{HD}, C^{HR}).$

Finally, λ changes according to the gap of δ and r:

(7.28) $\dot{\lambda} = \lambda(\delta - r)$.

Foreign Demand. As before, we assume that foreign demand is a function of foreign wealth A^* (a constant) and Π,

(7.29) $X^D = \beta\delta A^*/\Pi$.

Actual exports abroad, however, may be rationed when total demand Q^D exceeds aggregate supply Q^S. Specifically,

(7.30) $X = \min(X^D, X^R)$.

Pricing Behavior. Wages and prices are assumed to respond sluggishly to excess demand, according to Phillips-curve relationships. The value-added deflator is determined according to

(7.31) $P_{V_t} = P_{V_{t-1}} + P_{V_{t-1}} \cdot \phi \cdot (V^D - V^S)$.

The output price is given as

(7.32) $P = P_V + P_N$.

(Remember that the assumption that $Q = \min(V,N)$ justifies the additive pricing rule.) Thus, we allow the intermediate input costs to be passed through to final goods prices immediately. The wage equations are set as in (7.16)(b) or (7.16)(c) to allow for nominal or real wage rigidity.

The Complete Model. The entire disequilibrium model is presented in Table 7.4. In the case with slow real wage adjustment, given levels of P, W_C, K, B^*, E, λ, τ we can solve for $\dot{P}$, $\dot{W}_C$, $\dot{K}$, $\dot{B}^*$, $\dot{E}$, $\dot{\lambda}$, $\dot{\tau}$ as well as contemporaneous values of other variables (in the nominal-wage case, W replaces W_C). The system is thus implicitly a seven-dimensional system of nonlinear equations in P, W_C, K, B^*, E, λ, and τ. At any moment, four of the variables (P, W_C, K, B^*) are predetermined from past history, while three (E,λ,τ) must be determined by transversality conditions, that is, the initial values of E, λ, and τ are given as those values such that the transversality conditions are satisfied. As before, multiple shooting is the solution technique employed to find the initial values of E, λ, and τ.

SIMULATION EXERCISES

The four simulations are the same with this model as those studied in cases 1–4: a permanent rise in Π_N^* occurs under rigid real wages (simulations 5 and 7) and under rigid nominal wages (simulations 6 and 8). In simulations 5 and

Table 7.4. The Disequilibrium Model

Firm Behavior

(7.4.1) $W_Q = F_L(L^D, N^D, K)$

(7.4.2) $\Pi_N = F_N(L^D, N^D, K)$

(7.4.3) $Q^S = F(L^D, N^D, K)$

(7.4.4) $Q = \min(Q^S, Q^R)$

(7.4.5) $I^d = J^d[1 + (\phi_0/2)(J^d/K)]$

(7.4.6) $J^d = K \cdot (\tau - 1)/\phi_0$

(7.4.7) $I = \min(I^d, I^R)$

(7.4.8) $I = J[1 + (\phi_0/2)(J/K)]$

(7.4.9) $\dot{K} = J - dK$

(7.4.10) $L = L(Q,K; \Pi_N, W_Q)$

(7.4.11) $N = N(Q,K; \Pi_N, W_Q)$

(7.4.12) $\tau = (r+d)\tau - \partial[VC(W_Q, \Pi_N, Q, K)]/\partial K$
$\qquad + (J/K)^2(\phi_0/2)$

Household Behavior

(7.4.13) $U_1[C^{HD}, C^{MD}, (M/P)^D] = \lambda$

(7.4.14) $U_2[C^{HD}, C^{MD}, (M/P)^D] = \lambda/\pi$

(7.4.15) $U_3[C^{HD}, C^{MD}, (M/P)^D] = i\lambda$

(7.4.16) $C^H = \min(C^{HD}, C^R)$

(7.4.17) $U_2[C^H, C^{MD}, (M/P)^D] = \lambda/\pi$

(7.4.18) $U_3[C^H, C^{MD}, (M/P)^D] = i\lambda$

(7.4.19) $\dot{\lambda} = \lambda(\delta - r)$

Foreign Demand

(7.4.20) $X^D = \beta\delta A^*/\pi$

(7.4.21) $X = \min(X^D, X^R)$

Market Equilibrium

(7.4.22) $Q^D = I^D + C^{HD} + X^D + G^D$

(7.4.23) $C^{HR} = C^{HD} - \alpha_C(Q^D - Q)$

(7.4.24) $G^R = G^D - \alpha_G(Q^D - Q)$

(7.4.25) $I^R = I^D - \alpha_I(Q^D - Q)$

(7.4.26) $X^R = X^D - \alpha_X(Q^D - Q)$

Price and Wage Formation

(7.4.27) $P = P_V + P_N$

(7.4.28) $P_N = EP_N^*$

(7.4.29) $P_{Vt} = P_{Vt-1} + P_{Vt-1} \cdot \phi \cdot (V^D - V^S)_{t-1}$

(7.4.30)

(a) $W_{C_t} = W_{C_{t-1}} + W_{C_{t-1}} \cdot \psi \cdot (L - L^f)_{t-1}$

(b) $W_t = W_{t-1} + W_{t-1} \cdot \psi \cdot (L - L^f)_{t-1}$

Asset Market Equilibrium

(7.4.31) $\dot{E}/E = i - i^*$

(7.4.32) $CA = [Q - C^H - C^M/\Pi - I - G] + EB^*i^*/P$

(7.4.33) $E\dot{B}^*/P = CA$

Transversality Conditions

(7.4.34) $\lim_{t\to\infty} \Delta(t_0, t)\lambda(t) = 0$

(7.4.35) $\lim_{t\to\infty} \Delta(t_0, t)\tau(t) = 0$

6 there is no policy response, while in the latter cases there is a one-shot 4.8 percent increase in M at the time of the rise in Π_N^*. The results are shown in Table 7.5.

The first finding from simulations 5 and 6 is that the supply shock leads to classical unemployment ($Q^D > Q^S$) with real wage rigidity, and Keynesian unemployment ($Q^D < Q^S$) with nominal wage rigidity. As noted earlier, we specify that P_V is predetermined at the time of the shock and that P is flexible, with $P = P_V + P_N$. Given real wage rigidity, W/P_C is predetermined, which means that W/P_V tends to rise when Π_N increases, thus decreasing Q^S. With nominal wage rigidity, W is predetermined, which means that W/P_V is also unaffected in the period of the shock. Since W/P_V does not change, neither does aggregate supply, which is a function of W/P_V and K.

Thus with nominal wage rigidity, $Q^S = 0$ in the first period, while Q^D falls slightly. The result (in simulation 6) is slight unemployment, of 1.0 percent. With real wage rigidity, Q^S falls by 11.8 percent, and unemployment jumps to 14.4 percent (in simulation 5). In both cases we get a jump in the price level, which is a combination of the direct effects of higher P_N and the indirect effects of an exchange rate depreciation that occurs at the time of the supply shock. In simulation 5 there is excess demand in the first period, so that prices continue to rise in the midst of high unemployment. Thus, we find stagflation *par excellence.* In the nominal wage case, there is excess supply in the first quarter, so that P_V starts to fall (though very slightly) and the consumer price level falls by a very small amount. In both simulations 5 and 6, the capital stock begins to decline at the time of the shock.

One interesting feature of the model is that the economy crosses regimes in the process of adjustment. In the real wage case, the rise of prices over time raises Q^S and reduces Q^D, until in the first quarter of year 4 the economy enters Keynesian unemployment. In simulation 6 the slight fall in P_V, coupled with capital decumulation, quickly reduces Q^S below Q^D, so that the economy enters classical unemployment in the third quarter (at which point prices start to rise again). Under the perfect foresight assumption of the model, agents' plans from the beginning are based on the knowledge of the path of regimes over the entire adjustment horizon.

In simulation 7, the real-wage-rigid economy is subjected to a one-time monetary expansion on top of the supply shock. Unlike the case of real wage rigidity with output market clearing (simulation 3), the economy is no longer neutral with respect to M, because P_V is predetermined in the short run. As expected, higher M raises aggregate demand, but it perversely *reduces* aggregate supply. Since $Q = \min (Q^D, Q^S)$, the net effect is to reduce output! This surprising result is easy to explain. P_V is fixed, but W is flexible, since it is tied

Table 7.5. Oil Price Increase in the Disequilibrium Model

Simulation	1:1	1:2	1:3	1:4	2:1	3:1	4:1	5:1
				Year and quarter				
5. Real wage rigidity								
Q^D	0.6	0.1	−0.4	−0.9	−1.3	−2.7	−3.6	−3.6
Q^S	−11.8	−10.7	−9.7	−8.9	−8.1	−5.4	−3.3	−1.7
P^C	8.1	8.6	9.2	9.6	10.0	11.0	11.3	11.1
L	−14.4	−12.6	−10.9	−9.5	−8.2	−4.0	−1.7	−1.6
6. Nominal wage rigidity								
Q^D	−0.7	−0.5	−0.3	−0.2	−0.1	0.0	−0.1	−0.3
Q^S	0.0	−0.2	−0.4	−0.6	−0.8	−1.1	−1.2	−1.2
P^C	7.9	7.8	7.8	7.8	7.9	8.0	8.2	8.4
L	−1.0	−0.5	−0.4	−0.5	−0.6	−0.7	−0.6	−0.4
7. Real wage rigidity with money supply increase								
Q^D	11.4	9.5	7.8	6.3	4.9	0.5	−2.4	−4.0
Q^S	−13.7	−12.7	−11.9	−11.1	−10.4	−7.6	−4.9	−2.5
P^C	9.4	10.6	11.6	12.6	13.5	16.0	17.2	17.3
L	−16.7	−14.9	−13.2	−11.7	−10.2	−5.3	−1.4	−0.8
8. Nominal wage rigidity with money supply increase								
Q^D	8.6	8.0	7.3	6.7	6.1	4.0	2.4	1.2
Q^S	0.0	−0.1	−0.2	−0.3	−0.3	−0.5	−0.6	−0.6
P^C	9.1	9.5	9.9	10.2	10.6	11.7	12.3	13.0
L	0.0	0.0	−0.1	−0.1	0.0	0.0	0.2	0.4

to P_C. The monetary expansion depreciates the currency, raises P_C, and thereby raises W. Thus W/P_V increases, and V^S and Q^S fall. We could easily show that with real wage rigidity and $V^S < V^D$, a monetary *contraction* rather than expansion would raise domestic output. Note that the rise in M also substantially worsens the price situation by widening the gap $V^D - V^S$, raising P_C in the first quarter and inflation in later periods.

In simulation 8, the same monetary expansion is shown to have more desirable results in the nominal wage case. Again Q^D is increased, but Q^S is not affected in the first quarter since W/P_V is fixed. Because the economy was in a situation of excess supply ($Q^S > Q^D$), the rise in Q^D now raises output and reduces unemployment, though at the expense of high prices and slightly higher inflation. Note that the monetary expansion is effective only insofar as $Q^D < Q^S$. Once M is high enough so that $Q^D = Q^S$, further increases in M will have price effects but no output effects.

Appendix 7A: Notation Used in This Chapter

VARIABLES

A	Household wealth	P_C	Consumer price index
B	Bonds	P_N	Price of intermediate input
C	Consumption	P_V	Value added deflator
CA	Current account	Q	Gross output
C^H	Consumption of home goods	r	Real rate of interest
C^M	Consumption of foreign goods	R	Steady-state value of Q_K
		s_k	Share of K in total costs
D	Foreign debt	s_l	Share of L in total costs
E	Exchange rate	s_n	Share of N in total costs
F	Financial wealth	T	Taxes
G	Government consumption expenditure	τ	Tobin's q
		u	Instantaneous utility
H	Human wealth	U	Intertemporal utility
I	Total investment expenditure	V	Value added, gross domestic product
i	Nominal interest rate		
J	Gross fixed capital formation	W	Nominal wage
K	Capital stock	W_V	W/P_V
L	Labor input	W_Q	W/P
M	Money stock	Y	National income
N	Intermediate input	Π	P/EP^*
P	Price of gross output	Π_N	P_N/P

PARAMETERS

α	Household expenditure share on home goods
β	Household expenditure share on foreign goods
d	Rate of geometric depreciation of K
δ	Rate of time preference
Δ	Discount factor in two-period model
$\Delta(t_0, t)$	Discount factor in continuous-time model
ρ	$\log(Q_K)$
σ	Elasticity of substitution between N and V in Q function
σ_1	Elasticity of substitution between L and K in V function
ϕ	Cost-of-adjustment parameter in investment function

OTHER

Superscripts and subscripts

D	Demand
H	Home good
M	Foreign good
R	Ration limit
S	Supply
*	Foreign country variable

For all X:

$\overline{X}$	Steady-state value of X
$\dot{X}$	dX/dt (time rate of change)

8 Empirical Overview of Stagflation in the OECD

THE WESTERN industrialized economies have experienced more than a decade of unsatisfactory macroeconomic performance. We noted in the Introduction that almost every economy in the OECD has suffered from unemployment rates at levels not seen since the early postwar period, and many economies have continued to suffer from high levels of inflation. In spite of high unemployment and low growth, most governments have abjured expansionary policies out of the widespread conviction that such policies are ineffective and serve only to intensify inflation. In the next five chapters we analyze these macroeconomic developments in terms of the theoretical framework of the first part of this book. This chapter sets out the key ingredients of our diagnosis: the role of real wages and supply shocks in the simultaneous worsening of employment and inflation in the 1970s; the interaction of supply shocks and demand management in the deep world-wide recessions of 1974–75 and 1980–82; and the role of excess capacity in the worldwide productivity slowdown after 1973.

The most striking fact concerning the recent stagflation is its pervasiveness. As shown in Table 8.1, *all* twenty-four countries in the OECD suffered a slowdown in aggregate growth after 1973, the watershed year. Twenty-three of the countries (all but Switzerland) experienced higher inflation on average after 1973, although many countries have restored low inflation rates in the recent past (Table 8.2). The data also show the synchronization in aggregate output and price movements within the decade: deep recession and sharp inflation, 1973–75; partial recovery and moderating inflation, 1975–79; renewed recession and generally higher inflation, 1979–81.

The growth slowdown reflects two phenomena: a dramatic decline in resource utilization after 1973, as well as a sharp decline in productivity growth. The rise in unemployment, shown in Table 8.3, is the most direct

Table 8.1. GNP Growth Rates, 1960–1981 (in percentages)

Country	Major periods		Subperiods			
	1960–1973	1973–1981	1971–1973	1973–1975	1975–1979	1979–1981
Australia	5.1	2.7	4.5	1.9	2.6	3.7
Austria	4.9	2.6	5.6	1.8	3.6	1.6
Belgium	5.1	1.9	5.7	1.3	2.9	0.7
Canada	5.6	2.8	6.8	2.4	3.6	1.5
Denmark	4.5	1.4	4.6	−0.9	3.3	−0.2
Finland	5.2	2.5	6.9	1.9	2.6	3.0
France	5.6	2.6	5.6	1.7	3.9	1.0
Germany	4.5	2.0	4.3	−0.7	4.0	0.7
Greece	7.7	2.9	8.1	1.1	5.1	0.6
Iceland	5.6	2.7	6.7	0.7	4.0	2.0
Ireland	4.1	3.5	5.6	3.1	4.5	1.7
Italy	5.2	2.4	5.1	0.2	3.8	1.9
Japan	10.4	3.6	8.9	0.6	5.3	3.4
Luxembourg	4.4	0.9	8.5	−1.3	2.8	−0.7
Netherlands	5.0	1.7	4.8	0.8	3.1	−0.2
New Zealand	4.0	1.2	5.8	2.9	0.2	1.5
Norway	4.7	4.2	4.7	4.7	4.9	2.6
Portugal	6.8	3.0	9.6	−1.6	5.0	3.6
Spain	7.4	2.2	8.0	3.4	2.4	0.8
Sweden	4.2	1.5	3.0	3.3	1.1	0.6
Switzerland	4.5	0.6	3.2	−3.1	1.4	2.9
Turkey	6.3	4.1	6.4	7.7	3.5	1.6
United Kingdom	3.1	0.5	4.7	−0.8	2.4	−2.0
United States	4.2	2.3	5.7	−0.8	4.7	0.9
Total OECD	5.0	2.4	5.7	0.3	4.0	1.2

Source: International Financial Statistics, IMF.

indication of low resource utilization. Note that the European unemployment rate has risen monotonically since 1973, while the U.S. unemployment rate rose during 1974–75, fell in the next four years, and then rose again after 1979. The productivity slowdown during 1973–79 is shown in Table 8.4. Every economy experienced a slowdown in labor productivity growth, comparing 1973–79 with 1960–73, and all but three experienced a second decrease in 1979–81.

The sharp jumps in unemployment rates throughout the OECD during

Table 8.2. Inflation Rates, 1960–1981 (in percentages)

Country	Major periods		Subperiods			
	1960–1973	1973–1981	1971–1973	1973–1975	1975–1979	1979–1981
Australia	4.3	11.5	10.0	16.5	9.9	9.8
Austria	4.6	5.8	7.8	8.0	5.1	5.1
Belgium	3.9	7.1	6.6	12.5	5.8	4.7
Canada	3.6	10.0	7.1	13.0	8.3	10.3
Denmark	6.9	9.9	9.7	12.8	8.9	9.0
Finland	6.5	12.0	11.4	18.6	9.5	10.5
France	4.9	10.8	7.0	12.3	9.6	11.5
Germany	4.2	4.7	5.8	6.8	3.6	4.6
Greece	4.5	16.4	12.0	16.4	14.9	19.2
Iceland	14.3	42.4	24.3	40.2	39.2	51.4
Ireland	7.5	14.3	14.4	13.9	13.8	15.7
Italy	5.5	17.6	8.9	18.0	16.7	19.3
Japan	5.5	7.9	8.5	14.0	4.7	3.1
Luxembourg	4.1	6.9	7.7	7.9	6.5	6.5
Netherlands	5.9	7.5	8.9	10.2	7.4	5.2
New Zealand	5.6	14.1	9.1	9.0	15.9	15.6
Norway	4.2	9.8	7.0	10.2	7.1	14.7
Portugal	3.9	19.1	8.6	17.5	21.4	16.2
Spain	7.8	16.9	10.3	16.6	18.7	13.5
Sweden	4.9	10.6	7.3	11.6	10.0	10.8
Switzerland	5.4	3.9	8.9	7.0	2.0	4.7
Turkey	8.8	40.8	19.2	22.1	32.5	70.2
United Kingdom	5.2	15.8	7.8	20.8	13.6	15.2
United States	3.4	7.9	4.9	9.0	6.7	9.1
Total OECD	4.4	9.7	6.7	11.5	8.4	10.3

Source: International Financial Statistics, GNP/GDP deflators, for 1960–1980. 1981 is from OECD Economic Outlook, July 1982.

1973–75 and 1979–82 are cyclical phenomena, closely linked to supply shocks and monetary policy. But the steady climb in European unemployment rates, even during 1975–79, reveals a deeper trend at work. The level of unemployment that seems to be consistent with nonaccelerating inflation (termed NAIRU, for non-accelerating-inflation rate of unemployment) has risen sharply.

In the first section of this chapter we review the major supply and demand

Table 8.3.   Unemployment Rates, 1960–1981 (in percentages)

Country	1965–1973	1974–1981	1974–1975	1976–1979	1980–1981	1982:I
Australia	1.9	5.2	3.7	5.7	5.9	6.2
Austria	1.6	1.9	1.6	1.9	2.2	3.4
Belgium	2.4	7.3	4.1	7.7	10.0	12.3
Canada	4.8	7.3	6.1	7.7	7.5	8.6
Finland	2.4	4.7	2.0	5.9	5.0	5.9
France	2.3	5.1	3.5	5.1	7.0	8.2
Germany	0.8	3.4	2.7	3.5	3.7	5.5
Italy	5.6	6.9	5.6	7.1	7.9	9.1
Japan	1.2	2.0	1.7	2.1	2.1	2.2
Netherlands	1.3	4.5	3.4	4.2	6.2	8.9
Norway	1.7	1.9	1.8	1.9	2.0	2.0
Sweden	2.0	2.0	1.8	1.9	2.3	3.0
United Kingdom	3.2	6.1	3.4	5.9	9.4	12.4
United States	4.5	6.9	7.1	6.7	7.4	8.6
EEC[a]	2.9[b]	5.4	4.3	5.9	7.0	9.0

Source: OECD Economic Outlook, July 1982.
a. Germany, France, United Kingdom, Italy, Belgium, Netherlands.
b. 1966–1973.

factors that affected GNP, unemployment, and prices in the post-1973 decade. In the second section we demonstrate the importance of various supply shocks for the stagflation process. We describe the nature of the supply shocks in some detail and present econometric evidence of their importance in the 1970s. Finally, in the last section we discuss the productivity slowdown from a comparative perspective and investigate the question of whether the slowdown is an exogenous phenomenon or a by-product of the stagflation itself. All of these issues are taken up again in greater detail in later chapters.

Supply and Demand Factors in the Stagflation

The great challenge of macroeconomics is to explain the pattern in Figure I.1 at the beginning of the book, where we graphed the annual OECD inflation rate versus OECD unemployment. There are really two types of puzzles in that figure. First, how can one account for periods such as 1973–74 and

Table 8.4. Labor Productivity Growth, 1960–81 (in percentages)

Country	1960–1973	1973–1975	1975–1979	1979–1981
Australia	2.5	1.1	2.0	0.4
Austria	5.0	1.6	3.1	1.5
Belgium	4.1	1.3	2.9	1.7
Canada	5.4	−0.6	0.1	−0.5
Denmark	3.1	0.4	0.5	1.1
Finland	4.7	0.6	3.5	1.2
France	4.9	1.9	3.4	1.0
Germany	4.3	1.7	3.7	0.9
Greece	8.1	−1.1	4.1	−2.7
Iceland	3.3	−0.7	2.6	0.3
Ireland	4.5	2.4	2.6	1.7
Italy	5.5	−1.0	3.0	1.0
Japan	8.4	1.0	3.9	2.8
Luxembourg	NA	−3.2	2.6	−0.7
Netherlands	4.2	1.7	2.2	−1.2
New Zealand	1.7	1.5	−1.3	1.9
Norway	NA	3.1	2.6	0.8
Portugal	6.5	—	5.0	0.7
Spain	6.4	4.0	3.8	4.3
Sweden	3.5	0.9	0.5	0.1
Switzerland	3.1	−0.1	1.4	1.7
Turkey	4.8	7.7	2.7	1.4
United Kingdom	2.8	−0.8	2.5	0.8
United States	2.1	−1.1	0.8	0.2
Total OECD	3.9	0.1	2.4	1.0

Source: Annual percentage change in GDP per person employed, from OECD Historical Statistics of the Main Economic Indicators, 1960–1981.

1979–80, when both prices and unemployment are increasing sharply? And — what is less obvious, but perhaps more puzzling and important — why does it seem that ever-increasing rates of unemployment are needed merely to stabilize the inflation rate? (That is, why is the NAIRU increasing?) We propose that supply factors can help to resolve both of these issues.

DEMAND FACTORS

The cyclical swings and persistent stagflation reflect a complex interaction of demand and supply factors. On the demand side, the boom of 1971–73, recession of 1973–75, recovery of 1978–79, and recession of 1979–81 seem to be closely linked to fluctuations in the rate of growth of the world's major currencies. These shifts, in turn, are well explained by shifts in U.S. monetary policy (see McKinnon, 1982, for an exposition of the importance of global swings in monetary growth).[1]

Table 8.5 reports the annual money stock growth rates for the largest OECD economies during various subperiods to emphasize further the important role played by monetary policy in this period. One can see clear worldwide cycles in money growth in the table. During 1970–72, both nominal and real money growth increased dramatically in all of the large economies. This is the period of the Bretton Woods breakdown, when rapid U.S. money growth coupled with speculation against the dollar led to an

Table 8.5. Money Stock Growth, Nominal and Real, Selected Periods (annual percentage rates of change)

Country	1960–1970	1970–1972	1972–1974	1974–1979	1979–1981
Canada					
Nominal	5.9	12.7	5.1	7.1	8.2
Real	3.2	8.5	−3.8	−1.1	−2.7
France					
Nominal	9.4	13.4	12.4	10.8	11.1
Real	5.1	7.1	1.7	0.6	−2.0
Germany					
Nominal	8.1	13.5	6.1	9.3	1.2
Real	5.4	7.6	−0.8	4.9	−4.3
Japan					
Nominal	17.8	27.1	14.1	9.6	3.8
Real	11.4	20.8	−3.2	2.2	−2.5
United Kingdom					
Nominal	3.8	14.6	7.9	15.3	10.2
Real	−0.1	5.8	−4.1	−0.2	−4.1
United States					
Nominal	4.4	7.7	4.4	7.1	5.5
Real	1.6	3.8	−3.9	−0.8	−5.7

Definitions and Sources: Nominal money stock is M1, end-of-year, from the International Financial Statistics of the IMF (except for Canada, which is from the OECD). Real money is defined as M1/*CPI*, with the CPI also from IFS data.

enormous buildup of international reserves in all of the major economies. The counterpart of heavy foreign exchange intervention in support of the dollar was the rapid creation of domestic credit, particularly in Germany and Japan.

With the ensuing inflation in 1973 and 1974, monetary authorities in all of the countries reduced nominal money stock growth. *Real* money growth fell even more sharply (*M/CPI* fell in four of five countries of Table 8.5 from end-1972 to end-1974) as a consequence of the supply-shock-induced jump in prices. None of the economies, then, appears to have followed an accommodating monetary policy after the first shock.

There is somewhat more divergence in money growth behavior in the "intershock" period, 1974–79. In Canada, Germany, the United Kingdom, and the United States, M1 growth picked up again as policy turned moderately expansionary in view of the high unemployment during the period (remember that only the United States achieved by 1979 a return of unemployment rates to those of the early 1970s). In France and Japan, nominal money growth was lower during 1974–79 than during 1972–74.

During the second supply shock, policymakers once again rejected monetary accommodation, and real money balances fell sharply in all six countries. Though nominal M1 growth remained approximately unchanged in

Table 8.6. Money Supply, GNP, and Inflation in the OECD, 1964–1980

$$\dot{v}_t = 1.97 + 0.48\dot{v}_{t-1} - 0.10\dot{v}_{t-2} + 0.08\dot{v}_{t-3} + 0.61[\dot{m}_{t-1} - \dot{m}_{t-2}]$$
$$\quad (2.24) \quad (0.43) \qquad\qquad (0.33) \qquad (3.32)$$

$$\overline{R}^2 = .46, \text{D.W.} = 2.21$$

$$\dot{v}_t = 5.86 + 0.39\dot{v}_{t-1} - 0.22\dot{v}_{t-2} + 0.36\dot{v}_{t-3} + 0.61(\dot{m}_c)_{t-1}$$
$$\qquad (1.47) \qquad (1.18) \qquad (0.18) \qquad (4.47)$$

$$\overline{R}^2 = .61, \text{D.W.} = 1.90$$

$$\dot{p}_{c_t} = -13.8 + 0.34\dot{p}_{c_{t-1}} - 0.01\dot{p}_{c_{t-1}} + 0.09\dot{p}_{c_{t-2}} + 0.66\,\dot{m}_{t-1}$$
$$\qquad\quad (1.11) \qquad (0.01) \qquad (0.32) \qquad (1.76)$$
$$\quad + 0.72\,\dot{m}_{t-2} + 0.94\,\dot{m}_{t-3}$$
$$\qquad (1.82) \qquad\quad (2.30)$$

$$\overline{R}^2 = .76, \text{D.W.} = 1.54$$

Source: p_c is the consumer price index for the OECD, and v_t is real GNP. m is constructed from IMF data, and $\dot{m}_c = \dot{m} - \dot{p}_c$. The regressions are on annual data for 1964–1980. The numbers in parentheses are *t*-statistics.

Canada and France (which each experienced large effective exchange rate depreciations), nominal M1 growth declined in Germany, Japan, the United Kingdom, and the United States in this period.

It is worthwhile to recall a reason given in Chapter 6 for the uniformity of contractionary policies following the supply shocks, in spite of the high unemployment that those policies engendered. We argued earlier that there exists precisely such a tendency toward global overcontraction, since a demand expansion in one economy is treacherous when other countries are contracting. Each economy is induced to contract when all might plausibly agree to a common expansion (were the benefits to coordination better appreciated). We have a prisoner's dilemma writ large.

Some simple causality tests underline the importance of monetary fluctuations for OECD GNP and inflation. In Table 8.6 we regress the annual percentage change of OECD GNP ($\dot{v}$) on its own lags, and on lagged changes in (log) OECD nominal M1 balances ($\dot{m}$) or real M1 balances ($\dot{m}_c$, CPI deflated). In all cases, lagged monetary policy is a strong predictor of current OECD output and price changes. Money has a shorter lag in the output equations than in the price equations, as we might expect. The largest monetary decelerations came in 1973–74 and 1980–81, both times just ahead of the very deep OECD recessions. In both cases, the monetary decelerations represented a clear policy response to the sharp increases in inflation accompanying the OPEC oil price increases.

Table 8.7. Terms-of-Trade Losses Due to Rise in Energy Prices, as Percentage of GNP (cumulative losses for periods shown)

Region	1968–1972	1973–1974	1975–1978	1979–1981
Europe				
(OECD)	−0.1	6.2	−0.5	3.3
Japan	−0.3	8.2	−1.2	5.8
United States	0.0	2.4	−0.1	2.0

Source: The share of net energy imports in GNP is calculated as net imports of trade classification category S.I.T.C.3 as a percentage of GNP. Denote this share as s_t^m. The terms-of-trade loss in year t is calculated as $(\dot{p}_{n_t} - \dot{p}_{v_t}) \cdot \frac{1}{2}(s_{t-1}^m + s_t^m)$, where p_{n_t} is the (log) price of Saudi petroleum exports (in domestic currency) and p_v is the (log) GNP deflator. These annual losses are then summed over the years shown. This measure will be inaccurate to the extent that S.I.T.C.3 includes energy imports (for example, coal and natural gas), whose relative price changed differently from $\dot{p}_{n_t} - \dot{p}_{v_t}$ as defined above. (Note that intra-European trade in coal nets out of calculations.) S.I.T.C.3 imports are from OECD Trade Statistics Series A, and GNP data are from OECD National Accounts (for Europe-OECD) and the IMF (for Japan and the United States).

A second demand factor of great short-run influence was the international transfer of purchasing power to OPEC after the oil price increases of 1973–74 and 1979–80. Though most of our empirical work on this factor in the coming chapters stresses the supply-side consequence of higher oil prices, the contractionary demand factors must not be overlooked. The rise in oil prices in 1973–74 and 1979–80 led to a substantial transfer of income from the non-oil countries to OPEC. Since many of the OPEC countries (the so-called low absorbers) took many years to increase their spending in line with their higher incomes, the effect of the transfer was to raise the world's marginal propensity to save, as analyzed in Chapter 4. Table 8.7 gives an indication of the size of this transfer by computing the terms-of-trade loss (as a percentage of GNP) implicit in higher oil prices, for the United States, Europe, and Japan.

SUPPLY FACTORS

On the supply side, we argue that high real factor prices, for raw materials and for labor, substantially reduced aggregate supply relative to potential output during the period, with two implications. First, demand management alone could no longer restore noninflationary full employment, since firms were not willing to hire the full-employment labor force at prevailing factor prices. Second, the high factor prices reduced the profitability of capital, and

Table 8.8. Labor Share of Value Added, Manufacturing Sector, 1961–81 (in percentages)

Country	1961	1969	1973	1975	1979	1981
Belgium	58.3	60.6	67.9	77.0	75.7	76.9
Canada	67.3	68.5	65.8	69.2	65.8	NA
Denmark	68.6	72.2	74.8	74.5	76.5	74.5
France	65.9	65.8	68.7	74.1	74.6	75.9
Germany	52.6	52.6	58.8	60.5	59.2	63.3
Japan	39.6	40.3	44.5	53.8	49.8	NA
United Kingdom	69.9	71.0	71.4	80.2	79.7	82.8
United States	70.5	71.0	71.6	71.6	73.8	75.6

Source: Bureau of Labor Statistics (BLS) for all countries except France; Institut National de Statistiques et des Etudes Economiques, for France. There is a substantial difference in the French labor share according to the two sources, with the French national source (reported here) showing a considerably higher labor share of value added and a more sharply rising profile than the BLS series. The other series accord closely to national sources.

Table 8.9. Pretax Rate of Return to Capital, Manufacturing Sector
1961–81 (in percentages)

Country	1961	1969	1973	1975	1979	1981
Canada	14.9	14.4	15.3	13.1	13.4	12.7
France	NA	18.8	18.2	13.1	13.8	NA
Germany	24.2	20.5	16.5	13.7	14.9	13.0[a]
Japan	NA	39.4	32.4	18.5	21.2	20.2[a]
United Kingdom	12.0	10.3	9.2	5.5	5.9	4.1
United States	18.3	20.3	18.9	15.7	15.4	12.4

Source: OECD National Income Accounts.
a. 1980.

thereby played an important role in the slowdown of capital accumulation
and productivity growth in the 1970s and 1980s. Many of the major economies entered a low-profit, low-growth trap in which excess wage levels contributed to slow productivity growth, which in turn reinforced the excess of
wages over market clearing levels.

Some evidence for the shift of income from profits to labor is shown in the
following tables. In Table 8.8 we record the movements in labor's share of
income in manufacturing for eight major OECD economies from 1961 to
1981. The period 1961–69 was an era of stable factor shares, or even slightly
declining labor share of income. During 1969–75 this stability was broken,
with sharp increases in s_l everywhere but Canada and the United States. The

Table 8.10. Growth of Manufacturing Capital Stock, 1960–80 (annual
percentage rates)

Country	1960–1973	1973–1980	Of which: 1973–1975	1975–1980
Canada	4.8	3.9	4.8	3.5
France	5.7	3.8	4.5	3.5
Germany	6.5	2.1	2.5	2.0
Japan	12.8[a]	5.5	7.8	4.7
United Kingdom	3.5	2.4	2.7	2.3
United States	3.1	4.3	3.6	4.5

Definitions and Sources: The capital stock is the "gross capital stock at constant prices" of
Flows and Stocks of Fixed Capital, OECD, 1983.
a. 1964–73.

labor share stabilized or declined in most countries during 1975–78 (the period between the two oil shocks) but then increased sharply once again in 1979 and after.

The counterpart to this shift has been a remarkable decline in the pretax rate of return to capital in manufacturing during the same period. These rates of return are shown in Table 8.9; once again we see that a slow secular decline in the rate of return during the 1960s gives way to a sharp decline in the 1970s and early 1980s. In our view, this decline in profitability is a major factor in the slowdown in capital accumulation in the business sector during that period. In Table 8.10 we verify that the growth of the manufacturing capital stock slowed sharply in Europe and Japan after 1973.

Table 8.11. Price Changes of Primary Commodities, 1955–81 (annual percentage rate)

Commodity category	Major periods		Subperiods			
	1955–1971	1971–1981	1971–1973	1973–1975	1975–1979	1979–1981
Food						
Nominal	1.2	14.1	28.5	11.9	6.6	14.6
Real	−1.0	2.3	14.3	−4.7	−0.8	1.6
Nonfood Agriculture						
Nominal	−1.0	13.0	37.3	0.0	9.7	12.5
Real	−2.5	1.5	21.9	−14.3	1.8	−0.4
Nonferrous Metals						
Nominal	2.6	11.0	17.9	−0.4	7.7	21.5
Real	1.3	−1.0	4.7	−14.2	0.7	7.2
Oil						
Nominal	1.3	30.9	20.6	69.0	4.8	53.5
Real	−0.5	17.0	7.3	44.4	−2.7	36.2

Source: "Real prices" are computed as the ratio of commodity prices to an index of export unit values of manufactured goods of the developed economies. All commodity series are U.N. indexes of primary commodity export prices, for "total market economies." The series are from the 1967 U.N. Statistical Yearbook (p. 404) for 1957–60 (base 1963 = 100); the 1978 U.N. Statistical Yearbook (p. 481) for 1960–1975 (base 1970 = 100); and the U.N. Monthly Bulletin of Statistics, October 1981 (p. 168) for 1975–80 (base 1975 = 100). The series are spliced together at 1960 and 1975.

Raw Material Prices. We turn first to the raw material price increases. Table 8.11 provides data on raw material price changes in the past three decades. Observe that *non-oil* as well as oil prices rose sharply in real terms in the early 1970s (but also fell more than oil prices in the recessions of 1975 and 1979–82). The relative price of agricultural commodities rose on average in the 1970s, after falling for two decades in the 1950s and 1960s. Thus, in discussing the supply shocks of the 1970s, we must direct attention to a wide array of commodities of central importance to the production process. The nonferrous metals show no relative price trend.

In the theoretical models of earlier chapters, we have treated fluctuations in Π_N as exogenous shocks to the OECD economies, and as a *source* of OECD stagflation. Clearly, events in the OECD had some important effects on Π_N, so that causation in fact runs in both directions. For example, the self-reversing boom in some commodity prices during 1972–75 no doubt reflected the rapid growth in world liquidity and consequent output boom in the early 1970s. But the persistence of high real energy and other commodity prices in the face of the OECD growth slowdown does suggest that deeper supply factors have also been at work. Supply factors are easy to identify in the energy price increases since 1970: a substantial drop in the annual growth of world production of crude oil lies behind the huge price increases, as shown in Table 8.12. Though part of the slowdown in growth of crude oil production occurred in some OECD economies (particularly the United States), the major source of slowdown was in the production of the OPEC economies. As described by Nordhaus (1980), OPEC produced substantially below capacity after 1973. The lower production was the concomitant of OPEC pricing behavior.

There is still considerable debate over the nature of OPEC supply and price behavior and therefore in the interpretation of the shut-in capacity. Some economists have taken a rather extreme view of OPEC as a unified,

Table 8.12. Average Growth in Crude Oil Production, 1955–81 (annual percentage rate)

Production	1955–1973	1973–1979	1979–1981
World	7.1	2.2	−8.1
OPEC	10.0	−0.0	−14.7

Source: The 1955–1973 and 1973–1979 world production numbers are calculated from Table 5.5 in Bosworth and Lawrence (1982). The 1955–1973 OPEC observation is from Nordhaus (1980). The remaining data are from the OECD Economic Outlook, December 1982.

wealth-maximizing cartel, making supply decisions subject to optimizing intertemporal considerations. However, this position has been convincingly attacked on theoretical and empirical grounds (see Nordhaus, 1980, and the discussion that follows his paper). Salant (1976), among others, has modified this view in an important direction by treating the largest producers asymmetrically from the others, in a strategic game in which a monopoly cartel of large producers plays with a competitive fringe of small producers. This view helps to explain OPEC supply behavior since 1979, but as Bosworth and Lawrence indicate (1982, pp. 127 – 128), the model is not particularly helpful for the 1974 – 79 period.

Nordhaus (1980) offers a pragmatic view of OPEC pricing which recognizes the profound difficulties of OPEC's acting as a unified cartel. He suggests that OPEC has priced according to a "ratchet rule," in which run-ups in spot market prices (as opposed to OPEC posted prices) set a floor to OPEC posted prices. If demand or supply shifts tend to cause spot market prices to fall back below a newly raised OPEC posted price, the major OPEC suppliers (particularly Saudi Arabia) cut back production to maintain the floor. In this view, the 1973 price increase resulted largely from the same demand factors that pushed up the whole spectrum of commodity prices, but, unlike the prices of other commodities, oil prices were prevented from falling in the subsequent OECD recession. In 1979 – 80, it was a combination of rising OECD demand, falling Iranian oil exports, and speculative inventory buying that once again caused spot market prices to surge and thus led to the second major increase in OPEC posted prices. The deep world recession after 1981 and the sharp appreciation of the U.S. dollar put this ratchet rule to a severe test. In fact, the price of oil in terms of U.S. dollars fell somewhat, but the price of oil did not fall in terms of other foreign currencies.

Agricultural products represent the second major category of primary commodity price increases. As we saw in Table 8.11, both food and nonfood agricultural prices fell in real terms between 1955 and 1971 and then rose during 1971 – 81 (though of course not as dramatically as oil prices). As in the oil market, a combination of institutional changes and adverse supply developments contributed to the price increases. Bosworth and Lawrence list several factors of prime importance.

1. The Soviet Union experienced several crop failures in the 1970s. In previous decades the Soviets had absorbed crop failures principally by reducing domestic consumption, whereas in the 1970s they chose instead to import heavily from world grain markets.

2. As a result of policy errors, grain reserves in the major grain-produc-

ing economies (for example, the United States) were allowed to become depleted at the end of the 1960s and in the early 1970s so that the major Soviet purchases came at a time of very low reserve stocks.

3. Outside the Soviet Union and the United States, there was a significant slowdown in productivity growth after 1972. "Despite a great expansion of harvested land, actual production has remained below the trend growth rate [of 1960–1972]. This slow growth has been primarily the result of a decline in the rate of improvement in production yields." (Bosworth and Lawrence, 1982, p. 106).

Labor Costs. The second supply factor of importance, which affected Europe and Japan more than the United States until recent years, was the level of real labor costs. During the period 1969 to 1975 there was a sharp rise in real labor costs relative to productivity growth throughout the OECD. The gap between real wage costs and productivity levels has persisted since 1975, and in some important cases has widened substantially. The wage story must be told in phases. In the late 1960s and early 1970s, a real wage explosion (particularly in Europe and Japan) caused a major shift in income distribution away from profits and toward labor. Even *before* the oil shocks, therefore, many OECD countries faced a major problem of declining profitability and slowing growth. In the second phase real wages did not decelerate (outside of the United States) to make room for the raw material price increases, so the profit squeeze intensified. In the third phase low profitability and rising unemployment slowed the rate of capital accumulation and productivity growth. Real wage increases *were* reduced, but so too was productivity growth, with the result that the excess of wages over full-employment productivity persisted into the early 1980s.

There are several factors that contributed to the initial real wage burst during 1969–75 and that prevented a necessary readjustment of real wage levels in subsequent years. For the earlier period, three explanations stand out. First, the wage behavior in Europe during the period 1969–73 reflects in part a catching up of wages that were constrained by income policies during the mid-1960s, and in part a reaction to unusually high profits in the late 1960s. Second, the sustained period of high employment in the 1960s, as well as specific episodes of industrial strife late in that decade, led to important institutional gains in union power and coverage. Third, after the increases in real wages occurred, they were partially or fully ratified by expansionary policy in the early 1970s.

Soskice (1978) has provided a fascinating analysis of the wage explosion in terms of the first factor. With great attention to institutional detail, he records that European economies recovered from the recession in the mid-1960s with national unions committed to income policies and long-term wage agreements. It is because of these policies, in his view, that labor's share was stable or actually falling throughout Europe during the 1966–69 period. Country by country, dissatisfaction among the rank and file with union participation in income policies led to the dramatic wildcat strikes of 1969–70 that heralded the wage acceleration. Indeed, the widely recognized surge in labor militancy came first not in official union action but in the critical response of workers to union inaction. A provocative aspect of Soskice's argument is that the size of the wage settlements, "considerably greater than could be accounted for by conventional economic factors," served in part to "enable the unions to regain control of the situation, a desire common to governments and employers as well as unions" (1978, pp. 244–245).

To explain why the modest deceleration of real wages in the late 1960s was followed by enormous growth in real wages lasting until the mid-1970s, the second factor is important: the developments of the 1960s led to significant changes in the process of wage determination. For example, the upheaval in France in May 1968 brought with it the government-backed Grenelle Accords that called for a large, one-time increase in real wages and obliged employers to negotiate with unions on economic demands. In December 1968, the labor law conferred recognition for the first time on plant-based bargaining. The "Hot Autumn" of 1969 in Italy, tied to union negotiations in the metal sector, also created large gains in wages and longer-lasting institutional changes. The Italian Parliament enacted the "1970 Workers' Charter" on union rights, extending union powers at the plant level. Moreover, a rapid growth of membership in Italian unions occurred during this period, from 4.5 million in 1968 to 6 million in 1973 (Brandini, 1975, p. 97). Even more important, the three competing trade union federations in Italy embarked on a common program after 1969, substantially strengthening the common front of the labor movement. In Germany, wildcat strikes in the steel and coal industries in 1969 led the trade unions to abandon the incomes policy that had existed since the beginning of the "concerted action" policy in 1967. "Trade unions drew more of the active union elements into their policy-making forums, steering toward a more active wage policy to demonstrate their legitimacy" (Bergmann and Muller-Jentsch, 1975, p. 260). In the United Kingdom, new institutional changes that were designed to limit union power instead brought forth a tremendous flexing of that power. Widespread strike activity made union power a central election issue in 1970 and presaged, under a Conservative government, the 1971 Industrial Rela-

Table 8.13. Indicators of Labor Power, 1960–1980 (annual averages)

Country	Degree of unionization				Strike rates	
	1960	1970	1975	1979	1960–67	1968–75
Canada	0.25	0.27	0.31	0.33[a]	0.35	0.82
Denmark	0.47	0.51	0.58	0.69	NA	NA
Germany	0.30	0.30	0.35	0.37	0.01	0.03
Japan	0.17	0.23	0.24	0.23	0.09	0.10
Sweden	0.53	0.66	0.75	0.80	NA	NA
United Kingdom	0.42	0.46	0.50	0.54	0.12	0.45
United States	0.26	0.25	0.23	0.21[a]	0.33	0.53

Definitions and Sources: Degree of unionization is union membership per total employed workers. The strike rate is workdays lost due to strikes per total employed. Union membership data are from the Office of Productivity and Technology, Bureau of Labor Statistics, for all countries except the United States (which are from the BLS Handbook of Labor Statistics). The strike data are from OECD Main Economic Indicators.

a. 1978.

tions Act. In turn, the three years under the act until its repeal in 1974 by the new Labor government "witnessed the most direct confrontation between the unions and the government since the General Strike of 1926" (Goodman, 1975, p. 47).

Table 8.13 provides some (imperfect) quantitative indicators of the rise in labor power between 1969 and 1975, for assorted economies. In every country but the United States there is a strong increase in the degree of unionization between 1968 and 1975 and, as shown in the second column of the table, a rise in strike activity in each country.

IS THE PRODUCTIVITY SLOWDOWN AN INDEPENDENT SUPPLY SHOCK?

One of the major issues involved in understanding stagflation is the puzzling slowdown in productivity growth since 1973. The productivity puzzle remains unsolved, though many possible sources of the slowdown have been put under observation in recent years. We do not claim to give a definitive "solution" to the puzzle in this book, though some light will be shed on this central problem by comparing experiences across the OECD and analyzing various factors associated with the supply shocks and the demand response to them.

Comparative data, presented in Kendrick (1981) and Lindbeck (1983) among others, contain several important messages.

1. The slowdown occurred everywhere in the OECD, comparing average labor productivity or total factor productivity during 1960–73 and 1973–79.

2. The onset of the slowdown was sudden almost everywhere, beginning in 1973 or 1974. The United States is the major exception, since the slowdown was gradual and started as early as 1967.

3. The growth of measurable inputs per unit of labor (including capital, quality of labor, and so on) accounts for less than one-half of measured labor productivity growth since 1955 in all countries, according to estimates by Denison (1967) and Kendrick (1981).

4. The *change* in growth of measurable inputs per unit of labor accounts for less than one-sixth of the slowdown after 1973 in all countries except for Japan, where it accounts for about one-quarter.

5. Roughly one-third to one-half of the slowdown is accounted for by a decline in gains due to economies of scale, resource reallocation, and capacity utilization, according to Kendrick's estimates.

The suddenness of the slowdown, its universality, and the modest importance of capital per man-hour in the slowdown all suggest that global macro-

Table 8.14.   Productivity Growth in Historical Perspective (in percentages)

Country	Annual rate of increase in GNP per employed worker			
	1922–1929	1929–1937	1960–1973	1973–1979
Canada	2.1	−0.9	2.5	0.3
Denmark	2.1	1.1	3.5	1.1
France	5.8	−1.3	4.7	2.9
Germany	6.0	2.1	4.4	3.2
Japan	5.9	2.4	8.9	3.0
Sweden	3.3	1.9	3.3	0.6
United Kingdom	1.6	1.6	2.8	1.2
United States	2.1	0.4	2.1	0.3

Sources: For 1922–1937 the data are total product per man-year, from D. C. Paige et al., "Economic Growth: The Last Hundred Years," *National Institute Economic Review,* 1961, 24–49. For 1960–1979, the data are real GNP per employed worker, from the *Main Economic Indicators,* OECD.

economic phenomena have had a large role to play. It is hard to imagine that factors such as a slowdown in research and development expenditure or an exhaustion of the post-World-War-II boom would lead to such an abrupt universal productivity slowdown, in the absence of other macroeconomic factors. A common factor shared by all economies since 1973 has been the low profitability and high unemployment in the period, factors that we shall stress in our discussion in Chapter 12. In fact, the current productivity slowdown is not unlike that which occurred in the last experience of high global unemployment, the Great Depression. In Table 8.14 we present that comparison explicitly. Measuring "peak-to-peak" in 1922–29 and in 1929–37, we see that almost all countries experienced a pronounced slowdown in productivity growth during the eight-year period of high unemployment in the Great Depression. Of course, the 1937 "peak" was at far higher levels of unemployment than in 1979, so we might expect a larger slowdown after 1929 than after 1973, but the analogy to the present situation probably holds to some extent.

Sorting Out the Roles of Supply and Demand Variables

The rising unemployment and higher inflation of the 1970s resulted from both supply and demand factors. We have suggested that the *sharp* increases in unemployment during 1973–75 and 1979–82 are mostly demand-induced and resulted from the application of tight monetary policies to the supply shocks and high inflation in 1972–73 and 1979–80. The steady rise in unemployment during 1975–79 in most of the OECD, however, should be attributed to the fact that real wages remained above market-clearing levels in most economies (but probably not in the United States). In this interpretation, an end to the stagflation would require policies aimed both at demand and supply expansion, where the latter would include real-wage moderation.

THE ROLE OF REAL WAGES IN EMPLOYMENT DETERMINATION

A prominent view in the empirical macroeconomics literature is that real wages do not move countercyclically, as would be necessary if employment fluctuations were really caused by changes in real wage levels. This has caused some analysts to doubt the importance of real wages as a direct contributor to the high unemployment in the 1970s. This alleged empirical finding has been explained by the assumption that firms are typically rationed in their sales in the output market, with employment fluctuations reflecting shifts in output demand rather than in the real wage. Disequilibrium theorists have argued more persuasively that the real wage will be important for aggregate employment determination at certain times (in the classical regime) and that at other times demand rationing of firms will break the link (in the Keynesian regime). Our models in Chapters 5 and 7 explained in great detail how such regime switching may characterize adjustment to supply shocks. It appears from the evidence that the 1970s were characterized by extended periods of classical unemployment, with intervening periods of Keynesian recession.

The standard empirical results denying a real wage–employment link are deficient in two ways. First, the data have typically not been selected with care, in the sense that the wage variable has often not been appropriate for a labor-demand schedule. Second, almost all work to date has been based on U.S. data, in spite of the evidence that U.S. wage and price setting institutions differ markedly from those in Europe and Japan. In fact, the United States does stand out in the evidence given here as having relatively little direct link between real wage levels and employment or unemployment.

The regressions in Table 8.15 build from a standard labor demand schedule in log-linear form:

(8.1) $l_t = \alpha_0 + \alpha_1(w_t - p_{v_t}) + \alpha_2 t + k_t.$

The specification in Eq. (8.1) assumes the following: (1) that firms are always on the labor-demand schedule; (2) that Harrod-neutral technical change proceeds at a constant geometric rate; and (3) that firms can costlessly and instantaneously adjust the level of the labor input. We estimate a modified version of (8.1) that allows for a lagged adjustment of l to l^d, and in which time and a time shift variable ($t7580$) for 1975–1980 serve as a proxy for k:[2]

(8.2) $l_t = \alpha_0 + \alpha_1(w_t - p_{v_t}) + \alpha_2 t + \alpha_3 t7580 + \alpha_4 l_{t-1}.$

In the estimation, l is man-hours, w is hourly labor costs, and p_v is the value-added deflator (all variables are in log levels). All variables refer to manufacturing and are from the U.S. Bureau of Labor Statistics. The regressions are run on annual data for 1960–80.

Contrary to the common assertion, the real wage variable has a significant negative coefficient in eight of nine cases (all but the United States). As expected, the time trend, which proxies for productivity growth, is positive and the time shift variable is negative, again in all cases except that of the United States. The evidence for partial adjustment of the labor input comes from the highly significant estimates of α_4 in all but two cases.

Table 8.15. Man-hours – Real Wage Equation
$l_t = \alpha_0 + \alpha_1(w - p_{v_t}) + \alpha_2 t + \alpha_3 t7580 + \alpha_4 l_{t-1}$

Country	α_1	α_2	α_3	α_4	$\overline{R}^2$	D.H.
Belgium	−0.42**	0.024	−0.025	0.36	0.98	0.36
	(3.71)	(2.86)	(2.81)	(2.05)		
Canada	−0.54**	0.027	−0.017	0.79	0.91	1.63
	(2.05)	(2.21)	(1.71)	(4.69)		
Denmark	−1.22**	0.076	−0.030	0.29	0.94	−1.97
	(2.30)	(2.06)	(1.78)	(1.40)		
France	−0.51**	0.030	−0.016	0.61	0.88	−0.08
	(3.28)	(3.63)	(3.01)	(2.23)		
Germany	−0.67*	0.037	−0.012	0.60	0.87	NC
	(1.89)	(1.66)	(1.20)	(2.73)		
Japan	−0.67**	0.079	−0.029	0.46	0.93	−0.55
	(3.74)	(3.62)	(2.71)	(3.11)		
Sweden	−0.26**	0.013	−0.015	0.66	0.98	0.46
	(2.38)	(1.45)	(2.69)	(5.84)		
United Kingdom	−0.42**	0.011	−0.019	0.24	0.91	NC
	(2.17)	(1.26)	(3.12)	(0.87)		
United States	0.75	−0.021	0.002	0.61	0.70	3.50
	(1.24)	(1.03)	(0.22)	(3.11)		

Definitions and Sources: Numbers in parentheses are *t*-statistics. Single asterisk indicates significance at $p = 0.10$ (these symbols are included for the wage variable only). Double asterisk indicates significance at $p = 0.05$. D.H. is the Durbin H statistic.

l_t is (log) man-hours in manufacturing; w_t is (log) hourly compensation in manufacturing; p_{v_t} is the (log) ratio of nominal value added to real value added in manufacturing. These data are from the Office of Productivity and Technology, Bureau of Labor Statistics, U.S. Department of Labor. t is a time trend: 1 in 1955; 2 in 1956; and so on. $t7581$ is 0 for 1955–1974; 1 in 1975; 2 in 1976; and so on.

Of course these results do not in any way exclude a role for demand in recent years, for two key reasons. First, to some extent, contractionary demand policies operate by raising the product wage. A monetary contraction, for example, that causes the exchange rate to appreciate may well reduce p_v relative to w. But even more important, the regressions in Table 8.15 strongly suggest that demand variables should be *added* to the equations alongside $w - p_v$. Consider, for example, the residuals from the regressions for Japan, Germany, and the United States during 1973–75 (Table 8.16). In all three countries, manufacturing employment is underpredicted during the 1973 boom and overpredicted during the 1974–75 recession. The deep recession *cannot* be well accounted for by real wage shifts.

Table 8.16. Residuals in Man-hours Equation, Table 8.15

Country	1973	1974	1975
Germany	0.038	−0.008	−0.058
Japan	0.041	−0.018	−0.036
United States	0.012	−0.025	−0.087

In Chapter 10 we will present regressions that describe man-hours and the aggregate unemployment rate as a function of both supply and demand variables.

THE ROLE OF SUPPLY FACTORS IN INFLATION DETERMINATION

In Chapter 10 we introduce a model of wage-price dynamics to explain how excess real wage levels and raw material shocks help to explain the Phillips-curve movements of recent years. A major theme of this model is that

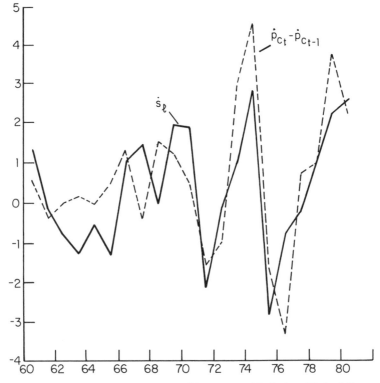

Figure 8.1. Changes in labor share of income and inflation, United States

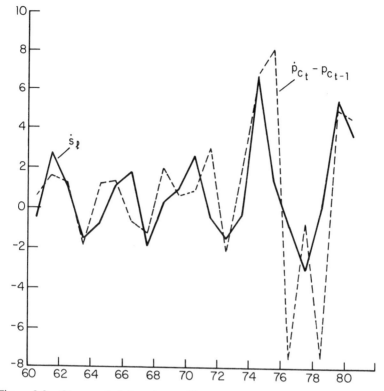

Figure 8.2. Changes in labor share of income and inflation, United Kingdom

inflation accelerates at a given unemployment rate when *real* wage targets exceed trend productivity growth adjusted for terms-of-trade changes.[3] The inconsistency of wage targets with adjusted productivity growth is strongest at times of external shocks, which squeeze, *deus ex machina,* the scope for real wage gains. Thus, the supply shocks are crucial in explaining the big bursts of inflation during 1973–74 and 1979–80.

Let us illustrate this proposition with a simple time-phased system of wage-price dynamics in an economy with a single final good. We write:

(8.3)   (a) $\dot{w}_t = \dot{p}_t + \tau,$

          (b) $\dot{p}_{v_t} = \dot{w}_{t-1} - \dot{\psi},$

          (c) $\dot{p}_t = \dot{p}_{v_t} + [(1 - s_v)/s_v]\dot{\pi}_{n_t}.$

Real wages grow at a target rate τ; value-added price change is given by *lagged* wage change minus trend productivity growth $\dot{\psi}$; and output price change is a function of $\dot{p}_v$ and the change in real input prices, $\dot{\pi}_n$.

The (log) labor share of value added is given as $s_{l_t} = w_t - p_{v_t} - \psi_t +$ constant, so that $\dot{s}_{l_t} = \dot{w}_t - \dot{p}_{v_t} - \dot{\psi}_t$. Using this definition and (8.3)(a) and (b), we may write that:

(8.4) $\dot{p}_t = \dot{p}_{t-1} + \dot{s}_{l_t}$,

that is, changes in inflation equal changes in labor's share of value added. Using (8.3) and (8.4), we may also write:

(8.5) $\dot{s}_{l_t} = (\tau - \dot{\psi}) + [(1 - s_v)/s_v]\dot{\pi}_{n_t}$,

that is, labor's share rises when real wage targets (τ) exceed productivity growth ($\dot{\psi}$), or when adverse supply price shocks occur ($\dot{\pi}_n > 0$).

Graphs of $\dot{p}_{c_t} - \dot{p}_{c_{t-1}}$ versus $\dot{s}_{l_t}$ for the United Kingdom and the United States confirm the basic message of this model (Figures 8.1 and 8.2). To a strong extent, increases in inflation in these two countries have been tied to periods of a rising labor share of value added, particularly as a result of terms-of-trade deterioration. (Note the sharp spikes in 1973–74 and 1979–80.) The same relationship is apparent in most of the other economies. We return to this relationship in Chapter 10.

There is another, more subtle link between supply factors and inflation that seems to explain part of the apparent rise in the "natural rate of unemployment." A better rendering of (8.3) allows for the effects of economic slack on inflation. We shall see that unemployment alone is not a good indicator of slack from an economic point of view, since high real wage levels reduce desired aggregate supply. Chapter 10 will show that an augmented Phillips curve that adds $w - p_v$ helps to account for the inflation performance in the 1970s.

Summary and Conclusions

In our view, the stagflationary era must be explained as the result of several interacting factors. The most important of the factors include:

1. Excessive real wage growth, beginning at the end of the 1960s, which led to a major shift in income distribution toward labor.

2. Overly expansionary monetary policies around the world during the period 1969–73, which left a legacy of high inflation for the next decade.

3. Various supply price shocks, particularly of energy and food prod-

ucts, which caused a jump in inflation and reduced the scope for real income gains.

By 1974, the major economies suffered from an inherited inflation and profit squeeze and were being buffeted by the import price shocks. A sharp rise in unemployment was probably inevitable in these circumstances, although nonaccommodative monetary policies were a major cause of the stagnation that descended upon the OECD.

The profit squeeze has not been alleviated easily. High unemployment has been required to slow real wage growth, to keep in line with reduced productivity growth. Low profitability has probably been a major source of the poor productivity performance, and thus has fed upon itself. Low profits result in reduced productivity gains, while low productivity gains with persistent real wage growth lower profits further.

The 1975–79 period allowed for some recovery, particularly in the United States, where the profit squeeze was least severe. The second round of OPEC price shocks, together with extremely contractionary monetary policies throughout the world, cut the recovery short. The combination of additional terms-of-trade losses and slow productivity growth has led to a further tightening of the profit squeeze. After a decade of stagflation, profitability remained lower in 1983 than it was in 1973.

The succeeding chapters give detailed analyses of key arguments. Chapter 9 provides empirical evidence on the role of high real wages during the period. We discuss various aspects of labor markets and wage determination, including the sources of real wage growth, models of wage setting under unions, and demographic changes in OECD labor markets. Chapter 10 shows how various supply factors can help to account for the shifts in the Phillips curve. In Chapter 11 we delve somewhat more deeply into the institutional aspects of wage setting, to show that different institutional forms have been variously suited to handle the problems of the 1970s and 1980s. Chapter 12 explores the productivity slowdown in a time-series and cross-section analysis. Finally, in Chapter 13 we summarize some of the policy implications of our study.

9   Real Wages and Unemployment

THE SLOW GROWTH and high unemployment occurring throughout the OECD in recent years have resulted from a complex interaction of contractionary supply and demand factors. In Chapter 8 we introduced evidence suggesting that an important supply factor has been the persistent excess of real wage levels above the marginal product of labor at full employment. We term this gap between real wages and productivity the "real wage gap," denoted w^x. In this chapter we seek to measure w^x, albeit imperfectly; to show that empirical measures of w^x convey important information about the evolution of unemployment; and to explain the development of w^x over time. In this last regard, we describe a series of theoretical models that help to explain why labor markets do not rapidly adjust to equate w^x to zero.

Measurement of the Wage Gap

To formalize the wage gap concept, let us begin with a value-added function in L, K, and t: $V = F(L,K,t)$. The marginal product of labor is $F_L(L,K,t)$, which we can measure at full employment, $F_L(L^f,K,t)$. With output-market clearing and competitive firms, $(W/P_v)^f = F_L(L^f,K,t)$ is the level of the wage for which labor demand will equal L^f. We define w_t^x as the percentage deviation of the actual wage W/P_v over $(W/P_v)^f$. In log-linear approximation, $w_t^x = (w - p_v) - (w - p_v)^f$.

Once this wage gap is constructed, we can relate w^x to labor inputs and to unemployment. On the basis of Chapter 3 we note that the elasticity of labor demand with respect to the product wage (assuming output-market clearing) is $\sigma_1/(1 - s)$, where s is labor's share in value added and σ_1 is the elasticity of substitution between L and K in V. Thus, we can conclude (as a log-linear approximation):

(9.1) $l^d - l^f = - [\sigma_1/(1 - s)]w_t^x.$

By construction, $l^d = l^f$ when $w_t^x = 0$. Hereafter we will denote $\sigma_1/(1 - s)$ as α.

The problem of measuring w^x lies in estimating the marginal product of labor at full employment. First, the data tell about average rather than marginal productivity; and second, productivity is measured at actual rather than full-employment levels. In principle, we should estimate the production technology directly, calculate F_L for $L = L^f$, and compare the result with W/P_V. Unfortunately, several technical limitations made this approach difficult. Most important, techniques for estimating the production technology almost always rely on market-clearing assumptions, which we are reluctant to make on a year-to-year basis. In addition, data problems, particularly for the capital stocks, made us hesitant to apply the full econometric machinery to the problem. Finally, we chose to offer several estimates of w^x, under alternative technological assumptions and methods of estimation, in order to show a robust range of estimates. The calculations that follow generally point to the conclusion that w^x has been positive, and growing, in most countries since about 1970.

The easiest case for calculating w^x is Cobb-Douglas technology, with $V_t = (e^{\gamma t}L_t)^\phi K_t^{1-\phi}$. Since $\partial V/\partial L = \phi(V_t/L_t)$, we have that full-employment marginal productivity is given by $\phi(V_t^f/L_t^f)$, where V^f is defined as the level of V when $L_t = L_t^f$. Hereafter, we denote $\partial V/\partial L$ as V_L. Then, in log terms, $w^x = (w - p_v) - (v_t^f - l_t^f) - \log(\phi)$. The problem, then, is to calculate *average* labor productivity at full employment (in logs, $v_t^f - l_t^f$). We choose two approaches, the first very pragmatic (which probably overestimates $v_t^f - l_t^f$ for recent years) and the second somewhat better theoretically.

In the first approach, we assume that $v_t - l_t$ equals $v_t^f - l_t^f$ at cyclical peaks, for which we choose the years 1960, 1973, and 1979. Second, we assume that $v_t^f - l_t^f$ grows at a constant exponential rate between 1960 and 1973, and a (possibly different) constant rate during 1973 and 1979 (note that we assume, in effect, that $v^f - l^f$ and $v - l$ grow at the same rates between cyclical peaks). Third, we assume that the growth rate of $v^f - l^f$ during 1979–81 equals a simple average of the growth rates of $v - l$ during 1979–81 and 1973–79.[1] These procedures yield an index for $v^f - l^f$ that must be compared with the index for $w - p_v$. We normalize the resulting $w^x[= w - p_v - (v^f - l^f)]$ to average 0.0 during 1965–69, under the assumption that wages were at the "right level" during that full-employment, low-inflation period. The final result for w^x (denoted w_1^x) is shown in Table 9.1 (top half), where we see that $w_1^x > 0$ for all countries outside of North America after 1973, and that it has increased sharply in recent years. (Note the measurement problems for France described in the table.)

This measure of w^x probably *understates* the wage gap, because it over-states $v^f - l^f$. (However, we shall see later that the Cobb-Douglas assumption may overstate w^x, so the errors go in both directions.) The problem is that while 1979 was a cyclical peak, it was far from a full-employment year. With $l_{79} < l_{79}^f$, $v_{79} - l_{79}$ is probably higher than $v_{79}^f - l_{79}^f$. During periods of high unemployment, observed productivity will tend to exceed full-employment productivity, assuming that firms remain on the production function. Intuitively, high unemployment causes a reduction in output of the least efficient, labor-intensive enterprises, thus raising measured productivity. To see this, note that $(v - l) = \gamma\phi t + (1 - \phi)(k - l)$, according to the production tech-

Table 9.1.   Real Wage Gap, Alternative Measures, 1965–81 (percentages; 1965–69 = 0.0)

Country	1965	1969	1973	1975	1979	1981
w_1^x						
Canada	−1.7	2.0	−1.4	−0.8	−1.4	NA
France[a]	0.3	−5.5	−0.3	2.9	−0.5	1.9
Germany	1.7	−0.2	8.0	11.3	8.6	12.2
Japan	2.3	1.6	9.8	21.0	21.1	NA
United Kingdom	−1.5	1.1	3.1	9.9	14.1	19.3
United States	1.2	0.0	3.1	−0.1	6.1	8.1
Average	0.4	−0.2	3.7	7.4	8.0	10.4
w_2^x						
Canada	−1.7	2.0	−1.4	−0.8	−1.4	NA
France[a]	0.3	−5.5	−0.6	2.9	3.1	4.1
Germany	1.5	0.0	8.6	13.8	15.1	17.7
Japan	3.4	0.6	6.6	14.7	16.2	NA
United Kingdom	−2.1	1.8	4.9	10.4	17.3	25.3
United States	0.6	0.6	5.1	1.3	6.3	7.4
Average	0.3	−0.1	3.9	7.1	9.9	13.6

Source: BLS.

a. As pointed out in Table 8.8, the BLS data for France disagree significantly with national sources (INSEE). While the BLS data are used in this and the next chapter, the INSEE data suggest far larger wage gaps for France than are shown. For example, using the INSEE data for French compensation, we find for w_1^x: −0.6 (1965); 0.8 (1969); 2.5 (1973); 7.3 (1975); 10.7 (1979); 9.7 (1981).

nology, so that $(v - l) = (v^f - l^f) - (1 - \phi)(l - l^f)$. Thus, when $l < l^f$, $(v - l)$ is greater than $(v^f - l^f)$. We return to this point in Chapter 12.

We now attempt to correct w^x for this bias. Our correction should also reflect the fact that firms may be off the technical production frontier during cyclical downturns. During such a downturn, particularly one caused by a demand contraction, it is usual that labor declines with a lag behind falling output. Consequently, productivity falls below $(v^f - l^f) - (1 - \phi)(l - l^f)$. After a short period, however, the labor input is reduced and the normal productivity relationship is restored. Empirically, we expect $v_t - l_t$ to be a positive function of U_t but a negative function of $\dot{U}_t$, and perhaps of $\dot{U}_{t-1}$. (Note that in the discrete-time context, $\dot{U}_t$ signifies $U_t - U_{t-1}$.) If we write $(v^f - l^f)$ as a function of time and a time shift after 1974, we arrive at an equation for $v - l$ of the form:

$$(9.2) \qquad v_t - l_t = \alpha_0 + \alpha_1 t + \alpha_2 t7581 + \alpha_3 U_t + \alpha_4 \dot{U}_t + \alpha_5 \dot{U}_{t-1},$$

where we expect $\alpha_1 > 0$, $\alpha_2 < 0$, $\alpha_3 > 0$, and $\alpha_4 < 0$. The results shown in Table 9.2 provide some support for the productivity equation, since the coefficient signs are as expected everywhere except Japan, and $\hat{\alpha}_4$ is negative in all cases (a "hat" over a coefficient signifies an estimated value). However, $\hat{\alpha}_3$ is significantly different from zero only in the cases of Canada and Germany.

Table 9.2. Productivity Equation, 1961–1981
$(v - l)_t = \alpha_0 + \alpha_1 t + \alpha_2 t7581 + \alpha_3 U_t + \alpha_4 \dot{U}_t + \alpha_5 \dot{U}_{t-1}$

Country	α_1	α_2	α_3	α_4	α_5	$\overline{R}^2$	D.W.
Canada	0.044	−0.035	0.008	−0.018	0.004	0.998	1.55
	(64.55)	(14.69)	(2.69)	(4.47)	(1.014)		
France	0.057	−0.017	0.005	−0.019	0.022	0.997	1.13
	(29.26)	(2.27)	(0.35)	(1.28)	(1.51)		
Germany	0.054	−0.016	0.011	−0.015	−0.00	0.999	1.21
	(66.71)	(5.86)	(2.72)	(3.16)	(0.02)		
Japan	0.104	−0.038	−0.033	−0.149	−0.080	0.977	1.52
	(38.87)	(4.10)	(0.75)	(3.02)	(1.73)		
United Kingdom	0.039	−0.028	0.017	−0.016	−0.001	0.992	0.93
	(20.79)	(3.16)	(1.06)	(1.46)	(0.16)		
United States	0.031	−0.014	0.003	−0.017	−0.004	0.984	1.31
	(24.67)	(3.58)	(0.52)	(3.00)	(0.79)		

Source: BLS. Note that v and l refer to the manufacturing sector. Numbers in parentheses are t-statistics.

By setting $U_t = \dot{U}_t = \dot{U}_{t-1} = 0$ in the estimated equation, we get an estimate for $v_t^f - l_t^f$ (up to a constant). This new estimate of $v_t^f - l_t^f$ may then be used to construct a second estimate of w^x (denoted w_2^x), as is done in Table 9.1 (second half), where we once again normalize w^x to 0.0 during 1965–69. According to the estimates of Eq. (9.2), recent values of $v_t^f - l_t^f$ are *lower* than we had estimated earlier in Canada, France, Germany, and the United Kingdom; higher than we had estimated earlier for Japan; and about the same for the United States. Consequently, the new estimates of w^x are higher everywhere in recent years than estimated earlier, except in Japan (where they are lower) and in the United States (where they are basically unchanged). Equation (9.2) allowed for the possibility of a slowdown in productivity growth after 1974, by including a post-1974 time shift variable. Indeed, we estimate that growth in $v^f - l^f$ did in fact slow markedly after 1974 in all the countries.[2] In Chapter 12 we discuss several possible reasons for this slowdown.

Even if we accurately measure $v^f - l^f$, we will still mismeasure w^x if average labor productivity is not a good proxy for marginal labor productivity. Remember that under the Cobb-Douglas assumption, $\partial V / \partial L$ and V/L stand in fixed proportion (which is the advantage of the assumption). If we write $V(K,L,t)$ more generally, V/L may not give a good indication of $\partial V / \partial L$. Therefore, we must show that our finding that $w^x > 0$ is robust to alternative assumptions about the production technology.

To explore a wide class of cases, let V be a CES function of K and L, with Harrod-neutral technical change:

$$(9.3) \qquad V_t = [\mu(A_t L_t)^{-\rho_1} + (1 - \mu)K_t^{-\rho_1}]^{-1/\rho_1}.$$

Here A_t is the time-dependent level of technical progress (with constant exponential technical progress, we have $A_t = e^{\gamma t}$), and the elasticity of substitution is $\sigma_1 = 1/(1 + \rho_1)$. In the Harrod-neutral case, V_L grows faster (slower) than V/L if and only if K_t grows faster than $A_t L_t$ and $\sigma_1 > 1$ ($\sigma_1 < 1$). Specifically, by differentiating (9.3) we derive:

$$(9.4) \qquad [V_{L_t}/(V_t/L_t)] = \mu/[\mu + (1 - \mu)(K_t/A_t L_t)^{(\sigma_1 - 1)/\sigma_1}].$$

Thus, in (9.4), the ratio of V_L to (V/L) is increasing in $K_t/A_t L_t$ for $\sigma_1 < 1$, and decreasing for $\sigma_1 > 1$.[3]

These results may have an important bearing on the computation of w^x. Suppose, for example, that the *true* w^x is zero, (that is, $W/P_V = V_L(L^f, K, t)$), but that we in fact measure w^x as log $[(W/P_v)/(V_t^f/L_t^f)]$. From (9.4), our *measured* w^x *will rise* as $K_t/A_t L_t$ increases, assuming $\sigma_1 < 1$. Put in words, the simple method of calculating w^x assumes that the full-employment share of labor is a constant; but with capital deepening and $\sigma_1 < 1$, the full-employment labor share should in fact rise over time.

To illustrate the quantitative importance of capital deepening for the calculation of w^x, we present a numerical example. Suppose that an economy begins in full-employment equilibrium with the share of labor equal to 60 percent. How will a 10 percent increase in K/AL^f affect the full-employment share of labor (s^f), for alternative values of σ_1? By use of (9.1) we calculate that s^f becomes 62.5 percent for $\sigma_1 = 0.5$; 60.6 percent for $\sigma_1 = 0.8$; 60.3 percent for $\sigma_1 = 0.9$; and stays at 60.0 percent for $\sigma_1 = 1$. Thus, the lower is the elasticity of substitution (σ_1), the greater is the rise in the full-employment labor share (s^f) for a given degree of capital deepening. When σ_1 is between 0.8 and 1.0, s^f is not greatly affected by the capital deepening. Incidentally, s^f is nearly linear in K/AL^f: if a 10 percent rise in K/AL^f raises s^f by 2.5 percentage points, a 20 percent rise in K/AL^f increases s^f by about 5.0 percentage points.

We have tried to estimate the change in K/AL^f during the period 1960–80, with the following (rough) findings.[4] The United Kingdom shows the greatest increase (since $\dot{A}/A$ is so small), with an approximate 30 percent increase over the two decades. Germany is next, with a 20 percent increase, and the other economies show a decrease. Thus, with $\sigma_1 = 0.8$, the full-employment share in the United Kingdom would have risen by approximately 1.8 percentage points (30×0.6) and in Germany by about 1.2 percentage points (20×0.6), and would have declined elsewhere. With σ_1 as low as 0.5, s^f rises in the United Kingdom by about 7.5 percentage points (relative to the actual 14.4 percentage point increase), and in Germany by about 5.0 percentage points (relative to the actual 11.0 percentage point increase).

The actual movements in K/AL^f have almost surely been too small to explain a large part of the observed increases in s^f. Indeed, in several economies it appears that K/AL^f has declined over time, so that with $\sigma_1 < 1$, our measures (based on $\sigma_1 = 1$) would *understate* the true wage gap.

The Wage Gap and Unemployment

By construction (see, for example, Eq. 9.1), labor demand (relative to full-employment labor input) is a negative linear function of w^x, assuming that firms are on their supply schedules. Though this assumption is not generally valid, we now show that the link between labor input (or unemployment) and w^x is nonetheless evident in the data.

Table 9.3 shows the strong cross-country link between w^x and labor input changes since 1970. For the large OECD countries we calculate manufacturing man-hours growth ($\dot{l}$) for 1960–70 and 1970–81, for comparison with w^x. The hypothesis is that $\dot{l}_{70-81} - \dot{l}_{60-70}$ is negatively related to the rise in w^x, $w_{71-80} - w_{60-70}$. Manufacturing man-hours growth slows everywhere after 1970, but the slowdown is smallest in Canada, France, and the United States, where the rise in w^x is also smallest. The man-hours slowdown is greatest in Japan, where the rise in w^x is also greatest, and is large in Germany and the United Kingdom, in line with the sharp increases in w^x in those countries.

The wage gap variable is a labor demand indicator, measuring L^D/L^f. It is only with some care that we may link w^x to unemployment rather than labor inputs. The problem is that unemployment measures L relative to labor supply (or to the labor force) rather than to our concept of L^f, which is labor supply when the economy is fully employed. In many economies, as actual employment deviates from L^f, the labor supply L^S also changes. At least four cyclical phenomena may be at work: (1) "discouraged workers" who are without jobs may drop out of the labor force and thus not be counted as unemployed; (2) "added workers" may join the labor force to supplement household income when another household member has become unemployed; (3) foreign workers who lose jobs may return to their country of origin and thus not be counted as unemployed, though they still represent potential labor supply in the event of a recovery; and (4) job losers who enroll in official job-retraining programs may be counted as out-of-labor-force or employed. Important examples of the discouraged worker effect (Japan), the

Table 9.3. Manufacturing Man-hours and the Wage Gap, 1960–81

Country	Man-hours growth			Rise in w^x
	1960–70	1970–81	Slowdown	(1971–81) minus (1960–70)
Canada	1.7	0.8	0.9	−0.6
France	0.8	−1.1	1.9	1.6
Germany	0.2	−2.6	2.8	9.9
Japan	2.7	−0.6	3.3	16.1
United Kingdom	−0.8	−3.2	2.4	9.6
United States	1.4	0.4	1.0	2.4

Definitions and Sources: Man-hours growth is the average annual change in manufacturing man-hours for the time intervals shown. The rise in w^x is the average value of w^x for 1971–81 minus the average value of w^x for 1960–70, shown as a percentage gap. The wage gap is w_1^x, shown in the top half of Table 9.1. The man-hours data are from the BLS.

foreign-worker effect (Austria, Germany, Switzerland), and the training-program effect (Sweden) are discussed in the next chapter.

These cyclical effects help to determine the relationship between unemployment and w^x. Define U as the percentage gap between L and L^S, approximately equal to $\log(L^S/L)$. Let us suppose that L^S is subject to effects (1)–(4) according to the simple relationship:

$$(9.5) \qquad L^S = (L^f)(L/L^f)^\beta.$$

Each 1 percent decline in labor input L reduces the labor force L^S by β percent. When β is positive, effects (1), (3), and (4) dominate (2); when β is negative, effect (2) dominates the others, since the labor force rises as labor use declines.

The unemployment rate is approximated by $\log(L^S/L)$, which from (9.5) equals $-(1-\beta)\log(L/L^f)$. Assuming that firms are on their short-run supply schedules, so that $L = L^D$, we know from (9.1) that $\log(L/L^f) = -\alpha w^x$. Therefore, we have under our labor supply assumptions:

$$(9.6) \qquad U = \alpha(1-\beta)w^x.$$

Countries with large β (for example, Switzerland, with an "exportable" foreign labor supply) will show a smaller rise in U for a given change in w^x.

Table 9.4 introduces unemployment rate equations in the spirit of (9.6), though lagged U_t and a time trend are also added to the regressions. We use

Table 9.4. Unemployment and the Wage Gap, 1961–81
$U_t = \alpha_0 + \alpha_1 U_{t-1} + \alpha_2 t + \alpha_3 w_t^x$

Country	α_1	α_2	α_3	$\bar{R}^2$	D.H.
Canada[a]	0.63	0.07	15.72	0.85	0.45
	(5.46)	(2.82)	(2.23)		
France	0.93	0.06	4.45	0.97	−0.38
	(8.24)	(2.05)	(1.51)		
Germany	0.55	−0.04	18.37	0.90	0.17
	(4.44)	(−0.92)	(3.53)		
Japan	0.35	−0.01	3.36	0.94	−1.30
	(2.72)	(−1.03)	(3.99)		
United Kingdom	1.13	−0.15	23.61	0.91	1.57
	(5.48)	(−2.01)	(4.20)		
United States	0.62	0.04	10.67	0.56	1.93
	(3.43)	(1.04)	(1.07)		

a. 1961–80. Numbers in parentheses are t-statistics.

w_1^x as the wage gap variable. The lagged U_t is included to allow for a lagged adjustment of labor inputs to a change in the real wage, along the lines of Table 8.15 in the previous chapter. As predicted, the coefficient on w^x is everywhere positive, and is significant in four of six cases. We shall see later that adding demand-side variables will improve the relationship between U and w^x and will make the relationship statistically significant in France. (Note as well the concern with the data for France, as explained in Table 9.1.)

The small coefficient on w_1^x for Japan seems to be well explained by the high cyclical sensitivity of the Japanese labor force, along the lines suggested earlier. In the next chapter we briefly describe some reasons for this high cyclical sensitivity.

Table 9.5 offers a different minimal test for w^x: that it helps to predict U_t, given lagged values of U and a time trend. (Technically, this is the test that w^x "Granger causes" unemployment.) For the two measures of w^x derived in the previous section we run the regression

$$(9.7) \qquad U_t = \alpha_0 + \alpha_1 U_{t-1} + \alpha_2 U_{t-2} + \alpha_3 U_{t-2} + \alpha_4 t + \alpha_5 w_{t-1}^x$$

and test for $\alpha_5 \neq 0$ (in which case w^x Granger causes U). The results are quite supportive of the general proposition of interest. For w_1^x, α_5 is significantly different from zero in five of six cases; and for w_2^x, in four of six cases. As in the unemployment regressions of Table 9.4, the links of w^x and U in France and the United States seem to be weakest.

The results of Tables 9.3, 9.4, and 9.5 are a bit surprising in light of a long history of papers in which the real wage is shown to be acyclical or even procyclical. Keynes wrote in the *General Theory* that a real wage squeeze was necessary to explain the supply response of firms to a demand contraction; though several studies on U.S. data seemed to cast doubt on this view. Recent work by Geary and Kennan purports to show that real wages and

Table 9.5. Tests of Granger-Causality w^x on U (at 5% probability level)

Country	w_1^x	w_2^x
Canada	Yes	Yes
France	Yes[a]	No
Germany	Yes	Yes
Japan	Yes	Yes
United Kingdom	Yes	Yes
United States	No	No

a. At 10% probability level.

employment are independent in other countries also, in contradiction to the findings here, but Grubb, Layard, and Symons have challenged those findings, reaching conclusions in unpublished work similar to those of Table 9.4 and Table 9.5.[5]

There are two ways to reconcile the conclusions of Tables 9.4 and 9.5 with the established literature. First, the United States is simply different, and the literature has mainly dealt with the United States. Second, even in Europe it is doubtful that real wages move countercyclically in all business cycles and likely that the supply shocks of the 1970s have strengthened the links between w^x and U in recent years. Malinvaud (1977) convincingly argued that different cycles may have different characteristics in this regard; the 1970s happened to be a period of adverse supply shocks that pushed firms onto their labor-demand schedules.

The Dynamics of the Wage Gap

Consider the measurement of w^x under Cobb-Douglas assumptions: $w^x = (w - p_v) - (v^f - l^f) + \text{constant}$. Taking first differences, and rewriting $(w - p_v)$ as $(w - p_c) + (p_c - p_v)$, we have

$$\dot{w}^x = \dot{w}_c + (\dot{p}_c - \dot{p}_v) - (\dot{v}^f - \dot{l}^f).$$

Loosely speaking, $\dot{w}_c$ is a negative function of the unemployment rate; $\dot{p}_c - \dot{p}_v$ is a positive function of supply shocks, such as $\dot{\pi}_n > 0$; and $\dot{v}^f - \dot{l}^f$ is a function, among other things, of the rate of capital accumulation, which in turn depends on profitability.

In very stylized terms, which must be modified on a country-by-country basis, we can identify at least three phases in the development of $\dot{w}^x$ since the early 1960s. After little change in the mid-1960s, the wage gap began to increase rapidly after 1969 (particularly in Europe) because of a "real wage explosion," in which w_c increased sharply. Though there is still much discussion about the genesis of this wage increase, it is fundamentally rooted in the long period of high employment and tight labor markets that raised real wage aspirations and shifted power to labor in wage bargaining. In a second phase, w^x increased further when the supply shocks caused $\dot{p}_c - \dot{p}_v$ to rise in the mid-1970s. Finally, in a third phase, w^x has risen in most countries since the late 1970s through a combination of further supply shocks and a sharp deterioration almost everywhere in productivity growth. Thus, while $\dot{w}_c$ has been low by postwar standards in the past three or four years (the United

Kingdom is an exception), $\dot{v}^f - \dot{l}^f$ has fallen as much or more, so that w^x has continued to rise.

Table 9.6 shows some of these trends, by decomposing $\dot{w}^x$ into $\dot{w}_c + (\dot{p}_c - \dot{p}_v) - (\dot{v}^f - \dot{l}^f)$ for the subperiods 1963–69, 1969–75, and 1975–81. The table has been organized to contrast the behavior of Europe and Japan with that of North America. In Europe, $\dot{w}_c$ rises sharply in the middle period, accounting for much of the rise in w^x in that period; while in North America, $\dot{w}_c$ does not change significantly (and indeed falls in the United States). France, Japan, and the United States appear to be most affected by higher $\dot{p}_c - \dot{p}_v$ during 1969–75. In the third period, real wage growth slows everywhere, but so does productivity, with the result that w^x either stabilizes or continues to rise. The terms-of-trade squeeze, as measured by $\dot{p}_c - \dot{p}_v$, worsens everywhere, with the largest effects occurring once again in France, Japan, and the United States.

It is discouraging to note from Table 9.6 that slower real wage growth after 1975 did not make major inroads into the profit squeeze, because of even larger declines in productivity growth. To some extent the productivity slowdown may be considered to be simply "bad luck." But, as noted in Chapter 8, we believe that to a large extent the post-1973 slowdown in productivity growth is a reflection of high unemployment and the profit squeeze itself (see also Chapter 12). In this sense, a high wage gap can beget an even higher wage gap. An economy can become stuck in a low-growth, low-profitability path, since an initial profit squeeze feeds upon itself through the effect of reducing capital accumulation and other contributions to productivity growth.

Some Theoretical Explanations of Slow Wage Adjustment

So far we have shown evidence that real wages were consistently above labor-market clearing levels, and we have traced out some of the dynamic implications of that finding. The purpose of this section is to offer some general theoretical arguments that might help to explain the failure of wages to adjust very rapidly to eliminate a wage gap.

We propose three basic reasons why real wages may persistently exceed full-employment levels. Most important, when wages are set in collective bargaining between unions and employers, unions may have strong incentives to demand high wages at the expense of employment, or to adjust to adverse shocks by reduced employment rather than by reduction in real wages. In certain cases, for example, an input price shock will be absorbed by

Table 9.6. Decomposition of Changes in the Wage Gap, 1963–1981 (annual rates)

Country	1963–69 $\dot{w}^x =$	$\dot{w}_c +$	$(\dot{p}_c - \dot{p}_v)$	$-(\dot{v}^f - \dot{l}^f)$	1969–75 $\dot{w}^x =$	$\dot{w}_c +$	$(\dot{p}_c - \dot{p}_v)$	$-(\dot{v}^f - \dot{l}^f)$	1975–81 $\dot{w}^x =$	$\dot{w}_c +$	$(\dot{p}_c - \dot{p}_v)$	$-(\dot{v}^f - \dot{l}^f)$
Europe and Japan												
France	-1.2	4.0	0.6	-5.8	1.4	5.8	1.1	-5.5	-0.2	3.0	1.3	-4.5
Germany	0.1	5.3	0.3	-5.5	2.0	7.5	-0.1	-5.4	0.1	3.8	0.9	-4.7
Japan[a]	0.5	8.2	2.7	-10.4	3.3	8.4	4.2	-9.3	0.2	1.2	6.0	-7.0
United Kingdom	0.7	3.2	1.8	-4.3	1.5	5.3	-0.3	-3.5	1.2	2.9	0.7	-2.1
North America												
Canada[b]	0.5	3.0	2.3	-4.7	-0.5	3.5	-0.2	-3.8	-0.2	1.7	0.1	-2.0
United States	-0.5	1.9	1.1	-3.5	-0.1	1.2	1.6	-2.9	1.4	0.3	2.6	-1.5

a. 1975–80 rather than 1975–81.
b. 1975–79 rather than 1975–81.

an optimizing union *entirely* in the form of reduced employment rather than real wage concessions. The same may be true of adjustments to higher payroll taxes, reduced productivity growth, and so on. In fact, payroll tax increases may have played a key role empirically in several economies (see Table 9.7).

The second factor involves the interaction of wage contracts and uncertainty. In typical labor markets, wage commitments must be made before the market-clearing wage level is known. Because of the costs of contracting, the wage agreements will not in general contain a rich enough array of contingencies to guarantee that the *ex post* contract wage will equal the market-clearing level. Thus, wage agreements were signed in 1973 and 1979 before the supply shocks were observed, and real wages were temporarily stuck above full employment levels for that reason alone. The United Kingdom in 1974 provides a case where bad timing alone greatly exacerbated the impact of the supply shock, as we will describe later.

Even after the supply shocks occurred, there was a great deal of confusion as to whether the disturbances represented transitory or permanent changes in the economic environment. We will use a model developed by Brunner, Cukierman, and Meltzer (1980) to argue that confusion over the persistence of the supply shocks slowed the downward response of real wages to the lower market-clearing level.

The third factor, also based on uncertainty, is that wage setters may fail to believe that a real wage problem exists. We will describe a model of Grossman and Hart (1981) in which employers suffer a productivity shock, but cannot credibly convey this fact to workers. The workers know that employers try to win wage concessions by falsely claiming an adverse shock. In the model, the workers accept real wage cuts only in conjunction with layoffs. This model demonstrates that the quality of labor-management relations can have important macroeconomic consequences. Indeed, in the next chapter we will present evidence that successful macroeconomic performance after 1973 is well correlated with the absence of labor disputes in the decade *before* 1973. The Grossman-Hart model is most persuasive in view of the novelty of the supply shocks in the 1970s. The period 1945 – 1972 was an era of steadily rising real incomes, and therefore, when the supply shocks hit, standard operating procedures and guidelines in union wage negotiations were often pointed in exactly the wrong direction.[6]

THE UNION WAGE MODEL

Several writers have recently analyzed the role of union wage setting as a factor in real wage rigidity over the business cycle (see, for example, Oswald,

1979; Calmfors, 1982; Grossman, 1982a, b; McDonald and Solow, 1981). McDonald and Solow provide a series of models that focus on the wage-employment trade-off and the outcomes that are likely to arise from wage bargaining, emphasizing the implications of demand shocks for real wage outcomes. We will adopt their simplest model and study the implications of certain supply shocks for wages and unemployment. We will then examine a number of realistic amendments to the model.

Consider a union with membership N that bargains over wages with an employer. In the model, the union is assumed to select the wage rate and the employer then to select the employment level $L \leq N$. The union randomly allocates the available jobs among its members, so that each has probability L/N of employment and $[1 - (L/N)]$ of unemployment. The union maximizes the expected utility of a representative worker:

$$(9.8) \qquad \max_{W/P} (L/N)\Omega(W/P) + [1 - (L/N)]\Omega_0.$$

$\Omega(W/P)$ is the utility level of an employed worker receiving W/P, and Ω_0 is the utility level of the worker if he is in the fraction $[1 - (L/N)]$ that becomes unemployed (and is therefore a function of factors such as unemployment benefits, alternative work available, and leisure). We assume that the union takes Ω_0 as given, exogenous to W/P and L.

The firm's demand for labor depends, of course, on the wage, technology, and the price of other factors (for example, intermediate inputs). We write in log-linear terms the labor-demand equation from Chapter 3:

$$(9.9) \qquad l = -\alpha w_q - \beta \pi_n + k.$$

Now, maximizing (9.8) with respect to W/P yields the first-order condition:

$$(1/N)[dL/d(W/P)]\Omega + (L/N)[d\Omega/d(W/P)]$$
$$- (\Omega_0/N)[dL/d(W/P)] = 0.$$

Multiplying through by (WN/PL), we have

$$(9.10) \qquad \alpha[\Omega(W/P) - \Omega_0] = [(W/P)d\Omega/d(W/P)],$$

where $\alpha = dl/dw_q = -(W/PL)[dL/d(W/P)]$ is the elasticity of demand from the labor-demand equation.

Equation (9.10) is an implicit relationship between W/P and Ω_0. Like a typical monopolist, the union sets an optimal markup of $\Omega(W/P)$ over Ω_0 that is an inverse function of the elasticity of demand for labor facing the union. For instance, suppose that $\Omega(W/P) = \log (W/P)$. Then, solving (9.10), $W/P = \exp [1/\alpha + \Omega_0]$. Thus, as the elasticity of demand falls, W/P rises.

The level of W/P depends on the elasticity of demand for labor and on Ω_0, but not directly on the level of demand for labor. Shifts in the level of demand, for example $dk > 0$, will alter W/P only indirectly by altering α or Ω_0, if those parameters are not constant. This fact has a remarkable implication. Suppose that π_n rises with α and Ω_0 constants. According to (9.10), the union's optimal real wage will remain unchanged. From (9.9), we see immediately that $dl = -\beta d\pi_n$, since $dw_q = 0$. Thus, an optimizing union absorbs an input price shock *entirely in the form of reduced employment at a given real wage,* if the shock does not affect the elasticity of labor demand or the level of utility in unemployment.

The elasticity of demand for labor with respect to the wage is not a constant for most production functions. Changes in Π_N will affect the optimal choice of W/P through an effect on α. In general, when $V(K,L)$ has an elasticity of substitution less than 1, the rise in Π_N will result in a rise in labor's share of income, a rise in α, and a fall in the optimal wage. Unions will respond to a supply shock by partial real wage rigidity, and some rise in unemployment. To illustrate this proposition, consider the following examples. When Q is Cobb-Douglas in K, L, and N, α is constant and W/P is invariant to Π_N. Instead, let $Q = \min(V,N)$, where $V = aL - bL^2$. It is then easy to derive the demand for labor as $L = (a/2b) - W_Q/[2b(1 - \Pi_N)]$. The elasticity of L with respect to W_Q is an increasing function of the wage and an increasing function of Π_N. Pursuing this example, if $\Omega(W_Q) = W_Q$, and $\Omega_0 = 0$, then by substitution into (9.10), we find:

(9.11) $W_Q = a(1 - \Pi_N)/2$, $L = a/4b$.

In this case W_Q absorbs the *full* brunt of the rise in Π_N, since the optimal union policy is to hold L constant. This example hinges strongly on the fact that α rises as Π_N rises, so that the union monopoly power declines after an oil shock.

More generally, as long as α is an increasing function of W_Q, as it will be if $Q(L,K,N)$ is CES with $\sigma < 1$, downward shifts in the labor demand schedule (whether from supply price shocks, or technical regress, or capital decumulation) will tend to cause partial real wage concessions and some rise in unemployment.

The union-wage model is useful for considering a second type of shock that was prevalent in the 1970s: an increase in payroll taxes. Suppose that take-home pay of workers is W/P while labor costs are $(1 + \tau)W/P$, where τ is an *ad valorem* payroll tax. Labor demand is then based on the equality of $\partial Q/\partial L$ with $(1 + \tau)W/P$, which causes (9.9) to be rewritten as

(9.12) $l = -\alpha(w_q + \tau) - \beta\pi_n + k$.

Table 9.7. Legally Required Employer Contributions to Social Insurance Funds, as a Percentage of Employee Compensation

Country	1966	1972	1978
Belgium	19.7	22.2	21.8
Canada	3.0[a]	3.8[b]	4.2
France	22.0	22.5	22.1
Germany	12.1	16.6	18.2
Italy	26.0	27.4	27.3
Japan	5.5[c]	5.9[b]	12.2
Netherlands	10.8	14.2	17.5
Sweden	8.3[a]	10.0	22.8[d]
United Kingdom	5.2[a]	5.9[e]	9.6
United States	5.5	6.2	7.4[f]

Source: Office of Productivity and Technology, Bureau of Labor Statistics.
a = 1968; b = 1971; c = 1965; d = 1979; e = 1973; f = 1977.

A rise in the tax rate of one percentage point is therefore equivalent to an (α/β) percent increase in π_n in its effect on labor demand and therefore on the union wage. For a constant α, a rise in τ is fully absorbed by a decline in l, with a constant level of take-home pay.

Table 9.7 gives an indication of movements in τ in several economies since the mid-1960s. In every country there is an increase between 1966 and 1978 in the share of total employee compensation accounted for by payroll tax contributions of employers. The change is negligible in France; small in Belgium, Canada, Italy, and the United States; and large in the remaining economies. The country-by-country comparison of changes in this ratio between 1966 and 1978, with the comparable change in w^x, suggests an important relationship between the variables. Countries with relatively large payroll tax increases—Germany, Japan, Netherlands, Sweden, and the United Kingdom—also tend to display relatively large increases in the wage gap. Belgium is the sole case of a large rise in w^x that is not also accompanied by a sharp rise in τ. The correlation coefficient between $(w^x_{78} - w^x_{66})$ and $(\tau_{78} - \tau_{66})$ is $r = 0.35$ for the seven countries with available data, and $r = 0.86$ if Belgium is removed from the list.[7]

THE ROLE OF UNCERTAINTY WITH WAGE CONTRACTS

We mentioned earlier two key channels through which uncertainty can play a role in real wage adjustment: wage contracting and asymmetric information. Let us turn to the contracting issue first. Because of the costs of continuous negotiation, wages are set at fixed intervals, typically before some relevant variables, like π_n, are fully known. Unexpected shocks can therefore push w_q above or below the level that would be selected with perfect foresight, assuming that contracts are not written with contingencies based on realizations of π_n.[8] Moreover, once a shock occurs, there may be a persistent deviation of w_q from the perfect foresight level if there is difficulty in determining whether the shock is temporary or permanent.

Suppose, for example, that π_n follows a stochastic process that makes it subject to both transient and persistent shocks. Suppose, in particular, that $\pi_{n_t} = x_t + v_t$, where x_t follows a random walk and v_t is white noise. Agents observe π_{n_t}, but not the individual components x_t and v_t, though they are assumed to know the stochastic processes generating x_t and v_t. Formally:

(9.13) $\pi_{n_t} = x_t + v_t,$

$x_t = x_{t-1} + \varepsilon_t,$

v_t is i.i.d. $N(0, \sigma_v^2),$

ε_t is i.i.d. $N(0, \sigma_\varepsilon^2),$

$\text{cov}\,(\varepsilon_t, v_{t+j}) = 0$ for all $t, j.$

Define $\pi_{n_{t+1}}^e = E(\pi_{n_{t+1}} | \pi_{n_t}, \pi_{n_{t-1}}, \ldots)$, so that $\pi_{n_{t+1}}^e$ is the tth period expectation of $\pi_{n_{t+1}}$ conditional on current and lagged π_n but *not* on x and v separately. We let $\pi_{n_{t+1}}^E$ denote $E(\pi_{n_{t+1}} | v_t, x_t)$, that is, the expectation of $\pi_{n_{t+1}}$ that is conditional on x and v separately. By a formula due to Muth (1961):

(9.14) $\pi_{n_{t+1}}^e = \lambda \sum_{i=0}^{\infty} (1 - \lambda)^i \pi_{n_{t-i}},$

where $\lambda = (a + a^2/4)^{\frac{1}{2}} - a/2$ and $a = \sigma_\varepsilon^2/\sigma_v^2$. That is, $\pi_{n_{t+1}}^e$ is a geometric weighted average of current and past values of π_n, where the relative weighting of current and past values depends on the relative variance of permanent and transitory shocks. $\pi_{n_{t+1}}^E$ is given by

(9.15) $\pi_{n_{t+1}}^E = x_t.$

In other words, the expected value of $\pi_{n_{t+1}}$, knowing the permanent component of π_{n_t}, is simply the permanent component itself.

If a permanent shock in fact occurs at time t, of size ε, the agent's expectation of $\pi_{n_{t+1}}$ will rise by $\lambda\varepsilon$ with $\lambda < 1$, though $\pi_{n_{t+1}}^E$ rises by the full amount of the shock. Agents will tend to underestimate $\pi_{n_{t+1}}$. Now, suppose that wages are being set in part according to the expectation of future π_n, in a contract of the form $w_{q_{t+1}} = a_0 - a_1\pi_{n_{t+1}}^e$, so that wages are reduced when $\pi_{n_{t+1}}^e$ rises. In highly competitive labor markets, the wage might be set to clear the labor market in expectation (for example, so that $E(w^x)$ is zero), while in unionized markets, considerations such as those in the previous section might prevail. When a permanent shock occurs, workers will only slowly raise $\pi^e_{n_{t+j}}$ and thus will persistently underestimate $\pi_{n_{t+j}}$. Wages will persistently exceed the full-information level. Each year workers will find that the somewhat "temporary" rise in input prices has lasted another year. Only after several years will it be widely appreciated that higher π_n, and lower w_p, are here to stay.

This model is important for an understanding of the past ten years (as pointed out by Brunner, Cukierman, and Meltzer, 1980). The supply shocks (particularly of oil prices) have been substantially permanent, as seen in Chapter 8, although there was much doubt during each episode that the shocks would persist. For example, some authorities argued strongly that the OPEC cartel would inevitably collapse, with real energy prices falling to pre-1973 levels. Thus Milton Friedman declared in early 1975:

> Almost regardless of our energy policy, the OPEC cartel will break down. That is assured by a worldwide reduction in crude-oil consumption and expansion in alternative supplies in response to high prices. The only question is how long it will take. It has taken a lot longer than I expected, partly because of the ill-advised energy policies we have been following under the demagogic influence of Senator Jackson and some of his colleagues. But the chances are good that even so the cartel will begin to disintegrate by 1976 and crude-oil prices will begin to tumble (*Newsweek,* February 17, 1975).

And indeed, for those taking a historical view, the only other supply shock since World War II was the temporary and wholly reversed rise in raw material prices during the 1951–52 Korean War boom.

THE ROLE OF ASYMMETRIC INFORMATION

The raw material price shocks provided a novel challenge to workers and firms and generated considerable confusion in wage bargaining. It was not widely understood by unions in 1973–74, for example, that external terms-of-trade shocks caused a downward shift in the labor demand schedule. In many cases the run-up in prices was seen to be a typical demand-induced inflation, in which workers could expect to get normal real wage gains. Only the hard experience of subsequent unemployment brought home a more realistic view.

Firm managers were of course in a much better position to understand the effects of higher Π_N on marginal costs and profitability, through a more complete knowledge of the firm's production technology and income data. It is one thing to understand the ramifications of higher Π_N, however, and another to convey them credibly to workers in the course of wage negotiations. Since firms have a natural incentive to overstate the need for real wage reductions, pronouncements by firms about a profit squeeze fall on skeptical ears. The result is that real wages do not fall as sharply as they would under full information by the work force, and unemployment becomes a cost of the asymmetry in information and lack of trust between firms and workers.

To illustrate this point, reconsider the case in which production is quadratic and worker utility is linear in real income (see the earlier section on the union wage model). We saw that a union would choose a *constant* employment level, with real wages a negative function of Π_N. Suppose now that the union does not observe the real input price faced by the firms (or alternatively does not know the production function governing its use). It cannot rely on the firm to tell it what Π_N is, since the firm would then have a strong incentive to cheat by stating a high value of Π_N. The wage cannot be conditioned on Π_N (since workers will not believe what the firm claims Π_N to be), with the implication that a rise in Π_N will lead to little wage moderation and therefore to some unemployment.

Grossman and Hart (1981), Hall and Lazear (1982), and others have examined the nature of contracts in cases where one party has key information that cannot be credibly conveyed to the other party (that is, where the possibility of self-serving deception prevents the simple transfer of information to the other side). They conclude that unemployment is a natural consequence, since wage contracts cannot be made contingent on the key information. Grossman and Hart (1981) have developed a particularly intriguing model of this situation, which we briefly describe. They consider a competitive market in which workers and a firm enter into an employment contract, so that the competitive firm maximizes its own utility (a function of profits) subject to the condition that the wage agreement yield the workers an expected utility at least as high as Ω_0. Once the workers have signed with the firm, they are unable to shift to other employment in the event that they are laid off or not fully employed. There are N workers, L of whom are employed. If the worker is employed he receives from the firm W_Q^E, and if unemployed, W_Q^U (W_Q^U may be thought of as severance pay or supplemental unemployment benefits). When the worker is employed, utility is $\Omega(W_Q^E - R)$, where R is the reservation wage or value of leisure; when he is unemployed, utility is $\Omega(W_Q^U)$.

The firm maximizes an expected utility function $E[V(\text{Profits})]$, where Profits $= Q(L,N) - W_Q^E L - W_Q^U(N - L) - \Pi_N N$, subject to the constraint that $(L/N)\Omega(W_Q^E - R) + (1 - L/N)\,\Omega(W_Q^U) \geq \Omega_0$. Π_N is treated as a random variable that is observed by the firm *after* the contract is settled. In the case where both the firm and the workers observe Π_N *ex post* (symmetric information), contracts can be written that make W_Q^E and W_Q^U contingent on the value of Π_N. The wages W_Q^E and W_Q^U will in general be made functions of Π_N.

Things are decidedly more complex when Π_N is not observed by the workers. Now W_Q^E and W_Q^U can only be conditioned on publicly observed information, of which the most relevant may be the level of firm employment itself. Grossman and Hart show that the optimal contract under these restricted conditions is one in which W_Q^E and W_Q^U are *increasing* functions of L, the employment level.

The idea is the following. Workers are prepared to accept wage cuts when firms declare that Π_N is high only if they are certain that the firm is not deceiving them. The contract is therefore designed so that firms will only ask for wage cuts when Π_N is high. This is accomplished by requiring the firm to cut employment along with the wage. For a firm facing a *low Π_N*, the lost profits from cutting employment are made to outweigh the benefits from a lower wage (remember, when Π_N is low, profit-maximizing firms will choose to employ a large work force). By adding the employment condition, the workers tell the firm: "If profits are low and wage cuts are necessary, prove it! Cut some employment." Of course, the end result is that some workers are left unemployed by a rise in Π_N, since the wage levels are only partially downward-flexible. In fact, Grossman and Hart demonstrate in their specific model that the employment level is always lower than in the case of symmetric information.

Though the Grossman-Hart model is rudimentary, it captures the important insight that the degree of trust between firms and unions might significantly condition the efficiency in the response to supply shocks. We will return to this issue empirically in Chapter 11, when we compare labor markets with consensual versus conflictual traditions of dispute resolution and wage setting.

We now turn to the role of the wage gap in empirical inflation and unemployment equations.

10 Price and Output Dynamics in Eight Economies

IN THIS CHAPTER we estimate inflation and unemployment equations for eight countries, to decompose supply and demand factors in the stagflation. The importance of real wage adjustment and import price shocks in the stagflation process is strongly evident in the estimates for most of the countries. We compare our estimated model with a mainstream Keynesian specification, to highlight further the aggregate supply considerations. We do not pretend to offer a complete structural model of macrodynamics for the eight countries; rather, our goal is to show that the basic aspects of the stagflation can be parsimoniously and consistently modeled for each of the countries, and that our representation is an improvement over typical "small" models of the macroeconomy. The key point is that a supply-side variable, measuring the real wage gap, has an important role to play in the Phillips-curve and unemployment equations. This variable has been almost universally ignored in macroeconometric models.

In the first section of this chapter we estimate a reduced-form price equation that can help to account for the rise in inflation in the 1970s in the presence of high and rising unemployment. Three factors seem to be crucial to this story: import price shocks, falling productivity growth, and a rising real wage gap in most countries. The relative importance of these factors varies widely across the eight countries under study. In the second section we present unemployment equations that extend the work of Chapter 9 by adding demand variables into a regression of unemployment on the wage gap. Once again, the wage gap variable is highly significant for all countries except the United States. In the third section some of the policy implications of the econometric findings are discussed.

Inflation Equations for the 1970s

The rise in inflation and unemployment in the 1970s has presented a deep challenge to the Phillips-curve model of inflation-unemployment dynamics. As we noted in the Introduction, models of inflation and unemployment that were popular in the 1960s postulated a stable trade-off of $\dot{p}_{c_t}$ and U_t, such as shown by the curve AA in Figure 10.1. Higher inflation was believed to buy a permanent reduction in unemployment, say in moving from the point A_1 to A_2. As the AA curve began to drift upward in the late 1960s and early 1970s, theorists and model builders adopted the Friedman-Phelps accelerationist hypothesis, which held that inflationary *expectations* could shift AA upward (say to BB), and that the curve would indeed shift upward whenever unemployment was pegged at a level lower than a key "natural" rate U^N. Thus, if policymakers tried relentlessly to hold unemployment at A_2, lower than U^N, the AA curve would shift upward, with ever-increasing rates of inflation. In this view, the only long-run sustainable inflation-unemployment choices are those with $U = U^N$.

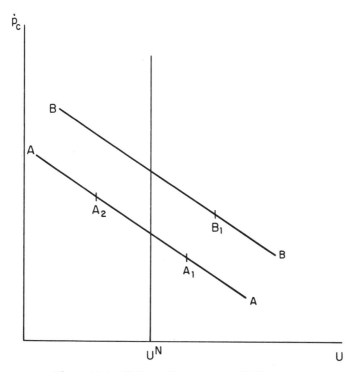

Figure 10.1. Shifts in the short-run Phillips curve

Although the accelerationist model proved useful in accounting for the shifts in AA, it has been distinctly unhelpful in explaining the data of the past decade, during which the trade-off moved to the northeast, from A_1 to B_1, without enjoying a sustained period of $U < U^N$. The professional responses to the new data have included the following points of view: (1) that there is not a stable short-run inflation-unemployment trade-off; (2) that demographic changes have pushed U^N upward, to historically unprecedented levels; or (3) that expectations have indeed shifted the trade-off, but that expectations are forward-looking, based on future policies rather than backward-looking extrapolations of recent inflation.

In our view, much of this discussion misses the point by insisting that expectations are the sole or the main factor that can shift the AA schedule. Several other identifiable and quantifiable factors have been responsible for raising AA in the 1970s. According to our simple derivations that follow, the AA schedule may be shifted by three factors in addition to expectations: import price shocks, changes in trend productivity growth, and the real wage gap. Since the last variable is the most novel addition to the Phillips curve, we consider its role first.

A typical Phillips-curve relationship like

$$(10.1) \qquad \dot{p}_{c_t} = \alpha_0 - \alpha_1 U_t + \alpha_2 \dot{p}_{c_{t-1}}$$

is a reduced form of underlying wage and price equations. A standard derivation of (10.1) is based on a wage equation such as

$$(10.2) \qquad \dot{w}_t = a_0 - a_1 U_t + a_2 \dot{p}_{c_t} + (1 - a_2)\dot{p}_{c_{t-1}},$$

in which nominal wage change is a function of the unemployment rate and the current and lagged consumer price change. The price equation typically makes $\dot{p}_{c_t}$ a function of the change in standard unit labor costs, $\dot{w}_t - \dot{\psi}_t$, and the unemployment rate:

$$(10.3) \qquad \dot{p}_{c_t} = b_0 - b_1 U_t + b_2(\dot{w}_t - \dot{\psi}_t).$$

Here ψ_t is the average productivity of labor measured at full employment, $\psi_t = v_t^f - l_t^f$. Combining (10.2) and (10.3), we find (10.1), assuming that $\dot{\psi}$ is treated as a constant, with $\alpha_0 = (b_0 + b_2 a_0 - \dot{\psi} b_2)/(1 - a_2 b_2)$; $\alpha_1 = -(b_1 + b_2 a_1)/(1 - a_2 b_2)$; $\alpha_2 = b_2(1 - a_2)/(1 - a_2 b_2)$. Significantly, the unemployment effect is a combination of effects from the wage equation and the price equation.

We argue that (10.1) should in fact be rewritten as

$$(10.1') \qquad \dot{p}_{c_t} = \alpha_0 - \alpha_1 U_t + \alpha_2 \dot{p}_{c_{t-1}} + \alpha_3 w_t^x,$$

where w_t^x is the wage gap defined in Chapter 9. The wage gap enters the

Phillips curve through a better specification of the price equation in (10.3). Specifically, $\dot{p}_c$ should be affected not merely by low levels of output (that is, high levels of U), but by *low levels of output relative to the desired supply of output*. If real wages are so high that firms want to hire little labor and produce little output, firms will not cut prices merely because measured unemployment is high. The incentive to cut prices is a function of both U and w^x.

Formally, let l^d be the demand for labor (as a function of factor costs), l the amount of labor currently employed, and l^f the full-employment labor input. Unemployment is then $l - l^f$, while $l^f - l^d$ is a linear function of w^x according to the results of Chapter 9:

(10.4) $l^f - l^d = \beta w^x.$

Now, most price equations write $\dot{p}_c$ as a positive function of $-U$, or $l - l^f$. Our argument is that $\dot{p}_c$ should properly be viewed as a function of $l - l^d$ instead. Since $l - l^d = (l - l^f) - (l^d - l^f)$, the excess demand term is $-U_t + \beta w_t^x$. Equation (10.3) is rewritten as

(10.3') $\dot{p}_{c_t} = b_0 - b_1(U_t - \beta w_t^x) + b_2(\dot{w}_t - \dot{\psi}_t).$

In fact, there are two other amendments to (10.1) that must be made before the price equation is estimated. First, we recognize that $\dot{\psi}_t$ has not been a constant in the past two decades and thus cannot be simply impounded in the constant term α_0. Noting that $\alpha_0 = (b_0 + b_2 a_0 - \dot{\psi}_t b_2)/(1 - a_2 b_2)$, we see that $\dot{\psi}_t$ should enter the price equation with a *negative* coefficient, $-b_2/(1 - a_2 b_2)$; the post-1973 slowdown in $\dot{\psi}_t$ therefore *raises* the Phillips curve.

The second, and somewhat more subtle, amendment to the price equation involves the inclusion of import prices for intermediate and final goods in (10.1'). In fact, an equation like (10.3') is appropriate for value-added prices but not for consumer prices in an open economy. Following our usual procedures, we write:

(10.5) $\dot{p}_t = s_v \dot{p}_{v_t} + (1 - s_v)(\dot{p}_{n_t}^* + \dot{e}_t)$

and

(10.6) $\dot{p}_{c_t} = \lambda \dot{p}_t + (1 - \lambda)(\dot{p}_t^* + \dot{e}).$

Here p is the domestic final good price, p^* is the foreign final good price, and p_v is the domestic value-added deflator. Combining these, we get

(10.7) $\dot{p}_{c_t} = (\lambda s_v)\dot{p}_{v_t} + (1 - \lambda s_v)[a(\dot{p}_{n_t}^* + \dot{e}_t) + (1 - a)(\dot{p}_t^* + \dot{e}_t)],$

where $a = \lambda(1 - s_v)/(1 - \lambda s_v)$. Thus, domestic consumer price inflation is a weighted average of value-added price inflation, on the one hand, and an index of foreign intermediate and final-good price inflation, on the other. We now make one major simplification, that changes in the economy's aggregate import price index provide a good approximation to $[a(\dot{p}_n^* + \dot{e}_t) + (1 - a)(\dot{p}_t^* + \dot{e}_t)]$. In that case we can write

$$(10.8) \qquad \dot{p}_{c_t} = (\lambda s_v)\dot{p}_{v_t} + (1 - \lambda s_v)\dot{p}_{m_t},$$

where p_{m_t} is the import price index. With this simplification we need not differentiate between p^* and p_n^* in the price equation.

Now, we regard (10.3′) as an equation for $\dot{p}_v$ rather than $\dot{p}_c$ (as it is now written). Combining (10.8) with an amended (10.3′) and with (10.2), we end up with the inflation equation to be estimated:

$$(10.9) \qquad \dot{p}_{c_t} = \beta_0 - \beta_1 U_t + \beta_2 \dot{p}_{c_{t-1}} + \beta_3 w_t^x - \beta_4 \psi_t + \beta_5 \dot{p}_{m_t},$$

where　$\beta_0 = (\lambda s_v b_0 + \lambda s_v b_2 a_0)/(1 - \lambda s_v b_2 a_2) > 0,$

$\beta_1 = (\lambda s_v a_1 b_2 + \lambda s_v b_1)/(1 - \lambda s_v b_2 a_2) > 0,$

$\beta_2 = (1 - a_2)\lambda s_v b_2/(1 - \lambda s_v b_2 a_2) > 0,$

$\beta_3 = \lambda s_v b_1 \beta/(1 - \lambda s_v b_2 a_2) > 0,$

$\beta_4 = \lambda s_v b_2/(1 - \lambda s_v b_2 a_2) > 0,$

$\beta_5 = (1 - \lambda s_v)/(1 - \lambda s_v b_2 a_2) > 0.$

Equation (10.9) shows that several factors can shift the Phillips curve. The accelerationist model has put too much stress on lagged inflation and its effects on expectations, and not enough on w^x, ψ, and $\dot{p}_m$, as the source of the upward movement of the Phillips curve in the 1970s. Price equations that leave out the three variables are likely to attribute the upward shift of the curve to "expectations" or inherited inflation, when the other factors are indeed at work. These equations will tend to find a highly autoregressive pattern of inflation (that is, a large $\hat{\beta}_2$), even in circumstances where the actual β_2 is close to zero.

In this model, policymakers face a long-run threshold of unemployment (like a "natural rate," U^N), such that when expansionary policies hold $U < U^N$, w^x will tend to rise continuously. This U^N is defined as the level of unemployment such that real wage growth is just balanced by trend productivity growth adjusted for terms-of-trade changes. Thus, let $\dot{\theta} = \dot{p}_c - \dot{p}_v$ in steady-state growth, and $\psi = \dot{v}^f - \dot{l}^f$. Then, from the wage equation (10.2) with $\dot{p}_{c_t} = \dot{p}_{c_{t-1}}$, we have: $\dot{w}^x = (\dot{w} - \dot{p}_c) + (\dot{p}_c - \dot{p}_v) - (\dot{v}^f - \dot{l}^f) = a_0 - a_1 U + \dot{\theta} - \psi$. The threshold, or "natural" unemployment rate, is then $U^N = (a_0 + \dot{\theta} - \psi)/a_1$. Holding U below U^N will result in rising w^x and therefore in continuing upward shifts in the short-run Phillips curve.

Equations (10.1) and (10.9) are now estimated for eight countries (those for which wage gaps may be constructed from Bureau of Labor Statistics data), as shown in Tables 10.1 and 10.2. In both cases the estimates allow for first-order serial correlation. The estimates of (10.9) also allow for simultaneous equation bias in w_i^x by use of Fair's method of instrumental variable estimation.[1] The equations are run with twenty-one annual observations from 1961 to 1981. Since we are estimating seven coefficients (β_0 to β_6 and the serial correlation component) with only twenty-one observations, it is not surprising to find fairly low t-statistics at many points in Table 10.2. The consistency of the coefficient signs and magnitudes across countries may add credence to the model even where individual parameters are statistically insignificant.

The naive Phillips curve in Table 10.1 is included to show why economists have lost faith, erroneously in our view, in a short-run inflation-unemployment trade-off. For all eight countries the unemployment term is statistically insignificant; it is near zero in Belgium and Canada, and actually of the wrong sign in Denmark and France. The lagged inflation term is somewhat more successful, and in Canada, the United Kingdom, and the United States the inflation process seems to be highly inertial, with $\hat{\alpha}_2 > 0.8$.

Table 10.1. Basic Phillips Curve Equation, 1961–81
$\dot{p}_{c_t} = \alpha_0 + \alpha_1 U_t + \alpha_2 \dot{p}_{c_{t-1}}$

Country	α_1	α_2	$\overline{R}^2$	ρ	D.W.
Belgium	−0.04	0.69	0.69	0.43	1.72
	(0.21)	(2.08)		(1.06)	
Canada	−0.02	0.95	0.84	0.31	1.60
	(0.05)	(4.91)		(0.99)	
Denmark	0.28	0.32	0.33	0.00	1.97
	(1.03)	(0.81)		(0.00)	
France	0.90	0.46	0.74	0.15	1.87
	(0.98)	(0.74)		(0.26)	
Germany	−0.18	0.73	0.61	0.37	1.92
	(0.68)	(1.82)		(0.81)	
Japan	−2.75	0.34	0.11	0.22	1.94
	(0.70)	(0.39)		(0.23)	
United Kingdom	−0.29	0.85	0.55	−0.05	1.99
	(0.43)	(3.24)		(0.15)	
United States	−0.93	0.97	0.75	0.39	1.67
	(1.59)	(3.50)		(0.89)	

Note: Numbers in parentheses are t-statistics.

Table 10.2. Augmented Phillips Curve Equations for Eight Countries, 1961–81
$\dot{p}_{c_t} = \alpha_0 + \alpha_1 \dot{p}_{c_{t-1}} + \alpha_2 w_t^x + \alpha_3 \dot{p}_{m_t} + \alpha_4 \dot{\psi}_t + \alpha_5 U_t$

Country	α_1	α_2	α_3	α_4	α_5	$\overline{R}^2$	ρ	D.W.
Belgium	0.40	10.43	0.27	−1.04	−0.55	0.95	−0.01	1.89
	(5.42)	(3.54)	(5.71)	(1.01)	(4.03)			
Canada	0.75	15.03[a]	0.21	0.02	−0.43	0.94	0.36	1.60
	(3.97)	(0.83)	(3.33)	(0.06)	(1.18)		(0.92)	
Denmark	−0.10	19.04	0.05	−2.59	−0.36	0.61	−0.02	1.74
	(0.36)	(1.63)	(0.43)	(1.82)	(0.99)		(0.07)	
France	0.40	10.92[a]	0.13[b]	−0.59	0.64	0.88	0.23	1.84
	(1.45)	(0.85)	(4.03)	(0.64)	(1.16)		(0.53)	
Germany	0.38	42.13	0.03	−0.34	−1.17	0.89	−0.24	2.22
	(2.90)	(7.86)	(1.14)	(1.26)	(9.73)		(1.15)	
Japan	0.38	22.33	0.13[b]	−0.37	−8.72	0.68	−0.01	1.99
	(2.97)	(1.16)	(2.59)	(0.24)	(1.38)		(0.07)	
United Kingdom	0.58	71.28	0.10	−0.03	−1.43	0.83	−0.61	2.16
	(3.66)	(3.88)	(1.25)	(0.05)	(2.53)		(2.53)	
United States	0.52	21.48	0.16	−1.18	−1.09	0.91	0.16	1.85
	(4.18)	(2.03)	(4.78)	(2.32)	(4.01)		(0.69)	

Source: The equations are estimated with two-stage least squares, allowing for first-order serial correlation, using Fair's method. Only w_t^x is regarded as endogenous. Excluded exogenous variables include w_{t-1}^x and log (p^m/p^x), where p^m is the unit value index for imports for the industrial countries, expressed in dollars, and p^x is the unit value index for exports. p^x and p^m are from the IMF *International Financial Statistics*. Numbers in parentheses are t-statistics.
a. w_{t-1}^x rather than w_t; these regressions are ordinary least squares.
b. $\dot{p}_{m_t}$ rather than $0.5 (\dot{p}_{m_t} + \dot{p}_{m_{t-1}})$.

In Table 10.2 we see that w^x, ψ, and $\dot{p}_m$ substantially raise the explanatory power of the Phillips curve (as measured by $\overline{R}^2$) in every case. The signs of these coefficients are in accord with theory in all cases: the coefficient on w^x is always positive, on $\dot{p}_m$ is always positive, and on $\dot{\psi}_t$ is always negative. Notably, the coefficient on U_t is more negative for *every* country than in Table 10.1, and it is statistically significant in four out of eight cases. Thus, the other variables tend to restore the negative slope of the Phillips curve. Also, the addition of w^x, $\dot{p}_m$, and ψ reduces in every case the coefficient on lagged inflation, $\dot{p}_{c_{t-1}}$. The estimates in the second column of Table 10.3 are striking. They show, for example, that if the Belgian wage gap (29 percent in 1981) were actually 0.0, Belgian unemployment could be lowered by 5.3 percentage points without increasing inflation. Or to put it differently, a rise in w^x from 0.0 to 29.0 percent requires a 5.3 percentage point rise in U to

Table 10.3. Shifts in Phillips Curve Due to Real Wage Gap (percentage of labor force)

Country	Unemployment increase needed to counteract 1 percentage point rise in w^x	w^x_{1981}	Increase in U_{1981} needed to counteract w^x_{1981}	$U_{1981} - U_{1969}$
Belgium	0.18	29.3	5.3	10.5
Canada	0.35	−3.6[a]	−1.4[a]	2.9
Denmark	0.53	7.0	3.7	8.8
France	−0.17	1.9	−0.3	5.3
Germany	0.36	12.2	4.3	3.4
Japan	0.03	23.0[a]	0.6[a]	1.1
United Kingdom	0.50	19.3	9.6	8.3
United States	0.19	8.1	1.6	4.1

Source: Calculations are based on regression estimates $[-\alpha_2/(100\alpha_5)]$ of Table 10.2.
a. 1980 value.

keep excess supply from changing. In Germany and the United Kingdom, excess supply (as measured by $\alpha_2 w^x_t + \alpha_5 U_t$) appears to be *less* in 1981 than in 1969, even though measured unemployment has risen several percentage points in that time interval. In the other countries except Canada and France, the rise in w^x eliminates a significant part, though not all, of the rise in excess supply due to higher U between 1969 and 1981.

The estimated equation suggests an interesting decomposition of the rise in inflation after 1965–69. For all variables x, let x_{65-69} be the simple average of x for the years 1965–69. For any year t, we can account for the difference in $\dot{p}_{c_t}$ and $\dot{p}_{c_{65-69}}$ as:

$$(10.10) \quad (\dot{p}_{c_t} - \dot{p}_{c_{65-69}}) = \alpha_1(\dot{p}_{c_{t-1}} - \dot{p}_{c_{64-68}})$$
$$+ \alpha_2(w^x_t - w^x_{65-69}) + \alpha_3(\dot{p}_{m_t} - \dot{p}_{m_{65-69}})$$
$$+ \alpha_4(\dot{\psi}_t - \dot{\psi}_{65-69}) + \alpha_5(U_t - U_{65-69})$$
$$+ (\varepsilon_t - \varepsilon_{65-69}).$$

The ε_t and ε_{65-69} represent the residuals from the regression equation of Table 10.2. Thus we can say, for example, that the rise in inflation between 1965–69 and year t *due to an increase in* w^x is $\alpha_2(w^x_t - w^x_{65-69})$. $\alpha_1(\dot{p}_{c_{t-1}} - \dot{p}_{64-68})$ represents the part due to differences in inherited inflation; $\alpha_3(\dot{p}_{m_t} - \dot{p}_{m_{65-69}})$ to differences in import prices; $\alpha_4(\dot{\psi}_t - \dot{\psi}_{65-69})$ to differences in trend productivity growth; $\alpha_5(U_t - U_{65-69})$ to differences in unemployment; and $\varepsilon_t - \varepsilon_{65-69}$ to unaccounted factors.

Table 10.4. Accounting for the Rise in Inflation since 1965–69 (in percentages)

Country	1970–72	1973–75	1976–78	1979–81
BELGIUM				
Total rise	1.1	7.3	3.4	2.7
of which:				
Inherited inflation	0.2	1.9	2.4	0.6
Wage gap	0.9	2.4	3.2	3.1
Import prices	0.7	3.6	0.9	3.1
Unemployment	0.2	−0.8	−3.4	−4.9
Productivity	0.0	0.4	0.6	1.2
Other	−0.8	−0.2	−0.3	−0.5
CANADA				
Total rise	0.1	6.1	4.5	6.9
of which:				
Inherited inflation	0.3	3.5	4.2	4.7
Wage gap	0.4	0.0	0.4	−0.1
Import prices	0.1	3.0	1.5	2.6
Unemployment	−0.8	−0.8	−1.6	−1.4
Productivity	0.0	−0.1	−0.1	−0.1
Other	0.1	−0.5	0.1	0.2
DENMARK				
Total rise	−0.1	5.0	3.6	4.8
of which:				
Inherited inflation	0.1	−0.4	−0.4	−0.4
Wage gap	0.8	2.1	1.9	1.8
Import prices	0.1	0.7	0.2	0.6
Unemployment	−0.1	−1.1	−2.9	−2.7
Productivity	0.0	3.4	5.0	6.0
Other	−1.0	0.3	−0.3	−0.4
FRANCE				
Total rise	2.1	7.2	5.6	8.7
of which:				
Inherited inflation	1.1	2.4	2.8	3.1
Wage gap	−0.5	−0.1	0.2	0.0
Import prices	0.5	2.0	0.8	1.8
Unemployment	0.5	0.9	2.0	3.1
Productivity	0.0	0.3	0.4	1.1
Other	0.5	1.7	−0.6	−0.4

Table 10.4 (*continued*)

Country	1970–72	1973–75	1976–78	1979–81
GERMANY				
Total rise	2.3	4.1	1.1	2.7
of which:				
Inherited inflation	0.3	1.4	0.7	0.6
Wage gap	1.4	4.1	4.4	4.4
Import prices	−0.1	0.4	0.1	0.3
Unemployment	0.3	−2.0	−3.9	−3.3
Productivity	0.0	0.1	0.1	0.5
Other	0.2	0.1	−0.4	0.2
JAPAN				
Total rise	0.8	10.7	1.8	0.2
of which:				
Inherited inflation	0.5	3.3	1.8	0.0
Wage gap	1.4	3.4	4.7	NA
Import prices	0.0	4.3	−0.8	3.0
Unemployment	−0.4	−2.7	−7.4	−7.7
Productivity	0.0	0.8	1.2	1.5
Other	0.9	−0.6	1.7	2.3
UNITED KINGDOM				
Total rise	3.4	12.2	9.3	10.2
of which:				
Inherited inflation	1.9	4.0	8.7	5.5
Wage gap	0.9	5.7	4.7	11.4
Import prices	0.1	2.3	1.1	0.6
Unemployment	−1.7	−1.5	−5.2	−8.1
Productivity	0.0	0.1	0.1	0.1
Other	2.3	1.6	−0.2	0.7
UNITED STATES				
Total rise	1.1	5.4	3.2	8.3
of which:				
Inherited inflation	1.4	2.2	2.4	4.3
Wage gap	−0.2	0.4	0.6	1.6
Import prices	0.6	3.7	0.8	2.4
Unemployment	−1.8	−2.7	−3.4	−3.3
Productivity	0.0	1.5	2.3	2.4
Other	1.1	0.3	0.6	0.9

This decomposition is undertaken for four subperiods after 1969 and is shown in Table 10.4. For each country, the "Total rise" signifies $\dot{p}_c$ during the subperiod minus $\dot{p}_{c_{65-69}}$. This change is accounted for by the six factors just mentioned. In general, the rise in inflation over 1965–69 is greatest in the two subperiods 1973–75 and 1979–81. (Japan and Belgium are the exceptions to this statement; in those cases, $\dot{p}_{c_{76-78}} > \dot{p}_{c_{79-81}}$.) And in most cases, the contribution of import prices explains the bulge in those years. Also, by 1976–78 the wage gap accounts for a significant fraction of the total rise in inflation in all countries except Canada, France, and the United States. In general, inherited inflation accounts for less than half of the rise in inflation for the most recent subperiod, a much smaller percentage than in the years 1970–72. The productivity slowdown also accounts for some of the inflation increase, though the measured productivity effect is generally smaller than the wage gap effect except in Denmark and the United States. Finally, note that in the United Kingdom and Germany, the wage gap effect is greater, in absolute value, than the disinflationary effects of higher unemployment. This adds further support to our early finding regarding the change in aggregate supply during the 1970s in these countries.

The decomposition in Table 10.4 is useful in indicating the proximate causes of inflation in any given year, but it certainly cannot provide an explanation of the fundamental factors at work in raising inflation in the course of several years. This is because an initial shock, say to $\dot{p}_m$, will work its way through the economy in various guises. First, the accounting would pick up a large direct contribution of $\dot{p}_m$ to the rise in inflation. Over time, w^x and *lagged* inflation would tend to rise and $\dot{\psi}$ tend to fall in response to the initial foreign price shock, so that w^x, $\dot{p}_{c_{t-1}}$, and $\dot{\psi}$ would account for a rising share of the increased inflation. In a fundamental sense, the continued rise in $\dot{p}_c$ might still be a result of the initial increase in $\dot{p}_m$, but the accounting in Table 10.4 does not pick up that relationship. A complete model of the determination of w^x, $\dot{p}_m$, $\dot{\psi}$, and $\dot{p}_c$ would be necessary for that purpose.

Unemployment Equations for the 1970s

The rise in the Phillips curve in the 1970s was only one side of the policy frustration in recent years. On the other side, a given real macroeconomic stimulus (for example, an increase in real money balances) has been widely perceived as providing less push to the real economy than predicted by standard macroeconometric models. Here, too, we believe that insufficient attention was paid to aggregate supply conditions, as measured by w^x. We now present an equation for unemployment in which changes in U reflect both aggregate demand and aggregate supply factors. For given w_t^x, a rise in real aggregate demand reduces U_t, while for given demand, a reduction in w_t^x also reduces U_t.

Once again, let us start with the conventional model. In demand-determined models of real output, we typically find equations such as

(10.11)   (a) $\dot{v}_t = \beta(v_{t-1}^d - v_{t-1})$,

    (b) $v_t^d = \gamma(m_t - p_{c_t})$.

Value-added v_t changes according to the lagged gap between aggregate demand, v_{t-1}^d, and actual output, v_{t-1}. Aggregate demand is a function of real money balances (and presumably fiscal policy, world output, and so on, which are suppressed in the illustration). Combining (10.11)(a) and (b), we find that v_t equals a geometric distributed lag of past real money balances.

The problem with (10.11) (a) and (b) is that there is no role for supply factors in output determination. Suppose, for example, that real wages are so high that desired supply v^s is actually far below v. We would expect that v would grow slowly, even with v^d well above v. In fact, in the strict disequilibrium models of Chapters 5 and 7, v_t would be determined as the minimum of v_t^d and v_t^s, so that the high real wage would be decisive in reducing output. Our amendment to (10.11)(a) is less extreme than the minimum rule, for reasons to be described. We rewrite $\dot{v}_t$ as a function of both $v_{t-1}^d - v_{t-1}$ and $v_{t-1}^s - v_{t-1}$:

(10.12) $\dot{v}_t = \beta(v_{t-1}^d - v_{t-1}) + \gamma(v_{t-1}^s - v_{t-1})$.

The last term is rewritten as $v_{t-1}^s - v_{t-1} = (v_{t-1}^s - v_{t-1}^f) + (v_{t-1}^f - v_{t-1})$, and $v_{t-1}^s - v_{t-1}^f$ is replaced by $-\alpha w_{t-1}^x$, according to the results of Chapter 9. Combining (10.12) with (10.11) (a) and (b), we then have

(10.13) $\dot{v}_t = \beta[(m_{t-1} - p_{c_{t-1}}) - v_{t-1}] - \gamma\alpha w_{t-1}^x - \gamma(v_{t-1} - v_{t-1}^f)$.

Finally, we introduce an Okun's law relationship to substitute the unemployment rate for v_t. Letting $U_t = \theta(v_t^f - v_t)$, we rewrite (10.13) as

(10.14) $\dot{U}_t = \theta\dot{v}_t^f - \theta\beta(m_{t-1} - p_{t-1})$
    $+ (\gamma\alpha\theta)w_{t-1}^x - (\beta + \gamma)U_{t-1} + \theta\beta v_{t-1}^f$.

Thus, $\dot{U}_t$ increases with w_{t-1}^x and decreases in $m_{t-1} - p_{t-1}$.

Before turning to the empirical estimates of (10.14), we should mention why we have chosen this specification, rather than one of two alternatives: full market clearing, with $v^d = v^s$, or the minimum rule, with $v = \min$

(v^d, v^s). The market-clearing model is clearly inappropriate for year-to-year modeling of output movements, for we have seen that the boom-bust cycles of 1972–75 and 1978–81 must be understood as deviations around an aggregate supply function. Moreover, these deviations are well explained by global demand factors, principally changes in money supplies in the major economies, as shown in Chapter 8.

Unfortunately, the same evidence is no more kind to the typical "min" rule of disequilibrium models, $v = \min (v^d, v^s)$. The output boom in the early 1970s seems to have been a period in which output was high even though v^s was low due to a sharp rise in real wages. Data for Germany (Table 10.5) illustrate this effect. Note the rise in w^x and M/P_C between 1969 and 1972, and the constant unemployment rate, in spite of the sharp fall in profitability. It seems that a major demand expansion (as measured by M/P_C) overcame the contractionary effect of a growing profit squeeze. v^s fell (relative to a trend path up to the early 1970s), but actual output remained high. In effect, firms were probably selling below marginal cost to meet demand, and profits fell in spite of high output. When Germany halted the rapid money growth in 1973, U doubled (to 2.6 percent from 1.3 percent) in the following year, then virtually doubled again in 1975 (to 4.7 percent).

We suspect, therefore, that demand expansions can raise production above firms' notional supply levels (v^s) in the short run. The long-run benefits of customer loyalty induce firms to meet demand at posted prices even when marginal costs are above that level. The direct evidence on unfilled orders, however, shows that not all demand is automatically and instantly met. Thus we take a compromise view that output adjusts according to both supply and demand factors, in the way summarized by Eq. (10.12). A nega-

Table 10.5. Aggregate Supply and Demand Measures for Germany, 1969–1973

Economic indicator	1969	1970	1971	1972	1973
Wage gap	−0.2	1.9	2.9	5.3	8.0
M/P_C (percentage deviation from trend)	0.8	1.0	3.2	6.2	−3.5
Unemployment rate	0.9	0.7	0.9	1.1	1.3
Profitability	0.21	0.19	0.18	0.16	0.17

Note: Unemployment in 1974 was 2.6 percent and in 1975, 4.7 percent. The M/P_C measure for Germany is calculated by regressing the logarithm of M/P_C on time for 1960–68, and then taking deviations of actual values from this time trend for 1969–73. M is end-of-year M1, from the International Financial Statistics of the IMF.

Table 10.6. The Unemployment Equation

$$U_t = \alpha_0 + \alpha_1 U_{t-1} + \alpha_2 w^x_{t-1} + \alpha_3(m - p_c)_{t-1} + \alpha_4 t + \alpha_5 D7481 + \alpha_6 T7481$$

Country	α_1	α_2	α_3	Shift variables	$\bar{R}^2$	ρ	D.H.
Belgium	0.73	7.02	−3.78	Not included	0.96	—	2.68
	(5.32)	(2.01)	(0.93)				
	0.23	10.56	−6.23	Included	0.97	0.57	
	(0.62)	(1.56)	(1.66)			(1.40)	
Canada	0.38	23.77	−5.36[a]	Not included	0.88	—	1.55
	(2.43)	(3.25)	(2.27)				
	0.33	25.69	−16.16[a]	Included	0.95	−0.60	
	(4.15)	(7.11)	(5.43)			(2.56)	
France	0.42	8.07	−4.31	Not included	0.98	—	NC
	(1.87)	(2.70)	(2.49)				
	−0.34	7.86	−5.77	Included	0.99	0.11	
	(1.25)	(2.82)	(4.36)			(0.29)	
Denmark	0.39	34.95	−15.26	Not included	0.90	—	1.47
	(2.92)	(2.79)	(3.11)				
	0.23	19.75	−20.92	Included	0.90	0.48	
	(1.00)	(0.82)	(2.91)			(1.43)	
Germany	0.41	17.57	−9.46	Not included	0.95	—	−0.53
	(4.10)	(4.55)	(3.86)				
	0.38	10.85	−8.93	Included	0.95	−0.40	
	(3.72)	(2.55)	(3.52)			(1.51)	
Japan	0.20	3.36	−0.31	Not included	0.94	—	−1.17
	(1.31)	(4.11)	(1.55)				
	0.30	2.40	−0.54	Included	0.95	−0.34	
	(1.53)	(2.75)	(1.44)			(1.05)	
United Kingdom	0.85	14.66	−9.32	Not included	.94	—	2.82
	(4.33)	(2.58)	(2.84)				
	0.63	21.97	−5.15	Included	.95	−0.62	
	(2.78)	(3.89)	(1.84)			(2.02)	
United States	0.32	−15.28	−11.17[b]	Not included	.63	—	5.84
	(1.50)	(1.03)	(2.20)				
	0.19	−8.97	−24.49[b]	Included	.93	−0.71	
	(2.60)	(1.73)	(1.55)			(3.52)	

Note: D7481 is a dummy variable, equal to 0.0 during 1960–1973, and 1.0 for 1973–1981. T7481 is a time shift variable, equal to 0.0 during 1960–1973; 1.0 in 1974; 2.0 in 1975; and so forth. Numbers in parentheses are t-statistics.

a. For Canada, the U.S. $m - p_c$ is used in the regressions.

b. For the United States, m is log (M2).

tive supply shock (for example, $\dot{w}^x > 0$) will reduce output for given demand, and a positive shock will raise output for given demand. Similarly, demand changes will induce output movements in the same direction, for constant levels of v^s.

Table 10.6 reports estimates of (10.14) for the eight countries under examination. For each country two equations are presented: in the first, $\dot{v}^f$ is treated as a constant, and v^f_{t-1} as a time trend; the equation is then a regression of U_t on $U_{t-1}, w^x_{t-1}, m_{t-1} - p_{c_{t-1}}$, and t. In the second regression we allow for a change in $\dot{v}^f$ after 1973, by adding slope and intercept shift variables for 1974–81. The second equation also corrects for possible first-order serial correlation. A few modifications were made to the basic equations, after some experimentation. For the United States and Canada, M2 is used as the money variable; in all of the other countries M1 is used. Also, in the Canadian regressions, U.S. $m - p_c$ proved to be far more important than Canadian $m - p_c$, so the U.S. values are used.

Table 10.6 provides rather striking confirmation of the joint importance of real wage and monetary factors in unemployment dynamics in most of the countries. In all cases except that of the United States, the coefficient on w^x_{t-1} is positive and is always statistically significant in at least one of the two regressions, and is generally significant in both. The coefficient on $m - p_c$ is also everywhere of the expected negative sign and is generally significant. To get an idea of the estimated importance of w^x for the path of unemployment, we can compute the effects of a one percentage point drop in w^x_t for a given path of real money balances. The point estimate of the one-year effect on U_t is $\hat{\alpha}_2$, and the point estimate of the long-run effect on U_t is $\hat{\alpha}_2/(1 - \hat{\alpha}_1)$. These measures are shown in the first two columns of Table 10.7. In the next two columns, we compute the one-year and long-run effects of reducing w^x_{1981} to zero. (Short-run effects are measured as $\hat{\alpha}_2 w^x_{1981}$ and long-run effects as $\hat{\alpha}_2 w^x_{1981}/(1 - \hat{\alpha}_1)$. For these computations we use the regressions with shift variables included.) In all countries except Canada (where $w^x_{1981} < 0$) and the United States, a return of w^x to zero in 1981 would have a beneficial effect on unemployment, and in many cases by a very significant amount, particularly in Belgium and the United Kingdom. In the United States, the estimated effect of reducing w^x is a perverse increase in unemployment, given the negative coefficient on w^x in the unemployment equation.

We can also perform a decomposition of the rise in U after 1965–69 as we did for inflation in Table 10.4. We start with the regression using slope ($T7481$) and intercept ($D7481$) dummy variables:

$$(10.15) \quad U_t = \alpha_0 + \alpha_1 U_{t-1} + \alpha_2(m - p_c)_{t-1} + \alpha_3 w^x_{t-1}$$
$$+ \alpha_4 t + \alpha_5 T7481 + \alpha_6 D7481.$$

Table 10.7. Effects on Unemployment of Reduction in w^x
(percentage of labor force)

Country	One-year effect of percentage point reduction in w^x (reduction in U)	Long-term effect	One-year effect of reducing w^x_{1981} to 0.0	Long-term effect	$U_{1981} - U_{1969}$
Belgium	0.1	0.1	3.1	4.0	10.5
Canada	0.3	0.4	−0.9[a]	−1.4[a]	2.9[a]
Denmark	0.2	0.3	1.4	1.8	8.8
France	0.1	0.1	0.2	0.1	5.3
Germany	0.1	0.2	1.3	2.1	3.4
Japan	0.02	0.03	0.6[b]	0.8[b]	1.1[b]
United Kingdom	0.2	0.6	4.2	11.5	8.3
United States	−0.1	−0.1	−0.7	−0.9	4.1

Source: Unemployment equation, shift variables included, from Table 10.6.
a. 1979.
b. 1980.

Next, we define $m^*_{c_{t-1}}$ as the level of real money balances that will keep U_t equal to U_{65-69}, *assuming that* $U_{t-1} = U_{65-69}$ and $w^x_{t-1} = w^x_{65-69} = 0$. Then m^*_c is defined implicitly by

(10.16) $U_{65-69} = \alpha_0 + \alpha_1 U_{65-69} + \alpha_2 m^*_{c_{t-1}}$
$$+ \alpha_4 t + \alpha_5 T7481 + \alpha_6 D7481.$$

$m^*_{c_{t-1}}$ may be regarded as the "full-employment level of real money balances." Subtracting (10.16) from (10.15), we have

(10.17) $(U_t - U_{65-69}) = \alpha_1(U_{t-1} - U_{65-69})$
$$+ \alpha_2[(m - p_c)_{t-1} - m^*_{c_{t-1}}] + \alpha_3 w^x_{t-1}.$$

In Table 10.8, $\alpha_1(U_{t-1} - U_{65-69})$ is the "inherited unemployment" effect; $\alpha_2[(m - p_c)_{t-1} - m^*_{c_{t-1}}]$ is the money supply effect; and $\alpha_3 w^x_{t-1}$ is the wage gap effect. These effects are averaged over the subperiods 1970–72, 1973–75, 1976–78, and 1979–81. In interpreting the table, it must be remembered that the decomposition refers to *proximate* effects only; no attempt is made to allocate the inherited unemployment among the ultimate causes. Thus, a high w^x which raises unemployment for several years will show up *both* as inherited unemployment and wage-gap unemployment.

In most economies, the wage gap and the money supply both show a growing contribution to unemployment (which feeds through naturally to a growing role for inherited unemployment). As we have already seen in Table

Table 10.8. Accounting for the Rise in Unemployment Since 1965–69

Country	1970–72	1973–75	1976–78	1979–81
BELGIUM				
Total rise	−0.3	1.4	6.2	8.9
of which:				
Inherited unem-				
ployment	0.0	0.1	1.2	1.8
Wage gap	0.3	1.9	3.2	3.1
Money supply	−0.1	−0.5	1.7	4.3
Other	−0.5	0.0	0.1	0.7
CANADA				
Total rise	1.8	1.8	3.6	3.3
of which:				
Inherited unem-				
ployment	0.4	0.5	1.0	1.2
Wage gap	0.5	−0.3	0.5	NA
Money supply	1.3	1.8	1.9	2.3
Other	−0.4	−0.2	0.2	NA
DENMARK				
Total rise	0.3	3.0	8.1	7.6
of which:				
Inherited unem-				
ployment	0.1	0.1	1.8	1.8
Wage gap	0.5	1.7	2.2	1.9
Money supply	−0.4	2.2	3.1	4.8
Other	0.1	−1.0	1.0	−0.9
FRANCE				
Total rise	0.9	1.4	3.1	4.8
of which:				
Inherited unem-				
ployment	−0.2	−0.3	−0.9	−1.4
Wage gap	−0.3	0.0	0.2	0.1
Money supply	1.4	1.8	3.8	6.1
Other	0.0	−0.1	0.0	0.0

Table 10.8 (*continued*)

Country	1970–72	1973–75	1976–78	1979–81
GERMANY				
Total rise	−0.3	1.7	3.3	2.8
of which:				
Inherited unemployment	−0.1	0.2	1.3	1.1
Wage gap	0.2	0.8	1.2	1.0
Money supply	−0.2	0.5	0.9	0.6
Other	−0.2	0.2	−0.1	0.1
JAPAN				
Total rise	0.0	0.3	0.8	0.9
of which:				
Inherited unemployment	0.0	0.0	0.2	0.3
Wage gap	0.1	0.3	0.5	0.5
Money supply	−0.1	0.0	0.1	0.1
Other	0.1	0.0	0.0	0.0
UNITED KINGDOM				
Total rise	1.2	1.0	3.6	5.6
of which:				
Inherited unemployment	0.5	0.6	1.9	2.5
Wage gap	0.2	1.2	1.8	2.5
Money supply	0.3	−0.7	−0.1	0.5
Other	0.2	−0.1	0.0	0.1
UNITED STATES				
Total rise	1.6	2.5	3.1	3.0
of which:				
Inherited unemployment	0.2	0.3	0.8	0.5
Wage gap	0.1	−0.2	−0.1	−0.5
Money supply	1.2	2.3	2.5	3.2
Other	0.1	0.1	−0.1	−0.2

10.7, the wage gap effect is relatively small in Canada, France, and the United States, and the money supply effect shows up as being particularly important in these economies.

Conclusions

The equations for inflation and unemployment in this chapter go far toward explaining the Phillips curve shifts in the 1970s. The standard Phillips curve framework is modified in two ways. First, import price shocks are allowed to have a direct effect on domestic inflation, which is shown to have been particularly large during the periods 1973–75 and 1979–81. Second, economic slack is written as a function of unemployment and the real wage gap, where the latter term helps to track shifts in aggregate supply in the past decade. The unemployment equation is similarly modified to allow for direct effects of the real wage gap. Both sets of equations strongly support our view that aggregate supply shifts have been, and continue to be, of the first order of importance in most of the major OECD economies.

If we are correct in our diagnosis, policymakers engaged in macroeconomic management must define the "current state" of the economy not only in terms of the inherited rates of inflation and unemployment but also in terms of the inherited state of aggregate supply, as measured by w^x. Short-run policy trade-offs become more complicated than simply balancing shifts in unemployment and inflation, because changes in unemployment and inflation also contribute to the dynamics of w^x, which affect the future trade-offs that the policymakers will face.

We now turn to a more detailed investigation of the role of labor market institutions in macroeconomic adjustment.

11 Labor Markets and Comparative Macroeconomic Performance

THE CROSS-COUNTRY macroeconomic experience since 1973 teaches two lessons: the deterioration in economic performance was pandemic in the OECD, and the extent of deterioration has depended on some key structural characteristics of the various economies. No economy escaped the slowdown in GNP growth after the watershed year of 1973, though interestingly, some countries escaped a rise in unemployment for reasons that we shall explore. Similarly, almost no country escaped a rise in inflation, on average, after 1973, though the dispersion of inflation experiences is much broader than that of growth or unemployment. Not surprisingly, countries that experienced a greater than average slowdown in growth after 1973 tend to show a smaller than average rise in inflation (measured as $\dot{p}_c[1979] - \dot{p}_c[1973]$), reflecting a short-run inflation-unemployment trade-off. Our most interesting finding is that some countries could buy a much greater decline in inflation, for a *given amount of slack,* than could others. The more favorable trade-off relates strongly to key labor market variables.

From our earlier work and our results later in this chapter, it appears that real wage moderation is a key to achieving low inflation and low unemployment after a supply shock. Two clusters of labor market characteristics can help us to explain the relative ease with which different countries were able to achieve wage moderation in the 1970s. The first, which has been termed labor market "corporatism" by political scientists, relates mainly to the level at which wage setting occurs. In countries with near-universal union coverage and highly centralized negotiations (for example, Austria and Sweden), it seems that wages were kept closer to market-clearing levels than in more decentralized systems (such as the United Kingdom). The second dimension involves the rate at which nominal wages adjust to exogenous shifts in labor demand. We will see that in economies such as that of the United States, with desynchronized bargaining, low wage indexation, and long-term contracts, nominal wages will tend to lag behind prices when inflation is increasing. In such a case, real wage moderation after a supply shock will then be achieved automatically by the temporary jump in inflation.

Two basic problems confront our attempt to explain differential macroeconomic performance of a group of countries. First, we must measure performance itself in a way that is meaningful on a cross-country basis. In the following section, we document the difficulties involved in using the aggregate unemployment rate in cross-country comparisons. We will find, for example, that some countries with the smallest rise in unemployment in the 1970s (for example, Japan and Switzerland) also show the largest slowdown in economic growth.

The second problem is deeper and more conceptual. Observed patterns of inflation and output across countries may differ for two reasons: economic structures may differ across countries, or policymakers' goals (and therefore policy instruments) may differ. Observed macroeconomic outcomes are in this sense a function both of "technology" (economic structure) and "tastes" (policy objectives). Ideally, we should aim to explain cross-country differences in terms of both factors. In practice this is quite difficult, since it may not be possible to estimate econometrically a policy preference function together with a structural model of the economy (see Taylor, 1982, for a good discussion of this issue and for a specific example in which "tastes" cannot be estimated on a cross-country basis). Our goal here is more modest and focuses exclusively on differences in structure rather than on policy goals: we aim to show that different countries faced different short-run output-inflation trade-offs in the past decade that can be traced in part to the structural labor market characteristics mentioned earlier. We try to link these structural characteristics to the models in Chapter 9 that sought to explain some of the microeconomic foundations behind real wage rigidity.

The plan of the chapter is as follows: in the next section we discuss various measures of economic performance and mention some of the problems of cross-country comparability; in the following section we show that important differences in performance can be explained by two labor market variables, termed "corporatism" and "nominal wage responsiveness." For a given set of macro policy objectives, we will indicate how different degrees of corporatism and nominal wage responsiveness should affect policy choices pursued by macroeconomic authorities and policy outcomes. A summary of key labor market characteristics for several economies is presented in an appendix to the chapter as a point of reference for the discussion.

Measuring Macroeconomic Performance

One of the difficulties of comparative work is that the meaning of economic variables of interest can differ substantially across countries. These differences have played havoc with attempts to explain why one country or another has "succeeded" or "failed" in its macroeconomic policies in recent years. An illustration of these problems is given in Table 11.1, where we show, for seventeen countries, two measures of the post-1973 decline in resource utilization. The first measure is the rise in average unemployment rate after 1973, measured as the 1974–80 average (U_{74-80}) minus the 1965–73 average (U_{65-73}). In principle, countries with low values of U_{74-80} minus U_{65-73} maintained high levels of resource utilization after the supply shocks. The second measure is the slowdown in aggregate economic growth after 1973, measured as the annual growth rate of GNP for 1965–73 ($\dot{v}_{65-73}$) minus the annual growth rate for 1973–80 ($\dot{v}_{73-80}$). We should expect small increases in unemployment to correspond to low values of the growth slowdown.

We find that the two measures are almost completely uncorrelated for the seventeen countries (excluding New Zealand), with $r = 0.08$. Switzerland and Japan, for example, appear to have full resource utilization according to the unemployment rate but the sharpest drop according to the growth slowdown. Leaving out these two countries, the remaining fourteen countries show a stronger positive correlation between these measures, with $r = 0.55$.

For cross-country comparisons, the growth variable is probably a better simple indicator of the degree of resource utilization than is the unemployment rate. In Japan and Switzerland the unemployment measure is seriously misleading regarding overall slack in the economy, and it is moderately misleading in Austria, Finland, Germany, and Sweden. In each case the cyclical behavior of the labor force hides the underutilization of resources. In Austria, Finland, Germany, and Switzerland, outmigration of foreign workers hid some of the decline in employment after 1973. In Japan, women workers withdrew from the labor force upon job loss and thus were not counted among the unemployed. And in Sweden, extensive official worker retraining programs kept unemployed workers out of the official statistics. Let us consider the most extreme cases in more detail.

Japan has the distinction of showing the third smallest rise in unemployment but the single largest fall in GNP growth rate among the seventeen countries. As judged from measures of capacity utilization, the growth rate variable is more accurate, for capacity measures show an extremely low level

Table 11.1. Indicators of Aggregate Resource Utilization: GNP Growth and Unemployment (in percentages)

Country	$\dot{v}_{65-73}$ (I)	$\dot{v}_{73-80}$ (II)	U_{65-73} (III)	U_{74-80} (IV)	GNP slowdown (I − II)	Unemployment increase (IV − III)
Australia	5.3	2.3	1.2	4.8	3.1	3.6
Austria	5.3	3.0	2.0	1.7	2.3	−0.3
Belgium	5.0	2.3	2.1	5.8	2.7	3.7
Canada	5.6	2.7	4.9	7.2	2.8	2.3
Denmark	4.1	1.6	1.1	5.5	2.6	4.3
Finland	5.0	2.9	2.4	4.6	2.1	2.2
France	5.2	2.9	1.2	4.6	2.3	3.4
Germany	4.3	2.3	0.9	3.5	2.0	2.6
Italy	5.2	2.8	5.6	6.7	2.4	1.1
Japan	9.8	3.8	1.2	1.9	6.0	0.7
Netherlands	5.1	2.1	1.4	4.1	3.0	2.7
New Zealand	3.5	0.9	NA	1.0	2.5	NA
Norway	4.1	4.8	0.8	1.0	−0.7	0.2
Sweden	3.4	1.8	2.0	1.9	1.6	−0.1
Switzerland	3.9	0.3	0.0	0.3	3.6	0.3
United Kingdom	3.1	0.9	2.3	4.6	2.2	2.4
United States	3.8	2.4	4.4	6.7	1.4	2.3

Source: Real GNP is from the International Financial Statistics of the IMF; unemployment is from OECD Main Economic Indicators. $\dot{v}_{x-y}$ is the annual average growth rate of real GNP between years x and y; U_{x-y} is the average unemployment rate for all years x to y (inclusive).

of capacity use throughout the period 1974–79. There seem to be three factors that keep unemployment low in Japan in spite of large deviations of output from potential. First, job losers (and particularly part-time women factory workers) are more likely than in other countries to move out of the labor force instead of into the pool of unemployed. From 1973 to 1975, for example, the female participation rate dropped from 54.0 percent to 51.7 percent, reflecting a sharp drop in female employment levels. If these job losers had remained in the labor force, the aggregate unemployment rate would have risen from 1.3 percent to more than 3.0 percent, rather than to the rate of 1.9 percent that it hit in 1975. A second factor holding U to low levels involves differences in data definitions for the classification of employment and unemployment (particularly the definition of job search). According to some Japanese studies, a reclassification based on U.S. concepts would raise U several percentage points in recent years and would result in a much steeper rise in U during 1973–83.[1]

Finally, differences in layoff policies in Japan from those elsewhere mean that Japanese firms are far more likely to hoard labor and reduce man-hours during cyclical downturns than are their counterparts in other economies. For this reason, Japan shows the greatest and most persistent procyclical productivity pattern of all the major economies. Thus, a growth slowdown shows up as a decline in output per employee rather than as a rise in U.

The reasons for low unemployment in Switzerland are notorious: the sharp decline in employment levels after 1973 fell almost entirely on foreign workers, who constituted more than 15 percent of the labor force. The job losers either returned to their country of origin, or they remained in Switzerland but were not counted among the officially unemployed. As in Japan, the low Swiss unemployment rates hide a major slowdown in economic growth and low levels of capacity utilization after 1973. Manufacturing production in Switzerland fell an astounding 13.0 percent between 1973 and 1975, and as late as 1980 Swiss industrial production was still below its 1973 peak. Yet almost none of this showed up in unemployment, given a drop in the labor force of over 8 percent between 1973 and 1977, and of 5 percent in 1975 alone.

In Sweden, a combination of restrictive labor laws that hinder layoffs and large-scale job retraining programs for job losers keep official unemployment rates low in spite of low GNP growth in recent years. If one adds to the rolls of the "officially unemployed" the numbers of workers not employed but in official retraining programs, we find that the unemployment rate rose slightly between 1973 and 1979 (by 0.4 percentage points), while it actually fell in the official statistics (by 0.4 percentage points).[2]

In Austria and Germany, like Switzerland, outmigration of foreign labor helped to moderate the post-1973 rise in unemployment. Lindbeck (1983) has tried to adjust the official unemployment statistics to measure this effect. Officially, $U_{79} - U_{73}$ in Austria is 1.0 percentage points; adding to U_{79} the change in stock of foreign workers in the period 1974–79, Lindbeck finds that U_{79} is raised 0.2 percentage points. Similarly, U_{79} in Germany is raised 1.3 percentage points; and in Switzerland, the most important case, U_{79} is raised 3.2 percentage points!

An International Comparison of Wage-Setting Institutions

Since much of the stagflation process is tied to the behavior of real wages, and particularly how they adjust to supply shocks, it is not surprising that structural differences in labor markets account for much of the cross-country differences in macroeconomic performance. In countries in which real wage moderation was easily achieved, both inflation *and* unemployment tended to remain relatively low in the 1970s. In countries in which real wage moderation could be achieved only after protracted political or economic conflict, the costs in terms of inflation and unemployment were much higher. Certain institutional arrangements seem to be conducive to real wage moderation after a supply shock, including the following: centralized wage negotiations (in which the rank and file do not, in general, vote to ratify contracts); high employer coordination (for example, in national employer federations); low shop-floor presence of unions; low wage indexation; infrequent collective bargaining; and, if negotiation is decentralized, a desynchronized schedule of bargaining. These six factors appear to fall along two dimensions: the level at which bargaining proceeds, and the capacity of labor to adjust nominal wages rapidly to changing labor market conditions (through indexation or wage recontracting). The level of bargaining and the extent of centralization of negotiation are often described by the term "corporatism" in political science analysis. A number of writers, including Cameron (1982), McCallum (1982), and Tarantelli (1982), have observed that corporatist economies outperformed others in the 1970s. (Tarantelli's work was a major stimulus to our own investigation of this topic.)[3] In this section we try to explain why this is so, in terms of the theory that we have developed. In the next section we turn to indexation and other aspects of the timing of wage setting.

Much of the discussion that follows involves institutional details concerning the wage-setting process. For the reader's convenience, we include in Appendix 11A a detailed outline describing major aspects of wage-setting practices in twelve countries, together with bibliographic references. We will refer to this appendix throughout the following sections.

CORPORATISM AND WAGE OUTCOMES

Corporatism is defined as a mode of social organization in which functional groups rather than discrete individuals wield power and transact affairs. In the sphere of labor markets, it has been defined as "institutionalized negotiation, bargaining, collaboration, and accord about wages and 'income policies' (and perhaps additional economic issues) between representatives of the major economic groupings in the society (most typically labor confederations and employers' associations) and often including, in addition, representatives of the government."[4] There are several structural characteristics that may be used to measure the degree of corporatism, as suggested by this definition: the extent to which wage negotiations proceed on the national level, rather than the plant level; the power of national labor organizations vis-à-vis their constituent members; the degree of organization on the employer side; and the power of plant-level union stewards (the more powerful they are, the *less* corporatism there is).

A key feature that distinguishes corporatist from noncorporatist settings is voting on collectively bargained agreements. In countries with national or branch-level bargaining (for example, Austria or Sweden) it is extremely rare for the rank-and-file union membership to vote on an agreement. In Canada, the United Kingdom, and the United States, plant-level ratification is a typical part of the negotiating process.

To get a sense of corporatist orientation, let us briefly consider an outstanding example of the phenomenon, Sweden. After a period of conflict and high strike activity in the early twentieth century, Sweden arrived at a system in the 1930s that has delivered nearly fifty years of relative labor peace and consensus. (As we shall see in Table 11.2, Sweden has the third lowest rate of strike activity among the countries under consideration.) The system is built around nearly universal union participation, which puts Sweden first in the extent of union coverage. Nearly 100 percent of blue-collar workers are represented in the national trade union confederation, LO, and a substantial majority of salaried workers are represented in two other union organizations, TCO and SACO-SR. Employers are represented, again almost universally, in the national employers' confederation, SAF.

The LO is organized along branch lines, with twenty-four member federations constituting the parent organization. The detailed wage negotiations typically take place at the branch level and then are further refined at the local level, but without exception are guided by a *central* agreement negotiated between LO and SAF. The branch-level agreement is considered binding for the constituent members of the branch. Rank-and-file voting on that agreement is virtually nonexistent, since negotiators at the branch level have vested powers to reach binding agreements.

The government plays an active, though behind-the-scenes, role in the national bargaining. There is an active tripartite (government, labor, employers) exchange of views leading up to negotiations, and the negotiating period is often selected to coincide with the national budget process. Tax policy (for example, reductions in payroll taxes) has been used as a form of "tax bribery" (in the words of Faxén, 1982) or "social contract" to encourage moderation in wage settlements.

During the 1950s to mid-1970s, a high degree of consensus at the national level was reached concerning the scope for overall real wage increases. The so-called EFO-Aukrust (or "Scandinavian") model took as its norm that labor should maintain a constant share of income in the tradables sector. (With value added separable from N in production, the constant-shares rule is appropriate to maintain full employment in the face of a rise in Π_N.) Thus the scope for nominal wage increases was measured as the sum of productivity increase plus nominal price increase of tradable goods. Though the pressure of terms-of-trade shocks, large inflation swings, and a sharp slowdown in productivity growth have severely strained the application of this norm, there remains nonetheless a basic commitment to a constant-shares strategy of wage setting. Indeed, in recent years much and perhaps most of the strains in bargaining have come between LO and the professional labor groups, rather than LO and SAF.

A recent large devaluation of the Swedish krona by the ruling Social Democratic party illustrates the possibility of real wage moderation in the Swedish context. When the Social Democrats returned to office at the end of 1982, after six years out of power, they instituted a large 14 percent devaluation of the Swedish krona vis-à-vis a basket of currencies. The policy was predicated on a tacit understanding with LO that nominal wage demands would not rise to keep pace with the devaluation-induced bulge in prices.

The Swedish case is typical of the highly corporatist economies in several regards:

1. A high degree of unionization, nearly total among blue-collar workers.

2. Highly centralized wage bargaining.

3. National or a few branch-level agreements as the basis for the entire economy's wage setting.

4. Low levels of strike activity, reflecting a high degree of social consensus concerning the norms of wage bargains.

5. Social Democratic rule for extended periods, resulting in very high levels of government participation in the economy (as measured by expenditure/GNP and revenue/GNP indicators).

Tables 11.2 and 11.3 provide some cross-country comparisons of these various factors, with Austria, Germany, the Netherlands, Norway, and Sweden ranked as the most corporatist economies and Australia, France, Italy, the United Kingdom, and the United States as the least. A rank ordering of seventeen countries, adapted from Crouch (forthcoming), is shown in Table 11.3. We construct an index (shown in the last column of the table) based on Crouch's analysis. Note that there are four indicators in Crouch's index: the

Table 11.2. Industrial Conflict, Union Membership, Industrial Relations, and Corporatism, Seventeen Countries, 1965–77

	Worker involvement in disputes per 1,000 employees	Worker involvement in disputes per 1,000 union members	Union membership as percentage of all employees	Percentage of cabinet seats held by labor parties
Australia	203.63[a]	431.73	46.12	22.44
Austria	10.34	19.63	52.60	64.70
Belgium	16.47[b]	23.99	68.00[g]	27.20
Canada	53.89[a]	182.69	28.28	00.00
Denmark	27.41[a,d]	50.48	52.88	63.10
Finland	127.07[a,c]	222.73	43.40	41.65
France	114.96[f]	577.29	20.00[g]	00.00
W. Germany	5.34[a]	16.85	31.80	55.00
Italy	348.06[b,e]	997.17	32.31	12.89
Japan	32.96	145.12	22.62	00.00
Netherlands	4.65	13.15	35.48	23.43
New Zealand	70.36[d]	189.87	36.65	22.44
Norway	3.05[a,b]	4.33	64.23	44.90
Sweden	4.18	5.74	70.10	90.38
Switzerland	0.21	0.68	29.35	28.57
United Kingdom	52.12[a,d]	115.12	45.51	71.79
United States	29.96	106.29	28.17	00.00

Source: Crouch (forthcoming).
Notes: Figures are annual averages.
 a. Excludes very small disputes.
 b. Excludes workers indirectly affected.
 c. Pre-1971, excludes workers indirectly affected.
 d. Excludes political strikes.
 e. 1969–74, excludes political strikes.
 f. Excludes disputes in agriculture and public administration.
 g. Estimates.

Table 11.3. Index of Labor Market Corporatism

Country	Union movement centralization	Low shop-floor autonomy	Corporatism indicators Employer coordination	Works councils	Corporatism rank order	Corporatism index
Australia	0.0	0.0	0.0	0.0	15.0	0.0
Austria	1.0	1.0	1.0	1.0	1.0	4.0
Belgium	?	?	0.0	?	9.0	0.5
Canada	0.0	0.0	0.0	0.0	16.0	0.0
Denmark	1.0	0.0	1.0	1.0	7.0	3.0
Finland	?	?	1.0	?	8.0	1.5
France	0.0	?	0.0	?	13.0	0.0
W. Germany	1.0	1.0	1.0	1.0	2.0	4.0
Italy	0.0	0.0	0.0	?	14.0	0.5
Japan	0.0	?	0.0	1.0	10.0	1.5
Netherlands	1.0	1.0	1.0	1.0	3.0	4.0
New Zealand	?	0.0	0.0	0.0	11.0	0.5
Norway	1.0	1.0	1.0	1.0	4.5	4.0
Sweden	1.0	1.0	1.0	1.0	4.5	4.0
Switzerland	?	?	1.0	1.0	6.0	2.0
United Kingdom	?	0.0	0.0	0.0	12.0	0.0
United States	0.0	0.0	0.0	0.0	17.0	0.0

Source: Columns 1–4: Crouch (forthcoming). Column 5: From Crouch data, as adapted by the authors.

degree of union centralization, the extent of shop-floor union power (or "autonomy"), employer coordination, and the presence of works councils. These are summed to produce the corporatism index (with some judgmental allowance for the "?" entries).

The case for Austria, Germany, the Netherlands, Norway, and Sweden as corporatist is clear. They each display the extensive, centralized unionization, low levels of strike activity, and high degree of Social Democratic rule that is characteristic of corporatism. In general, the plant or shop-floor role of the unions is slight. The case on the other end is equally clear. In Canada, the United Kingdom, and the United States, for example, unions are organized at the plant level, and the overall extent of unionization is rather low. National labor federations exist as umbrella organizations, but not as active participants in wage bargaining. The bargain is typically struck at the firm level and is subject to rank-and-file ratification. Strike activity is high in international comparison, and Social Democratic power is low or nonexistent.

More difficult cases are presented by the intermediate countries: Belgium, Denmark, Finland, and Switzerland. Although Belgium is highly unionized, the national union confederations are split along linguistic and religious lines, so that centralization is substantially reduced. Similarly in Finland, the labor movement is sharply divided between communist and socialist unions. In Switzerland the unions are substantially weaker, and are not well organized at the national level. Denmark, finally, is a case of extensive unionization with Social Democratic backing; but unlike the fully corporatist economies, Denmark has developed a strong shop-floor union representation, which reduces the extent of centralization. Crouch, therefore, places Denmark at the top of the second tier of countries in his rank ordering of corporatism.

A striking first piece of evidence on the importance of corporatism for macroeconomic performance is shown in Figure 11.1. For seventeen countries, we relate the post-1973 rise in "misery index" to the corporatism measure. (The use of the misery index follows Tarantelli, 1982, who established a similar relationship.) The change in the misery index is the *rise* in inflation plus the *slowdown* in real GNP growth after 1973:

$$(11.1) \qquad MI = (\dot{p}_{73-79} - \dot{p}_{65-73}) + (\dot{v}_{73-79} - \dot{v}_{65-73}).$$

We find a strong negative correlation between *MI* and the corporatism index ($r = -0.68$), which is statistically significant at $p = 0.01$ and is strongly evident in the figure.

Corporatist economies were able, on average, to achieve better inflation

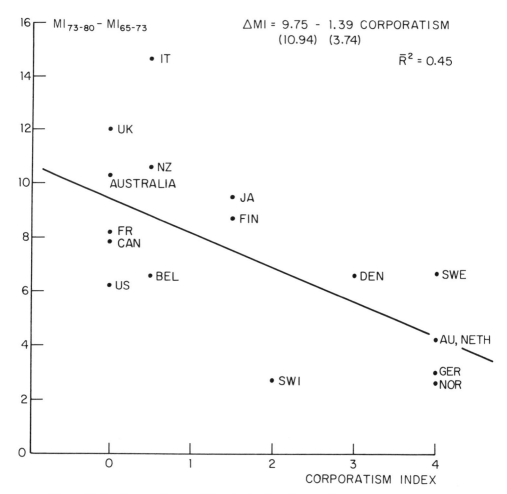

Figure 11.1. Corporatism and the rise in the misery index, seventeen countries

performance than noncorporatist economies for given levels of economic slowdown. We start with the basic fact that greater economic slack in the 1970s is associated with superior inflation performance on a cross-country basis. Measuring trend GNP growth as $\dot{v}_{65-73}$, we define our measure of 1973–79 slack as $-[\dot{v}_{73-79} - \dot{v}_{65-73}]$. The rise in inflation is measured similarly as $[(\dot{p}_c)_{79} - (\dot{p}_c)_{73}]$. A cross-section regression for the seventeen countries shows

$$[(\dot{p}_c)_{79} - (\dot{p}_c)_{73}] = \underset{(1.59)}{2.83} + \underset{(2.16)}{1.39} \; [\dot{v}_{73-79} - \dot{v}_{65-73}].$$

$$\bar{R}^2 = 0.19$$

On average, a 1 percentage point rise in GNP growth during 1973–79 is associated with a 1.4 percentage point rise in inflation between 1973 and 1979.

Corporatist economies do significantly better than average in this trade-off. For the same slowdown in GNP growth relative to trend, they achieved far greater moderation of inflation. Thus adding CI (corporatism index) to the regression, we find

$$[(\dot{p}_c)_{79} - (\dot{p}_c)_{73}] = \underset{(4.24)}{6.40} + \underset{(3.85)}{1.75} [\dot{v}_{73-79} - \dot{v}_{65-73}] - \underset{(4.12)}{1.54} \, CI.$$

$$\bar{R}^2 = 0.61$$

Each unit rise in the corporatism index is associated, for given GNP performance, with a reduction in inflation of 1.5 percentage points. Note that including CI raises the coefficient and statistical significance of the slack variable; for given CI, a 1 percentage point rise in average GNP growth during 1973–79 is estimated to raise 1979 inflation by 1.75 percentage points.

Some further correlations suggest some of the structural links underlying these results. Using an OECD "wage gap" measure that is available for all the economies, we can verify that higher CI is associated with greater real wage moderation after the first supply shock. The wage gap measure covers the entire economy and is normalized to 1972 = 0.0. It has various flaws that probably make it a less accurate indicator than the manufacturing-sector measure we used in Chapter 9, but the OECD measure is available for a much wider group of countries.[5]

Table 11.4 presents w^x_{OECD}, with the countries ranked according to CI. Looking at the average for w^x_{OECD} for 1973–79, the highly corporatist countries as a group have an average value of 0.2; the moderately corporatist countries, 4.7; and the low corporatist countries, *excluding the United States*, 5.1. The United States is a major exception to the rule, with a very low real wage gap and a thoroughly noncorporatist labor market. We will show later that the low nominal wage responsiveness in the United States helps to explain this anomalous result. A simple correlation of $(w^x_{OECD})_{73-79}$ and CI, again excluding the United States, shows $r = -0.64$.

As discussed earlier, for given measured economic slack we should expect more inflation moderation with a small wage gap. Presumably, this is one of the major channels through which corporatism affects the inflation performance. To test this proposition, we regress the inflation change on the slack variable and w^x_{OECD} using two-stage least squares, instrumenting the wage gap variable with the corporatism index and the nominal wage responsive-

Table 11.4. Real Wage Gap, OECD Measure, 1973–1980 (1972 = 0.0)

Country	1973	1974	1975	1976	1977	1978	1979	Average 1973–79
Austria	2.9	−0.9	3.1	2.1	3.4	4.5	1.1	2.3
Germany	0.7	3.7	2.0	−1.3	−1.5	−2.6	−3.6	−0.4
Netherlands	−1.9	1.4	3.5	−0.8	−0.6	−0.2	0.4	0.4
Norway	−0.8	0.4	3.4	5.5	6.7	4.5	−2.5	2.5
Sweden	−4.0	−4.4	−4.7	−4.3	−1.4	−4.0	−4.9	−3.6
Switzerland	1.7	2.1	3.3	2.1	2.1	3.2	3.2	2.5
Denmark	0.1	7.4	10.6	4.9	2.9	0.5	−1.3	3.6
Finland	−1.0	1.7	5.3	4.8	−1.2	−4.1	−5.1	0.1
Belgium	1.3	4.6	9.3	10.8	11.7	11.9	12.6	8.9
Japan	4.1	10.8	13.8	11.4	8.8	4.1	4.2	8.2
United Kingdom	0.0	7.1	10.5	4.0	−1.5	−1.7	0.0	2.6
France	1.4	4.9	7.7	7.4	8.0	6.3	4.5	5.7
Italy	2.0	1.9	6.0	2.6	7.8	6.8	5.1	5.0
Australia	4.1	15.0	12.4	9.1	10.6	5.4	5.2	8.8
Canada	−1.8	−0.3	4.4	5.7	6.7	5.9	3.5	3.4
United States	−0.9	−0.3	−1.7	−3.1	−3.4	−3.0	−2.3	−2.1

Source: OECD unpublished data. The wage gap measures may be found in the OECD Economic Outlook, various issues.

ness index (*NWR*) introduced below:

$$[(\dot{p}_c)_{79} - (\dot{p}_c)_{73}] = -109.3 + 2.72\ [\dot{v}_{73-79} - \dot{v}_{65-73}]$$
$$(1.74)\quad (2.32)$$
$$+\ 1.12\ w^x_{OECD}.$$
$$(1.79)$$

Although the wage gap is not quite significant at $p = 0.05$, the regression does suggest that a higher profit squeeze, *ceteris paribus,* contributes to inflation. We will see much more evidence on this point later.

One of the mechanisms linking *CI* and w^x_{OECD} is the higher level of consensus that apparently surrounds wage bargaining in the corporatist economies. As mentioned earlier in the context of Sweden, national-level bargaining has led in several of the more corporatist economies to explicit adoption of wage norms, or income distributional norms, as a basis for negotiation. The counterpart to this higher level of consensus has been a lower level of industrial strike activity on a long-term average basis. The simple correlation between strike activity, as measured in the first column of Table 11.2, and *CI* is $r = -0.50$.

There are several possible links between CI and w^x_{OECD} that merit our attention, some of which relate back to the three models of real wage rigidity from Chapter 9. In the political science discussion of corporatism, wage restraint on the part of unions is seen as the labor movement's concession in return for a greater role in economic policymaking.[6] In one such interpretation, by Panitsch, "Corporatist structures, in the form of economic planning and incomes policy bodies, involved the integration of trade unions in economic policy making in exchange for their incorporation of capitalist growth criteria in union wage policy and their administration of wage restraint to their members" (cited in Cameron, 1982, p. 6). Similarly, Hibbs (1978) argues that in Social Democratic countries, labor is able to abandon direct labor militancy in return for increased power over the political allocation of resources. Workers limit negotiated wage demands in return for an increased "social wage" (for example, extensive job retraining programs as in Sweden, or large-scale social welfare transfers).

This type of bargaining has been most evident in the so-called social contracts reached between the government and the trade union movement in several economies, in which moderation in wage bargaining has been quite explicitly exchanged for tax reductions or expansionary macroeconomic policies. This possibility was not allowed for in the simple union-wage model of the previous section, which implicitly studied a local union whose only bargaining power is on the wage variable. Unfortunately, little if any formal theoretical modeling of national-level bargaining has yet been carried out.

The corporatist structure is also particularly effective for overcoming the informational inefficiencies that were at the heart of the second and third models of real wage rigidity of Chapter 9 and this is *a fortiori* true when the economy is being hit by economy-wide disturbances. Though national bargaining may not allow effectively for the interfirm and interindustry variations in wages that are important for microeconomic resource allocation, it is singularly well equipped to draw attention to the magnitude and implications of economy-wide shocks. Moreover, in a bargaining environment that stresses consensual wage norms, negotiators are far more likely to absorb a terms-of-trade shock by a shared reduction in the real incomes of capital and labor. Remember that the wage response necessary to maintain full employment after a rise in Π_N will be one that keeps labor's share of income constant, assuming that K and L are weakly separable from N in the production process.

Some analysts have also pointed out that interunion rivalries in decentralized systems can forestall real wage moderation. To the extent that the *raison d'être* of a local union is to secure real wage increases for its members, unilateral wage concessions may make it vulnerable to challenges from competing unions. The importance of this political constraint on local union leadership is well described in Lange, Ross, and Vannicelli (1982) in the cases of France and Italy. A centralized system with a unified and dominant trade union organization can obviously avoid much of this problem, since much less union competition exists.

NOMINAL WAGE RESPONSIVENESS

Some international differences in the timing of nominal wage changes are described in Appendix 11A. There we summarize the major aspects of nominal wage responsiveness for the unionized sector of the OECD economies (there is little explicit information available about wage setting among nonunion workers). The timing in the organized sector has a strong influence on the nonorganized sector. Government wages are often patterned on contractual union wages, and nonunionized workers in union firms typically receive compensation in line with negotiated union settlements. According to the appendix, only in the United States is the union sector characterized by long-term, overlapping agreements, with low levels of wage indexation. The normal length of contracts in the other countries is about one year. As noted earlier, there are synchronized and centralized bargaining systems in the Scandinavian economies, moderate to high synchronization of contract negotiations in Germany and Japan, and low synchronization in France and the United Kingdom. In Japan, plant-level bargaining is effectively synchronized in the "spring wage offensive" *(shunto)*. In France and the United Kingdom, labor agreements are often written without fixed duration. The U.K. agreements are not legally binding and are typically subject to reopening at the request of one of the parties. Only under the Industrial Relations Act (1971–74) was there an attempt to institute legally binding agreements with obligations to maintain industrial peace for a fixed contract period. Under the labor government incomes policy (1975–78), the Trade Union Congress agreed to the twelve-month rule, forbidding two contract reopenings during a twelve-month period. The incomes policy collapsed in 1978–79.

Besides the United States, only Italy has long-term agreements. But in Italy the three-year bargaining cycle is basically synchronized, and extensive wage indexation (the *scala mobile*) allows for rapid responses of wages to changes in the price level during the contract period. The coverage of employees under the *scala mobile* is nearly universal in the industrial sector

Table 11.5. Growth of Selected Prices and Wages, Exchange Rate Appreciation, Germany, 1972–75 (annual rate, in percentages)

Measure	1972	1973	1974	1974:I	1974:II	1974:III	1974:IV	1975
Exchange rate appreciation	3.4	11.4	5.2	−4.8	22.3	−13.0	10.7	1.7
Consumer price index	5.4	6.9	7.0	9.9	6.6	3.8	5.4	6.0
Price index, consumer goods								
Import prices	0.0	14.7	14.7	19.1	−14.3	4.8	1.5	3.6
Export prices	4.2	5.4	12.7	33.0	8.3	4.5	5.7	5.9
Contractual wage index[a]								
Public sector	7.0	8.8	12.6	—	—	—	6.0	—
Metal industry	7.5	8.6	11–11.6	—	—	—	7.0	—
Chemical industry	5.6–7.8	9.9–10.8	12.9	—	—	—	6.8	—
Construction	6.4–7.9	9.7	11.2	—	—	—	6.6	—

Sources: The effective exchange rate is from International Monetary Fund, *International Financial Statistics*, various issues; contractual wage data are from *OECD Economic Surveys: Germany* (Paris: OECD, July 1975), p. 7; and price data are from *OECD Economic Surveys: Germany* (July 1975), p. 58, and other issues.

a. The ranges of values in the contractual wage indexes reflect regional differentiation of contracts.

(including nonunion workers), though the degree of protection of real wages offered by the indexing rules has varied widely. By 1975, the elasticity of wage change with respect to price change under the index had declined to about 0.5. An overhaul of the indexing scheme in 1975 restored the degree of indexation to more than 1.0, but by 1978, it had declined again to approximately 0.85.

The example of Germany provides a clear case of how centralized, synchronized, and short-term contracts allow for the rapid response of nominal wages to shifts in demand (in this case, to a shift in monetary policy). From 1970 to 1973, annual inflation rates climbed in Germany from 3.3 percent to 6.9 percent. Contrary to popular belief, the German economy showed no special immunity to inflation. The Bundesbank pursued a contractionary monetary policy after the breakdown in March 1973 of the Smithsonian agreement of December 1971, with growth of the money stock declining from 15.4 percent in 1972 to 11.4 percent in 1973 and 9.5 percent in 1974. Following that tightening of money, the German exchange rate appreciated sharply in 1973 and 1974. Although import and export prices showed a one-time jump after the oil price shock, the rate of inflation of consumer prices declined during the course of 1974, as shown in Table 11.5.

At the beginning of 1974, some relaxation of Bundesbank policy was expected in light of the prospect of recession. Inflation was "widely expected to accelerate to at least 10 percent, [and] average contractual wage increases reached about 14 percent."[7] But, according to the OECD,

> In pursuance of the agreed monetary policy targets, but contrary to widespread expectations, the Bundesbank did not accommodate the higher nominal wage increases by an easing of credit conditions. Consequently, businessmen were on average unable to fully pass on cost increases resulting from the high wage settlements and the upsurge in raw materials prices. The tight monetary situation produced an unexpected moderation in price inflation during 1974 [actual inflation of the consumer price index was 7 percent], to which business responded by cutting both investment and employment.[8]

Since wage contracts were fixed for 1974, the large nominal increases swelled real wages, with real compensation per hour climbing by 7.1 percent after a 6.0 percent increase in 1973.

Now the annual wage round enters the story. Late in 1974 the concerted action meetings took place, with government, union, and employer representatives present. These meetings were not designed to formulate an incomes policy but rather to enforce a "concertation of expectations," so that the implications of governmental policy as well as private action for the macroeconomy are clearly understood by all parties. The Bundesbank warned that the low targets for monetary aggregates would be maintained throughout 1975, and that substantial unemployment would result unless nominal wage increases were sharply cut. In the words of the OECD, "This message was taken seriously by employers and unions as wage increases fell drastically compared to the preceding round."[9]

In *all* major industries the increase in contractual wages plummeted in a matter of months. Each sector had a new bargaining round, so that no long-term contracts caused carry-overs from 1974. The last four rows of Table 11.5 illustrate the deceleration in wages, showing how Germany became a country with low inflation by 1975. The sharp appreciation of the mark resulted in only a temporary boom in the real wage gap (which was reduced—although not fully—by 1975), so that the tight monetary policy had only a modest effect on profits and real activity. In other words, tight monetary policy did not exacerbate the profit squeeze. And the converse is also probably true: an expansionary monetary policy, announced at the concerted action meetings, would not have eased the profit squeeze. Giersch's observation is relevant:

> Inflation in Germany would have much less chance [than in the United States], if any, of depressing real wage increases below the rise in distributable productivity . . . for more than a year, given the inflation sensitivity of the population and the annual nation-wide wage rounds. Prospects for a long wage lag in Germany have deteriorated in comparison to the 1960s when the great post-1967 expansion, supported by longer wage contracts, ended in a series of wild cat strikes in the fall of 1969.[10]

Given the institutional setting, stimulative monetary policy is neither needed nor able to moderate the growth of real wages.

In the United States, on the other hand, nominal price developments importantly affect the real wage. The rise in commodity prices during 1972–74 led to a reduction in real wages because nominal wages were largely tied to decisions made before the price spurt. The inflation was an efficient way to bring about the needed decline in real wages after the relative increase in the prices of primary goods. Since 1978, another jump in inflation—induced in part by the depreciation of the U.S. dollar—again has led to a significant slowdown in the growth of real wages. The pattern is illustrated in Figure 11.2: whenever current price inflation exceeds *lagged* wage inflation, the real

Figure 11.2. Inflation and the real wage in the United States, 1973–1978

wage change is typically negative. The reason for this is that the current changes in nominal wages are strongly linked to their own past value through the existence of long-term, overlapping contracts.

The differences in nominal wage responsiveness between the United States (and Canada to a lesser degree), on the one hand, and Europe and Japan, on the other, can be given econometric content. Nominal wage growth in all of the countries is well described as a negative function of the rate of unemployment and a positive function of the rate of consumer price change. In North America the link to consumer prices occurs with a lag, while in Europe and Japan the link of $\dot{w}$ to $\dot{p}_c$ is virtually instantaneous (at least with regard to annual data). Generally:

$$(11.2) \qquad \dot{w}_t = \beta_0 - \beta_1 U_t + \beta_2 \dot{p}_{c_t} + (1 - \beta_2)\, \dot{p}_{c_{t-1}},$$

with $\beta_2 < 1$ in the United States and Canada, and $\beta_2 \approx 1$ in Europe and Japan. Estimates of (11.2) are shown in Table 11.6, where we verify that β_2 is not significantly different from 1.0 outside of North America, and is so there. Thus, in Europe we can write

$$(11.3) \qquad \dot{w}_{c_t} = \beta_0 - \beta_1 U_t,$$

Table 11.6. Nominal Wage Equations for Manufacturing, 1960–81[a]

| Country | Independent variable | | Summary statistics | |
	Unemployment rate	First-year change of consumer prices (β_2)	$\overline{R}^2$	D.W.
Canada	−0.76	0.37	0.81	0.91
	(3.04)	(1.48)		
France	−0.47	0.89	0.66	2.39
	(−1.75)	(3.41)		
Germany	−0.62	1.53	0.41	1.33
	(−1.76)	(3.05)		
Japan	−9.04	0.88	0.79	1.26
	(−5.46)	(6.60)		
United Kingdom	0.04	1.22	0.83	2.37
	(0.13)	(7.37)		
United States	−0.45	0.52	0.82	1.01
	(−2.14)	(3.56)		

a. The dependent variable is the rate of change in nominal wages in the manufacturing sector. Numbers in parentheses are t-statistics.

while in Canada and the United States we have

$$(11.4) \qquad \dot{w}_{c_t} = \beta_0 - \beta_1 U_t - (1 - \beta_2)(\dot{p}_{c_t} - \dot{p}_{c_{t-1}}).$$

In Table 11.7 we create an index of nominal wage responsiveness (NWR), based on the length of wage agreements, the degree of explicit wage indexation, and the extent to which wage setting is highly synchronized. While we have seen that the United States and Canada take a low value on each of these dimensions, countries like Australia and Denmark rank high on each score. The resulting index accords well with the wage equations of the previous table: the index of nominal wage response is positively correlated with the weight attached to *current* prices in the wage equation. Table 11.8 shows what happens when we align nominal wage responsiveness with the coefficient estimate of β_2.

A second piece of evidence in shown in Table 11.9. We calculate the standard deviations of wage change and nominal GNP change during the period 1972–79 for eleven countries (the ones with Bureau of Labor Statistics wage data). In countries with low nominal wage responsiveness (particularly Canada and the United States), the standard deviation of $\dot{w}$ is low in absolute terms, and more important, low relative to the variance of nominal

Table 11.7. Index of Nominal Wage Responsiveness

Country	Duration of agreement	Degree of indexation	Synchronization	Responsiveness rank order	Responsiveness index
Australia	2	2	2	2	6
Austria	2	0	2	8.5	4
Belgium	2	2	0	8.5	4
Canada	1	1	0	15	2
Denmark	2	2	2	2	6
Finland	1	1	1	13.5	3
France	1	2	0	13.5	3
Germany	2	0	2	8.5	4
Italy	0	2	2	8.5	4
Japan	2	0	2	8.5	4
Netherlands	2	2	1	4	5
New Zealand	2	2	2	2	6
Norway	1	1	2	8.5	4
Sweden	1	1	2	8.5	4
Switzerland	0	0	0	17	0
United Kingdom	2	2[a]	1	8.5	5
United States	0	1	0	16	1

Note: All variables are on a scale between 0 and 2. The index scores have the following meaning. Under Duration of agreement, 0 = 3-year contract length; 1 = 1–3 years, or open-ended; 2 = 1 year or less. Under Degree of indexation, 0 = no indexation clauses; 1 = partial indexation, or reopening clause triggered by price increases; 2 = widespread indexation. Under Synchronization, 0 = no synchronization (for example, negotiations proceed throughout the year); 1 = partial synchronization (for example, industry-level bargaining, with key industry); 2 = centralized national settlements.
a. The degree of indexation, though normally low, was very high at the time of the first OPEC shock, under the mandate of prevailing incomes policies.

Table 11.8. Nominal Wage Responsiveness and the Coefficient on Prices in the Wage Equation

Country	NWR	$\hat{\beta}_2$
United Kingdom	5	1.22
		(7.37)
Germany	4	1.53
		(3.05)
Japan	4	0.88
		(6.60)
France	3	0.89
		(3.41)
Canada	2	0.37
		(1.48)
United States	1	0.52
		(3.56)

Note: Numbers in parentheses are *t*-statistics. $\hat{\beta}$ is the estimated coefficient on p_{c_t} in the wage equation of Table 11.6.

Table 11.9. Nominal Wage Responsiveness and the Relative Variance of Wages and GNP

Country	NWR	S.D.($\dot{w}$) (I)	S.D.($\dot{p}_v + \dot{v}$) (II)	Ratio (I : II)
Denmark	6	4.7	1.9	2.5
Netherlands	5	4.4	2.9	1.5
United Kingdom	5	6.3	4.3	1.5
Belgium	4	5.3	3.5	1.5
Germany	4	3.1	1.9	1.6
Italy	4	5.1	3.9	1.3
Japan	4	8.9	4.6	1.9
Sweden	4	4.3	2.7	1.6
France	3	2.7	1.0	2.7
Canada	2	3.0	3.7	0.8
United States	1	1.5	1.8	0.9

Source: $\dot{w}$ is from the BLS; $\dot{p}_v + \dot{v}$ is from the International Financial Statistics of the IMF.
Note: $r[NWR, \text{Ratio}] = 0.52$. NWR is the index of nominal wage responsiveness; S.D.($\dot{w}$) is the standard deviation of nominal wage change, 1972–79; S.D.($\dot{p}_v + \dot{v}$) is the standard deviation of annual changes in nominal GNP, 1972–79.

GNP growth. Fluctuations in nominal GNP do not translate rapidly into changes in nominal wage growth.

Other research has arrived at broadly similar conclusions regarding the special nominal wage stickiness in the United States versus Europe and Japan. In particular, see Branson and Rotemberg (1980) and Gordon (1982).

The degree of nominal wage responsiveness has had two major effects on macroeconomic performance after the supply shocks of the 1970s. First, in the absence of policy responses, nominal wage stickiness is likely to moderate the adverse supply consequences of a terms-of-trade deterioration. As we showed in Chapter 6, higher indexation tends to worsen both the price and output consequences of a supply shock. Countries with low NWR were better able to avoid the sharp profit squeezes that we have found in several countries. Second, the low-NWR countries were better placed to use expansionary aggregate demand policies to reduce unemployment, though this opportunity was not always adopted. Switzerland, for example, pursued aggressively tight monetary policies in spite of low NWR, in large part because the resulting unemployment could be exported abroad. The United States, on the other hand, adopted an expansionary monetary policy after 1974 with successful effect in reducing unemployment. After the second oil shock in 1979 though, the United States pursued several years of contractionary policies.

Some simple regressions confirm this message. The most desirable combination of labor market structures during the supply shock period consisted of high corporatism and low nominal wage response, as shown by the change in the misery index (MI) after 1973:

$$(MI_{73-79}) - (MI_{65-73}) = 6.43 + 0.93 \, NWR - 1.53 \, CI.$$
$$(4.83) \quad (2.97) \qquad (4.99)$$
$$\bar{R}^2 = 0.64$$

Each unit increase in NWR is associated with a near unit increase in MI, while a unit increase in CI reduces MI by 1.5. Once again, we stress that a key channel operates through W^x_{OECD}. Higher NWR allowed workers to maintain real wage growth until the late 1970s. Earlier we showed that W^x_{OECD} is negatively correlated with CI. Adding NWR as an explanatory variable for W^x_{OECD}, we find:

$$(w^x_{OECD})_{73-79} = 1.75 - 1.11 \, CI + 0.86 \, NWR.$$
$$(0.90) \quad (2.49) \qquad (1.87)$$
$$\bar{R}^2 = 0.29$$

Conclusions

Table 11.10 compactly describes the two important dimensions of wage setting in the era of stagflation. Corporatism measures the level at which wage setting proceeds, with highly corporatist economies characterized by centralized bargaining among national representatives. Nominal wage responsiveness is an amalgam of institutional bargaining features which help to determine how rapidly unexpected price changes (whether from demand management policies or supply shocks) can feed through into nominal wages. We have seen that macroeconomic "misery," as measured by higher inflation and slower GNP growth, is importantly related to these structural factors. High corporatism and low nominal wage responsiveness helped countries to avoid a serious profit squeeze and the worst of the stagflation of the past decade.

Interestingly, these two dimensions are largely uncorrelated ($r = 0.15$), so it appears that countries could benefit from one or the other of the favorable characteristics. Austria, Germany, Norway, Sweden, and Switzerland come closest to having both sets of favorable institutions, while the Commonwealth countries Australia, New Zealand, and the United Kingdom have had the least favorable structures.

Table 11.10. Summary of Labor-Market Indexes

		Corporatism		
		Low	Medium	High
	High	Australia New Zealand United Kingdom		Netherlands Denmark
Nominal wage responsiveness	Medium	Belgium France Italy	Finland Japan	Austria Germany Norway Sweden
	Low	Canada United States	Switzerland	

Note: Corporatism index: high = $3.0 \leq$ index; medium = $1.0 \leq$ index < 3.0; low = index < 1.0. Nominal wage responsiveness index: high = $5.0 \leq$ index; medium = $3 \leq$ index < 5.0; low = $0 \leq$ index < 3.

Appendix 11A: Wage-Setting Institutions for Twelve Countries

This appendix offers a summary of several aspects of wage setting for twelve OECD economies. It should be pointed out that in all countries, a continuing process of institutional change makes a summary statement hazardous. Therefore, interested readers should consult one of several more detailed studies on wage-setting practices for a better sense of continuing developments in labor-management practices. Some useful references include OECD (1979a and 1979b) and Faxén (1982).

AUSTRIA

Level of negotiation: Industry-level negotiations, which depend on approval of the Austrian Confederation of Trade Unions (OGB). Strong centralized employees' association. It is very unusual for workers to vote on collective bargaining agreements.

Coverage of bargaining: 400–500 agreements concluded. 52.6% unionization.

Synchronization: High. Key industries (for example, metals, construction) have great influence.

Contract duration: 1 year to 15 months.

Indexation: None.

Incomes policies: A Joint Wages and Prices Board must approve the timing of negotiations of new contracts. The Board is composed of private and governmental representatives.

Role of government: Extensive discussion among trade unions, employers, and government concerning the state of the economy. Formalized in meettings on 3-month basis.

CANADA

Level of negotiation: 70% of unions participate in national labor federation (CLC). There is no national confederation of employers' associations involved in collective bargaining. Negotiations are at local level, and are typically subject to ratification by local membership.

Coverage of bargaining: 18,000 collective agreements, covering about 30% of the labor force.

Synchronization: Low.

Contract duration: In 1960s, 2–3 years on average. In 1977, approximately 65% of major contracts for one year.

Indexation: Approximately 30% of contracts in 1977, though the effective rate of indexation in these contracts is generally low.

Incomes policies: Wage and price control policies during 1975–78.

Role of government: No active participation in the negotiating process.

FINLAND

Level of negotiation: Central trade union federation (SAK) and employer association (STK) generally reach a collective agreement, which provides the basis for branch-level negotiations. However, the trade unions are deeply divided between a Social Democratic majority and a Communist minority. Low level of consensus and high strike activity.

Coverage of bargaining: 43.4% unionization.

Synchronization: High.

Contract duration: 1–2 years.

Indexation: Reopening clauses in lieu of indexation.

Incomes policies: Number of "package deals" linking wage policy, exchange rates, and fiscal policies.

Role of government: Active government intervention in the wage-setting process.

FRANCE

Level of negotiation: Deep split among the major union confederations along policy/ideological lines. The principal labor confederations are the CGT, CFDT, CFTC, CGC. The major employers' confederation is the CNPF. Negotiations are at industry and plant levels, with growing plant-level organization since 1968. Bargaining is sporadic, and actual wages are only loosely tied to collective agreements.

Coverage of bargaining: Approximately 20% of the work force is covered by collective bargaining agreements, but the proportion is difficult to estimate since many agreements are defunct.

Synchronization: Low.

Contract duration: Indefinite life of agreements. Agreements continue in force until changed. Bargaining is typically annual or intermittent, depending on industry, and so forth. By statute, the national minimum wage is revised at least once a year.

Indexation: Widespread use of indexation. Important influence of SMIC (minimum wage), which is indexed by government policy.

Incomes policies: Stabilization program under Barre government, including price controls and wage guidelines.

Role of government: Activist intervention to influence wage setting. In recent years government policy has supported real wage increases and encouraged indexation.

GERMANY

Level of negotiation: Unions organized on branch basis (17 branch trade unions associated with DGB). Large proportion of employers organized in associations, the most important of which is the BDA.

Coverage of bargaining: 31.8% unionization.

Synchronization: Negotiations are throughout the year, though metal sector is considered to be key industry for setting wage pattern. (IG-Metall has a large plurality of OGB members.)

Contract duration: 1 year. (In the mid-1960s, contracts of 18 months to 2 years were frequent.)

Indexation: None. Under the Monetary Law of June 1948, explicit indexation is prohibited, though some indexation clauses were used in the long-term contracts of the 1960s.

Incomes policies: None.

Role of government: There are a number of important institutions in which tripartite discussions among the government, labor, and employers take place. The "Concerted Action" policy, suspended in the mid-1970s, was the most important of these institutions.

ITALY

Level of negotiation: Several national labor confederations (including GIL, CISL, UIL, CISNAL, CIDA). Confindustria is the major employers' confederation. There has been a growing extent of plant-level bargaining since 1969, though the basic wage framework is set at the national level. In general, plant-level agreements are subject to worker approval at the workplace.

Coverage of bargaining: Approximately 30% unionization.

Synchronization: High.

Contract duration: 3-year agreements on national level.

Indexation: Widespread indexation. Formal sliding-scale agreement covering all workers (so-called *scala mobile*).

Incomes policies: No formal machinery to link wage setting with macroeconomic policies of the government.

Role of government: Traditional role has been as mediator and facilitator of private-sector negotiations.

JAPAN

Level of negotiation: All bargaining is at enterprise level. The national confederations (SOHYO, DOMEI, and others) help to coordinate wage bargaining policies of *shunto* (spring wage offensive).

Coverage of bargaining: 34,000 unions, representing 22% of employees.

Synchronization: High, due to *shunto* (instituted in 1955).

Contract duration: 1 year.

Indexation: None. However, because of bonus system in which a substantial part of compensation is paid in two lump-sum installments, effective rate of nominal compensation is not firmly fixed by collective agreement.

Incomes policies: None.

Role of government: Little direct role.

NEW ZEALAND

Level of negotiation: Negotiations proceed at all levels: national, regional, industry, and workplace. It is not common for members to vote on the results of collective bargaining.

Coverage of bargaining: 37% unionization.

Synchronization: Moderate-high. Negotiations take place during September–March each year, with a strong influence of the metals unions.

Contract duration: 1 year.

Indexation: Typically, no explicit provisions. The Arbitration Court might adjust settlements to account for inflation.

Incomes policies: Extensive controls on wages and prices during 1974–1977.

Role of government: The role of the government has varied greatly over time, with periods of little intervention and periods of extensive controls. An arbitration court, at various times, has played a significant role in adjudicating labor disputes.

NORWAY

Level of negotiation: Centralized, although at times negotiations have proceeded at the local level. The national labor confederation, LO, has 37 national union members. NAF is the predominant employer confederation. Central settlements set the basic norms for the branches.

Coverage of bargaining: 64% unionization.

Synchronization: High.

Contract duration: 2-year agreements.

Indexation: Degree of indexation has varied over time, with a reduction in formal indexation after 1976.

Incomes policies: Continuing attempt to integrate fiscal policy with national settlements. Active pursuit of "social contract" agreements among government, labor, and employees. Price and wage freeze, 1979.

Role of government: Tradition of government interference in central bargaining, though emphasis is on the discussion stage.

SWEDEN

Level of negotiation: Highly centralized.

Coverage of bargaining: Approximately 95% of wage employees are members of LO. Approximately 75% of salaried workers are organized.

Synchronization: High.

Contract duration: Generally 1–2 years in the 1970s, 3 years in the 1960s.

Indexation: None. Contracts generally contain reopening provisions which are triggered by price level rises at specified rates.

Incomes policies: See Role of government.

Role of government: Although there is no formal machinery for government participation in bargaining, there are extensive discussions to implicitly or explicitly (for example, in 1978) link fiscal policies to wage bargaining outcome.

UNITED KINGDOM

Level of negotiation: National organizations, the TUC (Trade Union Congress) and CBI (Confederation of British Industry) are umbrella organizations that do not engage in negotiation. Negotiations are at the plant level, and are largely informal, fragmented, and autonomous. Frequently, agreements are referred to membership for ratification; in most cases, shop stewards are able to make binding agreements without membership approval.

Coverage of bargaining: 45% of the labor force.

Synchronization: Low.

Contract duration: Generally no fixed term, but bargaining is typically at 12-month intervals.

Indexation: Aside from explicit government incomes policies (for example, 1974), indexation is rare.

Incomes policies: A long tradition of government noninvolvement in private-sector wage setting was reversed in the period 1973–79, during which a variety of incomes policies and "social contracts" were put in place.

Role of government: Aside from formal incomes policies, government has little direct role in negotiations.

UNITED STATES

Level of negotiation: Predominantly plant level. Central labor organization (AFL-CIO) plays no role in wage bargaining. No national employers' federation that is engaged in the collective bargaining process. Large proportion of agreements must be ratified by membership.

Coverage of bargaining: 195,000 collective bargaining agreements, covering 25% of the labor force (1974).

Synchronization: Very low.

Contract duration: Predominantly 3 years.

Indexation: Indexing clauses are contained in about 60% of major agreements. Typical clause calls for 0–3% wage increase for 1% CPI increase.

Incomes policies: Wage guidelines, 1964–66. Wage-price controls 1971–73. Wage guidelines, 1979.

Role of government: No active participation in negotiating process.

12 Supply Shocks, Demand Response, and the Productivity Puzzle

THE OUTPUT and productivity slowdown of the 1970s seems a unique phenomenon when viewed against the background of the whole of the post–World War II period. Although our models may help to explain the slowdown in output growth, they do not in an obvious way explain the deceleration in growth of output per unit of input. The productivity slowdown has been widespread and has affected virtually all industrial countries. It also seems to have been fairly widespread sectorally, although this aspect has not yet been adequately investigated. Conventional growth accounting procedures (for example, Denison, 1979; Kendrick, 1981) that decompose the slowdown in terms of quantity, quality, and utilization of labor and capital inputs, research and development effort, environmental regulations, and so forth, leave one unsatisfied because there is a dominant characteristic of the slowdown that eludes such explanation.

With a few exceptions, the beginning of the phenomenon can be dated at about 1973, when a major break occurs in the slope of the various time series. Table 12.1 shows the growth of average labor productivity for the overall economy (GNP per employee) and the manufacturing sector (value added per man-hour) for several OECD economies during the period 1960–80. In no case, except possibly that of the United States, is there evidence of a sharp slowdown in productivity growth in the period before 1973. This central fact is confirmed econometrically in Table 12.2, where we examine a model that allows for a turning point t^*, with one trend growth rate of productivity for the years 1960 to t^* and another for t^* to 1981. The turning-point year is selected by minimizing the sum of squares deviations of productivity from the two trend lines.[1] In most cases the estimated turning point falls within the period 1972–75 (in 55 out of 72 cells in Table 12.2). In some cases it falls somewhere at the end of the 1960s (1968–70). Only the U.S. aggregate GDP

Table 12.1. Productivity Growth in the Aggregate Economy and the Manufacturing Sector (in percentages)

Country	Aggregate GDP per person employed			Value added in manufacturing per man-hour		
	1960–67	1967–73	1973–80	1960–67	1967–73	1973–80
Belgium	3.9	4.5	2.4	5.0	9.3	6.0
Canada	2.5	2.9	0.0	4.2	5.4	1.5
Denmark	2.9	3.2	1.1	5.9	7.3	4.1
France	5.0	4.7	2.6	5.5	6.1	4.6
Germany	4.0	4.8	2.8	5.7	5.3	4.6
Japan	8.6	8.3	3.0	9.7	11.3	7.1
United Kingdom	2.4	3.4	1.1	3.9	4.7	1.7
United States	2.7	1.6	0.2	3.5	3.6	1.4

Sources: Aggregate GDP per person employed is from the OECD Historical Statistics of the Economic Outlook, 1960–1980; manufacturing data are from the Bureau of Labor Statistics.

and GDP per employee series (but not manufacturing) dates the turning point around 1966–67.[2] The existence of a reasonably synchronized turning point should be rather disturbing for a growth-accounting approach to the measurement of productivity slowdown. Changes in research and development efforts, in conventional input qualities, and in environmental regulations are gradual processes; they can hardly explain sharp turning points, let alone the close synchronization of developments across countries. On the other hand, the very existence of such a watershed may provide a helpful lead for economic research. One may concentrate on the turning point itself, and then ask to what extent the worldwide shocks of the 1970s can help to explain the productivity slowdown. Though such an approach may still leave some questions open, it has the advantage of a search for common causes as well as enabling one to gain insight from the differences in response among countries or sectors.

The first and obvious candidate for analysis is the sharp increase in the price of energy. When the relative price of the input rises and it is a complementary factor of production, *gross output* per unit of the other factors, labor and capital, must fall. Under certain circumstances, *value added* per unit of labor (our principal productivity measure) will also decline. Profits must also fall, the extent of the fall depending on the extent of real wage rigidity. The profit squeeze will cause an investment slowdown, which in turn affects the accumulation of capital, thereby contributing to the slowdown in labor productivity. The direct effects of the supply shifts of 1973–74 and 1979–80

Table 12.2. Estimated Turning Point, Selected Output and Output per Employee Series (year of trend shift)

Country	Total economy, 1960–1980			Manufacturing, 1960–1982
	GDP	Domestic absorption	GDP per employee	Output per employee
Ten major OECD countries				
United States	66	66	67	72
United Kingdom	73	74	74	73
Belgium	73	73	73	75
France	74	74	74	75
Germany	75	74	73	69
Italy	75	75	71	66
Netherlands	74	72	73	73
Sweden	72	72	73	70
Canada	73	75	73	77
Japan	74	74	74	74
Nine smaller OECD countries				
Australia	73	72	69	73[a]
Austria	72	72	—	69
Denmark	74	72	—	73[b]
Finland	72	73	69	75
Ireland	68	75	68	76
New Zealand	74	73	73	—
Norway	68	75	71/2	70
Spain	74	74	68	72[c]
Switzerland	75	75	—	70

a. 1963–81.   b. 1955–80.   c. 1960–79.

help in part to explain the slowdown in productivity growth in the manufacturing sector of the major industrial countries and also to account for some international differences. This is shown in the following section, where the direct link between the raw material price shock and the productivity slowdown in manufacturing is explored for a cross section of ten OECD countries.

Raw materials by themselves do not give a complete answer even for manufacturing, let alone for the less material-intensive nonmanufacturing industries. But oil and raw material price shocks have not only caused factor substitution; they have also set in motion contractionary forces on the demand side and classical unemployment on the supply side. It will be argued that it is probably the interaction of depressed output levels (and greater output variability) with the direct effects of higher input prices that provides the main explanation for the aggregate productivity slowdown.

A common factor shared by almost all OECD economies since 1973 has been the low average level of capacity utilization and high unemployment in the period. Whether that unemployment has been supply-induced or demand-induced (or both), it is plausible that it has had a profound effect on productivity by (1) slowing the sectoral reallocation of labor from low- to high-productivity sectors; (2) stifling gains that resulted from the economies of scale in production and distribution; (3) reducing the within-firm upgrading of labor that occurs in a high-employment economy; and (4) inducing labor hoarding in many firms, in some cases for several years (an example is the notorious difficulty experienced by many British industries in reducing manpower since 1975).

Several pieces of evidence in addition to the cross-country synchronization lend plausibility to the importance of high unemployment for the productivity slowdown. One can compare the recent productivity slowdown with a similar phenomenon in the Great Depression, as shown in Table 8.14. We noted in Chapter 8 that almost all countries experienced a pronounced slowdown in productivity growth during the eight-year period of high unemployment, 1929–37.

Second, it seems that the productivity lost during a spell of high unemployment is not fully made up during the subsequent recovery to full employment. To the extent that the productivity decline in a recession reflects no more than labor hoarding, it is true that super-normal productivity growth during recovery will allow productivity to catch up to its early trend. To the extent, however, that the high unemployment reduces the shift of labor from the agricultural sector because of low demand in the industrial sector, or diminishes worker investments in human capital within the firm, or reduces the opportunities for "learning by doing," the years of lost productivity gains are not recoverable simply through a macroeconomic recovery. Though the *growth rate* of productivity might be restored by a resumption of full employment, the *level* of productivity will remain below the prerecession trend path. Thus, even if full employment were restored, productivity growth from 1973 to that point would still be low on average since the period was one of high average unemployment.

Dickens (1982) has offered such an analysis of U.S. data, showing that cyclical productivity losses in the United States are *not* made up in business cycle recoveries. Since, on average, the U.S. economy was heavily underutilized after 1973, he is able to attribute much of the U.S. productivity slow-down directly to the deep recessions of recent years. If his results extend to other OECD economies, a part of the puzzle is cleared up.

A major reason for the demand squeeze has come from the anti-inflation stance of macroeconomic policy in the major industrial countries. This is contrasted in the third section of this chapter with the more expansionary policies pursued by the middle-income developing countries, whose output and productivity both continued to grow during 1973–79, but at the cost of higher persistent inflation and large current account deficits. These data strongly support the argument that productivity growth and macroeco-nomic policy responses, via aggregate resource utilization, are closely linked.

Input Substitution, Demand, and the Productivity Slowdown

Since many researchers have argued for the importance of energy prices in the productivity slowdown, it is important to begin with an analytical dis-cussion of the channels through which energy prices might operate. It turns out that the arguments are often inaccurate and probably attribute to the direct effect of energy prices more of a role than they merit.

A convenient starting point is the three-factor production function $Q = Q[V(K,L,T),N]$, where V is a real value-added index, K and L are capital and labor, N represents the composite material input, and T repre-sents pure technical progress. Chapter 3 described the conditions permitting such separability of V and N, which we assume to hold in this discussion. At least two measures of labor productivity are suggested by the production function: gross output per unit of labor, Q/L; and value added per unit of labor, V/L. These measures will behave very differently after a rise in N.

Assume that the economy is always fully employed, so that K and L are given, while N may vary through net imports. (Alternatively, though K and L may fluctuate, we may want to measure productivity on a "normalized" full-employment basis.) Then $V(K,L,T)$ is also fixed at any given T and thus does not vary directly with changes in N. Gross output Q, however, does vary with N, as shown in Figure 12.1 (V is held constant in the background). The marginal product of N is given by the slope, which in turn must equal the product price of N, $\Pi_N(= P_N/P)$. Thus, the N-Q combination for a low Π_N is given at a point like A, and for a high Π_N at a point like B. Since L is held fixed in moving from A to B, productivity on a gross output basis (Q/L) falls.

Since we assume that V and L are held fixed while Π_N rises, productivity on

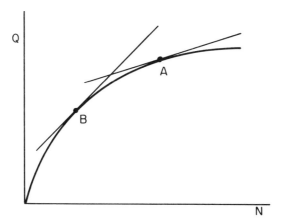

Figure 12.1. Gross output and intermediate inputs

a value-added basis is not directly affected by higher Π_N. But now let us measure value added not as V but as it is done in the national income account statistics, using a *double-deflation* procedure. Base-period GDP is defined as $Q_A - \Pi_N^A N_A$, and second-period GDP (after the oil price rise) is defined as $Q_B - \Pi_N^A N_B$. In other words, the base-period price of N is used to deflate the second-period quantity of the input. We can calculate double-deflated GDP by passing a line with slope Π_N^A through the production points A and B and measuring the intercept on the y-axis. This procedure is shown by the solid lines in Figure 12.2. Thus, using base-period measures of "real" value added, we find a fall in GDP from GDP^A to GDP^B. Measures of labor productivity based on GDP would, of course, show the same percentage decline. In sum, the double-deflation procedure yields a measure of value added that is partway between gross output and true value added. (See also Appendix 2B in Chapter 2.) If the GDP measures are rebased using post-shock relative prices Π_N^B instead of Π_N^A, then we would actually measure a *rise* in value added between A and B. This is shown by the dotted lines in Figure 12.2, with the results $(GDP^A)'$ and $(GDP^B)'$.

We mentioned in Appendix 2B the probable size of the GDP bias, by comparing GDP growth for ten small European economies using 1972 prices, 1975 prices, and a Divisia Index. The bias seems to add approximately 0.4 percentage points per year to the slowdown. In larger, less open economies, the bias would be correspondingly reduced. Lindbeck (1983) argues that the average bias across the OECD is about 0.1 percentage points for the aggregate economy and about 0.2 percentage points in manufacturing.

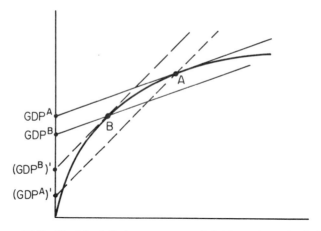

Figure 12.2. Double-deflation measures of GDP, under a rise in Π_N

We now turn to some estimates of the pure substitution effect of higher π_n on *gross output* measures of productivity. Starting with $Q = Q[V(K,L,T),N]$, and denoting the output elasticity of intermediate goods by β and that of capital with V by ϕ, we can write

(12.1) $\dot{q} = (1 - \beta)\dot{v} + \beta\dot{n} = (1 - \beta)[\lambda + \phi\dot{k} + (1 - \phi)\dot{l}] + \beta\dot{n},$

where λ is the rate of technical progress or "total factor productivity" in V. (Remember that lowercase variables signify logarithms of uppercase counterparts, and that $\dot{x} = dx/dt$).

Next we assume that the elasticity of substitution between V and N is constant (denoted by σ), from which it follows that

(12.2) $\dot{n} = \dot{q} - \sigma\dot{\pi}_n,$

where π_n is the (log) relative price of the intermediate input. Substituting into (12.1), we get

(12.3) $\dot{q} - [\phi\dot{k} + (1 - \phi)\dot{l}] = \lambda - \sigma(1 - \beta)^{-1}\beta\dot{\pi}_n.$

The left-hand side of Eq. (12.3) represents the change in factor productivity as measured in terms of gross output relative to the weighted capital and labor input. The capital share ϕ will be constant if $V(K,L)$ is a Cobb-Douglas production function. On the right-hand side of (12.3) we have a conventional time-shift factor (λ) which is augmented or reduced by a material-input price term according to whether relative raw material prices fall or rise over time. The coefficient of $\dot{\pi}_n$ in (12.3) is the product of the relative share of N and V in Q, $[\beta/(1 - \beta)]$, and the elasticity of substitution (σ). If we have constant proportions ($\sigma = 0$) or no change in input prices ($\dot{\pi}_n = 0$), this substitution term would be immaterial and the measurement of factor productivity would be invariant to the role of raw materials or to the choice of output measure (gross output or some GDP artifact).

In an earlier paper (Bruno, 1981) a similar framework was applied to four large industrial countries (the United States, the United Kingdom, Germany, and Japan), and direct estimates of the parameters (ϕ, β, σ, λ) were obtained from a two-equation system consisting of (12.3) and the associated factor price frontier. The model also allowed for some cyclical variation in factor utilization. This and related studies (Bruno and Sachs, 1982b; Lipton, 1981) suggested an estimate of σ on the order of 0.3–0.4 for the United States, the United Kingdom, and Germany, and 0.7–0.8 for Japan. Though the hypothesis gives a good explanation of the relative ranking of the productivity slowdown for the four countries as well as a quantitative fit for the lowest (Germany) and the highest (Japan), there was a sizable unexplained residual for the United Kingdom and a more moderate one for the United States. It could also be argued that the implied estimate of σ for Japan was somewhat high.

Table 12.3 gives the relevant average growth data for a wider sample of ten OECD countries for the periods 1955–73 and 1974–80. Column 4 shows the productivity slowdown measured under the assumption that $\phi = 0.35$ (obtained from a cross-section regression). Inspection of the figures for the drop in labor and capital inputs (columns 2 and 3) reveals that this measure is not very sensitive to the choice of ϕ (a change of ± 0.05 in ϕ changes the entries in column 4 by 0.06 on average). There is considerable variation in the estimated slowdown around the mean of 2.2 percent (from a base of 3.9 percent for 1955–73), with the figures ranging from less than 1 percent for Germany to more than 3 percent for Japan and Sweden.

As already noted in Chapter 2 (Appendix 2A) and Chapter 8, neither oil nor raw material prices were constant during the high growth period preceding 1972. Once the effects of the Korean boom had worked themselves out, the prices of these two types of goods declined steadily at a real annual rate of 0.5–1.0 percent from 1955 until 1971–72. The trend was reversed at the beginning of the 1970s, culminating in the price explosion of 1973–74. Raw material prices then came down again until a new shock hit both types of goods in 1979–80.

The magnitude of the total real input price shock ($\Delta\dot{\pi}_n$) is here measured by the differences in average growth of π_n during 1955–72 and 1973–79 (column 5, Table 12.3). Much of the cross-country variation in $\Delta\dot{\pi}_n$, though by no means all of it, stems from differential movements of the real effective

Table 12.3. Selected Data on Average Growth in Manufacturing and Aggregate Demand, Ten OECD Countries: Change in Annual Percentage Rate of Growth from 1955–73 to 1974–80

Country	Output (1)	Labor (2)	Capital (3)	Factor produc- tivity (4)	Materials input prices[a] (5)	Public consump- tion (6)	Domestic absorption (7)
United States	−3.1	−2.2	−0.9	−1.3	3.3	−0.7	−2.0
United Kingdom	−5.1	−3.3	−2.6	−2.0	6.4	−0.7	−2.1
Belgium	−5.4	−4.5	−1.4	−2.0	5.0	−1.6	−1.9
France	−4.2	−3.6	−0.1	−1.8	5.3	−0.7	−2.8
Germany	−4.8	−3.7	−4.2	−0.9	1.9	−1.6	−2.2
Italy	−3.7	−1.0	−1.8	−2.4	11.0	−1.6	−3.0
Netherlands	−4.7	−3.6	−1.4	−1.8	7.4	0.2	−2.7
Sweden	−4.9	−1.0	−2.4	−3.3	7.8	−1.2	−2.1
Canada	−4.1	−1.8	−0.8	−2.7	5.7	−3.6	−2.3
Japan	−8.5	−6.0	−3.7	−3.3	5.3	−1.5	−7.1
Mean	−4.9	−3.1	−1.9	−2.2	5.9	−1.3	−2.8

Source: Output and man-hour data from Bureau of Labor Statistics, U.S. Department of Labor; capital stock data based on Artus (1977) and updated; materials input prices based on OECD and wholesale price statistics of various countries. Public consumption from OECD, *National Income Accounts.*
a. Change from 1955–72 to 1973–79.

exchange rate that mitigated or accentuated the effect of the exogenous shock on domestic relative prices. It is important to stress again that even the external portion of the real price increases is only in part directly due to energy prices, since other raw material prices also changed in this period. (For more details on the large increase in primary non-fuel export prices, see Kravis and Lipsey, 1981.)

A first attempt at assessing the possible association between raw material prices and factor productivity growth is obtained by taking observations on average growth in each of the two subperiods, 1955–73 and 1974–80, for the ten countries listed in Table 12.3, a total of twenty observations (not detailed here), and pretending that they come from a common underlying production model. Obviously, such an approach ignores the possible inter-country differences in total factor productivity growth, as well as possible changes in that parameter over time, quite apart from possible differences in other parameters.

It is interesting to note that even this simple regression (Regression 1,

Table 12.4) yields a significant and quite plausible estimate for the input price term (-0.25). As long as basic country differences in production parameters are not correlated with the differences in raw material price changes, this might give an unbiased estimate of the $\dot{\pi}_n$ term in Eq. (12.3). However, while it can be argued that the shares, ϕ and β, and possibly the elasticity of substitution (σ), are similar in different countries, factor productivity (λ) almost certainly varies, and may have varied across subperiods.

One way of overcoming this statistical problem, at the cost of a severe cut in degrees of freedom, is by going to the first differences of average growth rates. If it is assumed that countries may differ in basic productivity growth but that level changes in this attribute over time are the same across countries, the problem is sidestepped. The resulting Regression 3 shows two things. With a value of β of about 0.35, the coefficient of -0.17 suggests an average elasticity of substitution of 0.32. At the same time, the significant

Table 12.4. Selected Regressions of Average Factor Productivity Growth in Manufacturing: Ten OECD Countries, 1955–73 (I) and 1974–80 (II)

Selected regressions	Constant	Input prices $(\dot{\pi}_n)$[a]	Public consumption $(\dot{g})$	Total domestic absorption $(\dot{a})$	$\bar{R}^2$	S.E.
Growth levels (I and II), 20 observations						
1	3.47	−0.25	—	—	0.21	1.56
	(0.43)	(0.10)				
2	0.29	−0.13	0.79	—	0.97	1.28
	(1.08)	(0.09)	(0.25)			
Growth increment (II − I), 10 observations						
3	−1.18	−0.17	—	—	0.19	0.70
	(0.60)	(0.09)				
4[b]	−0.96	−0.18	—	—	0.37	0.57
	(0.49)	(0.08)				
5	−0.76	−0.17	0.27	—	0.27	0.67
	(0.65)	(0.08)	(0.20)			
6	−0.56	−0.16	—	0.24	0.37	0.62
	(0.63)	(0.08)		(0.13)		

Note: Numbers in parentheses are standard errors.
a. Lagged one year.
b. Excluding Japan (number of observations is 9).

negative intercept (-1.18) suggests a common element of the slowdown that is not captured by the raw material factor. It is interesting to note that the exclusion of Japan, an outlier, from this regression only raises the $\Delta\dot{\pi}_n$ coefficient to 0.18, but the standard error falls (from 0.094 to 0.076), and $\bar{R}^2$ rises considerably (from 0.19 to 0.37).

Regressions 5 and 6 incorporate the deceleration in public expenditure and total domestic absorption, respectively (see columns 6 and 7 of Table 12.3). These variables seem to improve the explanatory power considerably and render the intercept insignificant.[3] Although there may be a statistical simultaneity problem with the use of these expenditure variables, they indicate that it may pay to introduce the degree of resource utilization in the analysis of productivity slowdown, which we shall do in the next section. At this stage we only point out the fact that the introduction of these demand-side variables hardly changes the estimate of the role of π_n, which seems reassuring as far as our assessment of the direct role of input substitution in manufacturing is concerned.

Value-Added Measures of Productivity Growth and Resource Utilization

We now turn to the measurement of productivity in the aggregate business sector. Most studies of the productivity slowdown have focused on value added per unit of labor, a measure which in principle (though not fully in practice) avoids the problem of raw material price changes. From (12.1), $\dot{v} = \lambda + \phi\dot{k} + (1 - \phi)\dot{l}$, so that labor productivity growth $\dot{v} - \dot{l}$ is the sum of total factor productivity growth λ, plus capital deepening times the capital share in value added, $\phi(\dot{k} - \dot{l})$. That is, $\dot{v} - \dot{l} = \lambda + \phi(\dot{k} - \dot{l})$. Since λ is unobserved, it is in fact calculated from the data as $(\dot{v} - \dot{l}) - \phi(\dot{k} - \dot{l})$. The productivity "puzzle" is that the declines in labor productivity are not fully accounted for by $\phi(\dot{k} - \dot{l})$, so that λ has apparently changed.

Several authors have concluded, on a wide range of data sets, that shifts in capital deepening after 1973 account for only a small part of the decline in $\dot{v} - \dot{l}$. One such decomposition, due to Kendrick (1981), is illustrated in Table 12.5. According to Kendrick's estimates for the business sectors of nine OECD economies, labor productivity growth was 3.0 percentage points slower on average across all economies during 1974–79 than during 1960–73. Approximately 0.4 percentage points can be traced directly to a decline in capital deepening, with the rest showing up in the total factor productivity (TFP) term. Kendrick also calculates changes in labor quality, based on the changing composition of the labor force, by age, sex, and education. In Table 12.5 we subtract Kendrick's estimate of the contribution of this factor in order to get an adjusted TFP, or "residual." Kendrick makes an interesting effort to account for the remaining TFP slowdown. His broad categories of remaining factors are reallocations of labor, volume changes (economies of scale and capacity utilization), government regulations, effects of research and development, diffusion of technical advances, and a final residual. The "diffusion" category basically measures changes in the average age of the capital stock and thus might be regarded as an additional component of the capital-deepening term (that is, the part due to *embodied* technical progress). Broadly speaking, each of these factors plays about an equal role; none of them stands out as the key to the productivity residual. Kendrick does not ask, however, why each of these terms should have declined in each of the countries (with few exceptions). For that perspective, we believe that we must return to the macro level to consider more generally the effects of low resource utilization on productivity growth.

The relationship of productivity to resource utilization is, in fact, a complicated topic in need of careful exposition. We believe that there are three distinct ways in which a change in resource utilization affects productivity. First, and most traditionally, at the beginning of a demand-led contraction workers are typically hoarded by firms in anticipation of an ensuing upturn. The firm is off the short-run production frontier, and measured productivity falls. Second, if the downturn persists, the hoarded labor is eventually laid off. Since firms will close down their least efficient operations and lay off their lowest-productivity workers, the effect of this second phase will be to *raise* average productivity even above its level at full employment. Third, the persistent operation of the economy at a high unemployment rate will have longer-term consequences on interfirm and intrafirm mobility of labor and capital that will depress the long-term potential growth of the economy.

To state this argument formally, we return to the distinction introduced in Chapter 9 between actual labor productivity and labor productivity at full employment. Let V^f be the maximum level of V that can be produced with fully employed labor, L^f. In logs, $v^f = \lambda t + (1 - \phi)l^f + \phi k$. Also, let L^m be the minimum amount of labor necessary to produce a given level of value added. In logs, $v = \lambda t + (1 - \phi)l^m + \phi k$. The three effects are captured by the hypotheses that (1) l adjusts slowly to l^m after a reduction in output; and (2) λ and k are positive functions of resource utilization.

As a specific illustration, let l^f be constant, and $\dot{l}$ be a function of $l^m - l$:

(12.4) $\dot{l} = \theta(l^m - l)$.

Table 12.5. Sources of Labor Productivity Growth in Nine OECD
Economies (in percentages)

Country	1960–73 (1)	1973–79 (2)	Slowdown (1) − (2)
BELGIUM			
Labor productivity	6.1	4.4	1.7
of which:			
Capital deepening	1.9	1.8	0.1
Labor quality	0.2	0.4	−0.2
Residual	4.0	2.2	1.8
CANADA			
Labor productivity	4.2	1.0	3.2
of which:			
Capital deepening	1.3	1.1	0.2
Labor quality	0.0	0.3	−0.3
Residual	2.9	−0.4	3.3
FRANCE			
Labor productivity	5.9	4.2	1.7
of which:			
Capital deepening	2.0	2.0	0.0
Labor quality	0.2	0.4	−0.2
Residual	3.7	1.8	1.9
GERMANY			
Labor productivity	5.8	4.3	1.5
of which:			
Capital deepening	2.6	2.2	0.4
Labor quality	0.0	0.2	−0.2
Residual	3.2	1.9	1.3
ITALY			
Labor productivity	7.8	1.6	6.2
of which:			
Capital deepening	2.0	0.8	1.2
Labor quality	0.9	0.6	0.3
Residual	4.9	0.2	4.7
JAPAN			
Labor productivity	9.9	3.8	6.1
of which:			
Capital deepening	3.3	2.0	1.3
Labor quality	0.7	0.6	0.1
Residual	5.9	1.2	4.7

Table 12.5 (*continued*)

Country	1960–73 (1)	1973–79 (2)	Slowdown (1) − (2)
SWEDEN			
Labor productivity	5.8	2.5	3.3
of which:			
Capital deepening	2.2	2.2	0.0
Labor quality	0.1	0.2	−0.1
Residual	3.5	0.1	3.4
UNITED KING-DOM			
Labor productivity	3.8	1.9	1.9
of which:			
Capital deepening	1.6	1.6	0.0
Labor quality	0.5	0.8	−0.3
Residual	1.7	−0.5	2.2
UNITED STATES			
Labor productivity	3.1	1.1	2.0
of which:			
Capital deepening	1.2	0.5	0.7
Labor quality	0.1	0.6	−0.5
Residual	1.8	0.0	1.8

Sources and Methods: The data are from Kendrick (1981), Table 7, pp. 140–141. Labor productivity is the annual growth of real gross product per labor hour in the business sector. Capital deepening is the annual growth in $k - l$, multiplied by ϕ, as in the text. Growth in labor quality is based on demographic shifts in age-sex composition of the labor force and changes in educational attainment of the labor force. The residual in this table is the simple difference of labor productivity and the other two components. It differs from Kendrick's "final residual," which allows for other factors to account for labor productivity.

Also, let $(\lambda + \phi \dot{k})$ be a rising function of capacity utilization, measured as $v - v^f$:

(12.5) $(\lambda + \phi \dot{k}) = \gamma_0 + \gamma_1 (v - v^f)$.

Now let us trace out the productivity implications of a permanent decline in $(v - v^f)$ of Δ percent, for an economy that begins in full-employment equilibrium with $v = v^f$ and $l = l^f$. Trend productivity growth $\dot{v}^f - \dot{l}^f$ equals $\lambda + \phi(\dot{k} - \dot{l}^f)$, or just $\lambda + \phi \dot{k}$, since l^f is constant. Thus, from (12.5), $\dot{v}^f - \dot{l}^f$ equals γ_0 before the downturn in utilization, and $\gamma_0 - \gamma_1 \Delta$ after the downturn. The time path of $v^f - l^f$ is given by the bent solid line in Figure 12.3.

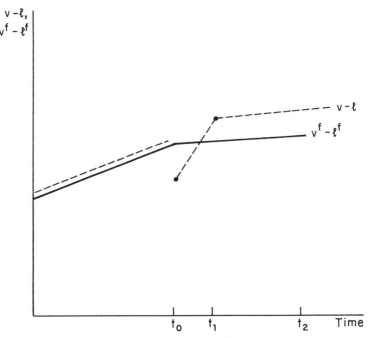

Figure 12.3. Productivity growth after a permanent reduction in capacity utilization (at t_0)

Actual productivity $(v - l)$ varies around that solid line. To find $v - l$, note that it may be written as $(v^f - l^f) + [(v - v^f) - (l^m - l^f)] - (l - l^m)$. By the definition of l^m, the term in brackets equals $-[\phi/(1 - \phi)](v - v^f)$, so that

$$(12.6) \qquad (v - l) = (v^f - l^f) - [\phi/(1 - \phi)](v - v^f) - (l - l^m).$$

According to (12.6), $(v - l)$ is reduced below $(v^f - l^f)$ when (1) capacity utilization is high (that is, $v > v^f$), since least-efficient firms and workers are drawn into production, and (2) labor is hoarded $(l > l^m)$. When $(v - v^f)$ falls, productivity must first fall, since v is reduced on impact but l is unchanged; after a bit of time, l is reduced to match l^m, and only effect (1) is left. The path of $v - l$ is shown as the bent dashed line in Figure 12.3. During full-employment growth $(t < t_0)$, $v - l$ equals $v^f - l^f$. When the downturn comes, $(v - l)$ temporarily falls below $v^f - l^f$ but eventually rises *above* it as the hoarded labor is eliminated. In the very short run, measured labor productivity growth is reduced; in the intermediate run (between t_0 and t_1 in the figure), it may actually be raised by the downturn; and in the long run (between t_0 and t_2), it declines as the long-term factors take over.

This kind of framework does a good job of accounting for the movements in $v - l$ after 1973. To implement the framework empirically, we write $\dot{v}_t^f - \dot{l}_t^f$ as a negative function of the unemployment rate, $\dot{v}_t^f - \dot{l}_t^f = a_0 - a_1 U_t$, and then integrate this relationship to find

$$(12.7) \qquad (v_t^f - l_t^f) = (v_0^f - l_0^f) + a_0 t - a_1 \sum_{i=0}^{t} U_i.$$

Thus, the level of full-employment productivity is a negative function of *cumulative* unemployment. Next, we assume that there is a one-year lag in the adjustment of l to l^m. Labor hoarding is a function of the rise in unemployment in a given year, $\dot{U}_t$, under the assumption that hoarded labor is eliminated by the second year after an increase in U. Finally, we replace $v - v^f$ in (12.6) by the unemployment rate. Putting these pieces into (12.7), our estimated equation is

$$(12.8) \qquad v_t - l_t = a_0 + a_1 t - a_2 \sum_{i=1}^{t} U_i + a_3 U_t - a_4 \dot{U}_t.$$

Table 12.6. Labor Productivity Equation, 1961–81

$$(v - l)_t = a_0 + a_1 t - a_2 \sum_{0}^{t} U_i + a_3 U_t - a_4 \dot{U}_t$$

Country	a_1	a_2 ($\times 100$)	a_3 ($\times 100$)	a_4	R^2	ρ	D.W.
Belgium	0.07	−0.35	1.35	−1.84	0.998	0.78	1.54
	(22.97)	(2.17)	(1.82)	(2.63)		(5.16)	
Canada	0.05	−1.28	1.66	−3.55	0.997	0.07	1.92
	(35.32)	(13.00)	(4.63)	(6.15)		(0.25)	
Denmark	0.06	−0.41	1.08	−0.51	0.997	0.26	1.92
	(39.24)	(6.13)	(3.08)	(1.84)		(0.98)	
France	0.05	−0.95	4.34	−3.88	0.999	0.23	1.87
	(25.20)	(4.54)	(2.67)	(3.37)		(0.92)	
Germany	0.05	−0.51	1.67	−1.78	0.999	0.07	1.85
	(63.13)	(7.17)	(4.43)	(3.93)		(0.25)	
Japan	0.10	−3.81	0.13	−8.21	0.997	0.59	1.73
	(23.73)	(2.58)	(0.02)	(1.58)		(2.72)	
United Kingdom	0.04	−0.55	2.37	−2.43	0.991	0.70	1.19
	(9.81)	(1.55)	(1.94)	(2.33)		(2.77)	
United States	0.03	−0.28	0.23	−1.14	0.981	0.50	1.71
	(7.15)	(1.06)	(0.27)	(1.81)		(1.98)	

Note: Numbers in parentheses are *t*-statistics.

Remember that a_2 reflects the impact of unemployment on full-employment productivity growth; a_3 measures the *positive* effect of U_t on $v_t - l_t$ that comes from eliminating the least efficient firms during a period of high unemployment; and a_4 captures the negative effect of labor hoarding on measured productivity.

The estimates of (12.8) for eight countries are shown in Table 12.6. The results appear to confirm strongly the three roles of capacity utilization in productivity growth. In every country, the level of labor productivity is a negative function of cumulative unemployment (significant in six of eight countries), a positive function of the level of unemployment (significant in four of eight countries), and a negative function of the change in unemployment (significant in five of eight countries). The effects of a permanent 1 percentage point rise in U in Germany are shown in Table 12.7 as an example of these results. In the first year, productivity growth is reduced by 0.6 percentage points and the productivity level is consequently 0.6 percentage points below the previous trend. In the second year, firms dis-hoard labor very substantially, which leads to a productivity boom and a *rise* in the productivity level relative to the previous trend (see Figure 12.3). In the remaining years, the growth in productivity is reduced by the presence of high unemployment, though the level of productivity continues to be above $v^f - l^f$ because of the labor-shedding phenomenon. By the fourth year, the slowdown in trend productivity growth pulls $v - l$ below the pre-shock trend path, so that an observer would begin to notice the productivity slowdown in the data.

Our earlier arguments suggested that the raw material price increases might have an impact on value-added productivity through measurement effects. To examine this question in the present framework, we add $\pi_{n_{t-1}}$ as an explanatory variable in (12.8), with the results shown in Table 12.8. The variable has the expected negative sign in seven of eight countries and is

Table 12.7. Simulated Productivity Response to a Permanent 1 Percentage Point Rise in the Unemployment Rate, Germany

Productivity growth and levels	Year				
	1	2	3	4	5
$\dot{v} - \dot{l}^a$	−0.6	1.3	−0.6	−0.5	−0.5
$v - l^a$	−0.6	0.7	0.1	−0.4	−0.9

Source: Based on regression results for Germany in Table 12.6.
a. Relative to previous trend.

Table 12.8. Labor Productivity Equation including π_n, 1961–81

$$(v - l)_t = a_0 + a_1 t - a_2 \sum_0^t U_i + a_3 U_t - a_4 \dot{U}_t - a_5 \pi_{n_{t-1}}$$

Country	a_1	a_2 ($\times 100$)	a_3 ($\times 100$)	a_4 ($\times 100$)	a_5	$\overline{R}^2$	ρ	D.W.
Belgium	0.07	−0.32	1.48	−1.45	−0.15	0.998	0.80	1.44
	(20.22)	(1.86)	(1.86)	(1.54)	(0.61)		(5.45)	
Canada	0.05	−0.97	1.54	−2.43	−0.27	0.998	0.36	1.78
	(23.24)	(5.59)	(3.85)	(3.99)	(2.11)		(1.31)	
Denmark	0.06	−0.49	0.71	−0.61	0.36	0.998	0.31	1.89
	(33.28)	(5.45)	(1.61)	(2.19)	(1.35)		(1.18)	
France	0.05	−0.87	5.73	−2.70	−0.37	0.999	−0.01	1.98
	(28.40)	(5.91)	(4.64)	(2.70)	(3.18)		(0.03)	
Germany	0.05	−0.33	2.15	−1.55	−0.26	0.999	0.01	1.89
	(57.89)	(2.98)	(5.33)	(3.53)	(2.02)		(0.04)	
Japan	0.10	−2.78	3.23	−4.97	−0.41	0.997	0.60	1.76
	(21.53)	(1.54)	(0.43)	(8.10)	(1.00)		(2.70)	
United Kingdom	0.04	−0.46	2.33	−1.58	−0.38	0.992	0.56	1.22
	(12.51)	(1.55)	(1.95)	(1.45)	(1.85)		(1.80)	
United States	0.03	−0.21	0.32	−1.12	−0.08	0.979	0.49	1.75
	(5.69)	(0.55)	(0.33)	(1.71)	(0.25)		(1.84)	

Note: Numbers in parentheses are *t*-statistics.

significantly negative in three cases. The measure of π_n that we use rises by 0.24 between 1972 and 1981, so that a coefficient of −0.30 signifies a level effect on productivity of about 7 percentage points. Notice that the inclusion of π_n has no major effect on the other coefficients, which remain of the same sign and same general magnitude as in the previous table.

Explaining the Links of Unemployment and Trend Productivity Growth

The cyclical effects of unemployment on measured productivity are conventional and well understood, though some discussions give too much weight to the labor-hoarding rather than the labor-shedding effects of unemployment (that is, they focus on a_4 rather than a_3). Our linkage of $\dot{v}^f - \dot{l}^f$ to U is less conventional, however, and merits an elaboration. We stress that until detailed microeconomic work confirms some of our hypotheses, we are operating at the level of conjecture rather than proof.

Some of the links of U to $\dot{v}^f - \dot{l}^f$ are fairly direct. A sustained rise in U and consequent fall in production will probably be accompanied by a loss of static and dynamic economies of scale. In industries where learning by doing is important, the mere fact of low output levels will result in losses of productivity relative to trend that will not simply be recaptured by a return to full employment. Kendrick (1981) assigns an average of 0.3 percentage points of the slowdown in residual in Table 12.5 to a loss of economies of scale (with a maximum 0.7 percentage points for Japan).

We follow Lindbeck (1983) in laying more stress elsewhere, namely on the effects of higher U in retarding the reallocation of resources among sectors, between firms within a sector, and even within firms. Most analysts of postwar OECD growth point to the large dividend in productivity that has resulted from the transfer of labor from agricultural to nonagricultural sectors. This analysis is based on the assumption that differences in the average productivity of labor in agriculture and nonagriculture elsewhere reflect comparable differences in *marginal* productivities, an assumption that seems to accord well with the cross-country evidence. Lindbeck summarizes the evidence of others[4] that approximately 0.3 percentage points of the productivity slowdown may be due to the reduced flow of labor from agriculture after 1973, with larger losses in Japan and Italy and smaller losses in the United Kingdom and the United States. More generally, Kendrick calculates the following contributions to the slowdown from reduced intersectoral reallocations of labor, across nine broad industry classifications: Belgium, 0.3; Canada, -0.1; France, 0.3; Germany, 0.2; Italy, 0.6; Japan, 1.1; United Kingdom, 0.3; United States, 0.3.

Even if the importance of the intersectoral resource flows for productivity is granted, the link to unemployment rates must also be made. In all countries, for example, the flow of labor from agriculture slowed sharply in the 1970s, but in many cases this reflected the substantial depletion of the agricultural labor force in the 1960s in addition to the high unemployment in the 1970s. But at least in France, Italy, and Japan, where a substantial part (greater than 10 percent) of the labor force remained in agriculture, the slow growth of industry and services rather than a depleted agricultural labor supply must be involved. More generally, high unemployment reduces sectoral mobility by (1) encouraging unions to fight layoffs and adopt restrictive practices; (2) spawning protective labor legislation and subsidization of declining firms; (3) reducing the start-up of new enterprises; and (4) reducing investments in new capital goods that are complementary to the labor reallocation process.

The estimates of Kendrick and others no doubt understate the contribution of resource reallocation, by ignoring within-sector and within-firm effects. Lindbeck (1983) quotes a detailed micro-study for Swedish manufacturing showing that at least 25 percent of labor productivity growth in the 1960s was the result of reallocation of resources, labor, and capital between various branches of manufacturing. He concludes that as much as "30–40% of the labour productivity slowdown—as an average for the OECD countries—may be due to various types of allocation factors."

Though future research efforts on resource reallocation will indeed be required, we can at least offer a framework for that analysis. Suppose the economy consists of several (finely subdivided) sectors producing a total GNP, V, which is broken down into $V_0 = V_0(K_0, L_0)$, a reference sector in which no disturbance occurs, and $V_i = V_i(K_i, L_i, T_i)(i = 1, 2, \ldots, n)$ representing the other sectors. K_i and L_i are the respective factor inputs, and T_i are exogenous shifts terms (technology, material input prices, and so on). Denoting relative output prices (in terms of V_0 as numéraire) by P_i, we have

$$(12.9) \qquad V = V_0(K_0, L_0) + \Sigma P_i V_i(K_i, L_i, T_i).$$

For changes we get

$$(12.10) \qquad \Delta V = (\partial V_0/\partial K_0)\Delta K_0 + \Sigma P_i(\partial V_i/\partial K_i)\Delta K_i + (\partial V_0/\partial L_0)\Delta L_0$$
$$+ \Sigma P_i(\partial V_i/\partial L_i)\Delta L_i + \Sigma (\partial V_i/\partial T_i)\Delta T_i.$$

Denote $\sum_{i=0}^{n} K_i = K$, $\sum_{i=0}^{n} L_i = L$, $\partial V_0/\partial K_0 = Z_V$, $\partial V_0/\partial L_0 = W_V$, and $RK/V = \phi$, $\Delta V/V = \dot{v}$. After some manipulation, we can rewrite (12.10) in the form

$$(12.11) \qquad \dot{v} - [\phi \dot{k} + (1 - \phi)\dot{l}] = \Sigma (T_i/V)\dot{t}_i$$
$$+ \Sigma (K_i/V)(P_i\partial V_i/\partial K_i - Z_V)\dot{k}_i$$
$$+ \Sigma(L_i/V)(P_i\partial V_i/\partial L_i - W_V)\dot{l}_i.$$

The left-hand side of Eq. (12.11) represents aggregate factor productivity as conventionally measured. The right-hand side consists of three terms: the first is the sum of the sectoral productivity shift factors; the other two are terms involving divergences of marginal factor productivities from real factor returns multiplied by the rates of change of factors by sector. The argument about sectoral reallocation is that during the 1960s, the contributions of the second and third factors to economy-wide productivity growth were positive (factors moving in the direction of higher marginal productivity) and large. High unemployment substantially reduced these contributions.

Another related empirical fact that may be invoked in this context is the existing evidence about the large increase in output growth variability after 1973.[5] At a time of severe fluctuations in output, the average optimal use of inputs per unit of output is necessarily greater than in a situation of greater certainty. Average factor productivity must therefore fall. This can be illustrated geometrically by comparing the mean cost of two points on opposite branches of a U-shaped cost curve with the point of minimum-cost production (assuming this is the equivalent output level under certainty). Under uncertainty producers may opt for flatter cost curves, but at the price of a higher minimum cost. Some such argument may account for the case of an outlier like Sweden, where the increase in relative variability of output growth was particularly large. It is also known that reallocation of factors was hampered in Sweden by government subsidies to ailing industries, which brings us back to the earlier argument.

Comparing OECD and the MICs

A major part of our argument here is that the depressed domestic output in OECD countries after 1973 has impeded the factor adjustment process that contributes to aggregate productivity change. When seen in this light, the observed productivity slowdown is directly linked to the choice of short-term and medium-term macroeconomic response strategy. The newly industrialized countries (NICs) and the much broader group of middle-income developing countries (MICs) can be brought into our story at this point to provide further evidence in favor of our interpretation. They provide an exception, during 1973–1979, to the OECD response of contractionary policies in the face of the supply shocks. Faced with similar input price shocks, these economies performed quite well in the 1970s in terms of output and general economic activity, while most OECD countries did poorly. Part of the answer, which was already mentioned in Chapter 4, has to do with the emergence of an international private capital market to which many of the MICs had access and where for a time they could borrow heavily at zero or negative real interest rates. The other side of the explanation — and the one more relevant to our present discussion — is that these countries by and large pursued highly expansionary domestic policies until 1980 or 1981. Let us now turn to an explicit comparison of the two groups of countries.

The difference in aggregate performance of the two types of countries in the 1970s will be illustrated by an international comparison of thirty-eight countries, nineteen OECD countries and nineteen MICs (see Table 12.9). While the OECD group covers almost all of the industrial market economies,

Table 12.9. Annual Average Rate of Change of Selected Variable,[a] by Country Group, 1960–73 and 1973–80[b]

Variable	19 OECD countries[c]		10 MICs[d]		19 MICs[e]	
	1960–73	1973–80	1960–73	1973–80	1960–73	1973–80
1. Gross domestic product	4.7 (1.8)	2.6 (2.2)	6.7 (4.9)	6.0 (3.8)	6.6 (3.6)	6.3 (3.4)
2. Employment	1.2	0.7	4.0	2.9	—	—
3. GDP per employed person	3.6	2.0	2.7	3.0	—	—
4. Gross investment	6.4	0.4	8.9	6.6	9.7	8.1
5. Public consumption	4.8	2.3	9.9	6.6	8.4	7.7
6. Import/export prices	−0.5	1.5	−0.5	−0.5	0.2	0.5
7. Consumer prices	4.7 (1.8)	10.8 (2.9)	6.3 (3.8)	18.5 (9.0)	7.2 (4.8)	19.5 (9.4)
8. Current-account deficit/GDP	1.5 (1.5)	0.9 (2.0)	3.9 (4.6)	8.0 (4.6)	0.3 (3.0)	3.6 (3.2)

Source: Line 1: for OECD: Divisia Index based on OECD accounts. Lines 4 through 6, 8: OECD, *National Income Accounts,* and IBRD World Tables for (LDC). Line 7: IMF, *International Financial Statistics.*

a. Numerals in parentheses are mean standard deviations.

b. Line 8, 1965–73 for first period, 1973–79 for some MIC countries in second period.

c. Comprising all OECD countries with the exclusion of Greece, Iceland, Luxembourg, Portugal, and Turkey.

d. Egypt, Israel, Kenya, Korea, Mauritius, Philippines, Singapore, Syria, Yugoslavia, Zambia.

e. As in d, with the addition of Ivory Coast, Morocco, Malaysia, Pakistan, Thailand, Greece, Turkey, Brazil, and Colombia.

the MICs comprise only about two-thirds, in terms of population, of the class of middle-income oil importers (as defined in the World Bank, *World Development Report 1981*). Aggregate employment data could be found for only ten of these, comprising 43 percent of the population of all MICs. Table 12.9 accordingly gives averages for both subgroups of MICs.

Note the group differences in average growth performance, comparing pre-1973 (period I, 1960–73) and post-1973 (period II, 1973–80). In contrast to the OECD group, the MICs hardly slowed down in terms of total GDP growth, and they may on average have *improved* their growth in labor productivity. Growth was by no means even during the subperiod in either group of countries. Table 12.10 gives more detail for a subsample of coun-

Table 12.10. Growth Rate of Gross Domestic Product (V) and Gross Domestic Product per Employed Person (V/L), in Nine Major OECD Countries and Ten MICs: 1966–80 (annual average rate of change, percent)

	1966–73		1973–75		1975–78		1978–80	
Country	V	V/L	V	V/L	V	V/L	V	V/L
Nine major OECD countries[a]								
United States	3.4	1.3	−0.8	−1.0	5.1	1.4	1.3	−0.2
United Kingdom	3.3	3.4	−0.8	−0.9	2.7	2.8	−0.0	0.5
Belgium	5.2	4.4	1.2	1.2	3.2	3.5	2.4	1.9
France	5.5	4.7	1.7	1.9	4.0	3.3	2.3	2.2
Germany	4.5	4.6	−0.7	2.1	3.8	3.9	3.2	2.0
Italy	5.3	5.3	0.2	−1.2	3.5	2.7	4.4	3.1
Sweden	3.6	3.0	3.3	0.9	0.2	−0.3	2.8	1.3
Canada	5.3	2.5	2.3	−0.6	4.1	1.6	1.5	−1.8
Japan	9.7	8.3	0.6	1.0	5.2	4.0	4.9	3.7
Mean	5.1	4.2	0.8	0.4	3.5	2.5	2.5	1.4
Ten middle income countries[b]								
Kenya	6.9	2.7	5.2	1.4	7.6	3.8	2.5	—
Mauritius*	3.7	−0.9	4.8	0.1	9.5	4.6	−1.4	−0.9
Korea*	10.1	6.4	8.2	5.0	11.7	7.0	1.7	0.9
Philippines	5.6	—	6.0	3.3	6.6	—	5.9	—
Singapore*	12.9	—	5.2	3.1	8.0	3.1	9.8	3.8
Yugoslavia*	5.7	2.9	7.6	2.2	7.4	3.1	4.0	0.3
Syria	6.4	—	25.3	20.2	4.7	1.2	7.1	—
Zambia*	3.2	−0.3	2.1	−0.6	0.5	2.8	−3.0	−5.2
Egypt	3.1	1.1	5.7	3.0	10.3	—	6.9	—
Israel*	9.6	6.1	4.2	3.3	2.2	−0.7	1.6	−0.2
Mean	6.7	—	7.4	—	6.9	—	3.5	—
Mean*	7.5	2.4	5.4	2.2	6.6	3.3	2.1	−0.2

a. Ten smaller countries not shown here are Australia, Austria, Denmark, Finland, Ireland, Netherlands, New Zealand, Norway, Spain, Switzerland.

b. Asterisk denotes the subsample of six countries for which all observations are available.

tries. Immediately after the first shock (1973–74) the difference between the groups was even sharper; there was only partial recovery for the OECD countries in 1975–78, while most MICs represented here grew faster during the period. The second shock (1978–80) was followed by a slump in both groups. All countries show a close relationship between GDP growth and labor-productivity growth.

Going back to Table 12.9, note the difference in the variability of output growth. For the OECD countries, the mean standard deviation of annual growth rose from fast growth (period I) to slow growth (period II). For the MICs, the opposite was true. The coefficient of variation rose from less than 0.5 in the OECD group to 0.8 after 1973, while for the nineteen MICs it fell from 0.7 to 0.6. This difference is in turn related to differential demand management (the data for growth in public consumption and gross investment in the samples are also given in Table 12.9).

The terms of trade on average deteriorated in the OECD group (relative to import/export prices, they fell by an average of 0.5 percent in period I and rose by 1.5 percent in period II), while they hardly changed for the MICs (slight deterioration for the entire group of nineteen; slight improvement for the subsample).[6] This difference probably stems from exports of primary commodities, which were sizable in most MICs.

The trade-off for the more expansionary stance of the MICs is indicated in the lower part of Table 12.9. The acceleration of inflation was greater in these countries (and the coefficient of variation higher). A more pronounced difference, which brings us back to the topic of Chapter 4, is the sizable increase in the relative foreign resource gap of the MICs shown by the rise in the real current-account deficit relative to GDP (with more or less constant average variability), while the OECD on average reduced an already small resource gap.[7]

The data just presented support the view that the more expansionary internal policies of the MICs have a lot to do with the difference in productivity performance between the two groups of countries. Paradoxically, it is also likely that the relative success of the MICs during 1973–79 would not have been possible if the OECD countries had also followed more expansionary policies and had had more buoyant investment demand, since competition for the OPEC surplus would have made this a much more costly option to pursue. But the most important conclusion for our present topic is that productivity and macroeconomic response are indeed closely linked.

If the view of the sources of the productivity slowdown in the OECD countries advocated here is correct, it would follow that this phenomenon is only as transitory or as permanent as the macroeconomic climate of the world economy. If input price shocks continue to hit the world economy frequently, but at uncertain intervals, and if cost-induced inflationary waves are going to be followed by contractionary demand policies in the leading industrial countries, then there is no reason to consider the slowdown as transitory. If, on the other hand, the system were to find an efficient way of smoothing the fluctuations in real input prices and of better coordinating economic activity and monetary policies across national frontiers, then one of the major sources of the slowdown would be removed. The best bet probably lies with neither of the two extremes. It may be that some learning and adaptation to the new environment would allow the pursuit of reasonable inflation rates without the enormous cost in unemployment that has been paid in the past. The upshot of the present discussion is that in this case aggregate productivity growth in the industrial countries might improve along with the hoped-for improvement in overall macroeconomic performance.

13 Lessons for Theory and Policy

IN THIS LAST chapter we draw some general lessons from the preceding analysis both for macroeconomic theory and for the conduct of macroeconomic policy. First, let us return to the doctrinal disputes mentioned in the Introduction. Our analysis has shown that the Keynesian aggregate demand framework and the basic notions of aggregate trade-offs (in particular the unemployment-inflation trade-off) are still highly relevant for theory and policy. However, aggregate demand considerations have to be embedded and reinterpreted within a broader scheme in which aggregate supply shifts now play a much larger role and in which open-economy considerations and the mutual interdependence of economies are explicitly taken into account. At the same time, our analysis does not deny the importance of some major contributions made by the rational expectations school. There is no doubt that a rational expectations approach considerably enriches one's understanding of the way asset markets work. In our framework we have indeed made use of that approach for both exchange rate and investment determination. However, we do not share that view for the equilibrium theory of business cycles, that is, for the process of adjustment in labor and commodity markets. The assumption of instantaneous clearing in these markets, and particularly in the labor market, does not stand up to the test of reality. Notions of disequilibrium and price rigidities seem to us to play a central role in the characterization of adjustment in these markets.

Within the realm of aggregate supply considerations, our analysis has stressed the central role of real factor prices in the macroeconomic adjustment mechanism, in particular that of raw material price shocks and of the nature of wage response. Without explicit and integral incorporation of these elements in macroeconomic theory and policy, any analysis of the major adjustment problems must, in our view, be seriously lacking. Once the importance of real factor prices is recognized, there is an immediate implication for the traditional dichotomy between short-term adjustment and long-term growth. The incorporation of real factor costs automatically entails explicit consideration of real profit behavior, which in turn affects the capital accumulation process and thus medium- and long-term growth. We have seen that supply shocks take quite a few years to work themselves through the system. Thus, short-term and long-term adjustment to real factor price shocks invariably have to be combined within one framework of analysis. It is hard to see a sound theory or a coherent policy being formed that does not explicitly take into account both the immediate and the longer-term repercussions of such shocks and the response to them.

The importance of real wage behavior for the understanding of macroeconomic phenomena again highlights one central requirement of macroeconomic theory. It would seem only natural that a theory for a country's (or several countries') response can only be formulated if one takes its specific institutional or structural features into consideration. However macro-theory, whether Keynesian or monetarist, has for a long time tended to consider one and the same basic model as applicable to all economies. Over the years it has gradually been recognized that at least two types of structural distinctions among countries are of major importance for the understanding of adjustment problems. One is the obvious division between closed and open economies. By now most economies, presumably even the United States, must be classified as "open" (even this, however, is often glossed over). The other distinction increasingly being made is between industrial and semi-industrial countries (in which financial markets, at least, tend to be much more segmented and imperfect). Our analysis highlights a third structural element — the importance of incorporating the structure of labor markets explicitly into macroeconomic theory that is applied across industrial economies. One central feature that has distinguished the United States, for example, from almost all other industrial countries is the nature of wage response. Our empirical analysis shows that the United States may also be different in other respects from the typical OECD economy, as for example in the timing of the productivity slowdown. The main point, however, is that both for its size and for the nature of its labor market, the United States is a much more "Keynesian" economy than the others, in the sense that aggregate demand fluctuations continue to play *the* major role in real GDP, profits, and investment fluctuations.[1] It is important to stress this point because so many textbooks are written and generalizations are made based on one economy that happens to be large and dominant but is nevertheless substantially different from its trading partners.

Of course, several problems remain in our specification of the macroeconomic adjustment process, most of them involving the interface of theoretical formulation and empirical estimation. We shall mention three such areas, although there may be many more loose ends in our study. One major problem with which we have tried to contend without success is finding a sound theoretical formulation that lends itself to empirical testing of the output and price adjustment mechanism over a period in which different market regimes may have taken place. There are known procedures for disequilibrium estimation of well-specified partial markets, but there are few if any successful attempts to estimate a disequilibrium model for an aggregate economy. In earlier work we made estimates of supply schedules and successfully incorporated demand factors in them, but these are rather ad hoc models that are not well-grounded in our basic theoretical framework.

Another area that has so far eluded systematic research is the specification of productivity changes for a system that is subject to supply and demand shocks. Again, we believe that our ad hoc estimates in Chapter 12 point to the importance of underutilization, output fluctuations, uncertainty, and disequilibrium factors, but we do not claim to have formulated any systematic theory to account for these very marked empirical developments.

Finally, let us point to a problem that has afflicted the study of foreign exchange markets in general. A beautiful theory exists, but one is hard put to point to any robust results on the actual behavior of exchange markets.[2] In our present context this is obviously of crucial importance for a quantitative assessment of the policy coordination problem.

Let us turn our attention now to some lessons for economic policy. In many ways these parallel the implications for economic theory. First to be stressed is a point made at the outset and now, we believe, amply supported by the empirical analysis. The economic developments of the last decade have reinforced the paramount importance and relevance of macroeconomic policy and, in particular, of demand management. Fluctuations in demand, mainly policy-induced, explain probably more than anything else the sharp gyrations in output and to a considerable extent also the fluctuations in inflation rates. However, this central role for demand factors can be fully appreciated only once we explicitly incorporate supply factors into the analysis. Clearly, the fact that real factor prices now play such a central role also implies that demand management alone cannot achieve the goals of price stability and full employment with smooth growth. Macro-policy must thus also incorporate elements of supply management.

Here we would like to stress a number of points. The first one involves the sharp movements in the price of energy and raw materials. Although we have not explicitly studied the problem, observations on the asymmetric response to upward or downward movements in real factor prices at least suggest that it is not only the rise in relative prices but also the unexpected large jumps and fluctuations that may cause adjustment problems. If this view is correct, then policies to smooth such fluctuations, particularly for raw materials prices, may be beneficial from a global welfare point of view (for a discussion of schemes such as buffer stocks and the like, see Bosworth and Lawrence, 1982). Another general observation has to do with the choice of policy targets for domestic macroeconomic policy. The adoption of *nominal* GDP targets can in our view of things lead to excessively contractionary policies for *real* GDP because such an approach does not distinguish the source of disturbances, whether they are from the demand or the supply side. Consider a one-time price increase that is caused by the pass-through of an import price shock. Keeping nominal GDP constant would in a case like that lead to a reduction in real GDP. In the framework in which we have conducted our discussion, policy should pay explicit attention not only to prices and unemployment as such but also to the behavior of real factor prices and real profits. The response to inflationary pressure should then depend on the underlying supply and demand factors at work.

Given an exogenous real supply price shock, what are the implications for policy response from the point of view of the individual economy? Can one point to obvious examples of polar responses in recent history? The appropriate policy response to a rise in Π_N, we have seen, depends on the nature of nominal wage behavior and the nature of demand and supply balance in the commodity market. If the commodity market gets back to equilibrium after the first impact of the rise in Π_N, and if nominal wages are sticky, a monetary expansion can raise prices and lower the product wage so as to reduce the unemployment effects of the shock. However, if wages are indexed or frequently negotiated, the monetary expansion may well lead to a general rise in wages and prices, with little downward pressure on the product wage. Even if the real consumption wage (W/P_C) is sticky, so that monetary policy is ineffective, a temporary fiscal expansion may raise home output. Fiscal policy works by raising demand on home goods, increasing Π (a real appreciation) and thus reducing W_Q and Π_N (Π_N^*/Π). This comes at the cost of a current-account deficit.

In a situation like this, wage moderation is obviously the key to less disruptive adjustment. In fact, we have seen that to keep employment unchanged one has to keep the real product (GDP) wage ($W_V = W/P_V$) constant relative to trend, which in turn implies a reduction in the growth of the consumption wage. At the same time the country may want to allow a one-time pass-through of the import price shock in terms of domestic consumer prices, and to pursue a combination of fiscal and monetary policies that will allow continued output growth and an increase in exports to finance the increased import requirements (ideally, a fiscal contraction combined with moderate nominal monetary expansion).

Consider two extreme, almost textbook examples of responses to the second oil shock, namely those of Japan and the United Kingdom. The key comparative data for the two countries are given in Table 13.1. Japan provides a striking example of improved macroeconomic response in 1979–81

Table 13.1. Adjustment to the Second Oil Shock: Japan versus the United Kingdom

Economic indicator	1976–78	1979	1980	1981
JAPAN				
$\dot{p}_c$	5.9	3.6	8.0	4.9
$\dot{p}_v$	5.1	2.6	3.0	2.7
$\dot{w}$	9.5	6.5	6.5	7.4
$\dot{w} - \dot{p}_c(\dot{w}_c)$	3.4	2.8	−1.4	2.4
$\dot{w} - \dot{p}_v(\dot{w}_v)$	4.4	3.9	3.5	4.7
$\dot{v}$ (GNP)	5.2	5.6	4.2	2.5
U	2.1	2.1	2.0	2.2
$w_t^x - w_{t-1}^x$	—	0.8	1.8	NA
Export volume	4.5	0.2	17.1	10.6
Real exchange rate $(-\dot{\pi})^a$	—	−5.3	4.9	4.2
UNITED KINGDOM				
$\dot{p}_c$	12.0	13.4	18.0	11.9
$\dot{p}_v$	12.5	15.1	19.2	12.0
$\dot{w}$	14.5	19.3	23.7	14.9
$\dot{w} - \dot{p}_c(\dot{w}_c)$	2.2	5.2	4.8	2.7
$\dot{w} - \dot{p}_v(\dot{w}_v)$	2.0	4.2	4.5	2.9
$\dot{v}$ (GNP)	2.3	1.4	−1.7	−2.2
U	5.6	5.4	6.8	10.7
$w_t^x - w_{t-1}^x$	—	8.8	0.4	4.8
Export volume	5.7	2.8	2.4	−1.0
Real exchange rate $(-\dot{\pi})^b$	—	−13.6	−5.1	7.8

a. Calculated as the change in nominal dollar exchange rate plus the difference between the U.S. and Japan's consumer price inflation.

b. Calculated as the difference between the change in nominal dollar exchange rate plus the difference between the U.S. and U.K.'s consumer price inflation.

relative to its own performance in 1973–75.[3] Compared to a deep recession in 1973–75, there was only a modest slowdown in growth in Japan after the second oil shock (consider the growth rate figures in the sixth row of Table 13.1), while the rest of the OECD countries slowed down much more sharply. There was an inflation blip in 1980 (in terms of $\dot{p}_c$ but *not* in terms of $\dot{p}_v$). The nominal wage grew at a more or less constant rate (only rising slightly by 1981). The real product wage ($\dot{w}_v$) virtually followed the textbook rule of constancy (relative to trend), while the consumption wage rate ($\dot{w}_c$) dropped sharply in relative terms. Thus the real wage gap hardly changed (eighth row, Table 13.1) nor did unemployment (U). On the demand side, output growth was maintained by a sharp rise in exports along with a substantial real depreciation in both 1980 and 1981.

The United Kingdom provides almost the polar opposite example.[4] After responding to the first oil shock with a wage explosion,[5] it repeated almost the same experience after the second oil shock. The inflation rate shot up much more than in the case of Japan in spite of the fact that the United Kingdom is less dependent on oil imports; in this case, there was an even larger increase in GDP prices (the GDP deflator in manufacturing, however, grew considerably more slowly than did the CPI). The collapse of the incomes policy of the labor government started off the Thatcher government with a legacy of a sharp wage push. In spite of a highly restrictive monetary policy, wages came down to earlier growth rates only by 1981. The real wage gap grew considerably between 1978 and 1981. Given the sharp real appreciation (following tight monetary policies), it is no wonder that exports hardly increased in spite of the domestic slack. Unemployment, of course, shot up to an unprecedented height.

The U.K. example also brings up a problem that has been common to a large number of industrial countries in the past decade. As Buiter and Miller (1981b) rightly point out, the required reduction in marginal labor costs could have been achieved by returning the North Sea oil revenues to the private sector in the form of a cut in payroll taxes, such as the employers' national insurance surcharge. In fact, in one industrial country after another the 1970s saw not only an increase in public sector expenditure on social services but also its finance by rising payroll taxes (see also Chapter 9). Wage cost moderation in a situation where the take-home pay is less than 50 percent of the gross wage cost to the employer could mean a lot more than just moderation of wage earners' demands. Wage moderation could come as well from fiscal management. In fact, under some circumstances a case could be made for a wage subsidy rather than a wage tax as a means of increasing employment and competitiveness. In a democratic society prone to a wage gap, real wage moderation requires some kind of social contract if it is not to be brought about by accelerating inflation or by double-digit unemployment. It may take the form of a tripartite agreement among government, employers, and trade unions in which taxes, wages, and demand management policy are thrown into the bargain.

Let us now consider the policy options of a representative industrial economy which finds itself in an unemployment equilibrium, the supply shock and its aftermath having worked themselves through the system. Suppose that inflation has been in large part wrung out of the system and the country is in a low-level unemployment equilibrium of the mixed classical-Keynesian type. The problem becomes one of engineering a return to full employment without at the same time reigniting inflation, or depending too heavily on current-account deficits and foreign borrowing.

Traditional models might suggest that a quick return to full employment would be consistent with the other objectives, as long as the economy's unemployment rate is not pushed *below* its equilibrium or "natural" rate. But in fact the argument is faulty if the wage gap remains high and is likely to increase in the event of a recovery. In that case inflationary pressures will reignite even with unemployment above the natural rate, as firms attempt to expand profit margins on the way back to recovery. The inflation rate is then like a compressed spring, held down by high unemployment yet ready to expand as soon as that weight is lifted. One senses that the reticence of policymakers to engage in expansion is at least partly founded on this interpretation of events.

If the economy can abandon either the inflation or the current-account target, it can probably use a mix of monetary and fiscal instruments to achieve its other aims. Thus, with the United States willing to run large trade deficits, its mix of expansionary fiscal policy and contractionary monetary policy in 1981 – 83 led to falling inflation and unemployment, at the expense of an extremely overvalued currency. If the inflation target were abandoned, rapid money growth and real exchange rate depreciation would probably reduce unemployment and current-account deficits, except where wages are extremely highly indexed.

We have stressed at several points that better international policy coordination may be required to allow countries even the modest success of meeting two out of three targets. For example, the willingness of countries to use expansionary monetary policies in fact depends on the choices made by other economies. The U.S. reliance on a mix of expansionary fiscal policies and tight monetary policies exported inflationary impulses to Europe and Japan and made it less likely that these other countries could ease their own monetary policies (they are reluctant, often for other political reasons, to follow the U.S. lead toward large budget deficits).

In an economy with a high wage gap, achieving all three targets requires a tool in addition to demand policies, whether it is termed "incomes policies" or "consensual tripartite negotiations" or "social contracts." A direct reduction in the wage gap remains the single most important positive supply shock that a country can engineer on its own. As we documented in Chapter 10, such a reduction would be likely to reduce inflation and unemployment simultaneously, as well as giving increased scope for expansionary policies to the macroeconomic authorities. Direct wage moderation is not the only path to reducing real labor costs. These costs can also be reduced by a cut in labor taxes, as we pointed out in Chapter 9.

In several European economies, favorable institutional change has taken place in the direction of wage moderation. After several years of bitter debate in Europe between the advocates and opponents of continued wage indexation, there have been a number of cases in which a compromise on partial indexation was successfully reached.[6] In 1981 the European Commission adopted guidelines indicating the need for reducing indexation in the face of external shocks or international noncompetitiveness. In Belgium, Denmark, France, and Italy, various private and public actions were taken in 1982 to limit the scope of indexation. In Sweden the new Socialist government undertook a very large 16 percent devaluation in October 1982, with the apparent understanding of the major trade union federation there that wage bargainers would accept the resulting reduction in real wages. The understanding seemed to be that a real wage reduction is a worthwhile price to pay for increased external demand and employment.

Other OECD economies seem to have been unable to engineer similar comprehensive arrangements. The trade union movements in those countries reflect skepticism that real wage levels are in any way responsible for the continuing high unemployment. It is particularly hard to overcome this skepticism when monetary contraction is clearly the major force behind unemployment increases, and when payroll taxes in addition to wage payments are a major factor in the overall rate of increase in labor costs. Meade (1982) and Malinvaud (1982) have responded independently to these doubts by proposing that adjustments in real wages be underwritten by "aggregate demand insurance," in which demand management policies are in place to prevent real wage reductions from depressing output in the short run.

Contractionary policies have been shown to achieve moderation of real wages, but at the cost of slower growth and continued high unemployment. Reductions in the wage gap should be easier to engineer on the upswing if trade unions, employers, and macroeconomic policymakers properly regard the real cost of labor as a target of policy and a matter for negotiation.

Notes
Bibliography
Index

Notes

Introduction

1. The Organization for Economic Cooperation and Development (OECD) comprises twenty-four industrialized market economies, including the economies of western Europe, North America, Japan, Australia, and New Zealand. The member countries are Australia, Austria, Belgium, Canada, Denmark, Finland, France, Germany, Greece, Iceland, Ireland, Italy, Japan, Luxembourg, the Netherlands, New Zealand, Norway, Portugal, Spain, Sweden, Switzerland, Turkey, the United Kingdom, and the United States.

2. Arthur Okun (1970).

3. For this equation, $\dot{p}_c = 7.50 - 1.34\,U$, $\overline{R}^2 = 0.35$, D.W. $= 1.49$, on annual data for 1960–69. The t-value of the unemployment coefficient is 2.40. The unemployment rate is calculated as $\Sigma\omega_i U_i$ where U_i is the unemployment rate of country i, and ω_i is the average share of country i's labor force in the total labor force of the following seven countries: Canada, France, Germany, Italy, Japan, the United Kingdom, and the United States. The average is calculated for the years 1965–80. Inflation is calculated as $\Sigma\omega_i \dot{p}_{c_i}$, where $\dot{p}_{c_i}$ is the consumer price inflation of country i.

4. M. Friedman (1968); E. S. Phelps (1968).

5. M. S. Feldstein (1982), pp. 63–64.

6. Formally, let $(\dot{p}_c)_{73-81}$ be the annual average rate of inflation between 1973–81, and $(\dot{v})_{73-81}$ the same for real GNP. $(\dot{p}_c)_{60-73}$ and $(\dot{v})_{60-73}$ are defined equivalently. Then, the rise in inflation is $(\dot{p}_c)_{73-81} - (\dot{p}_c)_{60-73}$, and the growth slowdown is $(\dot{v})_{60-73} - (\dot{v})_{73-81}$. These values are calculated for twenty-four countries on the basis of data in Tables 8.1 and 8.2.

7. J. G. Altonji (1982). The key coefficient on the real wage minus the expected real wage in the future "is almost always of the wrong sign and is often statistically significant" (p. 813). Several other studies are also discussed in this paper. See also Clark and Summers (1982), who conclude that "labor supply decisions are not very responsive to transitory changes in employment opportunities." One implication of the Lucas supply model is that output should be a positive function of unexpected

price shocks. A recent study by DeGrauwe and Nabli (1983) tests and largely rejects this proposition for economies in the EEC.

8. The weighted-average data are for yearly averages of money stocks, rather than end-of-year measures. The data are from the *International Financial Statistics* of the IMF, series L34x for the industrial countries (category 110).

1. Elements of a Theory

1. The subject matter of this section is discussed in detail in Chapters 2 and 3.

2. This line takes the algebraic form $W_Q = Y_0/L_0 - (K_0/L_0)R$ or, alternatively, $R = Y_0/K_0 - (L_0/K_0)W_Q$.

3. In technical jargon this is called "Hicks neutrality."

4. This statement is true independently of what happens to the share. The proof follows directly from the maximization of $Y = Q - \Pi_N N$ for given Π_{N_0}. When Π_N rises from Π_{N_0} to Π_{N_1}, we cannot have $Y_1 = Q_1 - \Pi_{N_1}N_1 > Q_0 - \Pi_{N_0}N_0$ because this would entail that $Q_1 - \Pi_{N_0}N_1 > Q_1 - \Pi_{N_1}N_1 > Q_0 - \Pi_{N_0}N_0$, which contradicts maximality of Y given Π_{N_0}.

5. We shall subsequently assume that technological progress takes a pure labor-augmenting form; thus, the real-wage axis will be redefined as wages in "intensity units" of labor, where the intensity units per man-hour are assumed to rise at a constant rate over time.

6. This specific problem is handled in detail in Appendix 2B.

7. Alternatively, if producers are unable to reduce the labor input for institutional or technological reasons (for example, "putty-clay" technology), then the production possibilities lie along the tangent to the point C and, with rigid wages, production will take place at F and not at B. Full employment is then retained, but profits must be squeezed by even more than at B.

8. It is, of course, by no means necessary that the real rate of interest in world capital markets remain invariant when a raw material price shock occurs. Part of the adjustment may occur through a downward shift in the real rate of interest. This has in fact happened after the first oil shock (the reverse seems to have happened after the second). In that case the long-run point will lie to the left of D on the new FPF. This is discussed further in the next section.

9. The topics of this section are analyzed in much greater detail in Chapter 4.

10. This, in turn, might have resulted from perceiving the oil and raw material price hikes as temporary, from less rigid domestic labor markets, from continued investment in oil-substituting equipment, or from a less buoyant world economy on the eve of the shock.

11. The subject matter of this section is analyzed in detail in Chapter 5.

12. Assuming that this can be properly measured. It is sometimes more conve-

nient to measure Q on the horizontal axis, as discussed later.

13. For convenience we here at first take the *nominal* wage to be rigid; real wage rigidity is discussed below.

14. The various parameters are thus marked on respective sides of the curve S in Figure 1.3.

15. Once aggregate demand shifts beyond D then, of course, we are at full employment, and only prices continue to rise with GDP remaining at V_f.

16. An alternative procedure in this case would be to plot the supply curve for a given base wage where the indexation is built into the S curve itself; such a steeper wage-indexed curve would pass through the points B and G. At the limit of full indexation it would be vertical (see the following section).

17. When both S and D contract, P could, in principle, move either way. However, with a relatively flat supply curve, there will in general be a net rise in P following upon a rise in Π_N.

18. This is the subject of Chapter 6.

2. Production, Technology, and the Factor Price Frontier

1. Note that W_V and Z_V are defined in terms of real V units. Subsequently we shall distinguish between these and the analogous measures in terms of gross final output units.

2. For convenience we use the vertical axis to measure V_L and not the horizontal one so as to have the slope measure the capital/labor rather than the labor/capital ratio.

3. This will be the case when the shift factor T in the production function appears as "weakly separable" from L, K, as for example $V = A(T)G_1(L,K)$. This is a specific example of an "if and only if" theorem due to Leontief (1947).

4. Thus $\dot{x} = dx/dt = X^{-1}dX/dt =$ proportionate rate of change of X.

5. This expression for the factor price frontier can be obtained directly by subtracting the quantity expression (2.3) from the equation $\dot{v} = s(\dot{v}_l + \dot{l}) + (1 - s)(\dot{v}_k + \dot{k})$. The latter, in turn, is obtained from logarithmic time differentiation of the Euler equation, $V = V_L L + V_K K$.

6. In the literature this is called a *value-added function* (see Arrow, 1974; Bruno, 1978a), but we do not want to confuse single-deflated value added (which is Y) with other concepts being used here.

7. This analysis easily generalizes to the case in which N is a vector of several inputs N_i with relative prices $\Pi_{Ni} = P_{Ni}/P$(where $i = 1,2, \ldots ,m$). We now have $Y = Q - \Sigma_i\Pi_{Ni}N_i = Y(L, K; \Pi_{Ni}, \ldots , \Pi_{Nm})$, $\partial Y/\partial\Pi_{Ni} = -N_i$, and $(\Pi_{Ni}/Y)(\partial Y/\partial\Pi_{Ni}) = -s_n/(1 - s_{ni})$, where $s_{ni} = \Pi_{Ni}N_i/Q$, $s_n = \Sigma_i s_{ni}$, and the rate of decline of real income (and the factor shares), holding L and K constant, will be $b =$

$(1 - s_n)^{-1} \Sigma_i s_{ni} \dot{\pi}_{ni}$. Note that the "technical regress" term, $-b$, is measured as a weighted Divisia Index of material input prices.

8. Logarithmic differentiation of (2.6) gives $\dot{y} = (L/Y)(\partial Y/\partial L)\dot{l} + (K/Y)(\partial Y/\partial K)\dot{k} + b$. Now $(L/Y)(\partial Y/\partial L) = (Q/Y)(L/Q)(\partial Q/\partial L) = (1 - s_n)^{-1}s_l$, and similarly for K.

9. Proof: The distance BA can be worked out from the elasticity $(\Pi_e/R)(\Delta R/\Delta \Pi_e) = s_e/s_k = -\Pi_e E/RK$, which implies $BA = \Delta R = -(E/K)(\Delta \Pi_e)$, where E/K is measured at A. But this is the same as the shift from F_0 to F', since in that case $E/K = \eta = $ constant. The tangent to F' at B is parallel to the tangent to F_0 at A. The rest of the argument follows by continuity.

10. Such a demand shortfall has accompanied the input price increases in the 1970s both on account of terms-of-trade effects on real income and wealth and from repercussions on demand management (see Chapters 5 and 10).

11. This illustration is based on an earlier study (Bruno, 1981).

12. Kravis and Lipsey's main contribution lies in showing that the properly measured index of manufacturing exports has grown by much less during the 1970s than the commonly used unit value index. Consideration of the domestic relative wholesale prices seems to bear out their contention. For recent detailed studies of primary commodity prices in the 1970s, see Enoch and Panić (1981); Bosworth and Lawrence (1982).

13. The use of translog production functions was pioneered by Jorgenson and his associates (see Christensen, Jorgenson, and Lau, 1973). For its application to the input of energy and raw materials, see Berndt and Wood (1979). Their estimates may be interpreted to suggest that a Cobb-Douglas specification for K and L and the separability assumption for the nonenergy material input may be close approximations. Similar results were obtained in a study on Japan (Lipton, 1981).

14. In the Norsworthy, Harper, and Kunze (1979) data for U.S. manufacturing, also reported in Berndt (1980), the energy share by 1977 was estimated at only 2.5 percent, compared with 63 percent for all other intermediate inputs. Data compiled for the United Kingdom by Louis Dicks-Mireaux and used in Bruno and Sachs (1982a) give these figures as 3.3 percent and 61 percent, respectively, in 1977. Of the 61 percent share of other intermediate inputs, roughly one-half (that is, about 30 percent) are from outside manufacturing, so that the ratio is at least 10 to 1.

15. The United States, the United Kingdom (see Bruno and Sachs, 1982b), and possibly Japan (see Lipton, 1981) lend themselves to a more sophisticated approach.

16. A more general two-level CES function was applied to U.K. data in Bruno and Sachs (1982b). The function is discussed further in Chapter 3.

17. This term is $-\frac{1}{2}\pi_n^2(s_n/s_k)(1 - \sigma)/(1 - s_n)$ and must be added on the right-hand side of Eq. (2A.1). In the estimates this turned out to be insignificant.

18. For a detailed discussion of the different patterns of wage behavior after the oil shock, see Chapter 9.

19. A partial regression of the FPF on the observations up to 1972 also yields a strong negative coefficient for Π_N (the same is true of the United Kingdom).

20. This regression is $r = 0.017t - 1.011w - 1.526\pi_n + 3.490j'$ (the standard errors of the coefficients are, respectively, 0.026, 0.985, 0.477, and 0.508), where j' is the corresponding FRB measure. This is not surprising in view of the fact that j and j' are very highly correlated. The estimated elasticity of j with respect to j' is 0.171 (± 0.030), which is consistent with the fact that the elasticity of r with respect to j' turns out to be 0.18 times that of the j coefficient (see column 1 in Table 2A.1). The capital utilization rate, J', fluctuates at a much higher amplitude than J, but its estimated effect on R is the same.

21. The outer curve corresponds to the minimum level of the index, reached in 1972, and the inner curve corresponds to the maximum, reached in 1974, only two years later.

22. Note that (2B.1) and (2B.2) are the same when $\Pi_N = 1$. This would happen when double deflation is carried out with a continuously shifting base year, which amounts to the use of a Divisia Index.

23. The countries included are Australia, Austria, Denmark, Finland, Ireland, the Netherlands, New Zealand, Norway, Spain, and Switzerland.

3. Factor Adjustment to Supply Price Shocks

1. We shall from now on speak about an "economy" meaning alternatively also a large sector like manufacturing.

2. Namely, cross derivatives of the production function with respect to its inputs are assumed positive. This implies that as the real price of one factor is raised (keeping other *prices* constant but letting output vary), the demand for any other factor must fall.

3. The very realistic possibility that Keynesian unemployment will be superimposed on the classical unemployment is taken up in Chapter 5.

4. First-period production is unaffected by this change of assumption, but its first-period allocation between consumption and investment will be affected (see Chapter 4).

5. If we denote the Hicks-Allen elasticity of substitution of factors i and j by σ_{ij}, the general condition for a fall in employment is $\sigma_{kn} + \sigma_{lk} \geq \sigma_{ln} + \sigma_{kk}$. This is automatically satisfied when $\sigma_{kn} = \sigma_{ln}$ (the case of N-separability), but it is obviously more general. For a proof see Appendix 3A.

6. The marginal product of the fixed-proportions bundle (K, E) stays the same $(R + \eta \Pi_e)$.

7. In a two-dimensional representation in W/P_V, Z/P_V space this will be shown as a movement up along a *given* FPF.

8. In the above two-level CES case the shares are $s_n = (1 - a)^\sigma \Pi_N^{1-\sigma}$ and $s_l/s_k = [(b/(1 - b)]^{-\sigma_1} (W_Q/R)^{1-\sigma_1}$, with $s_l + s_k + s_n = 1$.

9. The supply of real value added (v^s) can also be worked out directly from (3.11)

by using the fact that $\dot{v} - \dot{k} = (1 - s_n)^{-1} s_l(\dot{l} - \dot{k})$. Thus, $\dot{v}_s = \dot{k} - s_k^{-1} s_l \sigma_1 [\dot{w}_q + (1 - s_n)^{-1} s_n \tilde{\pi}_n]$.

10. The same condition applies to the relative short-run and long-run response of real value added (see the formula in note 9).

11. When $V(K, L)$ is CES with elasticity σ_1, the h function in log-linearized form will be $h = -\sigma_1 s_k^{-1} [s_n \pi_n + (1 - s_n) w_q]$ (see the analysis of the previous section). We ignore technical progress here.

12. Such an investment function can be derived from long-run optimization by firms, assuming static expectations. The case of rational expectations is discussed in Chapters 4 and 7.

13. This depends on the discriminant of the two-equation system $[(\phi' h')^2 + 4\psi' \phi' r_w']$, which may be positive or negative (r_w', the log slope of FPF, equals minus the ratio of factor shares). When the discriminant is negative, the dynamics are characterized by a spiral.

14. See Hicks (1970).

4. Savings, Investment, and Capital Flows

1. For recent closely related work, see Sachs (1981), Svensson (1981), Razin (1980), and Bruno (1982a).

2. Under a raw material price shock, capital may have to be adjusted downward. If one adds the realistic assumption of population growth or independent labor-augmenting technical progress, the interpretation is that capital should be lower relative to its previous trend growth, not necessarily that it should actually be reduced in absolute size. Depreciation could also be introduced. These modifications are ignored here only to keep the analysis to its essentials. Negative investment should be interpreted in this light.

3. The present analysis amounts to assuming investment behavior under perfect foresight (or rational expectations), without having to introduce costs of adjustments (or Tobin's q) explicitly, since the long-run (LR) adjustment from A to D in Figure 2.4 takes place in one period (see Chapter 7 for a multiperiod simulation model with costs of adjustment).

4. The idea that the present current account may reflect only future anticipated changes may manifest itself not so much in the case of a future price change, but in an analogous situation of future output changes (due to oil discoveries, say). These might here be represented as a rise in H_2 (with H_1 constant), causing a present current account deficit.

5. It is a straightforward extension of the model to assume that at the beginning of period 1 there is a net asset endowment B_0 (negative for net debt). We now have $B_0 + F_1 = F_2/R$, and therefore total assets $(B_0 + F_1)$ must replace F_1 in Eq. (4.14).

6. In Chapter 7 we take up an alternative formulation in which money demand appears explicitly within the household utility function. Note that with money in the

utility function, the money demand function has consumption rather than output in an equation like (4.15).

7. This could be represented by a tangent to the FPF at A^m with slope and W' intercept less than those of TS. Note that per employed person (instead of units of labor), the initial difference in K/L and Y/L between ICs and MICs would be much larger.

8. Partial empirical evidence given in Bruno (1983) for twelve to fifteen MICs shows an average annual drop in the manufacturing product wage of between 1.4 and 1.7 percent during 1973–75, while for OECD countries the real wage grew on average by 3.4 percent for seven major countries and 5.3 percent for the twelve smaller ones. In 1975–78 the MICs' real wage rose faster than among the OECD countries, and considerably above their own growth in labor productivity.

9. If, as is likely, for the aggregate economy the shock itself was smaller for a MIC than for an IC (see next section), the relevant FPF *a fortiori* shifts inwards by less, adding another component to the difference in response between countries.

5. Stagflation and Short-Run Adjustment

1. To put it differently, from an empirical point of view we need a framework to account for both the downward-sloping and the upward-sloping portions of the Phillips curve.

2. A detailed analysis of this model is given elsewhere (see Bruno, 1982a).

3. In Chapter 6, where we discuss two countries, we shall find it more convenient to resort to a p and q framework.

4. Thus instead of writing $\dot{q} = s_l \dot{l} + s_n \dot{n}$ we may write $q - \bar{q} = s_l(l - \bar{l}) + s_n(n - \bar{n})$ and now move the origin so that we can simply rewrite $q = s_l l + s_n n$.

5. In Appendix 5A, Eq. (5A.13), we give a slightly more general formulation for v^s involving also the domestic output of raw materials: $v^s = (1 - \theta_n)^{-1}[(1 - s_n)q + s_n \sigma(p_n - p)]$, where $\theta_n = P_N(N - H)/PQ < s_n$.

6. An alternative, which for the purposes of the present diagrammatic exposition would not be very different, is to consider the *nominal* wage as the given parameter (the meaning of the commodity supply curve will alter accordingly). This is more appropriate when the nominal, rather than the real, wage is the sticky price. In Chapter 6 we make use of the alternative formulation.

7. For simplicity we assume the supply of labor to be inelastic $(\bar{L})$.

8. Money might also affect the system through the domestic interest rate and the investment channel.

9. The fiscal variable is expressed in terms of the combined relative impact of government expenditure and taxes.

10. If there are marked differences between the propensities to consume out of wages and out of profits, the direction might be reversed. This possibility is ignored here. In any case, we assume $a_2 < a_1$.

11. For the same reasons, the demand curve may itself be upward-sloping (see Appendix 5A).

12. We should remember that the absolute price level, p, may rise even when the relative price, π, falls, provided the domestic price of the final export (import) good, $p^* + e$, rises sufficiently (this has certainly happened in all OECD countries in the 1970s).

13. The dynamics of adjustment of e and p are explicitly spelled out in Chapter 7.

14. As far as capital accumulation is concerned, the movement was, if anything, in the opposite direction.

15. Such a policy was followed by Sweden and Italy immediately after the first oil shock.

16. The capital stock, k, and the relative price, π, now appear as leftward-shifting variables while π_n is again ambiguous, but most likely to shift the curve to the left. The relative slopes of the curves L_q^d and L^d are implied by the assumption that the positive response of output supply to a fall in real wages dominates the response of output demand (for details see Appendix 5A).

17. In the example of Figure 5.2b there is Keynesian unemployment B_2B_1 over and above the classical unemployment B_1B.

18. A closed-economy treatment has been given by Malinvaud (1977). An open-economy disequilibrium framework similar to the present one is described in greater detail in Bruno (1982b). See also Neary (1980), Wijnbergen (1981).

19. Treatment of the case of an upward-sloping labor supply schedule ($l^s = a_5 w_c$, say) is only marginally different.

20. This corresponds to the case analyzed for the labor market in Figure 5.2b.

21. The same outcome could, of course, take place with a nominal appreciation and no wage or price change. It is here that the role of monetary policy obviously comes in.

22. The specific functional form taken in the C and K regimes will be different according to whether the economy is supply- or demand-constrained. Also there may be some additional ambiguity on the sign of w_c.

23. Actually this is the equation for the rate of change of MC, under cost minimization, which thus holds irrespective of market conditions. If this is to hold for prices as well, it is enough to assume a constant degree of monopoly (that is, $P/MC = $ constant, not necessarily $= 1$).

24. We are assuming that gross output $=$ value added in the intermediate goods industry.

25. C_2 is the derivative with respect to $1/\Pi$. According to the Slutsky decomposition, $C_2 = C_2' - C_N C_1$, where C_2' is the pure substitution effect ($C_2' > 0$) and C_N is the consumption of importables. For stability, a less restrictive assumption can be made (see Hanoch and Fraenkel, 1979). This formulation also ignores the possibility that there may be direct final consumption of the intermediate good. In the latter case the real wage and the labor supply curve would be affected directly by a change in Π_n^*.

26. Strictly speaking, one is allowed to use that relationship only when profits are maximized (that is, producers are on their supply schedule). An alternative, more general procedure is to use cost minimization $[n = \eta l + \sigma(w - p_n)]$ and then substitute for l, eventually including w_c as an additional variable in the demand curve.

27. In 1973 only Canada and Australia among the OECD nations were net exporters of S.I.T.C.3 "Mineral Fuels" (see *United Nations Yearbook of International Trade Statistics, 1976*). Once one considers other raw materials, there are additional net exporters for whom the terms of trade hardly worsened (for example, Sweden, Finland).

28. We definitely have $\delta_2 < 0$ in the fixed-proportions case ($\sigma = 0$), which is the one originally analyzed by Findlay and Rodriguez (1977).

29. The reason for this is the positive income effect coming from the increase in the output of the domestic intermediate-goods industry.

30. Again, we consider first the case $H = \overline{H}$, ignoring the constant level of employment in this industry.

31. The slope of the LL line in Figure 5.3 is thus $c_3/a_3 = 1/(1 - s_n) - \psi = c_1/a_1$. Therefore it must be less than the slope of the QQ line $[(c_1 + c_2)/(a_1 - a_2)]$.

6. Macroeconomic Adjustment and Policy Coordination in a Global Setting

1. As can be seen from Appendix 6A, the supply effect is represented by $B = [(1 - s_v)/s_v]\{\sigma + \alpha[1 - \theta(1 - \lambda)]\}$, and these results depend on B being (sufficiently) larger than ξ.

2. The two equations can be obtained from placing asterisks everywhere in Eqs. (6.14′) and (6.16), putting $\pi^* = p^* + e - p = -\pi$, and noting that $(1 - \mu^*) = \mu$. Here we assume $h^* = \delta^* - \xi^*\mu > 0$.

3. The static formulation $i = i^*$ is analogous to the dynamic assumption $i = i^* + \dot{e}$, to be employed in Chapter 7.

4. In the case under review one gets from Appendix 6A:

$$di/d\pi_n^w = d(b^* - \xi^*)/\Delta - h\xi^*/\Delta < 0.$$

5. By referring to the reduced-form equations for q and q^*, we may draw the following conclusions: Higher θ^* makes it more likely that a fall in m reduces q^* (that is, $d/d\theta^* [dq^*/dm] \geq 0$). If we ignore intermediate inputs ($b = b^* = \xi = \xi^* = 0$), then for $0 \leq \theta < 1$, $d/d\theta^*[dq^*/dm] > 0$. Thus, in this case there exists an intermediate value of foreign wage indexation, $\tilde{\theta}^*$, such that $dq^*/dm > 0$ if and only if $\theta^* > \tilde{\theta}^*$. When intermediate inputs are present, dq^*/dm may be positive even where $\theta = \theta^* = 0$. It remains true that higher θ^* will increase dq^*/dm.

6. This section was suggested by an early reading of Canzoneri and Gray, 1983.

The model here works off a different mechanism, but the basic principles are stated clearly in their paper.

7. The only case of full insulation of output that we have seen is for a small economy facing an export demand shock, under full *nominal* wage rigidity. As soon as partial wage indexation is introduced into that setting, however, the insulation property breaks down.

8. By inverting (6.1) we have $p = [a/(a + b)]w + [b/(a + b)]p_n + [1/(a + b)](q - k)$. In (6.18) we drop the last term.

9. Thus, the complete model in this illustration is:

$$p = \zeta w + (1 - \zeta)p_n$$
$$p = \zeta w* + (1 - \zeta)(p_n - e)$$
$$w = \overline{w}$$
$$w* = \overline{w}*$$
$$q = -\delta\pi - \psi i - \xi(p_n - p)$$
$$q* = +\delta\pi - \psi i - \xi(p_n^* - p*)$$
$$p_n = 0.5p + 0.5(p* + e) + \pi_n^w$$
$$p_c = p - (1 - \eta)\pi$$
$$p_c^* = p* + \eta\pi$$
$$\pi = p - e - p*$$

10. $\beta_0 = (1 - \zeta)/\zeta > 0$

$\beta_1 = 0.5(1 - \zeta)/\zeta + (1 - \eta) > 0$

11. When π rises there are two effects at work: there is a shift of final-goods demand abroad, and the relative price of inputs $(p_n - p)$ falls, since $(p_n - p) = -0.5\pi + \pi_n^w$. The reduction in $p_n - p$ raises aggregate demand. The assumption that $2\delta - \xi > 0$ is simply the assumption that the demand shift effect dominates the input price effect. To derive Eq. (6.20), note from the equations in note 9 to this chapter that $q - q* = -2\delta\pi - \xi(p_n - p) + \xi(p_n^* - p*)$. Also $p_n - p = -0.5\pi + \pi_n^w$, and $p_n^* - p* = 0.5\pi + \pi_n^w$. Thus, $(q - q*) = -(2\delta - \xi)\pi$, which is rearranged to yield Eq. (6.20).

12. In the dynamic model (Sachs, 1983b) utility is more realistically taken to be a function of the change in prices and the level of output.

13. For each country, π is the log (WPI) − log $(WPI*)$, where $WPI*$ is a weighted average of log (WPI) in the other two countries. All indexes have been converted to dollars using market exchange rates. The weights are based on the share of 1973 GNP accounted for by the three countries: United States, 0.64; Japan, 0.19; Germany, 0.17. U is the aggregate unemployment rate, and $U*$ is the weighted average U in the other two countries, using the GNP weights.

8. Empirical Overview of Stagflation in the OECD

1. McKinnon stresses instability in money *demand* as a key factor in the boom-bust cycle. We think rather that the data show that shifts in U.S. money supply with a world money multiplier effect are the source of the fluctuations.

2. T. J. Sargent (1978) has shown that if changing the labor input is costly, then current l can be written as a function of lagged l and future expected $w - p_v$. Under certain assumptions, expected $w - p_v$ can itself be written as a function of lagged wages and lagged labor input.

3. This view follows closely the work of Grubb, Jackman, and Layard (1982) and that of Modigliani and Padoa-Schioppa (1978).

9. Real Wages and Unemployment

1. One must take some position on the role of cyclical versus trend factors in the sharp productivity slowdown in France and Germany after 1979. This is clearly hard to do as of early 1983. Suppose that in 1976 one tried to forecast the 1973–79 rate by the procedure described in the text (averaging the rates of 1960–73 and 1973–75). The result would have been prediction of a post-1973 slowdown (the 1960–73 rate minus the 1973–79 rate) of 1.9 percent in the United Kingdom (2.7 actual); 0.7 percent in France (1.2 actual); 2.9 percent in Canada (2.6 actual); and 2.6 percent in Japan (3.2 actual). These estimates are thus fairly accurate and would have proved far superior to a simple extension of the 1960–73 productivity trend to 1974 and 1975.

2. Trend productivity growth based on estimates of Eq. (9.2), annual average (see Table 9.2):

	1960–1974	1974–1981	Slowdown
Canada	4.4	0.9	3.5
France	5.7	4.0	1.7
Germany	5.4	3.8	1.6
Japan	10.4	6.6	3.8
United Kingdom	3.6	0.4	3.2
United States	3.1	1.7	1.4

3. It is worthwhile to mention the implications of an alternative assumption on technical progress, namely Hicks-neutrality. With Hicks-neutral technical change, the production function is

$$V_t = A_t [\mu L_t^{-\rho_1} + (1 - \mu) K_t^{-\rho_1}]^{-1/\rho_1}.$$

Following the procedures in the text, we can differentiate V with respect to L, to show

$$[V_{L_t}/(V_t/L_t)] = \mu[\mu + (1 - \mu)(K_t/L_t)^{-\rho_1}]^{-1}.$$

According to this equation, V_L rises relative to V/L when K/L increases and $\sigma_1 < 1$, or when K/L decreases and $\sigma_1 > 1$.

4. To get a rough measure of K/AL^f, we compute $\dot{A}_t/A_t$ according to the relationship $\dot{v}_t = s_t(\dot{A}_t/A_t + \dot{l}_t) + (1 - s_t)(\dot{k}_t)$, where s_t is the labor share of value added. (In fact, s_t is taken to be the average share for $t-1$ and t.) L^f is assumed to grow, per annum, at the rate of increase of actual L during 1960–70. K_t is the gross capital stock from the OECD's *Flows and Stocks of Fixed Capital, 1955–1980*. With these procedures we arrive at the following rough estimates of the overall two-decade change in K/AL^f (in percentages): Canada, -19.5; France, -22.2; Germany, 20.8; Japan, -67.4; United Kingdom, 33.4; and United States, -17.8. Note that measures of technical progress in Canada, France, Japan, and the United States are so high that K/AL is estimated to have declined in absolute terms.

5. Geary and Kennan (1982); and Grubb, Layard, and Symons (1982). The most important problem with the Geary-Kennan analysis is that the wage is measured relative to the wholesale price index (*WPI*) rather than to P_V. This procedure is problematic in a period of supply shocks, which raise *WPI* relative to P_V. It appears that the real wage has decreased when measured as W/WPI, when in fact it has increased when measured as W/P_V. Grubb, Layard, and Symons show that when employment is regressed on W/WPI in an equation that also includes a real price of intermediate inputs (which Geary and Kennan exclude), the expected negative relation between the real wage and employment is found. The regression of Table 9.4 shows directly that when W/P rather than W/WPI is the explanatory variable, the wage-employment link is established. Also, Geary and Kennan do not allow for the productivity slowdown after 1973.

6. Consider a recent analysis of the real wage issue by a spokesman for the United Steelworkers of America:

> What we sought was . . . to keep real wages moving upward with the long-term trends of manufacturing sector productivity. In practice that required catching up with successive spurts of 1970's inflation through cost-of-living adjustments, and negotiating small periodic increases.
>
> This policy was essentially based on the view that the 1930's Depression resulted from the cumulative inability of American workers to buy back the ever-increasing flow of goods and services they were able to produce, during the 1920's. Purchasing power failed to rise as rapidly as productivity.
>
> During the 1950-to-1975 period the steel and auto wage patterns were approximately followed by workers in other industries, and led by some. The system worked tolerably well. It broke down in the 1970's as rapid inflation outstripped the ability of unorganized workers and others to keep up.
>
> The resulting shortage of consumer purchasing power has depressed sales in the economy. The added effects of artificially high interest rates, "free trade" in subsidized and dumped imports, an overvalued dollar, and other

policies to "wring inflation out" of the economy at the expense of unemployed workers, have produced the 1980's depression (James W. Smith, Assistant to the President, United Steelworkers of America, Letter to the Editor, Financial Section, *New York Times,* July 17, 1983).

An increase in real wages is argued to have an expansionary macroeconomic effect. Notably, in arguing for indexation, the statement makes no distinction between price increases due to terms-of-trade shocks and those due to domestic monetary policy. In fact in the 1970s, steelworkers' wages dramatically outstripped those of other industries, with a predictable effect on long-term steel industry employment.

7. In this calculation, w_1^x is used for the wage gap. τ is taken from Table 9.7. Note that the years 1966 and 1978 are adjusted as indicated in Table 9.7, so that w^x and τ data are taken for the same years. No wage gap data were constructed for Italy, the Netherlands, or Sweden.

8. There are almost no reported cases in which wage contracts linked the wage outcome to variations in π_n. To explain why this is so, we need a deeper theory of the costs of contracting. Blanchard (1979b) provides a useful starting point.

10. Price and Output Dynamics in Eight Economies

1. As excluded instrumental variables for w^x we include a measure of π_n^*, the world relative price of raw materials, and a time trend. By Fair's method, current and lagged values of the other variables in (10.9), as well as w_{t-1}^x, are also included in the instruments list. Our measure of π_n^* is log (P^M/P^X), where P^M and P^X are dollar indices of import and export unit values for the industrial countries as a whole, from the IMF. Specifically, P^M is $L75d$ and P^X is $L74d$, for country category 110, from the International Financial Statistics.

11. Labor Markets and Comparative Macroeconomic Performance

1. For an excellent discussion of these issues, see Hamada and Kurosaka (1983).

2. Based on data in the *OECD Country Survey of Sweden* (1980), Table E, p. 25.

3. See, for example, Cameron (1982); Faxén (1982); McCallum (1982); Crouch (forthcoming); Tarantelli (1982).

4. Cameron (1982), p. 5.

5. The variable uses actual rather than full-employment productivity, compensation per worker rather than compensation per hour, and output per worker rather than output per man-hour as the productivity measure. However, the OECD data have an advantage of applying to the entire economy rather than to the manufacturing section alone.

6. See Cameron (1982), pp. 5-9.

7. For this quotation and much of the subsequent discussion, see *OECD Eco-*

nomic Surveys: Germany (Paris: OECD, 1975), p. 7. Herbert Giersch (1977) offers a nearly identical story.

8. *OECD Economic Surveys: Germany* (1975), p. 7. The OECD points out that the overexpectation of inflation was not merely a result of failure to believe the monetary authorities. Rather, shifts in fiscal policy at the end of 1973 gave an indication of a more expansionary response to the developing recession.

9. Ibid., p. 8.

10. Giersch (1981), p. 30.

12. Supply Shocks, Demand Response, and the Productivity Puzzle

1. No attempt has been made to search for more than one break point.

2. This was already pointed out by Nordhaus (1982), but interestingly enough it seems to be the only such case among the OECD countries.

3. For the four large countries considered in Bruno (1981), the United States, the United Kingdom, Germany, and Japan, virtually all observations are now on the regression line (errors ranging between 0 and 0.1).

4. See Lindbeck (1983), p. 26, for some references.

5. An attempt to incorporate the role of output variability in cross-country regressions of the productivity slowdown is given in Bruno (1983). For the ten countries in Table 12.3, the coefficient of variation of output growth has on average grown by a factor of 2.5 in total GDP and a factor of 5 for the manufacturing sector. The role of demand and output variability in the U.S. context has been stressed by Mohr (1980).

6. There is reason to think that the average difference in the magnitude of the input price shock was similar for manufacturing in the two groups, but we have no data for the MICs.

7. There was some difference between large and small industrial countries, with the smaller ones tending to borrow more. For the nine major OECD countries, the change in percentage gap was from 0.5 ($\pm$1.0) to -0.4 ($\pm$1.3); for the remaining smaller ten, the change was from 2.3 ($\pm$1.9) to 2.0 ($\pm$2.7).

13. Lessons for Theory and Policy

1. Here too, however, imported inflation played a major role in the behavior of the price level.

2. For a recent critique see Meese and Rogoff (1983).

3. For a good analysis see Shinkai (1980).

4. For more details see Buiter and Miller (1981b).

5. For the difference between Japan and the United Kingdom after 1973, see also our factor price frontier figures in Chapter 2, Appendix 2A.

6. For an excellent recent discussion, see Emerson (1982).

Bibliography

Altonji, J. 1982. "The Intertemporal Substitution Model of Labor Market Fluctuations: An Empirical Analysis." *Review of Economic Studies* 49(159):783–824.

Argy, V., and J. Salop. 1979. "Price and Output Effects of Monetary and Fiscal Policy under Flexible Exchange Rates." *International Monetary Fund Staff Papers* 26(2):224–256.

Arndt, S. W., ed. 1982. *The Political Economy of Austria.* Washington, D.C.: American Enterprise Institute for Public Policy Research.

Arrow, K. J. 1974. "The Measurement of Real Value Added." In *Nations and Households in Economic Growth: Essays in Honor of Moses Abramowitz,* ed. P. A. David and M. W. Reder. New York: Academic Press.

Artus, J. 1977. "Measures of Potential Output in Manufacturing for Eight Industrial Countries, 1955–1978." *International Monetary Fund Staff Papers* 24 (March):1–35.

Bailey, M. N. 1978. "Stabilization Policy and Private Economic Behavior." *Brookings Papers on Economic Activity* 1:11–60.

——— 1981. "Productivity and the Services of Capital and Labour." *Brookings Papers on Economic Activity* 1:1–50.

Barkin, S., ed. 1975. *Worker Militancy and Its Consequences 1965–75: New Directions in Western Industrial Relations.* New York: Praeger.

Barro, R. J. 1976. "Rational Expectations and the Role of Monetary Policy." *Journal of Monetary Economics* 2(1):1–32.

Bergmann, J., and J. W. Muller-Jentsch. 1975. "The Federal Republic of Germany: Cooperative Unionism and Dual Bargaining System Challenged." In *Worker Militancy and Its Consequences 1965–75: New Directions in Western Industrial Relations,* ed. S. Barkin. New York: Praeger.

Berndt, E. R. 1980. "Energy Price Increases and the Productivity Slowdown in United States Manufacturing." Department of Economics Resources Paper no. 51, University of British Columbia.

Berndt, E. R., and D. O. Wood. 1979. "Engineering and Econometric Interpretations of Energy-Capital Complementarity." *American Economic Review* 69(3):342–354.

Bienaymé, A. 1978. "Incomes Policy in France." *Lloyds Bank Review* 128 (April):33–48.

Blanchard, O. 1979a. "The Monetary Mechanism in the Light of Rational Expectations." Harvard Institute of Economic Research Discussion Paper no. 682, Harvard University (January).

—— 1979b. "Wage Indexing Rules and the Behavior of the Economy." *Journal of Political Economy* 87(4):798–815.

Blanchard, O., and C. M. Kahn. 1980. "The Solution of Linear Difference Models under Rational Expectations." *Econometrica* 48(5):1305–12.

Blanchard, O., and J. Sachs. 1982. "Anticipation, Recession, and Policy: An Intertemporal Disequilibrium Model." *Annales de L'Insée* 47–48 (July–December):117–144.

Blanchard, O., and C. Wyplosz. 1979. "An Empirical Structural Model of Aggregate Demand." Harvard Institute of Economic Research Discussion Paper no. 687, Harvard University (March).

Blinder, A. S. 1979. *Economic Policy and the Great Stagflation.* New York: Academic Press.

Bodkin, R. G., 1969. "Real Wages and Cyclical Variations in Employment: A Reexamination of the Evidence." *Canadian Journal of Economics* 2(3):353–374.

Bosworth, B. P., and R. Z. Lawrence. 1982. *Commodity Prices and the New Inflation.* Washington, D.C.: Brookings Institution.

Brandini, P. M. 1975. "Italy: Creating a New Industrial Relations System from the Bottom." In *Worker Militancy and Its Consequences 1965–75: New Directions in Western Industrial Relations,* ed. S. Barkin. New York: Praeger.

Branson, W., and J. Rotemberg. 1980. "International Adjustment with Wage Rigidities." *European Economic Review* 13(3):309–332.

Braun, A. R. 1975. "The Role of Incomes Policy in Industrial Countries since World War II." *International Monetary Fund Staff Papers* 22(1):1–36.

Brecher, R. A. 1974. "Minimum Wage Rates and the Pure Theory of International Trade." *Quarterly Journal of Economics* 88(1):98–116.

Brock, W. C. 1974. "Money and Growth: The Case of Long-Run Perfect Foresight." *International Economic Review* 15(3):750–777.

Brunner, K., A. Cukierman, and A. H. Meltzer. 1980. "Stagflation, Persistent Unemployment and the Permanence of Economic Shocks." *Journal of Monetary Economics* 6(4):467–492.

Bruno, M. 1978a. "Duality, Intermediate Inputs and Value-Added." In *Production Economics: A Dual Approach to Theory and Applications,* vol. 2, ed. M. Fuss and D. McFadden. Amsterdam: North-Holland.

——— 1978b. "Exchange Rates, Import Costs, and Wage-Price Dynamics." *Journal of Political Economy* 86(3):379–404.

——— 1979. "Price and Output Adjustment: Micro Foundations and Macro Theory." *Journal of Monetary Economics* 5(2):187–212.

——— 1980. "Import Prices and Stagflation in the Industrial Countries: A Cross-Section Analysis." *Economic Journal* 90(359):479–492.

——— 1981. "Raw Materials, Profits and the Productivity Slowdown." National Bureau of Economic Research Working Paper no. 660 (December). Forthcoming in *Quarterly Journal of Economics.*

——— 1982a. "Adjustment and Structural Change under Supply Shocks." *Scandinavian Journal of Economics* 84(2):199–221.

——— 1982b. "Import Competition and Macro-economic Adjustment under Wage-Price Rigidity." In *Import Competition and Response,* ed. J. N. Bhagwati. Chicago: National Bureau of Economic Research and University of Chicago Press.

——— 1982c. "World Shocks, Macroeconomic Response, and the Productivity Puzzle." In *Slower Growth in the Western World,* ed. R. C. O. Matthews. London: Heinemann.

——— 1983. "Petrodollars and the Differential Growth Performance of Industrial and Middle-Income Countries in the 1970s." National Bureau of Economic Research Working Paper no. 1056 (January).

Bruno, M., and J. Sachs. 1979. "Macro-Economic Adjustment with Import Price Shocks: Real and Monetary Aspects." Falk Institute Discussion Paper no. 793 (January), and National Bureau of Economic Research Working Paper no. 340 (April).

——— 1981. "Supply versus Demand Approaches to the Problem of Stagflation." In *Macroeconomic Policies for Growth and Stability,* ed. H. Giersch. Kiel: Institut für Weltwirtschaft an der Universität Kiel.

——— 1982a. "Energy and Resource Allocation: A Dynamic Model of the Dutch Disease." *Review of Economic Studies* 49(159):845–859.

——— 1982b. "Input Price Shocks and the Slowdown in Economic Growth: The Case of U.K. Manufacturing." *Review of Economic Studies* 49(159):679–705.

Buiter, W. H. 1979. "Short-run and Long-run Effects of External Disturbances under a Floating Exchange Rate." *Economica* 45(179):251–272.

Buiter, W. H., and M. H. Miller. 1981a. "Monetary Policy and International Competitiveness." *Oxford Economic Papers* 33:143–175, Supplement.

——— 1981b. "The Thatcher Experiment: The First Two Years." *Brookings Papers on Economic Activity* 2:315–367.

Calmfors, L., and H. Horn. 1982. "Accommodation versus Non-accommodation Policies in a Model with a Trade-Union Determined Wage." Mimeo. Institute for International Economic Studies, University of Stockholm.

Cameron, D. R. 1982. "Social Democracy, Corporatism, and Labor Quiescence: The Representation of Economic Interest in Advanced Capitalist Society." Paper presented at the Conference on Governability and Legitimacy in Western European Democracies, Stanford University (October).

Canzoneri, M. B., and J. A. Gray. 1983. "Two Essays on Monetary Policy in an Interdependent World." International Finance Discussion Paper no. 219 (February).

Casas, F. R. 1975. "Efficient Macroeconomic Stabilization Policies under Floating Exchange Rates." *International Economic Review* 16 (October):682–698.

Christensen, L. R., D. W. Jorgenson, and L. J. Lau. 1973. "Transcendental Logarithmic Production Frontiers." *Review of Economics and Statistics* 55 (February):28–45.

Clark, Kim B., and L. H. Summers. 1982. "Labour Force Participation: Timing and Persistence." *Review of Economic Studies* 49(159):825–844.

Corden, M. 1978. "Keynes and the Others: Wage and Price Rigidities in Macro-Economic Models." *Oxford Economic Papers* 30 (July):159–180.

——— 1979. "Wages and Unemployment in Australia." *Economic Record* (March):1–19.

Crouch, C. (forthcoming). "The Conditions for Trade Union Wage Restraint." In *The Politics and Sociology of Global Inflation,* ed. Leon Lindberg and Charles Maier. Washington, D.C.: Brookings Institution.

Crouch, C., and A. Pizzorno, eds. 1978. *The Resurgence of Class Conflict in Western Europe since 1968.* Vol. 1: *National Studies;* and vol. 2: *Comparative Analyses.* New York: Holmes and Meier.

DeGrauwe, P., and M. Nabli. 1983. "Supply of Output Equations in the EC-Countries and the Use of the Survey Based Inflationary Expectations." Economic Paper no. 13, Commission of the European Communities (May).

De Larosière, J. 1980. "Exchange Rates and the Adjustment Process." *Finance and Development* 17(1):4–5. International Monetary Fund and International Bank for Reconstruction and Development.

Denison, E. F. (assisted by J.-P. Poullier). 1967. *Why Growth Rates Differ.* Washington, D.C.: Brookings Institution.

——— 1979. *Accounting for Slower Economic Growth: The United States in the 1970s.* Washington, D.C.: Brookings Institution.

Dickens, W. T. 1982. "The Productivity Crisis: Secular or Cyclical?" *Economic Letters* 9(1):37–42.

Dixit, A. 1981. "A Model of Trade in Oil and Capital." Discussion Paper in Economics no. 16, Woodrow Wilson School, Princeton University (August).

Dornbusch, R. 1976. "Expectations and Exchange Rate Dynamics." *Journal of Political Economy* 84(6):1161–76.

Dornbusch, R., and P. Krugman. 1976. "Flexible Exchange Rates in the Short Run." *Brookings Papers on Economic Activity* 3:537–575.

Drèze, J., and F. Modigliani. 1981. "The Trade-off between Real Wages and Employment in an Open Economy (Belgium)." *European Economic Review* 15(1):1–40.

Dunlop, J. T. 1938. "The Movement of Real and Money Wages." *Economic Journal* 49(19):413–434.

Emerson, M. 1982. "The European Stagflation Disease in International Perspective and Some Possible Therapy." Paper presented at the Conference of the Centre for European Policy Studies on European Policy Priorities, Brussels (December).

Enoch, C. A., and M. Panić. 1981. "Commodity Prices in the 1970s." *Bank of England Quarterly Bulletin,* March:42–53.

Fair, R. 1979. "Macroeconomic Models: The Open Economy." In *International Economic Policy: Theory and Evidence,* ed. R. Dornbusch and J. Frenkel. Baltimore: Johns Hopkins University Press.

Faustini, G. 1976. "Wage Indexation and Inflation in Italy." *Banca Nationale del Lavoro Quarterly Review* 119 (December):364–377.

Faxén, K.-O. 1982. *Incomes Policy and Centralized Wage Formation.* Stockholm: Swedish Employers' Confederation (SAAF) (February).

Feldstein, M. S. 1978. "Inflation, Tax Rates, and the Long-Term Interest Rate." *Brookings Papers on Economic Activity* 1:61–110.

——— 1982. "Inflation and the American Economy." *The Public Interest* 67 (Spring):63–70.

Feldstein, M. S., and L. Summers. 1977. "Is the Rate of Profit Falling?" *Brookings Papers on Economic Activity* 1:211–227.

Findlay, R., and C. Rodriguez. 1977. "Intermediate Imports and Macroeconomic Policy under Flexible Exchange Rates." *Canadian Journal of Economics* 10(2):208–217.

Fischer, S. 1977. "Wage Indexation and Macroeconomic Stability." In *Stabilization of the Domestic and International Economy,* ed. K. Brunner and A. Meltzer. Vol. 5 of the Carnegie-Rochester Conference Series on Public Policy. Amsterdam: North-Holland.

——— 1981. "Relative Shocks, Relative Price Variability, and Inflation." *Brookings Papers on Economic Activity* 2:381–431.

——— 1982. "Relative Price Variability and Inflation in the United States and Germany." *European Economic Review* 18(1/2):171–196.

Fleming, J. M. 1962. "Domestic Financial Policies under Fixed and Floating Exchange Rates." *International Monetary Fund Staff Papers* 9(3):369–379.

Flemming, J. S. 1976. "Adjust the Real Elements in a Changing Economy." In *Catch '76,* Institute for Economic Affairs Occasional Paper, special no. 47, Wolverhampton, England.

——— 1982. "U.K. Macro-policy Response to Oil Price Shocks of 1974–75 and 1979–80." *European Economic Review* 18(1/2):223–234.

Friedman, M. 1968. "The Role of Monetary Policy." *American Economic Review* 57(1):1–17.

—— 1977. "Nobel Lecture: Inflation and Unemployment." *Journal of Political Economy* 85(3):451–472.

Geary, P. T., and J. Kennan. 1982. "The Employment-Real Wage Relationship: An International Study." *Journal of Political Economy* 90 (August):854–871.

Giavazzi, F., M. Odenken, and C. Wyplosz. 1982. "Simulating an Oil Shock with Sticky Prices." *European Economic Review* 18(1/2):11–33.

Giersch, H. 1977. "A Discussion with Herbert Giersch: Current Problems of the West German Economy, 1976–1977." Studies in Economic Policy, American Enterprise Institute Study no. 147.

—— 1981. "Aspects of Growth, Structural Change, and Employment—A Schumpeterian Perspective." Paper presented at the 1979 Kiel Conference on Macroeconomic Policies for Growth and Stability, and published in *Macroeconomic Policies for Growth and Stability,* ed. H. Giersch. Kiel: Institut für Weltwirtschaft an der Universität Kiel, 1981.

Glyn, A., and B. Sutcliffe. 1972. *Capitalism in Crisis.* New York: Random House.

Goldfeld, S. 1973. "The Demand for Money Revisited." *Brookings Papers on Economic Activity* 3:577–638.

Goodman, J. F. B. 1975. "Great Britain: Toward the Social Contract." In *Worker Militancy and Its Consequences 1965–75: New Directions in Western Industrial Relations,* ed. S. Barkin. New York: Praeger.

Gordon, R. J. 1975. "Alternative Response to External Supply Shocks." *Brookings Papers on Economic Activity* 1:183–206.

—— 1977. "World Inflation and Monetary Accommodation in Eight Countries." *Brookings Papers on Economic Activity* 2:409–468.

—— 1982. "Why U.S. Wage and Employment Behavior Differs from That in Britain and Japan." *Economic Journal* 92(365):13–44.

Gray, J. A. 1976. "Wage Indexation: A Macroeconomic Approach." *Journal of Monetary Economics* 2(2):221–235.

Griliches, Z. 1967. "Distributed Lags: A Survey." *Econometrica* 35(1):16–49.

—— 1980. "R&D and the Productivity Slowdown." *American Economic Review* 70(2):343–348. Papers and Proceedings of the Ninety-Second Annual Meeting.

Grossman, G. M. 1982a. "International Competition and the Unionized Sector." National Bureau of Economic Research Working Paper no. 899 (June).

—— 1982b. "Union Wages, Seniority and Unemployment." Discussion Paper no. 21, Woodrow Wilson School, Princeton University.

Grossman, S., and O. Hart. 1981. "Implicit Contracts, Moral Hazard, and Unemployment," *American Economic Review* 71(2):301–307. Papers and Proceedings of the Ninety-Third Annual Meeting.

Grossman, S., O. Hart, and E. Maskin. 1982. "Unemployment with Observable Aggregate Shocks." National Bureau of Economic Research Working Paper no. 975 (September).

Grubb, D., R. Jackman, and R. Layard. 1982. "Causes of the Current Stagflation." *Review of Economic Studies* 49(5/159):707–730. Special issue for the July 1981 Cambridge University Conference on Unemployment.

———— 1983. "Wage Rigidity and Unemployment in OECD Countries." *European Economic Review* 2:11–40.

Grubb, D., R. Layard, and J. Symons. 1982. "Wages, Unemployment and Incomes Policy." Centre for Labour Economics Working Paper no. 479, London School of Economics.

Hall, R. E., and E. P. Lazear. 1982. "The Excess Sensitivity of Layoffs and Quits to Demand." National Bureau of Economic Research Working Paper no. 864 (February).

Hamada, K. 1974. "Alternative Exchange Rate Systems and the Interdependence of Monetary Policies." In *National Monetary Policies and the International Financial System,* ed. R. A. Aliber. Chicago: University of Chicago Press.

———— 1979. "Macroeconomic Strategy Coordination under Alternative Exchange Rates." In *International Economic Policy: Theory and Evidence,* ed. R. Dornbusch and J. Frenkel. Baltimore: Johns Hopkins University Press.

Hamada, K., and Y. Kurosaka. 1983. "The Relationship between Production and Unemployment in Japan: Okun's Law in Comparative Perspective." Paper presented at the International Seminar in Macroeconomics, Maison des Sciences de l'Homme, Paris (June), and forthcoming in *European Economic Review.*

Hamada, K., and M. Sakurai. 1978. "International Transmission of Stagflation under Fixed and Flexible Exchange Rates." *Journal of Political Economy* 86 (October):877–896.

Hanoch, G., and M. Fraenkel. 1979. "Income and Substitution Effects in the Two Sector Open Economy." *American Economic Review* 69(3):455–458.

Hart, O. D. 1982. "Optimal Labour Contracts under Asymmetric Information: An Introduction." Discussion paper, International Centre for Economics and Related Disciplines, London.

Hayashi, F. 1983. "Tobin's Marginal *q* and Average *q*: A Neoclassical Interpretation." *Econometrica* 50(1):213–224.

Helliwell, J. F. 1983. "Stagflation and Productivity Decline in Canada, 1979–1982." National Bureau of Economic Research Working Paper no. 1185 (August).

Helpman, E. 1976. "Macroeconomic Policy in a Model of International Trade with a Wage Restriction." *International Economic Review* 17(2):262–277.

Hibbs, D. A., Jr. 1978. "On the Political Economy of Long-Run Trends in Strike Activity." *British Journal of Political Science* 8(2):153–177.

Hicks, J. R. 1970. "Elasticity of Substitution Again: Substitute and Complements." *Oxford Economic Papers* 22(3):289–296.

———— 1974. *The Crisis in Keynesian Economics.* New York: Basic Books.

———— 1975. "What Is Wrong with Monetarism." *Lloyd's Bank Review* 118 (October):1–13.

Hill, T. P. 1979. *Profits and Rates of Return.* Paris: Organization for Economic Co-operation and Development.

Holland, D. M., and S. C. Myers. 1980. "Profitability and Capital Costs for Manufacturing Corporations and All Nonfinancial Corporations." *American Economic Review* 70(2):320–325. Papers and Proceedings of the Ninety-Second Annual Meeting.

Hudson, E., and D. W. Jorgenson. 1978. "Energy Prices and the U.S. Economy, 1972–76." *National Resource Journal* 18 (October):877–897.

—— 1979. "The Economic Impact of Policies to Reduce U.S. Energy Growth." In *Directions in Energy Policy,* ed. B. Kurnsunoglu and A. Perlumutter. Cambridge: Ballinger.

Johansen, L. 1982. "A Note on the Possibility of an International Equilibrium with Low Levels of Activity." *Journal of International Economics* 13(3/4):257–266.

Johnson, H. 1953–54. "Optimum Tariffs and Retaliation." *Review of Economic Studies* 21(55):142–153.

Kendrick, J. W. 1981. "International Comparisons of Recent Productivity Trends." In *Contemporary Economic Problems,* ed. William Fellner, Washington: American Enterprise Institute.

Kindleberger, C. P. 1967. *Europe's Postwar Growth: The Role of Labor Supply.* Cambridge, Mass.: Harvard University Press.

Korpi, W., and M. Shalev. 1980. "Strikes, Power and Politics in the Western Nations, 1900–1976." *Political Power and Social Theory* 1:301–334.

Korteweg, P. 1979. "The Economics of Stagflation: Theory and Dutch Evidence." Institute for Economic Research Discussion Paper no. 7903/M, Erasmus University (April).

Kouri, P. J. K. 1976. "The Exchange Rate and the Balance of Payments in the Short Run and the Long Run: A Monetary Approach." *Scandinavian Journal of Economics* 78(2):280–304.

—— 1979. "Profitability and Growth in a Small Open Economy." In *Inflation and Unemployment in Open Economies, Studies in International Economics,* vol. 5. ed. A. Lindbeck. Amsterdam: North-Holland.

—— 1981. "Balance of Payments and the Foreign Exchange Market: A Dynamic Partial Equilibrium Model." National Bureau of Economic Research Working Paper no. 644 (March).

Kouri, P. J. K., J. Braga de Macedo, and A. J. Viscio. 1982. "Profitability, Employment and Structural Adjustment in France." National Bureau of Economic Research Working Paper no. 1005 (October).

Kravis, I. B., and R. E. Lipsey. 1981. "Prices and Terms of Trade for Developed Country Exports of Manufactured Goods." National Bureau of Economic Research Working Paper no. 774 (September).

Lange, P., G. Ross, and M. Vannicelli. 1982. *Union, Change and Crisis: French and*

Italian Union Strategy and the Political Economy 1945–1980. London: Allen and Unwin.

Lawson, T. 1982. "Incomes Policy and the Real Wage Resistance Hypothesis: Econometric Evidence for the U.K., 1955–1979, Version II." Faculty of Economics, Cambridge University.

Layard, R. 1982. "Introduction: Special Issue on Unemployment." *Review of Economic Studies* 49(5/159):675–677. Special issue for the July 1981 Cambridge University Conference on Unemployment.

Lehment, H. 1982. "Economic Policy Response to the Oil Price Shocks of 1974 and 1979: The German Experience." *European Economic Review* 18(1/2): 235–242.

Leontief, W. W. 1947. "A Note on the Interrelations of Subsets of Independent Variables of a Continuous Function with Continuous First Derivatives." *Bulletin of the American Mathematical Society* 53(4):343–350.

Lindbeck, A. 1983. "The Recent Slowdown of Productivity Growth." *Economic Journal* 93(364):13–34.

Lipton, D. 1981. "Accumulation and Growth in Open Economies." Ph.D. diss., Harvard University (October).

Lipton, D., J. Poterba, J. Sachs, and L. Summers. 1982. "Multiple Shooting in Rational Expectations Models." *Econometrica* 50(5):1329–34.

Lipton, D., and J. Sachs. 1983. "Accumulation and Growth in a Two-Country Model: A Simulation Approach." *Journal of International Economics* 15(1/2):135–159.

Lucas, R. E., Jr. 1967. "Optimal Investment Policy and the Flexible Accelerator." *International Economic Review* 8(1):78–85.

Lucas, R. E., Jr., and L. A. Rapping. 1970. "Real Wages, Employment, and Inflation." In *Microeconomic Foundations of Employment and Inflation Theory,* ed. E. S. Phelps et al. New York: W. W. Norton.

Malinvaud, E. 1977. *The Theory of Unemployment Reconsidered.* Oxford: Blackwell.

—— 1982. "Wages and Unemployment." *Economic Journal* 92(365):1–12.

Marion, N. P., and L. E. O. Svensson. 1982. "Structural Differences and Macroeconomic Adjustment of Oil Price Increases in a Three-Country Model." National Bureau of Economic Research Working Paper no. 839 (January).

—— 1983. "World Equilibrium and Oil Price: An Intertemporal Analysis." NBER Working Paper no. 1074 (February), forthcoming in *Oxford Economic Papers.*

McCallum, J. 1982. "Inflation in the Seventies: A Cross-country Analysis." School of Business Administration and Economics Discussion Paper 81-10-1, Simon Fraser University.

McCracken, P., et al. 1977. "Towards Full Employment and Price Stability." A Report to the OECD by a Group of Independent Experts (June).

McDonald, I. M., and R. M. Solow. 1981. "Wage Bargaining and Employment." *American Economic Review* 71(5):896–908.

McKinnon, R. 1982. "Currency Substitution and Instability in the World Dollar Market." *American Economic Review* 72(3):320–333.

Meade, J. 1982. "Domestic Stabilisation and the Balance of Payments." *Lloyds Bank Review* 143 (January):1–18.

Meese, R. A., and K. Rogoff. 1983. "Empirical Exchange Rate Models of the Seventies: Do They Fit Out of Sample?" *Journal of International Economics* 14(1/2):3–24.

Miller, M. H. 1976. "Can a Rise in Import Prices Be Inflationary and Deflationary? Economists and U.K. Inflation, 1973–74." *American Economic Review* 66(4):501–519.

Modigliani, F. 1979. Roundtable Discussion in *International Economic Policy: Theory and Evidence,* ed. R. Dornbusch and J. Frenkel. Baltimore: Johns Hopkins University Press.

Modigliani, F., and T. Padoa-Schioppa. 1978. "The Management of an Open Economy with '100% Plus' Wage Indexation." Essays in International Finance no. 130, Department of Economics, Princeton University.

Modigliani, F., and L. Papademos. 1978. "Optimal Demand Policies against Stagflation." *Weltwirtschaftliches Archiv* 114(4):736–781.

Mohr, F. M. 1980. "The Long-Term Structure of Production, Factor Demand and Factor Productivity in U.S. Manufacturing Industries." In *New Developments in Productivity Measurements and Analysis,* ed. J. W. Kendrick and B. N. Vaccaro. Chicago: University of Chicago Press and the National Bureau of Economic Research. Studies in Income and Wealth, 44.

Mork, K. A., and R. E. Hall. 1978. "The Energy Price Shock and the 1974–75 Recession." Energy Laboratory Working Paper no. 17, Massachusetts Institute of Technology.

Mundell, R. A. 1963. "Capital Mobility and Stabilization Policy under Fixed and Flexible Exchange Rates." *Canadian Journal of Economic and Political Science* 29(4):475–485.

——— 1964. "A Reply: Capital Mobility and Size." *Canadian Journal of Economics and Political Science* 30(3):421–431.

Mussa, M. 1979. "Macroeconomic Interdependence and the Exchange Rate Regime." In *International Economic Policy: Theory and Evidence,* ed. R. Dornbusch and J. Frenkel. Baltimore: Johns Hopkins University Press.

Muth, J. F. 1961. "Rational Expectations and the Theory of Price Movements." *Econometrica* 29:315–335.

Nadiri, M. I. 1980. "Sectoral Productivity Slowdown." *American Economic Review* 70(2):349–352. Papers and Proceedings of the Ninety-Second Annual Meeting.

Neary, P. 1980. "Non-Traded Goods and the Balance of Trade in a Neo-Keynesian

Temporary Equilibrium." *Quarterly Journal of Economics* 95(4):403–429.

Nordhaus, W. D. 1972. "The Worldwide Wage Explosion." *Brookings Papers on Economic Activity* 2:431–464.

———— 1980. "Oil and Economic Performance in Industrial Countries." *Brookings Papers on Economic Activity* 2:341–388.

———— 1982. "Economic Policy in the Face of Declining Productivity Growth." *European Economic Review* 18(1/2):131–157.

Norsworthy, J. R., and M. J. Harper. 1979. "Productivity Growth in Manufacturing in the 1980's: Labour, Capital and Energy." *Journal of the American Statistical Association:* 17–26. Paper presented at the Annual Meeting of the American Statistical Association, Business and Statistics Sector.

Norsworthy, J. R., M. J. Harper, and K. Kunze. 1979. "The Slowdown in Productivity Growth: Analysis of Some Contributing Factors." *Brookings Papers on Economic Activity* 2:387–421.

Obstfeld, M. 1980. "Macroeconomic Policy and World Welfare under Flexible Exchange Rates." Department of Economics Discussion Paper no. 63, Columbia University.

OECD. 1979a. "Collective Bargaining and Government Policies." Proceedings of a conference held in Washington, D.C., by the Organization for Economic Cooperation and Development (July).

———— 1979b. *Collective Bargaining and Government Policies in Ten OECD Countries.* Paris: Organization for Economic Cooperation and Development.

———— 1979c. *Wage Policies and Collective Bargaining Developments in Finland, Ireland and Norway.* Paris: Organization for Economic Cooperation and Development.

———— 1980. "Productivity Trends in the OECD Area." CPE/WP2(79), 1st revision (April).

Okun, A. M. 1970. *The Political Economics of Prosperity.* Washington, D.C.: The Brookings Institution.

Oswald, A. J. 1979. "Wage Determination in an Economy with Many Trade Unions." *Oxford Economic Papers* 31 (November):369–385.

Otani, I. 1978. "Real Wages and Business Cycles Revisited." *Review of Economics and Statistics* 60(2):301–304.

Paige, D. C., F. T. Blackaby, and S. Freund. 1961. "Economic Growth: The Last Hundred Years." *National Institute Economic Review* 16 (July):24–49.

Paldam, M., and F. L. Rasmussem. 1980. "Data for Industrial Conflicts in 17 OECD Countries 1948–77." Institute of Economics Paper 80-4/5, University of Aarhus.

Perry, G. L. 1975. "Determinants of Wage Inflation around the World." *Brookings Papers on Economic Activity* 2:403–435.

Phelps, E. S. 1968. "Money, Wage Dynamics and Labor Market Equilibrium." *Journal of Political Economy* 76(4), part 2: 678–711.

———— 1978. "Commodity Supply Shocks and Full-Employment Monetary Policy." *Journal of Money, Credit, and Banking* 10(2):206–221.

Pitchford, J. D. 1977. "Inflation in Australia." In *Worldwide Inflation,* ed. L. Krause and W. Salant. Washington, D.C.: The Brookings Institution.

Posner, M. V. 1978. "Problems of the British Economy." In *Public Policies in Open Economies,* ed. K. Brunner and A. Meltzer. Vol. 9 of the Carnegie-Rochester Conference Series on Public Policy. Amsterdam: North-Holland.

Rasche, R. H., and J. A. Tatom. "Energy Resources and Potential GNP." *Federal Reserve Bank of St. Louis Review* 59(6):10–24.

Razin, A. 1980. "Capital Movements, Intersectoral Resource Shifts and the Trade Balance." Institute for International Economic Studies Seminar Paper no. 159, University of Stockholm.

Rodriguez, C. A. 1977. "Flexible Exchange Rates and Imported Inputs: A Dynamic Analysis of the Interactions between the Monetary and Real Sectors of a Small Open Economy." Department of Economics Discussion Paper 76–7708, Columbia University (March).

Sachs, J. 1979. "Wages, Profits, and Macroeconomic Adjustment: A Comparative Study." *Brookings Papers on Economic Activity* 2:269–319.

———— 1980a. "Factor Costs and Aggregate Supply in the Open Economy." Ph.D. diss., Harvard University.

———— 1980b. "Wages, Flexible Exchange Rates, and Macro-Economic Policy." *Quarterly Journal of Economics* 94(4):731–747.

———— 1981. "The Current Account and Macroeconomic Adjustment in the 1970s." *Brookings Papers on Economic Activity* 1:201–282.

———— 1983a. "Energy and Growth under Flexible Exchange Rates: A Simulation Study." National Bureau of Economic Research Working Paper no. 582 (November). In *Economic Interdependence and Flexible Exchange Rates,* ed. J. S. Bhandari and B. H. Putnam. Cambridge: MIT Press, 1983.

———— 1983b. "International Policy Coordination in a Dynamic Macroeconomic Model." National Bureau of Economic Research Working Paper no. 1166 (July).

Saito, K. 1977. "The Japanese Economy in Transition." *Finance and Development* 14(2):36–39.

Salant, S. W. 1976. "Exhaustible Resources and Industrial Structure: A Nash-Cournot Approach to the World Oil Market." *Journal of Political Economy* 84(5):1079–93.

Salop, J. 1974. "Devaluation and the Balance of Trade under Flexible Wages." In *Trade, Stability and Macroeconomics: Essays in Honor of Lloyd A. Metzler,* ed. G. Horwich and P. Samuelson. New York: Academic Press.

Samuelson, P. A. 1962. "Parable and Realism in Capital Theory: The Surrogate Production Function." *Review of Economic Studies* 29(3):193–206.

Sargent, J. R. 1979. "Productivity and Profits in U.K. Manufacturing." *Midland Bank Review* (Autumn):7–13.

Sargent, T. J. 1973. "Rational Expectations, the Real Rate of Interest, and the Natural Rate of Unemployment." *Brookings Papers on Economic Activity* 2:429–472.

——— 1978. "Estimation of Dynamic Labor Demand Schedules under Rational Expectations." *Journal of Political Economy* 86(6):1009–44.

Schmid, M. 1979. "Oil, Employment, and the Price Level: A Monetary Approach to the Macroeconomics of Imported Intermediate Goods under Fixed and Flexible Rates." Unpublished manuscript, University of Western Ontario (November).

Shinkai, Y. 1980. "Oil Crises and the Stagflation (or its absence) in Japan." Institute of Social and Economic Research Discussion Paper no. 110, Osaka University (November).

Sidrauski, M. 1967. "Rational Choice and Patterns of Growth in a Monetary Economy." *American Economic Review* 57:534–544.

Soderstrom, H. T., and S. Viotti. 1979. "Money Wage Disturbances and the Endogeneity of the Public Sector in an Open Economy." In *Inflation and Employment in Open Economies,* essays by members of the International Institute for Economic Studies, University of Stockholm, ed. A. Lindbeck. Amsterdam: North-Holland.

Solow, R. M. 1979. "Alternative Approaches to Macroeconomic Theory: A Partial View." W. A. Mackintosh Lecture, Queen's University, Kingston, Ontario (March).

——— 1980. "What to Do (Macroeconomically) when OPEC Comes." In *Rational Expectations and Economic Policy,* ed. S. Fischer. Chicago: University of Chicago Press.

Soskice, D. 1978. "Strike Waves and Wage Explosions, 1978–80: An Economic Interpretation." In *The Resurgence of Class Conflict in Western Europe Since 1968,* vol. 2: *Comparative Analyses,* ed. C. Crouch and A. Pizzorno. New York: Holmes and Meier.

Spitaller, E. 1976. "Semi-Annual Wages Equations for the Manufacturing Sectors in Six Major Industrial Countries." *Weltwirtschaftliches Archiv* 112(2):300–337.

Steigum, E., Jr. 1980. "Keynesian and Classical Unemployment in an Open Economy." *Scandinavian Journal of Economics* 82(2):147–166.

Svensson, L. E. O. 1981. "Oil Prices and a Small Oil-Importing Economy's Welfare and the Trade Balance: An Intertemporal Approach." Institute for International Economic Studies Seminar Paper no. 184, University of Stockholm (October). Forthcoming in the *Quarterly Journal of Economics.*

Tarantelli, E. 1982. "The Economics of Neocorporatism." Chapter 1 of unpublished manuscript. Bank of Italy, Rome.

Tarshis, L. 1939. "Changes in Real and Money Wages." *Economic Journal* 49 (March):150–154.

Taylor, J. B. 1979. "An Econometric Business Cycle Model with Rational Expectations: Some Estimation Results." Department of Economics, Columbia University (June).

—— 1980a. "Aggregate Dynamics and Staggered Contracts." *Journal of Political Economy* 88(1):1–23.

—— 1980b. "Output and Price Stability: An International Comparison." *Journal of Economic Dynamics and Control* 2:109–132.

—— 1981. "On the Relation between the Variability of Inflation and the Average Inflation Rate. In *The Costs and Consequences of Inflation,* ed. K. Brunner and A. Meltzer. Vol. 15 of the Carnegie-Rochester Conference Series on Public Policy. Amsterdam: North-Holland.

—— 1982. "Policy Choice and Economic Structure." Occasional Paper no. 9, Group of Thirty, New York.

Tobin, J. 1969. "A General Equilibrium Approach to Monetary Theory." *Journal of Money, Credit, and Banking* 1(1):15–29.

—— 1979. "Comment on Bruno and Sachs, 'Supply versus Demand Approaches to the Problem of Stagflation.'" Presented at the 1979 Kiel Conference on Macroeconomic Policies for Growth and Stability, and published in *Macroeconomic Policies for Growth and Stability,* ed. H. Giersch. Kiel: Institut für Weltwirtschaft an der Universität Kiel, 1981.

Torrington, D., ed. 1978. *Comparative Industrial Relations in Europe.* London: Associated Business Programmes.

Treadway, A. B. 1969. "On Rational Entrepreneurial Behavior and the Demand for Investment." *Review of Economic Studies* 36(2/106):227–239.

Turnovsky, S. J., and A. Kaspura. 1974. "Analysis of Imported Inflation in a Short-Run Macro-economic Model." *Canadian Journal of Economics* 7(3):355–380.

van Wijnbergen, S. 1981. "Inflation, Employment and the Dutch Disease in Oil Exporting Countries: A Short Run Disequilibrium Analysis." Development Research Center, World Bank (April).

Index